PEDAGOGICAL CASES IN PHYSICAL EDUCATION AND YOUTH SPORT

Pedagogical Cases in Physical Education and Youth Sport is a completely new kind of resource for students and practitioners working in physical education and youth sport. The book consists of twenty richly described cases of individual young learners, each written by a team of authors with diverse expertise from across the sport, exercise and movement sciences. These cases bring together knowledge from single sub-disciplines into new interdisciplinary knowledge to inform best practice in physical education teaching and coaching in youth sport settings.

At the heart of each case is an individual young person of a specified age and gender, with a range of physical, social and psychological characteristics. Drawing on current research, theory and empirical data from their own specialist discipline, each chapter author identifies the key factors he or she feels should be taken into account when attempting to teach or coach the young person described. These strands are then drawn together at the end of each chapter and linked to current research from the sport pedagogy literature to highlight the implications for planning and evaluating teaching or coaching sessions.

No other book offers such a rich, vivid and thought-provoking set of pedagogical tools for understanding and working with children and young people in sport. This is an essential resource for any student on a physical education, coaching, kinesiology, human movement studies or sport sciences course.

Kathleen Armour is Professor and Head of the School of Sport Exercise and Rehabilitation Sciences at the University of Birmingham, UK. Her main research interest is career-long professional learning for teachers and coaches, and its impact on young people's learning in physical education and sport.

PEDAGOGICAL CASES IN PHYSICAL EDUCATION AND YOUTH SPORT

Edited by Kathleen Armour

Routledge
Taylor & Francis Group

LONDON AND NEW YORK

First published 2014
by Routledge
2 Park Square, Milton Park, Abingdon, Oxon OX14 4RN

and by Routledge
711 Third Avenue, New York, NY 10017

Routledge is an imprint of the Taylor & Francis Group, an informa business

British Library Cataloguing in Publication Data

A catalogue record for this book is available from the British Library

Library of Congress Cataloging-in-Publication Data

Pedagogical cases in physical education and youth sport / edited by Kathleen Armour.
   pages cm
  1. Physical education and training—Case studies. 2. Physical education for youth—Case studies. 3. Sports for children—Case studies. 4. Coaching (Athletics)—Case studies. I. Armour, Kathleen.
  GV341.P37 2014
  613.7—dc23
  2013029640

ISBN: 978-0-415-70244-7 (hbk)
ISBN: 978-0-415-70245-4 (pbk)
ISBN: 978-0-203-79592-7 (ebk)

Typeset in ApexBembo
by Apex CoVantage, LLC

MIX
Paper from
responsible sources
FSC® C013604
www.fsc.org

Printed and bound in Great Britain by
CPI Group (UK) Ltd, Croydon, CR0 4YY

CONTENTS

CONTRIBUTORS

Manolis Adamakis: Department of Physical Education and Sport Science, National and Kapodistrian University of Athens, Greece.

Caroline Andries: Department of Physical Education and Physiotherapy, Universiteit Brussel, Belgium, International Centre for Ethics in Sport (ICES).

Kathleen Armour: School of Sport, Exercise & Rehabilitation Sciences, University of Birmingham, England.

Don Bailey: School of Human Movement Studies, The University of Queensland, Australia.

Dean Barker: Department for Food and Nutrition, and Sport Science, University of Gothenburg, Sweden.

Natalie Barker-Ruchti: Department for Food and Nutrition, and Sport Science, University of Gothenburg, Sweden.

Emma Beckman: School of Human Movement Studies, The University of Queensland, Australia.

Jan Bourgo: Department of Movement and Sports Sciences, University of Ghent, Belgium.

Mark Campbell: Department of Physical Education and Sport Sciences, University of Limerick, Ireland.

Greet Cardon: Department of Movement and Sports Sciences, University of Ghent, Belgium.

Tania Cassidy: School of Physical Education, Sport and Exercise Sciences, University of Otago, New Zealand.

Paul Castle: Institute of Sport and Exercise Science, University of Worcester, England.

Fiona Chambers: Sports Studies and Physical Education, School of Education, University College Cork, Ireland.

Diakai Chatziefstathiou: Department of Sport Science, Tourism and Leisure, Canterbury Christ Church University, England, United Kingdom.

Laura Claxton: Department of Health and Kinesiology and Department of Educational Studies, Purdue University, USA.

Marc Cloes: Department of Sport and Rehabilitation Sciences, University of Liege, Belgium.

Jean Côté: School of Kinesiology and Health Studies, Queen's University, Canada.

Kristine De Martelaer: Department of Physical Education and Physiotherapy, Universiteit Brussel, Belgium, International Centre for ethics in sport (ICES).

Christine De Medts: Department of Movement and Sports Sciences, University of Ghent, Belgium.

Vicki Ebbeck: Sport and Exercise Psychology, Oregon State University, USA.

Anne-Marie Etienne: Department of Psychologies and Clinics of Human Systems, University of Liege, Belgium.

Steven L. Fischer: School of Kinesiology and Health Studies, Queen's University, Canada.

Iain Fletcher: Institute of Sport and Physical Activity Research, University of Bedfordshire, UK.

Emmanouil Georgiadis: Exercise and Sport Psychology, School of Science, Technology and Health, University Campus Suffolk, UK.

Markus Gerber: Institute of Exercise and Health Sciences, University of Basel, Switzerland.

Jacqueline Goodway: Department of Human Sciences, The Ohio State University, USA.

Lisa Griffiths: Institute of Sport and Exercise Science, University of Worcester, England.

Mark Griffiths: School of Sport, Exercise & Rehabilitation Sciences, University of Birmingham, England.

Brendon J. Gurd: School of Kinesiology and Health Studies, Queen's University, Canada.

Leen Haerens: Department of Movement and Sports Sciences, University of Ghent, Belgium.

David J. Hancock: School of Kinesiology and Health Studies, Queen's University, Canada.

Stephen Harvey: Institute of Sport and Physical Activity Research, University of Bedfordshire, UK.

Pilvikki Heikinaro-Johansson: Department of Sport Sciences, University of Jyväskylä, Finland.

Samuel Hodge: Department of Human Sciences, The Ohio State University, USA.

Stéphanie Hody: GIGA-Neurosciences, University of Liege, Belgium.

Terhi Huovinen: Department of Sport Sciences, University of Jyväskylä, Finland.

Anne-Marie Jackson: School of Physical Education, Sport and Exercise Sciences, University of Otago, New Zealand.

Boris Jidovtseff: Department of Sport and Rehabilitation Sciences, University of Liege, Belgium.

Margarita Jimenez-Silva: Language and Culture Pedagogy, Arizona State University, USA.

Ian Kenny: Department of Physical Education and Sport Sciences, University of Limerick, Ireland.

Charlotte Kerner: Institute of Sport and Physical Activity Research, University of Bedfordshire, UK.

Emilie Lachance: Department of Physical Activity Sciences, University of Quebec at Trois Rivieres, Quebec, Canada.

Jean Lemoyne: Department of Physical Activity Sciences, University of Quebec at Trois Rivieres, Quebec, Canada.

Matthieu Lenoir: Department of Movement and Sports Sciences, University of Ghent, Belgium.

Francois-Xavier Li: School of Sport, Exercise & Rehabilitation Sciences, University of Birmingham, England.

Doune Macdonald: School of Human Movement Studies, The University of Queensland, Australia.

Eileen McEvoy: Youth Physical Activity, Department of Sport Sciences, University of Jyväskylä, Finland.

Ann MacPhail: Department of Physical Education and Sport Sciences, University of Limerick, Ireland.

Johnny Maeschalck: Department of Physical Education and Physiotherapy, Universiteit Brussel, Belgium, International Centre for ethics in sport (ICES).

Kyriaki Makopoulou: School of Sport, Exercise & Rehabilitation Sciences, University of Birmingham, England.

Cliff Mallett: School of Human Movement Studies, The University of Queensland, Australia.

Motohide Miyahara: School of Physical Education, Sport and Exercise Sciences, University of Otago, New Zealand.

Gyozo Molnar: Institute of Sport and Exercise Science, University of Worcester, England.

Alexandre Mouton: Department of Sport and Rehabilitation Sciences, University of Liege, Belgium.

Niamh Murphy: Sports Studies and Physical Education, School of Education, University College Cork, Ireland.

Orla Murphy: Sports Studies and Physical Education, School of Education, University College Cork, Ireland.

Yvonne Nolan: Sports Studies and Physical Education, School of Education, University College Cork, Ireland.

Nikos Ntoumanis: School of Sport, Exercise & Rehabilitation Sciences, University of Birmingham, England.

Rick Petosa: Department of Human Sciences, The Ohio State University, USA.

Arja Piirainen: Department of Health Sciences, University of Jyväskylä, Finland.

Stacey Pope: Institute of Sport and Physical Activity Research, University of Bedfordshire, UK.

Caroline Poulin: Department of Chiropractics, University of Quebec at Trois Rivieres, Quebec, Canada.

Uwe Pühse: Institute of Exercise and Health Sciences, University of Basel, Switzerland.

Laura Purdy: Institute of Sport and Exercise Science, University of Worcester, England.

Shirley Rietdyk: Department of Health and Kinesiology and Department of Educational Studies, Purdue University, USA.

Claire J.L. Rossato: Department of Sport Science, Tourism and Leisure, Canterbury Christ Church University, England, United Kingdom.

Melissa Savage: Department of Health and Kinesiology and Department of Educational Studies, Purdue University, USA.

Jon Shemmell: School of Physical Education, Sport and Exercise Sciences, University of Otago, New Zealand.

Nektarios Stavrou: Department of Physical Education and Sport Science, National and Kapodistrian University of Athens, Greece.

Jon Swain: Department of Sport Science, Tourism and Leisure, Canterbury Christ Church University, England, United Kingdom.

Deborah Tannehill: Department of Physical Education and Sport Sciences, University of Limerick, Ireland.

Thomas J. Templin: Department of Health and Kinesiology and Department of Educational Studies, Purdue University, USA.

Gay L. Timken: Sport Pedagogy/Physical Education Teacher Education, Western Oregon University, USA.

Daniel Tindall: Department of Physical Education and Sport Sciences, University of Limerick, Ireland.

Stewart Trost: School of Human Movement Studies, The University of Queensland, Australia.

Raili Välimaa: Health Education, Department of Health Sciences, University of Jyväskylä, Finland.

Lynn Van den Berghe: Department of Movement and Sports Sciences, University of Ghent, Belgium.

Hans van der Mars: Sport Pedagogy/Physical Education Teacher Education, Arizona State University, USA.

Lore Vandevivere: Department of Physical Education and Physiotherapy, Universiteit Brussel, Belgium, International Centre for ethics in sport (ICES).

Gemma van Vuuren-Cassar: Department of Childhood Studies, Canterbury Christ Church University, England, United Kingdom.

Tine Vertommen: Department of Physical Education and Physiotherapy, Universiteit Brussel, Belgium, International Centre for ethics in sport (ICES).

Phillip Ward: Department of Human Sciences, The Ohio State University, USA.

Doris L. Watson: Sport Pedagogy/Physical Education Teacher Education, University of Nevada-Las Vegas, USA.

Mary Yannakoulia: Department of Nutrition and Dietetics, Harokopio University, Greece.

INTRODUCTION

Kathleen Armour

SCHOOL OF SPORT, EXERCISE & REHABILITATION SCIENCES, UNIVERSITY OF BIRMINGHAM, UK

What is a 'pedagogical case'?

A 'pedagogical case' is a mechanism designed to make cutting edge, multidisciplinary research on learners in human movement available and accessible to practitioners and students learning about practice. This volume focuses on individual children and young people as learners in physical education and youth sport. The pedagogical cases method, however, could equally be employed in wider human movement settings; for example, focusing on learners at different points in the life course and in educational contexts beyond human movement.

In essence, the pedagogical cases in this book consist of an analysis of the learning needs of individual children and young people from multiple sub-disciplinary perspectives (in and beyond our field), and a pedagogical synthesis of those perspectives. The mechanism has been designed to help students and professional practitioners bridge the gap between research/theory and practice. Each chapter has been written by a multidisciplinary team of academics from an internationally recognized university in the broad field of sport and exercise sciences/kinesiology/human movement sciences. Using a common pedagogical case template, the chapters have been developed as stand-alone cases, and each one represents a unique blend of features. The specific focus of a chapter is easily identifiable from the chapter title, subtitle and key words.

Each chapter in this book constitutes a unique 'pedagogical case'. A pedagogical case can be defined by its three core elements: (i) a case narrative about a learner (a child or young person in this volume), (ii) a series of sub-disciplinary perspectives on the case narrative, and (iii) a pedagogical perspective that seeks to synthesize all the contributions to generate interdisciplinary knowledge on effective practice that could support the case learner to learn effectively. The chapters have been developed around the focal point of a 'case narrative' of a richly described individual child or young person. The case narrative includes details of, for example, context, age, gender, ability/disability, family, and an individual's unique blend of physical, social and psychological characteristics. The case narratives are based on real learners in a composite sense in that they are grounded in existing theory and research. The characteristics and features of the focal learner in each chapter will, therefore, be instantly recognizable to teachers and coaches. The individual children and young people named in the chapters are, however, fictitious, to ensure there are no ethical concerns with the wide dissemination and analysis of the pedagogical cases.

The author teams have created their pedagogical cases based on the expertise they had available, and the particular issues they wanted to raise about the learner from the perspective of both classic and new research in their respective fields. The contributors had the flexibility to be creative within the common chapter template and this has resulted in considerable variety in the style adopted. The chapters are all similar in structure, however, in that they begin with the case narrative and then continue with a perspective on the narrative from at least three sub-disciplines and, finally, from pedagogy. Taken as a whole, the book covers a wide range of young learners and illustrates ways in which research can inform practice in these and similar cases.

As was noted earlier, the author teams originate from some of the leading institutions in our field. It is a field (or discipline) that is labeled differently across the world; for example: Sport and Exercise Sciences, Kinesiology, Human Movement Sciences, Physical Education etc. Nonetheless, whatever the label, most university departments or schools in the field share considerable common ground, are multidisciplinary in nature, and have overlapping interests outside the field. As individuals, the contributors to each chapter (each pedagogical case) are acknowledged experts in their own sub-discipline. In order to write these chapters, the experts collaborated across sub-disciplinary boundaries (often for the first time) to produce a complex pedagogical case. Many of the author teams reported that it was a fascinating, yet challenging, project. The resulting cases are interesting at a number of levels and it is intended that they will generate discussion, debate, challenge and, of course, professional communication and learning.

The chapters are presented in this book in chronological order, from the youngest to the oldest case narrative learners (ranging from age 5 to 16). This is, however, only one way in which these unique and complex cases could be read. It would also have been possible to cluster the cases differently; for example, around gender, ability/disability, relationship to sport/physical activity, geographical context and sub-disciplinary perspective. This means that any specific ordering of chapters is bound to be somewhat arbitrary and given that each chapter is stand-alone, they are accessible in any order.

Complex and dynamic young learners

It is important to emphasize that although each chapter begins with a narrative about a young person, there is no suggestion that all young people who share similar characteristics would benefit from exactly the same pedagogical approaches. Such a claim would be seductive in its simplicity, but pedagogically crass. Instead, the cases are presented as learning tools that illustrate how we might study specific individual children and young people from different sub-disciplinary perspectives, and then use that knowledge to inform effective, evidence-based pedagogies in physical education, physical activity and sport settings. Of course, the information presented in the cases could be adapted as appropriate to meet the needs of young learners who share some of the same characteristics. It is also important to clarify that the young people are not to be understood as 'deficit' cases to be 'fixed'. Instead, they are presented as complex and dynamic young learners who deserve to be taught and coached by practitioners (pedagogues) who draw on a wide range of multidisciplinary knowledge to devise appropriate (interdisciplinary) learning encounters.

Practice is always multidisciplinary and interdisciplinary

It is a fundamental tenet of this book that interdisciplinary knowledge is at the root of the theory and practice of that area of study known as 'pedagogy' (see Chapter One for an in-depth discussion). Debates rage about the definitions of multi/inter/trans/cross/post-disciplinary knowledge and these are summarized in Chapter One. Yet, teaching/coaching *practice* in physical education and youth sport settings is *always* both multi and interdisciplinary; how else could a practitioner function? Yet, too often in academia and in teacher/coach education, the range of sub-disciplines contributing to what is labeled as 'pedagogy' is narrow, drawn mainly from the social sciences and education theory. Moreover, academics working in multidisciplinary departments in the wider field of sport sciences (or kinesiology/movement sciences) tend to work alongside each other in parallel or divergent tracks that can become increasingly difficult to bridge. Over time, the gap between these different areas of increasingly specialized knowledge can become a chasm as each develops its own critical mass of staff, advocates, research, programmes of study and students. For professional practitioners who seek to work across these sub-disciplinary boundaries, this trend is highly problematic.

Professions in the field

Teaching is a profession; coaching is more complex and in most parts of the world, it still aspires to full professional status. In the case of teaching, it might be anticipated that formal continuing professional development (CPD) would be the mechanism for ensuring teachers continue to grow their sub-disciplinary knowledge and skills across a career. As is reported widely from international research, however (see Chapter One for details), CPD rarely offers these opportunities. Indeed, registering for a postgraduate degree is often the only way in which teachers can gain access to further study and cutting-edge research in some of the sub-disciplines that underpin their practice. In many countries (although not all, as is apparent in some of the chapters in this book), this elite academic group is a very low percentage of the total teaching workforce. For coaches, the problems are more challenging. Coach education is often even more limited and variable in content and quality than teacher education. Yet, for a child or young person attempting to learn a movement skill, physical activity or sport, their requirements from both groups of practitioners – physical education teachers and youth sport coaches – are almost identical: they need a teacher or coach who can 'diagnose' their individual learning needs and design and deliver informed and effective learning sessions, opportunities and experiences. I use the term 'diagnose' deliberately. Although some find it problematic because it is suggestive of a 'medical' model, I think this is a misunderstanding of the term. Diagnosis is used in many other professions to signal the starting point for action; in other words, it reminds us that an analysis of an individual learner's needs, and professional capability to meet those needs, should be the starting point for teaching and coaching practice.

Our young clients

Ultimately, of course, this book is about children and young people, and meeting their individual learning needs in physical education and youth sport. Children and young people are the 'clients' of the profession of teaching and the professional group that is youth coaching. In using the term 'client', I am signaling that children and young people have a *right* to learning experiences that meet their individual needs, and teachers and coaches have a *responsibility* to meet those needs (Armour 2011). For practitioners, the minimal steps to be taken in order to meet the individual needs of diverse learners include: (a) diagnosing the complex strengths, weaknesses and developmental needs of each learner; (b) assessing personal capacity to meet the needs of the learners and addressing personal professional deficits (which can include collaboration with colleagues, attending a course and reading new research); and (c) planning curricula/sessions informed by up-to-date knowledge from relevant fields and professional experience. Of course, any pedagogical encounter demands much more, including alignment with existing policies and curricula, but the chapters in this book – the pedagogical cases – have been designed as pedagogical tools that can help practitioners in each of these three steps.

Pedagogical cases as learning tools

Pedagogical cases are presented here to be debated and discussed. As I emphasize several times, they have been designed as *learning tools* and as a starting point for generating ideas about ways to link theory, research and practice. As was noted earlier, the mechanism of a pedagogical case could be used in any field of practice. What makes the cases in our field so interesting is that learners in physical activity settings are required to engage so much of themselves in the learning process and their successes and failures are always highly visible. To serve these learners well, physical education teachers and youth sport coaches need to be knowledgeable across a very wide range of areas that they can synthesize in practice. This book, therefore, uses pedagogical cases as a mechanism to support practitioners in their personal professional learning so they, in turn, can better support the endlessly diverse young learners who rely upon them. As was noted earlier, pedagogical cases are not blueprints for practice; indeed, one of the clear features to emerge from the chapters is the powerful impact of local, national and international cultural context on what is possible in practice. Nonetheless, the cases do offer a mechanism for communication about practice across these and other boundaries.

How is the book organized?

As was noted earlier, given that each pedagogical case has been written as a stand-alone chapter, it is possible to read them in any order. Readers might find it helpful, however, to read Chapter One first (Pedagogical Cases Explained), as it offers a more detailed analysis of some of the issues that have only been touched upon in this Introduction. The 20 case chapters that follow have been written using a common template, as described earlier, although each team of authors has interpreted the framework in different ways. This is an important point. In some chapters, for example, the case narrative is written from the perspective of a young person; in others, a practitioner or researcher acts as narrator; and in others, the voice of the young person is present throughout each section. The case narratives also vary between those structured around an event, to those structured around a young person's thoughts on an issue and so on. What this means for the reader is that although the overall structure will soon become familiar, the individual chapters retain the capacity to offer something unique.

Looking ahead

The concept of 'Pedagogical Cases' has been developed to contribute something new to both the academic and practice aspects of our physical activity/human movement fields. This is the first of a set of volumes under the series title, 'Pedagogical Cases in Sport, Exercise and

Movement'. In the future, volumes will be developed that focus on different categories of learner and different settings (exercise, older exercisers, elite youth sport, specific sports etc.). It would also be desirable to develop a web-based repository of digital pedagogical cases in order to increase modes of access for practitioners, and this is currently under construction. In other words, 'Pedagogical Cases' is a project! Importantly, if these and subsequent pedagogical cases stimulate debate and discussion in professional practitioner communities, and further collaborative and translational research in relevant research communities, they will have served their purpose.

And finally . . . profuse thanks to the contributors

Those who edit books are always indebted to their chapter contributors. In this book, the thanks are even more profuse than usual. The contributors were asked to engage in a project and a style of collaborative writing that had little precedent. Although I offered guidance in the form of the book rationale and chapter template, they were left to create the detail and to put flesh on the skeleton concept of a Pedagogical Case. At the outset, none of us – including me – was quite sure how it would all turn out. As the draft chapters came in, however, it became apparent that the teams were creating something new and exciting. Enjoy.

Reference

Armour, K.M. (2011) *Sport Pedagogy: An Introduction for Teaching and Coaching.* London: Pearson.

1

PEDAGOGICAL CASES EXPLAINED

Kathleen Armour

SCHOOL OF SPORT, EXERCISE & REHABILITATION SCIENCES, UNIVERSITY OF BIRMINGHAM, ENGLAND

Key words: pedagogical case; professional learning tool, theory and practice; physical education; and youth sport.

Why pedagogical cases?

In the Introduction to this book, a "pedagogical case" was defined as a translational research mechanism and professional learning tool. A pedagogical case comprises three elements: (i) a case narrative about a learner (in this volume, a child or young person); (ii) multidisciplinary perspectives (usually three) on the case narrative; and (iii) a pedagogical perspective that seeks to draw the strands together to generate interdisciplinary knowledge. Each chapter in this book constitutes a unique pedagogical case written by a multidisciplinary team of authors, including teams from some of the leading departments in our international field. Taken as a whole, the book covers a wide range of individual young learners and contexts. The intention is that these pedagogical cases are viewed as learning tools that can generate discussion/debate, facilitate communication across traditional boundaries, and offer access to cutting edge research and theory.

In her Presidential Address to the 2012 American Educational Research Association (AERA), Arnetha Ball challenged researchers to "move away from research designed as mere 'demonstrations of knowledge' towards research that has the power to close the *knowing-doing gap* in education" (Ball 2012: 283, emphasis in original). Ball argued passionately that although it is important for researchers in education to conduct research that can create new knowledge, "*to know is not enough*" because knowing "is not sufficient to address social problems, mitigate inequalities, or advance innovative methods of instruction" (p. 284). Noting also that "there is a gap between what we know and what is widely done in the educational arena" (p. 285), Ball made a case for more translational research to close persisting knowledge-practice or research-practice gaps. She argued that what is required is "persistent, collaborative, and generative work" (p. 285) and "resources and mechanisms to promote the use of research to improve education" (p. 292). This book introduces the concept of pedagogical cases as a translational research mechanism and a professional learning tool for practitioners. The purpose of the cases is to make a contribution to closing the knowledge/research/practice gap for practising and aspirant teachers and coaches who work with children and young people in physical education/ youth sport settings.

In this chapter, the concept *pedagogical case* is explained, including discussion about its genesis and potential application. Questions about whether these integrative pedagogical cases should be labelled as multidisciplinary or interdisciplinary – or indeed something else – are also considered. Importantly, as was noted in the Introduction, the cases presented in this book are positioned firmly as tools to stimulate discussion and debate, rather than an attempt to provide a blueprint for practice. The book should be helpful, therefore, as a conduit for critical discussion among those with an interest in learning more about how research can contribute to practice.

The teams of contributors for each pedagogical case comprise a lead pedagogy author and three contributors from any other sub-disciplines that could offer helpful insights into the specific case. In practical terms, the task for each chapter team was to (a) create a research-based narrative that describes an individual child or young person; (b) identify current research knowledge from each of the sub-disciplines that could be relevant to understanding the young person as a learner; and (c) explore the pedagogical implications for meeting the needs of that learner. Given that the author teams are drawn from different countries, each pedagogical case also reflects key features of local and national cultural context.

Neither *pedagogical* nor *cases* are new terms or concepts. It is clear, therefore, that this book builds on a large body of existing theory and research in these areas. What is different, however, is that those terms have been put together and developed in a way that results in a new resource for professional learning in our field. In order to begin to explain the rationale for pedagogical cases, it is helpful to analyse the two constituent terms of the concept: *pedagogy/ pedagogical* and *cases*.

The "pedagogical" in pedagogical cases

In a recent book I reviewed the literature on the concept of pedagogy (see Armour 2011, for a fuller analysis). It became apparent that although there is some confusion in the use of the term (Stone 2000) *learning* – rather than mere transmission or instruction – is at its core (Watkins and Mortimore 1999). The work of Leach and Moon (1999) is widely cited, and these authors defined pedagogy as the relationship between four key elements of an educational encounter: teachers, learners, the learning task, and the learning environment. Alexander (2008) highlighted the "extraordinary richness of pedagogy as a field of intellectual exploration and empirical enquiry" and exhorted educators to reveal the "values, beliefs and theories . . . [that] . . . shape what both teachers and students do" (p. 183). He also argued that pedagogy "mediates learning, knowledge, culture and identity" (p. 183), and this point is certainly evident in the pedagogical cases presented in this book.

Within the field of physical education and youth sport, Tinning (2008) has written extensively on the concept of *sport pedagogy*. Tinning has argued that although the term *sport pedagogy* is amorphous, it is generally accepted as a "subdiscipline of the field of kinesiology" (p. 412). Tinning also argues for an understanding of pedagogical work related to physical activity, bodies, and health wherever it takes place, linked to other cultural players in the field such as those working in obesity/health. Certainly in the pedagogical cases presented in this book, a wide range of expertise contributes to an understanding of the cases. Importantly, each case takes, as its starting point, the needs and interests of an individual child or young person and his or her engagement in sport and physical activity.

In the specific field of physical education, Kirk, Macdonald, and O'Sullivan (2006) defined pedagogy "by its three key elements of learning, teaching and curriculum" stating that they "understand these three elements to be interdependent" (p. xi). In my earlier book entitled *Sport Pedagogy, An Introduction for Teaching and Coaching* I drew on the work of these authors and others such as Rovegno (2003), Grossman (1989), and Shulman (1987) to define sport pedagogy as having three complex dimensions that are made even more complex as they interact to form each pedagogical encounter: (i) knowledge in context; (ii) learners and learners; and (iii) teachers/teaching and coaches/coaching (Armour 2011). I also argued that the historical divisions and barriers between physical education teaching and youth sport coaching should be challenged. The point was made that the needs and interests of young learners should be prioritised, especially as many will try to learn across different sport/physical activity contexts. As Akkerman and Van Eijck (2013: 60) have argued, "the learner should be approached . . . as a whole person who participates in school as well as in many other practices". In short pedagogical, within the concept of pedagogical cases signals that the complex learning needs of learners are identified as the core of professional practice.

"Cases" in pedagogical cases

Case within the concept of pedagogical cases is central to the book's design and structure. In taking a case study approach as an organizing framework, I have drawn on numerous sources. For example, Lawrence Stenhouse (1979: 4) advocated for the wider use of case studies as a resource for practitioners. He argued for cases based on a "differential response to diagnostic assessment of [learner] needs" and for the development of mixed method case studies, and their ". . . patient accumulation". Stenhouse argued that taking this approach would lead to new resources that could be shared. He also believed these resources could support practitioners in educational contexts to "make refined judgments about what educational action to take in particular cases lodged in particular contexts" (p. 4). In other words, it would appear that Stenhouse was arguing for the use of cases that, in Ball's (2012) terms, could act as a translational mechanism.

There is a rich literature debating the value of case studies and case study research in education and other fields (Stake 2005). Classically, case studies are criticised for being descriptive, singular, and lacking in generalizability, but Thomas (2011) dismisses such criticisms, arguing that:

> At its best, case study provides the most vivid, the most inspirational analysis that inquiry can offer. Einstein did it; Newton did it. Sociologists do it; psychologists do it. Doctors do it; teachers do it; lawyers do it; nurses do it. It is done across the disciplinary and methodological spectrum . . . Case study provides a form of inquiry that elevates a view of life in its complexity . . . It's the realization that complexity in social affairs is frequently indivisible that has led to case study's status as one of the most popular and most fertile design frames open to the researcher.
>
> (Thomas 2011: preface)

Yet, despite the widespread use of case study as method in educational research, there have been relatively few examples of cases developed in interesting ways as professional learning tools. This is not to claim that no case studies have been published, but instead to note that there are very few collaborative and generative case studies on learners that draw on different sub-disciplinary perspectives. It is this gap that has driven the development of pedagogical cases.

A notable exception in the field of sport pedagogy is the work of Wathne (2011), which appeared in the journal *Sport, Education and Society*. The author used her rather unique combination of medical and sociological academic knowledge to offer a detailed analysis of the issues faced by an obese girl who was exhorted to take exercise to reduce her weight. In a paper entitled: "Movement of large bodies impaired: The double burden of obesity: Somatic and semiotic issues", Wathne pointed out that although it is recognised that obesity is both a medical and a social problem, "A traditional medical approach does not adequately consider social factors that may predispose and maintain the condition" (p. 415). Weaving together a detailed somatic and semiotic analysis of Berit, her young patient, Wathne illustrates vividly that when offered a traditional exercise prescription approach to weight loss, Berit faced unique challenges at multiple levels:

> Berit's body is very much a *constant presence,* a factor to be reckoned with, in all her undertakings . . . Berit seems obliged by her bodily structure to pause and inwardly pose questions like: *What will this particular movement achieve? Where will this situation land me?* This is the phenomenological or corporeal dimension to the equation.
>
> (p. 426, emphases in the original)

Wathne's conclusion is that "people in Berit's situation are effectively 'double trapped' by their obese bodily condition – physically and in terms of cultural codes" (p. 427). In pedagogical cases, the approach is different to Wathne's study in that each chapter offers multiple authors/perspectives, including an integrative pedagogical analysis. Nonetheless, Wathne's paper does provide an example of the depth of insight that can be developed by moving beyond single sub-disciplinary perspectives, and her paper formed part of the inspiration for this project.

To summarise these two sections, pedagogical cases can be understood as a translational mechanism that utilises research from a range of perspectives to analyse the complex learning needs of learners. Individual young people are the focal point for each chapter in this book, and they are presented as complex and diverse learners. Statements about the purposes of education systems or curricula usually claim to place the learning needs of individual pupils at the heart of policy and practice, so perhaps this book illustrates the challenges of delivering such claims in practice. It is possible that future editions of pedagogical cases will take different focal points; for example, learners at different ages and stages of the life course; groups of learners who share one or more characteristics or interests; learners in specific contexts; or even practitioners themselves. In all future iterations of the concept, however, the fundamental purpose will be the same: to act as a multidisciplinary and, at times, interdisciplinary translational research mechanism and a professional learning tool.

Transcending single disciplines in professional learning and practice: the multi-inter-trans-cross-post debate

Questions about what kinds of knowledge teachers or coaches have/need/use are clearly relevant to the kinds of continuing professional development that might be required over a career. In his classic work based on research that observed neophyte teachers, Shulman (1987) outlined a knowledge base of teaching in the form of seven categories: content knowledge, general pedagogical knowledge, curriculum knowledge, pedagogical content knowledge, knowledge of learners and their characteristics, knowledge of educational contexts, and knowledge of educational ends, purposes, and values. Shulman identified "pedagogical content knowledge" as distinctive because it is "most likely to distinguish the understanding of the content specialist from that of the pedagogue" (p. 8). The pedagogical cases presented in this book do focus on aspects of pedagogical content knowledge, particularly in the final section of each chapter. In addition, however, they cut across Shulman's classification, making a contribution to knowledge of learners, pedagogy, content, curriculum, contexts, and educational ends. Indeed, in adopting an approach that recognises multiple perspectives and complexity, it could be argued that pedagogical cases are illustrative of Shulman's suggestion that we should "express wonder at . . . the extensive knowledge of teaching" (p. 7).

Each of Shulman's (1987) proposed categories of teacher knowledge is complex in itself and in its overlap with the others. This complexity is exemplified in physical education and youth sport because the range of possible content knowledge is extensive, including knowledge of specific sports and physical activities, and technical knowledge. Moreover, practitioners are required, routinely, to draw on content knowledge from a wide range of sub-disciplines within and beyond the sport sciences, which are then synthesised in practice. This means that teachers and coaches are *always* engaged in "interdisciplinary work" as defined by Gardner and Boix-Mansilla (1999):

> . . . any individual who not only applies more than one discipline but actually strives to combine or synthesise these stances is engaged in that rare but precious practice called interdisciplinary work.
>
> (p. 87)

This point is one of the cornerstones of the concept of pedagogical cases. Academics and researchers can choose – indeed, are often encouraged – to focus on specialised fields of study and specific disciplines or sub-disciplines. Yet, for practitioners in physical education and youth sport, this high degree of specialisation is simply not feasible. If practice is to be informed and effective (i.e., professional), then teaching or coaching a group of children will require knowledge of a range of human movement sciences, social sciences including education, aspects of the humanities, and technical knowledge. Added to this is a need to understand how all of this knowledge applies to a specific group of young learners and the different individuals within that group. In other words, the cognitive challenge *alone* for the professional practitioner is daunting.

Classifying pedagogical cases as multidisciplinary and, at times, interdisciplinary, is to enter a conceptual quagmire. A Google search quickly reveals the parameters of the debate, although not its subtleties. For example, Dictionary.com somewhat confusingly defines *multidisciplinary* as "combining several specialized branches of learning or fields of expertise" and *interdisciplinary* as "combining or involving two or more academic disciplines or fields of study". From an applied perspective, *The Miller-Keane Encyclopedia and Dictionary of Medicine, Nursing, and Allied Health* explains that an interdisciplinary team is "a group of health care professionals from diverse fields who work in a coordinated fashion toward a common goal for the patient"; whereas a multidisciplinary team is "a team of professionals including representatives of different disciplines who coordinate the contributions of each profession, which are not considered to overlap, in order to improve patient care". On the other hand, a transdisciplinary team is "composed of members of a number of different professions cooperating across disciplines to improve patient care through practice or research". From a different field, the Committee on Facilitating Interdisciplinary Research, Committee on Science, Engineering, and Public Policy (2004) acknowledges that debates about the meanings of these terms are ongoing, concluding that research is dynamic and so establishing clear boundaries is probably fruitless. Regarding interdisciplinary research, they too point to the need for a minimum of two disciplines working together to "advance fundamental understanding or to solve problems whose solutions are beyond the scope of a single discipline or area of research practice".

The more complex debates around these concepts can be found in academic texts. For example, Repko (2011) in a book entitled *Interdisciplinary Research: Process and Theory* explored the debates in depth. Clearly it is impossible here to do justice to the level of debate presented in that text. In summary, however, Repko argues that interdisciplinarity is a process of "making whole". Noting that *disciplines* (and *sub-disciplines*) themselves are also contested terms (see later discussion), Repko draws on a range of existing definitions to offer an "integrated" definition of interdisciplinary studies:

> Interdisciplinary studies is a process of answering a question, solving a problem, or addressing a topic that is too broad or complex to be dealt with adequately by a single discipline, and draws on the disciplines with the goal of integrating their insights to construct a more comprehensive understanding.
>
> (p. 16)

For Repko, this is completely different to the notion of multidisciplinary, with which it is sometimes confused. He identifies multidisciplinary studies as "the placing side by side of insights from two or more disciplines . . . [that] . . . makes no attempt to integrate the insights produced by these perspectives" (p. 17). In other words, it is the level of integration that separates the two concepts. At the other end of the spectrum, total integration that moves completely beyond disciplines is labelled as *transdisciplinary studies*. Accepting these definitions, it is apparent that the pedagogical cases presented in this book do generate both multidisciplinary and interdisciplinary knowledge, although the level of interdisciplinarity achieved varies from case to case.

Within the broad field of sport and exercise sciences (including kinesiology and human movement science) Abernathy and colleagues (1996) produced a text entitled *The Biophysical Foundations of Human Movement*. Although the book title itself signalled an enduring divide in the field between biophysical and psycho/socio/cultural approaches to human movement, the authors argued for the development of "integrative perspectives" to overcome what they perceived to be the problems of increased specialisation. In the most recent edition of their book, Abernathy *et al.* (2013) debate the nature of human movement studies as a discipline and a profession. They conclude that human movement studies can justifiably be classified as a discipline, and that its sub-disciplines are functional anatomy; biomechanics; exercise physiology; motor control, sport and exercise psychology (that bridges the biophysical and sociocultural foundations); pedagogy; and the sociology, history, and philosophy of sport and exercise. They argue that

> . . . the field of human movement studies is probably most accurately depicted as *multidisciplinary*, whereas the desirable direction is to make it more *cross-disciplinary* and ultimately *interdisciplinary* or transdisciplinary.
>
> (p. 7, emphases in the original)

The aspiration is to cross what these authors view as arbitrary boundaries by "synthesising material from the sub-disciplines" (p. 7), and they feel this is most likely to happen as the discipline matures. Based on an historical analysis of the development of the field, they also view the current emphasis on physical activity/health as an opportunity to develop new alliances and rediscover old ones – such as with medicine and physical education (see, however, Armour and Harris 2013, for a critical discussion on this issue and the need to develop new health pedagogies). Ageing is also identified as an area of potential growth for the discipline but in all these examples, the authors point to the dangers of specialisation and fragmentation, and the continuing imperative to integrate knowledge "in order to advance our knowledge in a consolidated manner" (p. 23). Without suggesting that the pedagogical cases presented in this book achieve all that is required, it could certainly be argued that they make an attempt to integrate knowledge from the sub-disciplines around a core focus.

The human movement field is not alone in facing problems deriving from disciplinary specialisation. Lee (2010) commented that in education more widely, researchers tend to examine the world from their own disciplinary silos, whereas what teachers need is holistic knowledge. Lee uses a single pupil case study as a framework to argue for the development of a "science of learning" to reflect the fact that in learning, "systems of physiological, cognitive, and socio-emotional development are symbiotically linked" (p. 653). In Lee's view, researchers rarely "focus on intersections across the cognitive, the psychosocial, and the physiological" meaning that we are unable to understand individual young learners "inside a complex and dynamic ecological system" (p. 644). The fact that Lee even has to make these points signals a problem in "education science"; indeed she reports a need to justify to educationalists her "forays into human development and studies of biological systems of living organisms" (p. 644). Interestingly, for children and young people learning in areas such as physical education, sport and movement, physiological, cognitive, and socio-emotional aspects of development are linked very visibly. Pedagogical cases, therefore, can be understood, in Lee's terms, as a mechanism for developing an integrative science of learning and a shared language in human movement fields. This mechanism could, of course, be used in many other areas of education too.

Pedagogical cases and professional learning

The comment by Thomas (2011, cited earlier) about the range of fields in which case study is used is pertinent to the genesis of this book. The inspiration for developing pedagogical cases as a professional learning tool came, in part, from a professional field other than education (see later discussion). Indeed, inspiration for the concept and the book can be traced through a number of sources ranging from the personal, professional, theoretical, and practical. The personal aspect undoubtedly transfuses all the other sources. Ball (2012) argued that if effective generative research is to materialise, personal voice will be important because it:

> . . . represents the point at which researchers demonstrate individual approaches taken in an effort to help address the knowing-doing gap through an ability to combine research knowledge, personal knowledge, and knowledge gained from the research context based on their own engagement with reflection, introspection, and critique.

(p. 290)

Pedagogical cases as a tool is certainly an attempt to address the "knowing-doing gap" in teaching and coaching. In this context, personal voice has its roots in my career as a researcher who, from the 1990s, has undertaken a programme of research on physical education teachers' and coaches' professional development. In addition, I have a personal interest in narrative and case study research because experience suggests that practitioners find these forms of knowledge to be accessible and engaging. I also draw on decades of pedagogical experience as a university professor who has designed and delivered undergraduate and postgraduate programmes in physical education/sport pedagogy. In this regard, my perception is that pedagogy is a sub-discipline that lacks inspirational multidisciplinary and interdisciplinary learning tools, and that this vacuum continues into career-long professional development (CPD) for teachers and coaches. Each of these points is considered in turn.

(i) CPD research in physical education and youth sport

Teaching is a profession and, as Brunetti (1998) argued, members of a profession have both a right and a responsibility to engage in appropriate and effective career-long professional learning. Given that professions exist to serve their clients, this requirement makes sense. Nonetheless, a vast range of international literature on teachers' professional development suggests that traditional and current models fail to support teachers to learn effectively. In a much-cited comment, Borko (2004: 4) described CPD for teachers as "woefully inadequate". Day (2002: 431) identified schools and teachers as "the single most important asset in the achievement of the vision of a learning society", and there is certainly a growing awareness of the importance of teachers' professional learning (Wayne *et al.* 2008). In 2001, for example, the UK Government claimed that: "We need teaching to become a learning profession" (Department for Education & Employment [DfEE], 2001: 2). In the USA, Guskey (1994; 2002) argued that there is no single form of CPD that is appropriate for all teachers; instead an "optimal mix" of activities is needed for teachers at different stages of development. Yet, existing models of professional development have been described as largely ineffective (Garet *et al.* 2001) and James and colleagues (2007: 63) have argued for new forms of CPD that are "continuous and progressive". It has certainly been suggested that teachers need to engage in more collaborative forms of professional learning in teacher networks or professional learning communities (Day and Sachs 2004; Lieberman and Miller 2008). There are also enduring questions about the specific impacts of CPD on either teachers' or pupils' learning (Desimone 2009; Garet *et al.* 2001; Guskey and Yoon 2009; Timperley 2008).

In physical education, research on CPD has mirrored findings in the wider educational field. PE teachers have argued that formal professional development fails to meet their needs (Armour and Yelling 2004a; 2004b; 2007) being largely designed in a traditional off-site, standalone course style focussed on disseminating new policies or updating knowledge of single sports. It has been argued widely that PE teachers need CPD that is both situated and capacity building (Armour, Makopoulou and Chambers, 2012; Ko, Wallhead and Ward 2006; Makopoulou and Armour, 2011a; 2011b; O'Sullivan and Deglau 2006).

The situation in sport coaching is even more complex, but with some similar challenges. Jones, Armour and Potrac (2004) found that CPD activities were described by top level coaches as being narrow, failing to offer coaches scope to develop their own style, and largely irrelevant to the development of an effective coach. Indeed, Jones and Wallace (2005) argued that most coaches are "disillusioned with professional development programmes, which they criticise as being 'fine in theory' but divorced from reality" (p. 121). In echoes of the research on PE-CPD, Nelson, Cushion and Potrac (2006) were critical of coach CPD that is largely organized around traditional courses delivered out of context and without sustained follow-up support. In essence, therefore, despite the different characteristics of the teaching and coaching workforces, with the former having acknowledged professional status and the latter often comprising volunteers, both groups have found that traditional forms of professional development tend to lack the depth, challenge, and relevance they require.

(ii) Narrative as a powerful form of CPD

In 2006, I conducted a review of narrative research in physical education and its value as a professional learning tool for teachers (Armour 2006). Entitled: "The way to a teacher's heart: Narrative research in physical education", the review considered narrative forms of professional knowledge as "powerful professional development" (Clandinin 2001: viii). Underpinning the review was a belief that narrative research has "an unrivalled capacity to reach teachers – to really engage them – and, as a result, to change them and their practices" (Armour 2006: 467). Hinchman and Hinchman (1997) defined narratives as follows:

> Narratives (stories) in the human sciences should be defined provisionally as discourses with a clear sequential order that connect events in a meaningful way for a definite audience and thus offer insights about the world and/or people's experiences of it.
>
> (p. xvi)

In narrative research, it is not only stories "of" that are important. In the context of schools, stories that are created around schools and teachers are also a key feature of, what Clandinin and Connelly (1995) term "the professional knowledge landscape". Importantly, in the context of this book of pedagogical cases, Keats Whelan *et al.* (2001) argue that what practitioners sometimes need is the opportunity to retell and relive stories of practice in order to *imagine new storylines.* These authors conclude that although stories are often used by practitioners as a conservative force (reinforcing decisions taken and accepted storylines), the potential exists for them to be dynamic and revolutionary: "We want, instead, to draw attention to storytelling with diverse responses that leads to restorying with growth and change . . . We are arguing for restorying of the landscape" (p. 154). This is an important principle underpinning the concept of pedagogical cases. In adopting a research-based narrative centred on a young person as the heuristic, the contributing authors offer their different perspectives for debate and challenge. It is anticipated that the cases may generate debate not only between professional pedagogues and students, but also within and between sub-disciplinary specialisms.

(iii) Integrative and inspirational learning tools in education and sport pedagogy

The third aspect of personal voice can be traced through my experiences of teaching pedagogy in a university as a sub-discipline within the multidisciplinary field of sport and exercise sciences/kinesiology/human movement studies. Within the broad human movement field, it could be argued that pedagogy should be an exciting and relevant area of study because (a) all students have personal experience of being taught, coached, or instructed in physical activity settings; (b) pedagogy is the place where different strands of subject knowledge come together in the context of the moving person; and (c) teaching offers a secure career that in some countries – but not all – is also highly valued. Yet, individual pedagogy faculty are unlikely to be experts in all the disciplines required to make sense of human movement. Moreover, faculty from within the core sport sciences are often reluctant to teach pedagogy courses given that they are fully occupied with teaching and research in their own areas of interest and expertise. Instead, students (just like teachers and coaches) are expected to bring their knowledge from specialist sub-disciplines into the pedagogy context in order to integrate and apply it. Yet, there are few effective mechanisms that have been designed specifically to help them to do this integrative work.

In many ways, the generic problems identified earlier regarding the development of integrative knowledge are crystallised in the field of sport and exercise sciences where there is an added tension centred on the hierarchy of valued sub-disciplinary knowledge. In his classic comment, Bernstein (1971) claimed that:

> How a society selects, classifies, distributes, transmits and evaluates the educational knowledge it considers to be public reflects both the distribution of power and the principles of social control.
>
> (p. 47)

An increasing tendency towards the medicalisation of exercise (for example, the exercise prescription approach) and a growing emphasis on physical activity as part of public health agendas (Sallis *et al.* 2012) has resulted in biophysical knowledge being valued above socio-cultural knowledge (in which pedagogy tends to sit). Indeed, in the UK, a recent House of Lords Select Committee investigated the quality of research on elite athletes in sport and exercise sciences, and its translational value for improving the health of the nation. This high profile investigation focussed only on biomedical sub-disciplines with one witness dismissing other aspects of the broad field as "more esoteric areas" (House of Lords 2012: 12). Looking across the pedagogical cases presented in this book, however, it is apparent that attempting to engage young people successfully in physical activity and sport requires an understanding that goes far beyond biophysical or biomedical knowledge.

Within the specific sub-discipline of sport pedagogy (or sport and exercise pedagogy) it might be expected that research-based material would be routinely available to practitioners, yet as was noted in the Introduction to this book, there are problems of access once a student has left university. There is certainly interesting work being developed continuously by academics that would be of value to practising teachers and coaches. One example of an integrative approach in the physical activity/health area is that suggested by Haerens *et al.* (2011). These authors draw on the work of Metzler (2005) and Jewett, Bain, and Ennis (1995) to argue for the development of a pedagogical model for health-based physical education. The proposed model is based on a central theme: "pupils valuing a physically active life, so that they learn to value and practice appropriate physical activities that enhance health and wellbeing for the rest of their lives." (p. 321). It is argued that this theme signals the importance of affective learning to address the traditional "priority given to learning in the motor domain [that] . . . stems from a traditional disciplinary mastery orientation to physical education" (p. 334). Moreover, the theme "requires that teachers' beliefs are oriented toward self-actualization and social reconstruction" (p. 336). What this proposed model does very well is to illustrate the complexity of the process of learning in health-related aspects of physical education, and the need for a broad range of integrated knowledge in order to be successful. Yet, it is difficult to see how teachers and coaches can keep up-to-date with new developments in their subject field *unless* there is a specific enabling mechanism. Moreover, such mechanisms need to be updated regularly and made widely available and accessible. These latter two challenges remain to be addressed over the coming years as the pedagogical cases project evolves.

Returning to an earlier point about the personal experiences and challenges I have faced as a pedagogy professor, it is clear that I am not unique. A special edition of the respected *Journal of Teaching in Physical Education* (2011) focussed on a wide ranging critical review of the state and status of doctoral programmes in sport pedagogy and physical education teacher education (PETE) in the USA. The contributing authors raised critical questions about the number and quality of applicants to pedagogy-related doctoral programmes, and about the content of such programmes. Van der Mars (2011) concluded that pedagogy professors need to collaborate more with faculty from other relevant areas to "show that we can play with others" and move out of the "PE bubble" (p. 205) to address complex problems such as obesity. Ward *et al.* (2011: 184) suggested that D-PETE graduates should be required to study at least two sub-disciplinary areas; and Parker *et al.* (2011: 175) argue for the development of "a common core or shared technical language or culture" to assure the quality and competence of PETE doctoral students. Here again, we return to the same problems identified earlier about the need for open critique and sharing of professional knowledge (Stenhouse 1979).

Shulman (1987) among others has lamented the lack of sharing mechanisms for professional knowledge; indeed, he also referred specifically to the way in which *cases* are used in other professions. He described the loss of such sharing tools and mechanisms tools as resulting in "individual and collective amnesia":

> Unlike fields such as architecture (which preserves its creations in both plans and edifices), law (which builds a case literature of opinions and interpretations) medicine (with its records and case studies) . . . teaching is conducted without an audience of peers. It is devoid of a history of practice.
>
> (p. 11/12)

It is certainly true that observing professional learning in two of these fields provided part of the inspiration to develop pedagogical cases.

Learning from other professions

I would argue that the richness of pedagogical encounters in physical education and youth sport, and the demands of teaching and coaching in dynamic physical activity/sport/human movement settings, deserve the kinds of professional educational tools that are readily available in other fields. Indeed, the inspiration for developing this particular mechanism came from learning about the kinds of case-based learning experiences available to practitioners in medicine and law. It is interesting that Ball (2012) also refers to these fields, among others, arguing that they have found better ways than teaching of closing the knowing-doing gap. In the case of medicine, it might be speculated that the pressure to avoid making errors in professional practice has led to the kinds of robust professional development opportunities from which we, in education, could learn.

Picture two scenes

Scene one

Picture the scene. An audience of 500 specialist medical practitioners (intervention cardiologists) at a conference in a session entitled "Live Cases". There are large screens around the room streaming leading practitioners in another country performing live medical procedures on patients in a hospital location. A panel of leading experts on a stage at the front of the room discusses each case in real time. The panel focuses on the unique features of the case, the decision-making process of the practitioners, *and the research evidence base supporting the decisions made.* Members of the audience ask questions. At the end of the procedure, the practitioners who were performing the procedure explain what they did and why, and again the audience asks questions. This is followed by a session on cases that have been treated previously, and where the outcomes are known. The audience is given information on the case in stages, and at each stage they are asked to identify the best course of action for that case, and the evidence base supporting their decisions. It is a rich and compelling educational process for all participants. The patients being treated are completely anonymous as only the procedure is on screen.

Scene two

Picture another scene. Law students at a university in a series of seminars entitled "Landmark Cases". Prior to the seminars, the students are provided with readings on selected case law that might be relevant to the session. Upon arrival at the seminar, details of complex cases are provided, but not the outcomes. The students debate the cases and are asked to predict what happened and why, drawing on case law in relevant fields. The debates are lively and contributions are evidence-based. Finally, the legal rulings are shared and the decision-making by the judges explained. It is a lively session that is intellectually challenging with clear relevance for practice.

Both scenes described are real, and they share key factors that are relevant to this discussion:

- they are professional learning experiences based on complex cases;
- the cases are unique but their features are also rooted in a wider evidence base;
- participants must be able to understand the complexities of the individual case and draw on an established evidence base to engage in the discussions;
- the cases are integrative; and
- in the medical example, the individuals at the heart of the case are real but anonymous – thereby avoiding ethical concerns about wide dissemination.

This is not to suggest that these two fields have everything right, nor that professional development for PE teachers and youth sport coaches is devoid of some of these features. However, as noted earlier, I would claim that few existing professional development opportunities in our field offer the same degree of education in multidisciplinary and interdisciplinary knowledge in an applied individual context. Yet, at heart, professional practice in education contexts is about meeting the needs of the individual learner. Dewey (1958) stated that "education in order to accomplish its ends both for the individual learner and for society must be based on experience – which is always the actual life-experience of some individual" (p. 113). Moreover, Pajak (2012) highlighted the unique and dynamic challenges of teaching:

> . . . successful teachers, working as true scientists, make adjustments along the way for what they learn about the students, about the learning process, and about themselves, in pursuit of an ephemeral truth that can change as often as one moment to the next.
>
> (p. 1205)

Just like others cited in this chapter, Pajak focuses on understanding teaching as inherently complex; not only about the "narrowly prescribed goals of academic achievement" but also understanding "students' human development needs as well as development of their social, emotional, physical, linguistic, and aesthetic capabilities" (p. 1208). Perhaps one of the key contributions that pedagogical cases can make to the literature is to illustrate just how futile it is likely to be to conceive of education in any other way.

Conclusion

> The quality of an education system cannot exceed the quality of its teachers and principals.
>
> (OECD 2011: 235)

> Increasingly, researchers have recognised the complex interactive nature of coaching, highlighting its multifaceted, integrated and dynamic character.
>
> (Jones, Bowes and Kingston 2010: 15)

As has already been emphasised, pedagogical cases are offered as a professional learning resource for students and practitioners, and a translational research mechanism. They may also serve as a focal point for academic discussion and debate within sport/exercise pedagogy and across sub-disciplines in the wider fields upon which they draw. Hochstetler (2013: 197) argues that "Perhaps the most essential aspect of teaching and learning . . . is developing connections or relations . . . [including] . . . between themes and subject matter of various sorts". No one who has attempted to teach or coach young people in physical education and youth sport can doubt the truth of that statement.

The pedagogical cases presented in this book certainly attempt to make connections between sub-disciplines in the field and beyond. The aim is to help professional teachers and coaches to better serve their young clients by offering access to research and theory that can both inform and challenge established practice. At this stage, pedagogical cases as presented in this book might best be described as prototypes or proof of concept. As was noted in the Introduction, none of the chapter authors had worked in this way previously and most reported learning much in the process. In the next set of cases, the intention is to develop the tool even further by working to achieve greater levels of synthesis that can offer the possibility of generating new pedagogical knowledge. In her AERA presidential address, Ball (2012) was convinced of the need to address the knowing-doing gap in education research, but she posed the question: How? (p. 287). Perhaps one response is to use a mechanism such as the pedagogical cases presented in this book.

References

Abernathy, B., Kippers, V., Hanrahan, S. J., Pandy, M.G., Mcmanus, A.M. and Mackinnon, L. (2013) *The Biophysical Foundations of Human Movement.* Australia: Macmillan.

Abernathy, B., Kippers, V., Mackinnon, L., Neal, R. J. and Hanrahan, S. (1996) *The Biophysical Foundations of Human Movement.* Australia: Macmillan.

Akkerman, S.F. and Van Eijck, M. (2013) 'Re-theorising the student dialogically across and between boundaries of multiple communities', *British Educational Research Journal,* 39(1): 60–72.

Alexander, R. (2008) *Essays on Pedagogy.* London: Routledge.

Armour, K.M. (2006) 'Narrative research in physical education: the way to a teacher's heart', in D. Kirk, D. Macdonald and M. O'Sullivan (eds.) *Handbook of Research in Physical Education* (pp. 467–487). London: Sage.

Armour, K.M. (2011) *Sport Pedagogy: An Introduction for Teaching and Coaching.* London: Pearson.

Armour, K.M. and Harris, J.P. (2013) 'Making the case for developing new "PE-for-Health" pedagogies', *Quest,* 65(2): 201–219.

Armour, K.M., Makopoulou, K. and Chambers, F.C. (2012) 'Progression in PE teachers' career-long professional learning: conceptual and practical concerns', *European Physical Education Review,* 18: 62–77.

Armour, K.M. and Yelling, M.R. (2004a) 'Continuing professional development for experienced physical education teachers: towards effective provision', *Sport, Education and Society,* 9(1): 95–114.

Armour, K.M. and Yelling, M.R. (2004b) 'Professional development and professional learning: bridging the gap for experienced physical education teachers', *European Physical Education Review,* 10(1): 71–94.

Armour, K.M. and Yelling, M.R. (2007) 'Effective professional development for physical education teachers: the role of informal, collaborative learning', *Journal of Teaching in Physical Education,* 26(2): 177–200.

Ball, A.F. (2012) '2012 Presidential Address. To know is not enough: knowledge, power and the zone of generativity', *Educational Researcher,* 41(8): 283–293.

Bernstein, B. (1971) 'On the classification and framing of educational Knowledge', in M.F.D. Young (ed.) *Knowledge and Control* (pp. 47–69). London: Collier Macmillan.

Borko, H. (2004) 'Professional development and teacher learning: mapping the terrain', *Educational Researcher,* 33(8): 3–15.

Brunetti, G.J. (1998) 'Teacher education: a look at its future', *Teacher Education Quarterly,* Fall: 59–64.

Clandinin, D.J. (2001) 'Foreword', in C.M. Clark (ed.) *Talking Shop* (p. viii). New York: Teachers College.

Clandinin, D.J. and Connelly, F.M. (1995) *Teachers' Professional Knowledge Landscapes.* New York: Teachers' College Press.

Committee on Facilitating Interdisciplinary Research, Committee on Science, Engineering, and Public Policy (2004) *Facilitating Interdisciplinary Research.* Washington DC: National Academy Press.

Day, C. (2002) 'The challenge to be the best: reckless curiosity and mischievous motivation', *Teachers and Teaching: Theory and Practice,* 8(3/4): 421–434.

Day, C. and Sachs, J. (2004) 'Professionalism, performativity and empowerment: discourses in the politics, policies and purposes of continuing professional development', in C. Day and J. Sachs (eds.) *International Handbook on the Continuing Professional Development of Teachers* (pp. 3–32). Milton Keynes: Open University Press.

Department for Education and Employment – DfEE (2001) *Learning and Teaching: A Strategy for Professional Development.* Nottingham: DfEE Publications.

Desimone, L.M. (2009) 'Improving impact studies of teachers' professional development: toward better conceptualisations and measures', *Educational Researcher,* 38(3): 181–199.

Dewey, J. (1958) *Experience and Education.* New York: Touchstone.

Gardner, H. and Boix-Mansilla, V. (1999) 'Teaching for understanding in the disciplines – and beyond', in J. Leach and B. Moon (eds.) *Learners and Pedagogy* (pp. 78–88). London: Paul Chapman.

Garet, M.S., Porter, A.C., Desimone, L., Birman, B.F. and Yoon, K.S. (2001) 'What makes professional development effective? Results from a national sample of teachers', *American Educational Research Journal*, 38(4): 915–945.

Grossman, P.L. (1989) 'A study in contrast: Sources of pedagogical content knowledge for secondary English', *Journal of Teacher Education*, 40: 24–31.

Guskey, T.R. (1994) 'Results-oriented professional development in search of an optimal mix of effective practices', *Journal of Staff Development*, 15: 42–50.

Guskey, T.R. (2002) 'Professional development and teacher change', *Teachers and Teaching: Theory and Practice*, 8(3/4): 381–391.

Guskey, T.R. and Yoon, K.S. (2009) 'What works in professional development', *Phi Delta Kappan*, March: 495–501.

Haerens, L., Kirk, D., Cardon, G. and De Bourdeaudhuij, I. (2011) 'Toward the development of a pedagogical model for health-based physical education', *Quest*, 63: 321–338.

Hinchman L.P. and Hinchman, S.K. (1997) 'Introduction', in L.P. Hinchman and S.K. Hinchman (eds.) *Memory, Identity, Community: The Idea of Narrative in the Human Science* (pp. xiii–xxxii). New York: University of New York.

Hochstetler, D. (2013) 'Pedagogy and the teacher within: reflections on Thoreau and kinesiology in higher education', *Quest*, 65(2): 186–200.

House of Lords (18 July 2012) 'Sport and exercise science and medicine: building on the Olympic legacy to improve the nation's health', *Select Committee on Science and Technology*. London: The Stationery Office Ltd.

James, M., McCormick, R., Black, P., *et al.* (2007) *Improving Learning How to Learn: Classrooms, Schools and Networks*. London: Routledge.

Jewett, A.E., Bain, L.L. and Ennis, C.D. (1995) *The Curriculum Process in Physical Education*. Dubuque, IA: Brown & Benchmark.

Jones, R.L., Armour, K.M. and Potrac, P. (2004) 'Constructing expert knowledge: a case-study of a top-level professional soccer coach', *Sport Education and Society*, 8(2): 213–229.

Jones, R.L., Bowes, I. and Kingston, K. (2010) 'Complex practice in coaching: studying the chaotic nature of coach-athlete interactions', in J. Lyle and C. Cushion (eds.) *Sport Coaching. Professionalism and Practice* (pp. 15–26). London: Elsevier.

Jones, R.L. and Wallace, M. (2005) 'Another bad day at the training ground: coping with ambiguity in the coaching context', *Sport, Education and Society*, 10: 119–134.

Keane, C.B. and Miller, B.F. (2003) *The Miller-Keane Encyclopedia and Dictionary of Medicine, Nursing, and Allied Health*, ed. B.F. Miller and M.T. O'Toole, 7th ed., Philadelphia: Saunders.

Keats Whelan K., Huber, J., Rose, C., Davies, A. and Clandinin, D.J. (2001) 'Telling and retelling our stories on the professional knowledge landscape', *Teachers and Teaching: Theory and Practice*, 7(2): 143–156.

Kirk, D., Macdonald, D. and O'Sullivan, M. (2006) *The Handbook of Physical Education*. London: Sage.

Ko, B., Wallhead, T. and Ward, P. (2006) 'Professional development workshops – what do teachers learn and use?', *Journal of Teaching in Physical Education*, 25: 367–412.

Leach, J. and Moon, B. (1999) *Learners and Pedagogy*. London: Paul Chapman.

Lee, C.D. (2010) '2010 Presidential Address. Soaring above the clouds, delving into the ocean's depths: understanding the ecologies of human learning and the challenge for education science', *Educational Researcher*, 39(9): 643–655

Lieberman, A. and Miller, L. (2008) *Teachers in Professional Communities*. New York: Teachers College.

Makopoulou, K. and Armour, K. (2011a) 'Physical education teachers' career-long learning: getting personal', *Sport, Education and Society*, 16(5): 571–591.

Makopoulou, K. and Armour, K. (2011b) 'Teachers' professional learning in a European Learning Society: the case of physical education', *Physical Education and Sport Pedagogy*, i-First Article: 1–17.

Metzler, M.W. (2005) *Instructional Models for Physical Education*, 2nd ed., Scottsdale, AZ: Holcomb Hathaway.

Nelson, L.J., Cushion, C.J. and Potrac, P. (2006) 'Formal, nonformal and informal coach learning', *International Journal of Sport Science and Coaching,* 1(3): 247–259.

OECD (2011) *Lessons from PISA for the United States: Strong Performers and Successful Reformers in Education.* Online. Available HTTP: <www.oecd.org/dataoecd/32/50/46623978.pdf> (accessed 21 September 2013).

O'Sullivan, M. and Deglau, D.A. (2006) 'Principles of professional development', *Journal of Teaching in Physical Education,* 25(4): 441–449.

Pajak, E.P. (2012) 'Willard Waller's sociology of teaching reconsidered: what does teaching do to teachers?' *American Educational Research Journal,* 49(6): 1182–1213.

Parker, M., Sutherland, S., Sinclair, C. and Ward, P. (2011) 'Not surprised, but concerned: the professoriate's reaction to PETE doctoral education in the United States', *Journal of Teaching in Physical Education,* 30(2): 157–177.

Repko, A.F. (2011) *Interdisciplinary Research: Process and Theory.* London: Sage.

Rovegno, I. (2003) 'Teachers' knowledge construction', in S. Silverman and C. Ennis (eds.) *Student Learning in Physical Education: Applying Research to Enhance Instruction* (pp. 295–310). Champaign, IL: Human Kinetics.

Sallis, J.F., McKenzie, T.L., Beets, M.W., Beighle, A., Erwin, H. and Lee, S. (2012) 'Physical education's role in public health: steps forward and backward over 20 years and HOPE for the future', *Research Quarterly for Exercise and Sport,* 83(2): 125–135.

Shulman, L. (1987) 'Knowledge and teaching: Foundation of a new reform', *Harvard Review,* 57: 1–22.

Stake, R. E. (2005) 'Qualitative case studies', in N.K. Denzin and Y.S. Lincoln (eds.) *The Sage Handbook of Qualitative Research* (pp. 443–466). Thousand Oaks, CA: Sage.

Stenhouse, L. (1979) 'Presidential address: the study of samples and the study of cases', Published in the *British Educational Research Journal, 6,* 1, 1980. Available HTTP: <www.spanglefish.com/Action ResearchCanada/documents/Stenhouse,_1979.pdf> (accessed 21 September 2013).

Stone, E. (2000) 'Iconoclastes: poor pedagogy', *Journal of Teaching for Education,* 26(1): 93–95.

Thomas, G. (2011) *How To Do Your Case Study.* London: Sage.

Timperley, H. (2008) *Teacher professional learning and development.* UNESCO/International Academy of Education. Online. Available HTTP: <www.ibe.unesco.org/fileadmin/user_upload/Publications/Educational_Practices/EdPractices_18.pdf> (accessed 21 September 2013).

Tinning, R. (2008) 'Pedagogy, sport pedagogy, and the field of kinesiology', *Quest,* 60: 405–424.

Van der Mars, H. (2011) 'Reflecting on the state of U.S. Doctoral PETE problems . . . Houston, we've had a problem', *Journal of Teaching in Physical Education,* 30(2): 189–208.

Ward, P., Sutherland, S., Woods, M.L., Boyce, B.A., Goc Karp, G., Judd, M., Parker, M., Rikard, G.L., and Sinclair, C. (2011) 'The Doctorate in Physical education teacher education in the 21st century, contexts and challenges', *Journal of Teaching in Physical Education,* 30(2): 178–188.

Wathne, K. (2011) 'Movement of large bodies impaired: the double burden of obesity: somatic and semiotic issues', *Sport, Education and Society,* 16(4): 415–429.

Watkins, C. and Mortimore, P. (1999) 'Pedagogy: what do we know?' in P. Mortimore (ed.) *Understanding Pedagogy and its Implications* (pp. 1–19). London: Paul Chapman.

Wayne, A.J., Suk Yoon, K., Zhu, P., Cronen, S. and Garet, M.S. (2008) 'Experimenting with teacher professional development: motives and methods', *Educational Researcher,* 37(8): 469–479.

2

SOPHIE

A preschooler who is 'busy' – but not very active

Leen Haerens, Greet Cardon, Matthieu Lenoir, Jan Bourgo, Christine De Medts and Lynn Van den Berghe

DEPARTMENT OF MOVEMENT AND SPORT SCIENCES, UNIVERSITY OF GHENT, BELGIUM

Key words: 5-year-old female, motor delay, fundamental movement skills, overweight, physical activity and health, motor development, physiology, pedagogy.

Sophie

Sophie is a 5-year-old female preschooler who lives with her parents and is an only child. Both her mom and dad work very hard; her dad always works late shifts and is usually in bed in the mornings when it's time for Sophie to prepare for school.

Sophie and her parents live in a small house just outside the city centre of Ghent in Belgium. They don't have a garden, but they don't mind as they have a sunny terrace where they can sit outside. Although there is a playground nearby, the family does not often go there; Sophie never asks for it and they prefer to stay at home during their leisure time. Sophie's parents are very protective, hence avoiding situations in which she could fall or hurt herself in any other way. As her parents make her constantly aware of possible dangers, Sophie tends to avoid activities such as climbing on the playground equipment, and she is rather resistant to trying new things. Some children in Sophie's class have already learnt to ride a bicycle, but Sophie shows no interest in trying this activity.

During Physical Education (PE), Sophie always gets tagged first in chasing games. She finds it very difficult to catch a ball without dropping it, and jumping with two feet at the same time seems to be impossible. Sophie notices that some children in her class engage in very "dangerous" actions, such as rolling head over heels or jumping from a plinth. Although Sophie is not really aware of it, most of the other children are a lot more physically able than she is. PE lessons are stressful for Sophie, so she does not enjoy them at all. The other children have noticed that Sophie seems to be scared of many things.

The preschool teacher has become increasingly aware that Sophie experiences problems during PE lessons. While running, she barely moves her arms, and even when a big softball is used, she has difficulty throwing. Many other children in the class are able to throw and catch such a ball with confidence. The teacher has also noticed that Sophie is genuinely fearful during these lessons and that she always tries to avoid activities such as jumping from a bench, even from a low height.

Sophie is one of the 20 preschoolers in the class group, and she behaves very well. She is not as easily distracted as some children: she can sustain work on a task and she always pays attention to the teacher. Sophie clearly enjoys herself when she is in a classroom setting where she can sit down quietly and draw or play. Sophie also prefers to do most activities on her own. The teacher has noticed that Sophie still has problems with zipping her jacket or walking down the stairs, but feels reassured that she is academically advanced and so she generally does really well in the classroom. During recess, Sophie usually holds the teacher's hand when walking around or she sits on a bench talking to a friend. Other children, meanwhile, are a lot more active more of the time; they run around, climb on the playground towers or constantly go up and down the slides.

Every two years, all children in Belgian schools undergo a medical assessment[1]. Although the medical doctor has noted that Sophie is a little overweight, this has not been recorded as a health problem at this stage. Sophie's hearing and sight are excellent, she answers standard questions well and, when asked, she draws an age-appropriate picture of her mother. The medical doctor reported back to her parents and teacher that Sophie's health is perfectly fine. He also provided Sophie's parents with information about healthy eating guidelines in the form of a little booklet. He emphasized the point that healthy eating is really important for Sophie because she is a little overweight compared to the parameters for her age.

At home, Sophie is always very enthusiastic when she talks about school and her preschool teacher. From what she says, it would appear that Sophie really enjoys school. Sophie's parents don't notice any problems because she is their first and only child, and they don't have much contact with other children from this age group. Moreover, they believe that Sophie is sufficiently active because she seeks a lot of attention and, like many preschoolers, appears 'busy' most of the time.

Sophie's mom has to start work early in the morning so she always helps Sophie getting dressed to avoid losing much time. Once she is dressed, Sophie is allowed to watch television while having breakfast so that her mom can get ready for work. Sophie's mom then drives Sophie to school, dropping her off on the way to work. Sophie's dad works late shifts, so he sleeps a little longer in the morning. On her way back from work, Sophie's mom drives via the school and takes Sophie home. After school, Sophie relaxes in front of the TV with a snack. Her mom, meantime, can cook the evening meal without interruption.

Although a lot of the children in Sophie's class attend early morning gym or swimming lessons at the weekend, Sophie's parents are reluctant to encourage it. On Saturday mornings they prefer to sleep a little longer, and they are convinced that a 5-year-old child needs her rest after a very busy school week. Early-start gym or swimming lessons are also expensive, so although some of the other parents have suggested the family joins in, they have never really considered it.

During the weekend, Sophie's parents catch up with household tasks such as ironing and cleaning. Sophie spends her time drawing, colouring, doing puzzles or playing computer games; all activities she enjoys. On Sundays, Sophie and her parents visit Sophie's grandparents. Sophie really enjoys these visits as her grandmother always bakes a cake.

Physical activity (PA) levels and sedentary behaviours in preschoolers

Regular PA is critical for the health and well-being of preschool children as it leads to improved motor, musculoskeletal, and psychosocial development and a reduced risk of being overweight or obese (e.g. Janz *et al.* 2009; Lobo and Winsler 2006). Furthermore, active preschoolers are more likely to remain active in later life, making them at lower risk for diseases and/or obesity (Okely, Salmon, Trost and Hinkley 2008). According to the recently released health related guidelines (Australian Government 2012), preschoolers should be physically active for at least three hours daily. PA can be accumulated throughout the day through light activities such as standing up, moving around and playing as well as through engagement in more vigorous activities such as running and jumping. According to the reviews undertaken by Hinkley *et al.* (Hinkley *et al.* 2008; Hinkley *et al.* 2010) the majority of preschoolers are insufficiently active to gain health benefits. The promotion of PA in young children should, therefore, be the shared responsibility of parents, communities, and schools.

For preschoolers, the *home* and especially the *parents* play a major role in PA promotion. Children with active parents tend to be more active, and children who spend more time outdoors are more active than children who spent less time outdoors (Hinkley *et al.* 2008; Cardon and De Bourdeaudhuij 2008). In particular, the period of time at home after the school day ends offers lots of opportunities for children to be active. It is interesting to note, therefore, that when looking at PA patterns in preschoolers, this period of the day is often spent being largely inactive (Verbestel *et al.* 2011).

Results from focus groups with parents and preschool teachers in different European countries have pointed to some important factors in encouraging PA for young children. Examples include: increasing safety in the *neighbourhood* by addressing problems with traffic, teenage gangs etc.; and promoting a wide range of activities in the *community* (e.g. not only the most popular or traditional sports) (De Craemer *et al.* in press). The most frequently identified barriers for preschoolers are a lack of playgrounds adapted for young children and the lack of appropriate sport grounds, swimming pools and green spaces.

After the home, schools and *preschool teachers* have many opportunities to address low levels of PA. Recess is, of course, an ideal setting for PA (Cardon *et al.* 2008). According to a study of 583 Belgian preschoolers, however, activity levels during recess (unstructured free outdoor play) are rather low. Preschoolers spend 61% of their recess time being sedentary while only 11% is spent in moderate to vigorous PA (Cardon *et al.* 2009). Although providing playground markings and loose toys during recess appears to promote activity in slightly older children, these strategies do not appear to be as effective in preschoolers (Cardon *et al.* 2009). Instead, active supervision, including playing with the children, and stimulating them to play actively, are essential to promote PA (Cardon *et al.* 2009).

Further research on PA levels in recess found that longer recess time was associated with lower PA levels for preschoolers. This might be explained by the boost of activity at the start of recess, when entering the playground, and its subsequent drop. Interestingly, the density of children in the playground was shown to be the strongest predictor of activity during recess. Increasing available play space by rescheduling recess time was shown to be an effective strategy to promote PA and decrease sitting during recess (Van Cauwenberghe *et al.* 2012a).

The promotion of PA in preschoolers can also happen in a more structured way. In Flanders, the inclusion of PE in preschool programmes is mandatory. Yet, direct observations of PE lessons involving 272 preschoolers in 16 schools found that preschoolers were very active during only 18% of lesson time (on average 16 minutes), while 51% of the PE lesson time was spent sitting or standing (Cardon *et al.* 2010). In these classes, the teachers spent most of the time giving instructions because, according to the preschool teachers, motor learning is the main objective of preschool PE sessions. Motor learning is indeed very important for preschool children (see next section), but it does not necessarily correlate with high activity levels. As this study demonstrated, the inclusion of a PE lesson contributes only minimally to overall PA levels in preschoolers. It is important, therefore, to integrate PA throughout the entire day; PE can contribute to overall PA, but cannot 'claim' to be delivering PA alone.

Recently, sedentary behaviours have emerged as a new focus of research in preschoolers (e.g. Marshall and Ramirez 2011). Sedentary behaviour is not only the absence of PA nor the opposite, but rather a unique set of behaviours that involve sitting or lying down and that require very low levels of energy expenditure. Evidence shows it is not only important to accumulate sufficient amounts of activity; it is equally important to interrupt time spent in sedentary behaviours, even for very young children (Okely *et al.* 2008). More specifically, preschoolers should not sit still for longer than one hour at a time. Additionally, it is recommended that TV viewing should not exceed one hour daily (Australian Government 2012). Evidence, however, shows that preschoolers spend 50–80% of their awake time in sedentary pursuits. More specifically, screen time, and especially TV viewing, is very prevalent in most preschoolers. Studies in the US and Australia indicate that most 4- to 7-year-old children watched TV or played computer games for more than two hours daily (Heelan and Eisenmann 2006; Salmon, Telford and Crawford 2004). In Belgium, parental reports indicated that preschool children's screen time was on average 74 minutes on weekdays and 140 minutes on weekend days (Cardon and De Bourdeaudhuij 2008).

The reported findings on preschoolers' engagement in PA and sedentary behaviours might be counterintuitive. It is common, however, to find that preschoolers are perceived to be much more active than they actually are (Reilly 2008). Findings from focus group conversations conducted within the European ToyBox project showed that parents and preschool teachers believe that most preschoolers are sufficiently active (De Craemer *et al.* In press). Preschoolers are indeed often busy and demanding. When using objective measurement instruments like accelerometers or direct observations, however, it is very clear that most preschoolers spend the majority of their time being sedentary both at home and in preschool (Cardon and De Bourdeaudhuij 2008).

Motor development and learning in preschoolers

After the first two years of life, the repertoire of subcortically controlled reflexes has been replaced by voluntary movements, the so-called motor milestones. These include activities such as sitting, standing, walking alone, grasping and manipulating objects, to name just a few. The child is able to move independently against gravity and inertia, and has started to deliberately explore the environment (Haibach, Reid and Collier 2011).

Between the ages of 2 and 6, multiple new coordination patterns emerge that allow the child to move faster or better. Children can cope with more difficult challenges such as climbing a tower in the playground, can interact with other children by playing ball games, and make progress academically through improved manipulative skills such as drawing or handling scissors. Such skills are called fundamental movement skills (FMS) and can be divided into stability, locomotion and manipulation (Gabbard, 2008; Haibach, Reid and Collier 2011).

By the age of 5, fundamental movement patterns should be quite well developed. They will form the basis for the development of skills needed for future academic achievement (e.g. writing), playing music instruments, and participation in a range of sports and other physical activities. More specifically, a 5 year old who is developing at a typical rate should master the following:

- basic *locomotion skills* such as running (forward/backward), jumping (hopping, skipping, galloping, jumping on/from one or two feet, downwards and upwards etc.); and
- *manipulation skills* such as catching (at the age of 5, a ball is generally caught with two hands without touching the trunk), throwing, kicking and striking.

The child is also able to maintain *balance* in increasingly challenging situations, for example, walking on a balance beam or standing on one foot for a couple of seconds. Basic forms of climbing and rolling are also mastered. It has been demonstrated, for example, that a 5 year old should be able to execute a basic forward roll (e.g. Haibach, Reid and Collier 2011; Gabbard 2008). At this age, these skills are not fully established, but they will further develop and refine during the upcoming years if the child has enough opportunities to engage in them.

There is strong evidence that the optimal time frame within which to develop motor coordination and fundamental movement skills is *before* the age of seven (Vandorpe *et al.* 2012). This means that after that age, children with motor development delays will struggle to compensate for the delay when learning skills, such as those required for sport. This finding can also be viewed more positively; because in preschoolers, the central nervous system and the perceptual-motor system in general are still so sensitive to additional stimulation that a minimal effort can lead to a significant improvement in motor skill (Rietmuller, Jones and Okely 2009; Bardid *et al.* submitted).

From the age of 6 years onwards, FMS are refined, elaborated upon and, above all, *adapted* to changing individual constraints, task demands and environmental characteristics. As an example of this process, a solid basis for locomotion might be transferred to the mastering of more complex locomotion skills such as those required to run over hurdles with a specific technique. Nonetheless, the optimal development of these fundamental movement skills is a process that should not be taken for granted. Motor development is not a passive process that solely depends on the maturation of the central nervous system. The basic topography and the chief functions of the brain are mainly determined by genes inherited from the parents, but the number of neuronal connections and the quality of neuronal networks depend, to a very large extent, on the stimuli the brain receives in the early years. The brain can be considered as the engine that drives motor development, while the stimulation of the brain to explore new movement possibilities is the fuel feeding the engine. What a child needs, therefore, for optimal motor development, is the opportunity to *stimulate* the central nervous system *repeatedly*, with a large amount of *variability*, and sufficient *feedback*. Each of these three prerequisites is discussed briefly below.

Stimulating

Mastering a new motor skill, or in other words developing a novel coordination pattern, implies changes in neural connections in the brain. The neuronal connectivity in the brain is stimulated by trying to execute a new skill. Repetition of a given coordination pattern will result in the stabilization of neural connections; the higher the number of repetitions, the stronger the newly established connections. A child will only become a proficient 'line drawer' after a sufficient number of trials, and this is the case for any new skill learnt in this age group.

Repeatedly

A new motor skill cannot be mastered without trying, and trying also implies making mistakes. This trial-and-error process, and more particularly the mistakes that are made, are not a waste of time. When young children have the opportunity to explore and make errors, they will learn the difference between a movement solution that works and one that does not work in a given situation. At the level of the central nervous system, this means that connections that do not result in a satisfactory coordination pattern are abandoned, while the successful ones are consolidated.

Variability

This brings us to the issue of *variability*, which is inherently connected to motor development. There is solid evidence to suggest that a lack of movement variability in the first years of life is associated with developmental delays or deviations (Hadders-Algra 2010). In the preschool years, children expand their skill repertoire by (a) executing variations on a given motor skill, and (b) applying different motor skills to solve a movement problem. For example, a child of 5 years old should be able to run on a solid surface as well as on an unstable layer such as sand when on holiday. In both cases the child is running, but with subtle variations that are the result of environmental constraints. When the child wants to climb a sand dune, he or she might switch from walking to creeping when the slope becomes too steep.

Feedback

Feedback is information on the process and outcome of an intended action. It is essential for a child to know whether his/her solution for a given movement problem was a good one or one that needs modification or even deleting. Feedback can be generated intrinsically, meaning that it is generated by the mere execution of the movement through proprioceptive or visual information. A child that has just managed to kick a ball into the goal does not need an external source of feedback to realize that his/her coordination pattern was acceptable. Extrinsic feedback can be generated by different sources: school teachers, coaches or parents, but also by the child's peers.

When exercise physiology comes into play

Physical activity (PA) is a complex set of behaviours encompassing any bodily movement produced by skeletal muscles that results in energy expenditure above resting level. *Exercise*, on the other hand, can be seen as a form of PA that is planned, structured and repetitive. *Exercise physiology* can be defined as the study of how the human body, from a functional standpoint, responds, adjusts and adapts to PA and exercise.

Basic study areas in the domain of exercise physiology are bioenergetics and metabolism, and the cardiovascular, pulmonary, nervous, muscular, endocrine, immune and skeletal systems. In exercise physiology research, this is one example of a research question: how does the cardiovascular system, which includes the heart, blood vessels and blood, respond to meet the demands of the body during exercise? Knowledge generated from such studies can be applied to different settings (health and fitness clubs, clinical settings etc.) and different environmental circumstances (health and humidity, altitude etc.).

Pediatric exercise physiology especially deals with growth, maturation and development during childhood and hence generates important knowledge for the pedagogy of PE. It is generally agreed that there is considerable variation in biological characteristics, especially during childhood. *Growth* refers to measureable changes in size of the body or any of its parts, and there are wide variations in endpoints such as stature. *Maturation* refers to the tempo and timing of progress towards the mature biological state, which is also quite variable. *Development* reflects the biological changes that occur during growth, such as the age changes in maximal oxygen uptake (i.e. the highest rate of oxygen consumption, expressed in liter.min^{-1}, attainable during maximal or exhaustive exercise) and the significant differences between boys and girls. Growth, maturation, and development interact with one another, but have a different timing (Bourgois and Vrijens 2001). It is clear, therefore, that PE teachers and coaches are likely to be responsible for groups of 5 year olds that are very divergent in terms of growth, maturation and development.

Over the last two decades, there has been an exponential progression in pediatric exercise physiology research on PA, and the beneficial health and performance effects of PA and exercise in the age group 8–18 years. There is, however, very little data on preschoolers. There are a number of explanations for this gap in the research: lack of large-scale longitudinal studies and randomized control studies; difficulties inherent in measuring health, fitness and activity in preschoolers; general failure to control for potential intrinsic and extrinsic confounders (e.g. naturally occurring physiological shifts in growth and maturation and environmental influences); and ethical considerations (Cumming and Riddoch 2008). Moreover, decelerated or accelerated physiological responses, adjustments and adaptations to PA and exercise, and relevance and functional impact on current or future health and well being, are particularly apparent in the 8–16 age range (Malina and Bouchard 1991; Armstrong and Van Mechelen 2008).

In the research that does exist on the preschool age group, the main areas covered are measurement of PA levels and sedentary behaviours, and motor development and learning (see earlier sections) and their relationship with health indicators such as adiposity, psychosocial health and cognitive development (LeBlanc *et al.* 2012; Timmons *et al.* 2012; Tremblay *et al.* 2012). In a systematic literature review that found 22 articles representing 18 unique studies and 12742 enrolled participants, Timmons *et al.* (2012) found mixed evidence in preschoolers about the relationship between increased or higher PA and improved measures of adiposity and cardio-metabolic health indicators.

Anthropological studies suggest that PA is inherent in our genes (Booth *et al.* 2000). Most young children enjoy active play and will invent ways of passing time, which provide large amounts of PA. This activity will incorporate a wide variety of movements, using many muscle groups, and promoting cardio-respiratory development, muscle strength, muscle endurance, speed, power and flexibility (Cumming and Riddoch 2008). Yet, Sophie's behaviour and lifestyle tell a different story. There is growing evidence to suggest that preschool children spend increasing amounts of time being sedentary, both in and outside of school (LeBlanc *et al.* 2012).

From a genetic and molecular point of view, physical *inactivity* is physiologically abnormal. The discrepancy between gene functioning and physically inactive behaviour and lifestyle contributes to the development of a range of chronic diseases, which can be tracked into adulthood (Booth *et al.* 2000). So, despite the fact that PA in children shows little or no relationship with their aerobic fitness (probably because children rarely experience enough PA to promote aerobic fitness), a physically active lifestyle that begins during childhood is one factor (of many) that appears to influence growth and maturation in positive ways.

Children clearly adapt to the stress imposed by PA. Regular PA has no apparent effect on statural growth and maturation, but it is an important factor in the regulation of body weight. Children who participate frequently in PA usually have more fat-free mass, and less fat mass than those who are not active. PA also enhances bone mineralization and density although it is important to note that bone growth in width – but not in length – is increased by regular PA (Malina and Bouchard 1991). Taking into account the points covered in the earlier sections, it is clear that PA has a wide range of other benefits that are crucial to ongoing physiological functioning (Armstrong and Van Mechelen 2008). We can conclude, therefore, that preschool children should be given the best possible chances to participate in PA and exercise.

Pedagogical comment on the case study based on expert inputs

One of the stated aims of all compulsory PE programmes in the world is to improve motor skill competence and to educate for lifelong engagement in PA for health (Pühse and Gerber 2005). Current evidence shows that PE 'is currently the pill not taken' (McKenzie and Lounsbery 2009), largely because there is a lack of evidence and consensus on how resources for PE can be most effectively spent in different age groups (Haerens *et al.* 2011). The contributions in this chapter illustrate clearly that if we put the needs of the individual child at the heart of our pedagogies, as suggested by Armour (2011), very different approaches will be needed across age groups. In preschoolers, the focus clearly needs to be on the development of motor coordination and FMS through engagement in a wide range of physical activities. If children do not develop a solid basis in motor coordination and FMS between the ages of two and seven, they are unlikely to become competent in more advanced sports-related skills or activities in elementary or secondary school.

In Belgium, children from all social backgrounds experience formal PE from the age of three. Furthermore, in contrast to the situation in other countries, specialized PE teachers deliver most of the lessons. Internationally, most of the specialist resources for PE are directed towards older children in secondary schools (from around age 11). The evidence-based information provided in this chapter raises questions about the wisdom of this policy. The importance of providing high quality PE lessons for young children is clear, and it could even be argued that the resources allocated to older children will remain largely ineffective if no solid basis is provided at a younger age.

Integrating the evidence to discuss the pedagogy of PE in preschoolers

If children like Sophie are insufficiently active (less than 180 minutes per day), this not only has important contemporary health consequences (such as increased risk of developing obesity), it also causes the brain to receive insufficient stimuli necessary for optimal motor development.

When children with lower motor competence, like Sophie, grow older, they begin to compare themselves with others, and they start to notice their lack of competence. This knowledge means that they are less likely to experience success and enjoyment, which might cause them to become even more inactive and develop fewer motor skills. To break this *negative spiral of disengagement* (Stodden *et al.* 2008), children like Sophie need to develop their motor competence at very young age.

There could also be a positive side to this story. If specialized PE teachers deliver PE effectively to preschoolers and manage to promote movement experiences in the wider context of the child (school, home and community), young children will develop a solid base in motor coordination and FMS. This can lead to a *positive spiral of engagement*. For this to happen, it seems clear that 'Movement education' for preschoolers should be a shared responsibility of the entire school team because children develop motor competence through both structured and unstructured activities.

Structured PE lessons can have dramatic positive effects on preschoolers' motor competence development and their engagement in PA in and beyond school, even if the time is limited (Robinson and Goodway 2009). In the case of Sophie, a targeted intervention through preschool PE could work a small miracle for her motor development. Ideally, PE lessons include activities that can develop:

- locomotion skills like running, jumping, and crawling;
- manipulation skills like catching, throwing, rolling and kicking; and
- stability skills like climbing and standing on one foot.

These activities should preferably be provided in the curriculum through a wide range of activities. For example, in order to develop the skill of 'kicking', teachers can modify the size or type of the goal or balls to vary the degree of difficulty. Variations can also involve the use of materials such as sticks or rackets (De Medts *et al.* 2008; De Medts *et al.* 2012). In this way, the motor skill of 'kicking' is developed in variety of situations that require different solutions to the same motor problem. Furthermore, research in Belgium has found that additional emphasis is needed on the development of balancing skills (e.g. walking or climbing on stable or unstable surfaces) in a wide range of variations (wide versus small, low versus high, or flat versus sloping surfaces) (Van Cauwenberghe *et al.* 2012b).

Clearly, providing a variety of activities is important but not sufficient. Young children also benefit from receiving feedback and encouragement from teachers and peers. Even at the preschool stage, peers can serve as providers of help, encouragement and feedback. Preschoolers can offer help when climbing over an obstacle, they can hold hoops to crawl through or as targets and they can be taught to applaud or support each other to encourage perseverance in a task. Using child-friendly drawings, they can also provide some simple feedback, for example, on the best placement of the hands on a bench or on the number of goals scored by their friends (De Medts *et al.* 2008; De Medts *et al.* 2012).

While the goals of PE lessons in preschool aim at developing motor coordination and FMS, efforts to make the PE lesson as physically active as possible are clearly an asset too (Cardon *et al.* 2010). In order to use time effectively, preschool PE teachers should try to design activities that do not require lengthy explanations (e.g. about rules or techniques), complex and time-consuming organization, a lot of management (e.g. re-arrangement of equipment or directing pupils) or long waiting times. To reduce sedentary time, it is preferable that children remain standing instead of sitting when instructions are needed. When lesson management is required (e.g. re-arranging materials) it is appropriate to allow some free play if possible.

Sophie's case, in conjunction with the research evidence, emphasises the fact that PE can never be considered the only channel through which physical activities are provided to preschoolers. Schools, parents and policy-makers have a shared responsibility, and preschoolers like Sophie will only accumulate three hours of PA per day if a wide range of activities is incorporated throughout the day at school and at home. Moreover, it is vital for Sophie to engage in activities in different contexts so there are sufficient repetitions and variations to stimulate adaptations to tasks in flexible ways. PE teachers are, however, the 'professionals' who serve as an intermediary between the school, home and community. They have a crucial role to play (a) in advocating for more and adapted movement opportunities and (b) in increasing awareness among colleagues, parents and policy-makers about preschoolers' PA and movement patterns, and the opportunities to provide remediation where needed.

At *school,* structured opportunities for movement can easily be incorporated into the overall curriculum. For example, Sophie's preschool class teacher always asks the children to work on tasks (e.g. drawing) while sitting at a desk (De Decker *et al.* in press). The teacher could, however, use a more activating approach by allowing and even encouraging the class to include more variety in their postures. They could do some tasks at a standing table, for example, and also be allowed to walk around the room without having to ask for permission (www.toybox-study.eu; De Decker *et al.* in press). Activities such as educational walks or fun activity breaks every 30 minutes also add to the amounts of PA. Importantly, class teachers and PE teachers have a vital role in informing parents about delays in motor development, especially in cases like Sophie where the parents are unaware of the problem – and indeed are exacerbating it by protecting her from activity.

Alongside structured activities, unstructured opportunities to move during the regular school day or in recess are also very important. In preschoolers, multiple short recess periods are preferable to single, longer periods because preschoolers' activity patterns are typically characterized by short bouts of activity. During recess, it is important to allow preschoolers access to as much available space as possible. In some urban preschools, with a small playground, it might be helpful to double the play space of the children by using different recess time schedules for different groups. Teachers who supervise during preschool recess tend to attract children, often girls, to join them for instance by holding their hand. This is an ideal opportunity for these teachers to encourage those children to be active.

In many *communities,* there is a pressing need to advocate for safe playgrounds that are adapted for young children. Furthermore, many local sports clubs and preschools in Belgium offer after-school structured PA programs for preschoolers. Enrolling Sophie in such a program could help her to become more active and to gain better motor skills. It is important to note, however, that many of these activities are delivered in sport-specific ways that might not provide the wide variety of movement experiences required by a 5 year old. To illustrate, some of these clubs will organize young children into large-sided adult-like team games (e.g. soccer teams) despite their age. Although 'kicking' a ball is a central skill in soccer, 'soccer training' for 5 year olds should be much broader including tasks that require skills such as striking, catching and throwing.

Conclusion

To conclude, the messages from all four experts who have contributed to this chapter are unequivocal: Sophie and young learners facing similar challenges are heavily reliant on informed adults and the opportunities they provide. It is vital, therefore, that teachers, coaches, parents and policy-makers understand the importance of appropriate forms and amounts of PA for young children, and the consequences of getting it wrong.

Note

1. In Flanders (Belgium), schools are supported by centres with medical and psychological staff that provide the right support for children with special needs (e.g. learning problems). As part of a preventive health strategy, a medical doctor of such a centre investigates all school-aged children every two years. Investigations include intellectual and motor development, sight and hearing, dental inspection and measurements of height and weight. Results of these investigations are reported back to the parents.

References

Armour, K. (2011) *Sport Pedagogy: An Introduction for Coaching and Teaching,* 1st edn, Edinburgh: Pearson Education Limited.

Armstrong, N. and Van Mechelen, W. (2008) *Paediatrics Exercise Science and Medicine,* 2nd edn, Oxford: Oxford University Press.

Australian Government Department of Health and Ageing (2012) *Physical activity guidelines.* Online. Available HTTP: <www.health.gov.au/internet/main/publishing.nsf/Content/health-pubhlth-strateg-phys-act-guidelines#rec_0_5> (accessed 10 September 2012).

Bardid, F., D'hondt, E., Descamps, S., Depooter, G., Verhoeven, L., Lenoir, M. and Deconinck, F. (2013) 'The effect of a targeted motor skill intervention in preschoolers with low motor competence', submitted.

Booth, F.W., Gordon, S.E., Carlson, C.J. and Hamilton, M.T. (2000) 'Waging war on modern chronic diseases; primary prevention through exercise biology', *Journal of Applied Physiology,* 88: 774–787.

Bourgois J. and Vrijens, J. (2001) 'Growth, maturation and development: consequences for a long-term build-up training programme in rowing', in W. Fritsch (ed.) *Rudern-Entwickeln, Kooperieren, Vermitteln: Berichtsbandzum 4. Konstanzer Rudersymposium 1999,* Sindelfingen: Sportverlag, Schmidt & Dreisilker, GmbH.

Cardon, G. and De Bourdeaudhuij, I. (2008) 'Are preschool children active enough? Objectively measured physical activity levels', *Research Quarterly for Exercise & Sport,* 79: 326–332.

Cardon, G., Labarque, V., Smits, D. and De Bourdeaudhuij, I. (2009) 'Promoting physical activity at the pre-school playground: the effects of providing markings and game equipment', *Preventive Medicine,* 48: 335–340.

Cardon, G., Van Cauwenberghe, E., De Bourdeaudhuij, I., Gubbels, J. and Labarque, V. (2010) 'Predictors of activity engagement during pre-school PE', paper presented at the European Congress on Physical Activity and Health among 0–6 years old, *Science & Sports,* 25: 7.

Cardon, G., Van Cauwenberghe, E., Labarque, V. Haerens, L. and De Bourdeaudhuij, I. (2008) 'The contribution of preschool playground factors in explaining children's physical activity during recess', *International Journal of Behavioral Nutrition & Physical activity,* 5: 11.

Cumming, S. and Riddoch, C. (2008) 'Physical activity, physical fitness and health: current concepts', in N. Armstrong and W. Van Mechelen (eds.) *Paediatrics Exercise Science and Medicine,* 2nd edn, Oxford: Oxford University Press.

De Craemer, M., De Decker, E., De Bourdeaudhuij, I., Deforche, B., Vereecken, C., Duvinage, K., Grammatikaki, E., Iotova, V., Fernández-Alvira, J.M., Zych, K., Manios, Y. and Cardon, G. (2013)

'Physical activity and beverage consumption in preschoolers: focus groups with parents and teachers', *BMC Public Health*, 13: 278. doi:10.1186/1471-2458-13-278

De Decker, E., De Craemer, M., De Bourdeaudhuij, I. and Cardon, G. (2013) 'Influencing factors of sedentary behavior in European preschool settings: an exploration through focus groups with teachers', *Journal of School Health*, 83: 654–661.

De Medts, C., Bertrands, E. and De Scheppere, G. (2012) *Kleuterstappen in beweging. Bewegingszorg voor het jonge kind*, Leuven: Acco.

De Medts, C., Coens, H. and Van Damme, E. (2008) *Hop Pompom, bewegingsontwikkeling kleuters*, Antwerpen: Zwijsen.

Gabbard, C.P. (2008) *Lifelong Motor Development*, 5th edn, San Francisco, CA: Pearson Benjamin Cummings.

Hadders-Algra, M. (2010) 'Variation and variability: key words in human motor development', *Physical Therapy*, 90: 1823–1837.

Haerens, L., Kirk, D., Cardon, G. and De Bourdeaudhuij, I. (2011) 'Toward the development of a pedagogical model for health-based physical education', *Quest*, 63: 321–338.

Haibach, P.S., Reid, G. and Collier, S.H. (2011) *Motor Learning and Development*, Champaign, IL: Human Kinetics.

Heelan, K.A., Eisenmann, J.C. (2006) 'Physical activity, media time, and body composition in young children', *Journal of Physical Activity and Health*, 1: 1–14.

Hinkley, T., Crawford, D., Salmon, J., Okely, A.D. and Hesketh, K. (2008) 'Preschool children and physical activity: a review of correlates', *American Journal of Preventive Medicine*, 34: 435–441.

Hinkley, T., Salmon, J., Okely, A.D. and Trost, S.G. (2010) 'Correlates of sedentary behaviours in preschool children: A review', *International Journal of Behavioral Nutrition and Physical Activity*, 7: 66–76.

Janz, K.F., Kwon, S., Letuchy, E.M., Eichenberger Gilmore, J.M., Burns, T.L., Torner, J.C., Willing, M.C. and Levy, S.M. (2009) 'Sustained effect of early physical activity on body fat mass in older children', *American Journal of Preventive Medicine*, 37: 35–40.

LeBlanc, A.G., Spence, J.C., Carson, V., Gorber, S.C., Dillman, C., Janssen, I., Kho, M.E., Stearns, J.A., Timmons, B.W. and Tremblay, M.S. (2012) 'Systematic review of sedentary behavior and health indicators in the early years (aged 0–4 years)', *Applied Physiology, Nutrition, and Metabolism [Physiologie Appliquée, Nutrition et Metabolisme]*, 37: 753–772.

Lobo, Y.B. and Winsler, A. (2006) 'The effects of a creative dance and movement program on the social competence of Head Start preschoolers', *Social Development*, 15: 501–519.

Malina, R.M. and Bouchard, C. (1991) *Growth, Maturation and Physical Activity*. Champaign, IL: Human Kinetics Books.

Marshall, S.J. and Ramirez, E. (2011) 'Reducing sedentary behaviour: a new paradigm in physical activity promotion', *American Journal of Lifestyle Medicine*, 5: 518–530.

McKenzie, T.L. and Lounsbery, M.A.F. (2009) 'School physical education: the pill not taken', *American Journal of Lifestyle Medicine*, 3: 219–225.

Okely, A.D., Salmon, J., Trost, S.G. and Hinkley, T. (2008) 'Discussion paper for the development of physical activity recommendations for children under five years', Canberra: Department of Health and Ageing, Government of Australia. Online. Available HTTP: <www.health.gov.au/internet/main/publishing.nsf/content/E6DB023029F7D7D6CA25705100815E68/$File/physical_discussion.pdf> (accessed 21 September 2013).

Pühse, U. and Gerber, M. (2005) *International Comparison of Physical Education: Concepts, Problems, Prospects'*, Aachen: Meyer & Meyer.

Reilly, J.J. (2008) 'Physical activity, sedentary behaviour and energy balance in the preschool child: opportunities for early obesity prevention', *Proceedings of the Nutrition Society*, 67: 317–325.

Rietmuller, A.M., Jones, R.A. and Okely, A.D. (2009) 'Efficacy of interventions to improve motor development in young children: a systematic review', *Pediatrics*, 124: 782–792.

Robinson, L.E. and Goodway, J.D. (2009) 'Instructional climates in preschool children who are at risk. Part I: Object control skill development', *Research Quarterly for Exercise and Sport*, 80: 533–542.

Salmon, J., Telford, A. and Crawford, D. (2004) *The Children's leisure activities study (CLASS)* Summary report. Centre for Physical activity and nutrition research. Online. Available HTTP: <www.deakin.edu. au/health/cpan/behavioural-epide/class_report-final-1.pdf> (accessed 21 September 2013).

Stodden, D.F., Goodway, J.D., Lagendorfer, S.A., Roberton, M.A., Rudisill, M.E., Garcia, C. and Garcia, L. (2008) 'A developmental perspective on the role of physical competence in physical activity: An emergent relationship', *Quest,* 60: 290–306.

Timmons, B.W., LeBlanc, A.G., Carson, V., Gorber, S.C., Dillman, C., Janssen, I., Kho, M.E., Spence, J.C., Stearns, J.A. and Tremblay, M.S. (2012) 'Systematic review of physical activity and health in the early years (aged 0–4 years)', *Applied Physiology, Nutrition, and Metabolism,* 37: 773–792.

Tremblay, M.S., LeBlanc, A.G., Carson, V., Choquette, L., Gorber, S.C., Dillman, C., Duggan, M., Gordon, M.J., Hicks, A., Janssen, I., Kho, M.E., Latimer-Cheung, A.E., LeBlanc, C., Murumets, K., Okely, A.D., Reilly, J.J., Spence, J.C., Stearns, J.A. and Timmons, B.W. (2012) 'Canadian directives with regard to physical activity in young infants (0–4 years)', *Applied Physiology, Nutrition, and Metabolism [Physiologie Appliquée, Nutrition et Metabolisme]* 37: 357–769.

Van Cauwenberghe, E., De Bourdeaudhuij, I., Maes, L. and Cardon, G. (2012a) 'Efficacy and feasibility of lowering playground density to promote physical activity and to discourage sedentary time during recess at preschool: a pilot study', *Preventive Medicine,* 55: 319–321.

Van Cauwenberghe, E., Labarque, V., Gubbels, J., De Bourdeaudhuij, I. and Cardon, G. (2012b) 'Preschooler's physical activity levels and associations with lesson context, teacher's behavior, and environment during preschool PE', *Early Childhood Research Quarterly,* 27: 221–230.

Vandorpe, B., Vandendriessche, J., Vaeyens, R., Pion, J., Matthys, S., Lefevre, J., Philippaerts, R. and Lenoir, M. (2012) 'Relationship between sports participation and the level of motor coordination in childhood: a longitudinal approach', *Journal of Science and Medicine in Sport,* 15: 220–225.

Verbestel, V., Van Cauwenberghe, E., De Coen, V., Maes, L., De Bourdeaudhuij, I. and Cardon, G. (2011) 'Within- and between-day variability of objectively measured physical activity in preschoolers', *Pediatric Exercise Sciences,* 23: 366–378.

3

KATE

Recognizing and addressing developmental coordination disorder

Thomas J. Templin, Shirley Rietdyk, Laura Claxton and Melissa Savage

DEPARTMENT OF HEALTH AND KINESIOLOGY AND DEPARTMENT OF EDUCATIONAL STUDIES, PURDUE UNIVERSITY, USA

Key words: 6-year-old female, development coordination disorder, motor development, biomechanics, pedagogy.

Kate

Kate is a 6-year-old first grade student at Richards Elementary School in the USA. During class, Ms. Kim, the physical education (PE) teacher, noticed that Kate was experiencing gait and balance issues during different activities. While Kate was a very successful learner in her regular classroom and related well to her teacher and classmates, she clearly had difficulties with gross motor activities. Her class teacher, Mrs. Smith, reported that Kate is a typical 6 year old with a very pleasant and warm personality, but she had noticed that Kate has some physical and emotional issues at times. She observed that Kate had difficulty with handwriting and sequencing activities in the classroom, and that she lagged behind in recess activities. She appeared very "clumsy" and "out of sorts" when playing with the other children. These issues were even more apparent in the PE setting. In fact, Kate's natural enthusiasm tended to wane in PE classes and in recess as she struggled to keep up with her classmates in various movement activities. Given her success in most classroom activities, her teachers have been surprised to see a real sense of frustration on Kate's face in physical activity settings.

The special education teacher at the school determined that additional consultation with Kate's parents and perhaps other professionals was needed. It was clear that special testing was required to determine the nature of Kate's difficulties. Ms. Kim, a PE specialist and a graduate from the local university, suggested a consultation with three university Kinesiology professors in the areas of biomechanics, motor development, and pedagogy.

The principal of Kate's school, the special education teacher, university professors, and Ms. Kim met with Kate's parents. The meeting revealed the following: Kate was born after a difficult pregnancy; she had frequent ear infections when she was a toddler and ear tubes were used to address the infections; she was a late walker; she broke her leg at age three; she has difficulty in activities such as climbing stairs and using eating utensils; and she shies away from playing with her older sister and neighborhood children.

Subsequent to this meeting, Kate was tested by the professors using the Movement Assessment Battery for Children (Henderson and Sugden 2007) as well as the Bruininks-Oseretsky Test of Motor Proficiency (Bruininks and Bruininks 2005)[1]. It became clear through the tests of balance, auditory memory, sequential and symmetrical movement, and writing activities that Kate was significantly below the norm for a child of her age on these assessments. She was referred to her pediatrician and a physical therapist for further assessment, and Kate was diagnosed with developmental coordination disorder (DCD). Many children with DCD succeed with minor accommodations and do not need special education services, but due to Kate's motor, sequence, and memory challenges she qualified for special education services under the disability category, Other Health Impairment[2] (H.R.1350, IDEA 2003). A conference was held with Ms. Kim, and an Individual Education Plan (IEP) was set in motion.

What is developmental coordination disorder?

DCD "encompasses a complex presentation of sensory and motor impairment in children that can result in significant restrictions of daily activities and participation in life roles" (Hiller 2007: 1). While the exact cause of DCD is unknown to date, it is a disorder that leads to difficulties with fine and gross motor skills. While children may otherwise be very successful in other classroom learning, challenges with movement activities are typical. Whithall and Clark (2012: 259) state four diagnostic criteria for DCD in relationship to the *Diagnostic Statistical Manual IV-TR* (DSM-IV-TR) (APA 2000):

- Performance in daily activities that require motor coordination to be substantially below that expected given the person's chronological age and intelligence.
- The disturbance in performance significantly interferes with academic achievement or activities of daily living.
- The disturbance is not due to a general medical condition (e.g., cerebral palsy or muscular dystrophy) and does not meet criteria for pervasive developmental disorder.
- If mental retardation is present, the motor difficulties are in excess of those usually associated with it.

Hiller (2007: 2) points out various characteristics of DCD including: "information processing deficits (particularly visuo-spatial); reliance on visuo-spatial memory for learning movements; being perceived externally as having poor effort and reduced motivation; secondary effects of lower fitness levels or restricted social skills; and co-morbidity with learning delay (LD), developmental language disorder (DLD), and attention deficit and hyperactivity disorder (AD/HD)."

DCD has been associated with incompetence in motor activity, low motivation and confidence to participate in motor activity, withdrawal or exclusion from participation, low academic performance, low social esteem, low popularity, low levels of physical fitness, and increased long-term health risk factors that clearly suggest that the disorder will compromise quality of life (Hodge, Lieberman and Murata 2012; Whitall and Clark 2012; Rivilis *et al.* 2011).

Prevalence

The prevalence of children with DCD is currently between 6 and 13 percent of all school-aged children in the Unites States (Whithall and Clark 2012). The DSM-IV-TR puts the prevalence of DCD at 6 percent of the population, but other estimates vary widely: from 2 percent in the UK (Lingam *et al.* 2009) to as high as 19 percent in Greece (Tsiotra *et al.* 2006), making it one of the most common developmental disorders of childhood. It has been reported that boys experience DCD more than girls, and children from low social-economic status have an increased incidence of DCD (Hiller 2007). DCD is generally first identified during lower elementary years (Clark *et al.* 2005). While DCD usually presents itself at an early age, the motor gap with one's peers may (but not always) be closed by adolescence. This absence or continued presence of the gap is dependent on instruction in "fundamental motor skills that are often prerequisites for more task-specific skills and demanding physical activities" (Hodge *et al.* 2012: 280).

Diagnosis

As presented in the case narrative above, the diagnosis of DCD is commonly tied to a two-step process (Watkinson *et al.* 2001). First, a teacher or carer may notice some abnormality in gross or fine motor movement. This observation should be made over enough time so that a consistent pattern can be observed. The second step involves a more formal assessment conducted by professionals trained in the assessment of DCD. The characteristics and criteria addressed earlier serve as barometers for the diagnosis as various instruments are employed to assess DCD. For example, the following tests of static and dynamic balance and mobility, hand-eye coordination, and fine motor ability may be used:

- Developmental Coordination Disorder Questionnaire (Wilson *et al.* 2000)
- Movement Assessment Battery for Children, 2nd edition (MABC-2) (Henderson and Sugden 2007)
- Bruininks-Oseretsky Test of Motor Proficiency (Bruininks and Bruininks 2005)
- McCarron Assessment of Neuromuscular Development (McCarron 1982)

Whithall and Clark (2012: 261) state that "in 2001 and 2006, researchers agreed on test performance cut points that classified those at or below the 5th percentile as having DCD and those that are between the 6th and 15th percentile to be 'at risk' for DCD."

A motor development perspective

Developing the ability to control the body is an inherently complex and difficult process that extends well into the second decade of life (Haddad *et al.* 2012). When watching typically developing (TD) children in the playground, movement appears to be fluid, coordinated, and relatively efficient. This level of control requires children to have sufficient postural control, learn to appropriately coordinate their body parts in relation to one another, and have sufficient muscle strength and neural maturation. This complexity can best be understood by considering a simple movement such as shooting a basketball. To accomplish this task, a child must plan the movement and evaluate the demands of the task (e.g., how far is the basket), plan a response (e.g., what muscles and how much force do I need to generate so that the ball reaches the hoop), execute the response (appropriately activate the appropriate muscles and coordinate the appropriate segments), and then use feedback to evaluate their performance. To further complicate matters, children must learn to generate task-appropriate movements within a dynamically changing environment (Newell 1986). For example, the movement patterns required to shoot a basketball when standing at the free throw line are very different to those required to make a layup. From a motor development perspective, we investigate the mechanisms underlying the development and maturation of movement patterns in TD children and children with movement disorders. Children with motor disorders, such as DCD, can have difficulties with any of these steps of movement planning.

There are a variety of techniques that can be used to assess motor development, including standardized "paper and pencil tests" and laboratory equipment that is capable of examining movement patterns at a high spatial and temporal resolution. Standardized tests offer a powerful way to quickly assess motor development and performance in multiple gross and fine motor domains. These types of tests have many advantages over laboratory assessments such as being inexpensive, quick to administer and, unlike most laboratory assessments, have established age-appropriate norms. Although standardized motor tests can be beneficial to assessing the developmental skill level of children, they mostly provide descriptive information about motor deficits. This information is often critical to the diagnosis of motor disorders and the assessment of training efficacy, however, these tests do not provide mechanistic information. To better understand the mechanisms contributing to DCD, more sophisticated laboratory equipment is needed.

Typical laboratory equipment includes a force plate, motion capture system, and electromyography (EMG). Force plates are common in the assessment of balance. They measure the reaction forces exerted on the ground by the child's body. These reaction forces are often used to calculate the instantaneous locations of the vertical ground reaction force vector, also called the center of pressure (CoP). Force plates are able to examine reaction force data at a high sampling rate (1000 samples per second is not uncommon) and discriminate body movement to a high spatial resolution (within a fraction of a millimeter). Thus, force plates can be used to perform a sensitive balance assessment on children. Motion capture systems employ the use of multiple cameras to examine movement in three dimensions. This equipment works by placing markers on the segments of interest. Cameras then record marker position in three dimensions at a high spatial and temporal accuracy. Motion capture systems are typically used to calculate information such segmental coordination and angles as a movement pattern unfolds. Finally, EMG uses electrodes that are placed over a muscle of interest to measure muscle activity, such as when a muscle is activated and how muscles are timed with movements. It is important to note that researchers commonly synchronize and then use these devices simultaneously to capture different aspects of movement.

From research using force plates, we know that 4- to 6-year-old children with DCD have difficulty controlling their balance when sensory information important for maintaining balance (visual and somatosensory) is removed or altered (Cherng *et al.* 2007). For example, we could have Kate stand on a force plate and measure her CoP movement under four different conditions that manipulate sensory information: standing on the force plate (a solid surface) with her eyes open, standing on a force plate with her eyes closed (removing visual information), standing on a soft surface (a foam mat would be placed on top of the force plate that reduces the accuracy of the somatosensory information from the feet) with her eyes open, and standing on a foam surface with her eyes closed (removing visual information and providing inaccurate somatosensory information). We would expect that for all four conditions, Kate would show a larger amount of CoP movement than a TD 6-year-old, which would indicate that she is less stable overall. This difference would be even more prominent in the conditions when Kate was standing on the soft surface (with the reduced accuracy of the somatosensory information on her feet). It is thought that children with DCD have a deficit in sensory organization that makes it more challenging for them to cope with these types of altered sensory inputs (Cherng *et al.* 2007).

Often we are not just standing (as in the above example), but are standing and performing a concurrent task like texting on our cell phone. It is important to investigate these types of concurrent tasks as they are more similar to the activities of daily life (Haddad *et al.* 2013). In the case of Kate, we would expect that she would have even more difficulty maintaining balance when given a concurrent cognitive task such as naming simple objects (Laufer, Ashkenazi and Josman 2008). For example, we could have Kate stand on a force plate on a solid surface and a soft surface while simultaneously naming pictures of simple objects (e.g., ball, table) appearing on a computer screen. We would keep track of her CoP movement and the number of mistakes she makes while naming the objects. We would expect Kate to exhibit more CoP movements (less stability) and more mistakes on the naming task than TD 6-year-olds in both stance conditions. Kate would also exhibit even more CoP movement when given the cognitive task than TD children. This result would demonstrate that Kate has difficulty in dual task situations where she must control her balance and simultaneously complete a concurrent task.

Motion capture systems can be used to provide insights into coordination problems and solutions that children with DCD use in order to perform movement tasks. For example, through the use of motion capture, research has demonstrated that 7- to 8-year-old children with DCD coordinate their arm and hand movements differently when catching a ball as compared with TD children (Utley, Steenbergen and Astill 2007). According to this research, if we had Kate catch a ball and monitored how her arm segments were moving, she would exhibit smaller ranges of motion and fix her arms more rigidly as compared to TD children. This stiffening of her arms would make her less adaptable and less able to catch the ball. When TD children learn skills such as ball catching, although they start out with more rigid movements, over time their arm movements become much more flexible. We would expect that Kate would have difficulty moving on to this more flexible and adaptable step in skill acquisition and would need additional help with this process (Utley *et al.* 2007). EMG analyses have also demonstrated that children with DCD have problems timing the activity of their muscles (Geuze 2005). This is important because most movement requires a variety of muscles to be activated and timed in a specific sequence. Movement can be extremely uncoordinated if this timing is off or if the latency of muscle activation is too slow. These issues suggest that the higher motor centers of children with DCD have difficulty executing and planning movements.

Finally, a recent push in motor development has been to stop thinking of motor and cognition abilities as developing separately. Rather, motor skills and cognition are believed to be integrally linked (Diamond 2000). For example, although DCD is typically characterized as a motor disorder, children with DCD also have difficulties with cognitive tasks that involve executive functioning abilities (Piek *et al.* 2004; Piek *et al.* 2007). Executive functioning abilities refer to our ability to coordinate thoughts and actions and are typically measured using working memory tasks, planning/problem-solving tasks, and inhibitory control tasks (Welsh, Pennington and Groisser 1991). In inhibitory control tasks, children must inhibit a conflicting thought or action in order to perform a task correctly (Carlson and Moses 2001). For example, if we gave Kate a battery of executive functioning tests, we would expect to see deficits in performance across all of these tasks. These findings would suggest that Kate's ability to plan, monitor, and control both motor and cognitive abilities are potentially controlled by the same underlying brain mechanisms (Diamond 2000).

A biomechanical perspective

Locomotion is a fundamental skill that allows children to interact with their peers and participate in physical activity. Because walking appears automatic, it is not readily apparent that gait is mechanically unstable. In order to remain upright, the body's center of mass (the position where the entire mass could be considered to be located) must remain within the base of support (the area bounded by the outermost edges of the feet). Two-thirds of the body's mass is located in the head, arms and trunk, creating an unstable top-heavy system, which can easily destabilize as gravity acts to accelerate the upper body away from the vertical. In order to take a step with the left foot, the body is propelled forward and upward by forcefully pushing against the ground with the right foot. Then, the landing of the left limb must be controlled or the inertial mass of the upper body will collapse the landing limb. Simultaneously, the footfalls must be planned so that the center of mass (COM) remains within the base of support when both feet are in contact with the ground. A complex environment, including uneven paths, ramps, and obstacles, further compounds the inherent instability of locomotion. Therefore, locomotion requires strength and coordination, and the control of both propulsion and equilibrium. Equilibrium is controlled by information, or feedback from the sensory systems (e.g., vision), about an impending loss of balance and providing appropriate corrective torques to prevent loss of balance. In this section, we discuss how children with DCD walk and navigate complex environments compared to their typically developing peers. We will see that the gait patterns adopted by children with DCD reflect a reduction in balance control and contribute to these children appearing unsteady or "clumsy."

There is a range of gait assessments available to assess the impact of DCD on mobility. These assessments range from visual observation to pressurized walkways to full-body motion analysis synchronized with one or more force plates. It is important to note that the more detailed quantitative gait analyses have revealed DCD-related changes that cannot be detected through visual observation. Therefore, a detailed assessment conducted in a gait laboratory is recommended if this opportunity is available. The reader is cautioned that current literature regarding gait in children with DCD has been limited to small samples of children and narrow age ranges. This is especially critical given the heterogeneous presentation of DCD, and care must be taken when considering the gait of one individual child, like Kate, relative to the findings summarized below.

While children with DCD can establish a rhythmic locomotor pattern, it is shortened in time and space (Deconinck *et al.* 2006a). As noted above, walking requires the control of both propulsion and equilibrium. Children with DCD demonstrated changes consistent with reduced propulsion, including shorter steps and decreased plantarflexor angle (Deconinck *et al.* 2006a).

Propulsion may be reduced due to lack of muscle strength or as a protective adaptation to maintain equilibrium. Children with DCD also demonstrate a forward trunk inclination, less hip flexion, and greater knee flexion during stance, which may be a strategy to lower the COM to a more stable position (Deconinck *et al.* 2006a). The authors describe these changes as a "safer walking strategy." In addition, gait changes including poor head control, uncoordinated limb-to-limb transitions, wider dynamic base of support (Larkin and Hoare 1991), and asymmetry (Rosengren *et al.* 2009) have been observed.

When children with DCD were examined with more challenging locomotor tasks, further changes were observed. The support phase lengthened, and stride length and gait speed were markedly reduced when walking in the dark. However, typically developing children showed virtually no changes when walking in the dark (Deconinck *et al.* 2006b). The authors concluded that these changes are consistent with a greater reliance on visual feedback for the control of locomotion in children with DCD. Another study examined the control of equilibrium while stepping over obstacles, and found that children with DCD were not different from typically developing children during the approach to the obstacle. However, they had significantly greater COM displacement in the medial-lateral plane during crossing, consistent with reduced ability to control the momentum of the COM (Deconinck *et al.* 2010). Another method to challenge locomotion is to add a concurrent task, such as speaking or carrying a tray of marbles (Cherng *et al.* 2009). As above, gait changes in response to the extra challenge were greater in children with DCD than in typically developing children. These findings highlight the extra challenge of children with DCD to accomplish tasks that appear smooth, easy, and seamless in typically developing children. These observations also highlight the importance of assessing a range of challenging locomotor tasks, such as obstacle crossing, reduced lighting and concurrent tasks, in order to fully assess Kate's locomotor skills.

Given the relationship between mobility and optimal development, it is important to ensure that interventions positively impact these gait impairments. Specific training in this population is beneficial (Pless and Carlsson 2000; Sigmundsson *et al.* 1998; Sugden and Chambers 1998), so gait training should be included in any intervention. However, it is difficult to train a child in every conceivable environment and task they will encounter. Therefore, it is important that future research also examines non-specific training that improves coordination and balance, and determines how the improvement translates to everyday motor tasks (Haddad *et al.* 2013). For example, Taekwondo training will result in the ability to kick higher and faster. Kicking higher and faster also requires upper body control and the ability to balance on one foot during a dynamic, powerful movement. Therefore, generalized improvements in strength, coordination, and balance will likely also occur. Interestingly, Taekwondo training for three months improved sensory organization and standing balance in 23 children with DCD (Fong, Tsang and Ng 2012). In turn, these improvements may lead to improved propulsion and equilibrium control during challenging gait tasks, even though gait was not specifically trained. However, gait was not assessed in the intervention study, so this hypothesis, while reasonable, has not been proven.

The PE teacher should work with a qualified clinician, if possible, to determine ideal interventions that can be practiced in PE classes. If a clinician is not available, it is important to encourage a range of locomotor tasks, from walking to skipping to hopping in a variety of environments, as task-related practice is beneficial for children with DCD (Pless and Carlsson, 2000; Sigmundsson *et al.* 1998; Sugden and Chambers 1998). For example, the PE classes should be developed to include challenging locomotor tasks, such as: walking on tumbling mats, walking through sand, traversing slopes, stepping over obstacles, walking under structures, walking in the dark, counting while walking, carrying a tray with marbles, etc. These tasks should be tailored to match Kate's current locomotor skills and her motivation to participate. The tasks should become progressively more challenging as Kate's skills develop. Activities that require coordinated movements of the lower limbs and displacement of the upper body, such as movements similar to those in Taekwondo, should also be included, as they have been shown to be beneficial to standing balance (Fong *et al.* 2012), and may also be beneficial for locomotion.

In summary, the gait research highlights subtle but significant differences in locomotion that appear to result in greater instability and therefore higher risk of falls in children with DCD. These changes may lead Kate to avoid activities that involve locomotion, which in turn will further impair her motor development and social interactions with peers. Thus, it is important to encourage and motivate Kate to participate in activities that will build her locomotor skills.

A pedagogy perspective

Based on the information on DCD, and the motor development and biomechanics perspectives outlined above, it is clear that Ms. Kim and Kate's parents must provide "extra motor practice conditions" for Kate (Whitall and Clark 2012: 277). The question remains for Ms. Kim: what specific teaching approaches and "interventions" should be used to support Kate in physical education or in the home? The pedagogy professor has expertise in instructional strategies, and he refers Ms. Kim to the various principles that she learned in her Adapted Physical Education (APE) class at university. The professor reminded her of the following resources: Hodge *et al.* (2012), Lieberman and Houston-Wilson (2009) and Hodge *et al.* (2003). These resources address DCD, the principles of instruction grounded in three theoretical orientations, and interventions that assure activities that are simple, safe, repetitive, and motivational. The following dialogue between the professor and Ms. Kim illustrates the processes they went through to come to an understanding of how best to support Kate as a learner in movement:

Prof.: Do you remember anything from your APE class about working with children with motor deficits?

Ms. Kim: I remember something about a top–down or bottom–up approach; something about what the child is missing in terms of perceptual and motor skills and how you address that gap – I think that's bottom up. Top-down would be more of a skill-specific emphasis, like learning a sport skill and making sure that the child works on the skill more intensely and repetitively in problem solving situations.

Prof.: You are on track. You may recall that both approaches are linked to different theoretical orientations. The bottom–up approach is connected to a sensory-integration approach (SI). Research has shown that children may need help in adapting to their physical environment that, in turn, helps them to improve their ability to process sensory input.

Ms. Kim: What does that mean for working with Kate?

Prof.: It means that you need to present more verbal cues and demonstrations and that you may have to physically assist Kate in trying a skill. The increased repetition of a task, such as repeatedly throwing or kicking a ball, or physically assisting her while running, will help. Emphasize SI movements that engage the full body like walking, running, hopping, and jumping. Since, Kate is so young, she needs assistance and, in fact, another approach called the General Abilities Approach (GA) (Pless and

Carlsson 2000) may be really important here. It aligns with the bottom-up or SI approach. Using this approach, you will engage Kate in balancing activities, eye-hand and eye-foot activities, and reflex activities.

Ms. Kim: I remember a Specific Skill (SS) approach – should this approach be used with Kate?

Prof.: This top-down approach is often important to employ in addition to others. It is generally used for students with more severe motor difficulties, but this approach may work for Kate. In fact, most texts recommend this approach, and research suggests it can be a more effective approach than the general and sensory integration approaches (Pless and Carlsson 2000). As Kate becomes more comfortable with her movement abilities, it will become important for her to work on improving the specialized motor skills involved in game play and other problem solving situations. Be sure to integrate different motor skills using "different equipment, activities, and spaces" (Hodge *et al.* 2012: 282) in the SS approach as Kate develops more confidence and ability.

Prof.: What are some other principles that you remember from training or have learnt through experience of working with children with a range of motor abilities? What, for example, would you tell my students who are still preparing to be teachers?

Ms. Kim: My experience has taught me quite a few things. I suspect my work certainly reinforces various intervention strategies (Clark, *et al.* 2005; Fox and Lent 1996; Hodge *et al.* 2012); for example:

- Prepare an Individual Education Plan that gives a comprehensive picture of where your student is currently functioning, what should be addressed next, and how it should be addressed.
- Ensure that the student gets plenty of practice going from simple to more complex activity phases once he or she is able to master a task repeatedly. This practice should be sequentially distributed, aided by verbal cues, and progressive from more stable and stationary environments to those that involve more movement or less stable movement activities.
- Engage your students and others (parents, therapists, special educator) in *goal setting*. Goals should be measurable, small, and attainable; essentially, they should be realistic.
- Don't focus on motor skill development alone, but work diligently to increase self-esteem. Children will feel better about themselves as their movement skills develop.
- Involve the children in activities of their choice, and this will serve as an incentive to engage in movement in both predictable and non-predictable ways (also helping to build self-esteem).
- Modify activities that require fast movements and responses.
- Avoid activities that involve competition with peers that may lower self esteem and promote isolation or even humiliation. Establish an instructional/practice instead of a wholly competitive environment.
- Provide feedback and praise your students often! Avoid having the student engage in repeated inaccurate and ineffective performance of tasks without feedback or coaching. Be sure your feedback is instructive and positive.
- Use safety equipment such as helmets in ball games.
- Assess the progress of your students regularly and employ the MABC-2 test to assess improvements.

Prof.:   I really like the fact that you mentioned building Kate's self-esteem. Kate is not very motivated or confident, so it seems logical to start with small objectives and more accommodations so she may see and feel success quickly.

Ms. Kim: Do you have any other suggestions?

Prof.:   Yes. Start a peer program in your PE class when working on individual activities. Assigning a peer to help Kate could be beneficial to improving her self-esteem, developing skills, and also facilitating relatedness with classmates (Lieberman and Houston-Wilson 2009). Working on leadership skills can also be helpful in building self-esteem. Let Kate be a leader in areas in which she is competent in order to develop some confidence (Hodge *et al.* 2003); for example, select activities that she performs routinely in your class (e.g., warm-ups, attendance).

Ms. Kim: Those are great ideas and could benefit all my students, not just Kate. Kate will have an IEP, so will a special education teacher will be responsible for making sure that Kate gets what she needs?

Prof.:   Yes. The special education teacher will be Kate's teacher of record (TOR). The TOR is responsible for the IEP and leading the collaborative efforts between you, therapists, and parents in order to help Kate improve her challenges with DCD.

Ms. Kim: I know I am responsible for input into Kate's IEP; for example, levels of performance, goal suggestions, objective suggestions, assessment procedures, accommodations, but how would those be written for Kate?

Prof.:   The TOR needs to know Kate's current level of performance. This information helps the TOR decide what goals and objectives are most important for Kate to work on throughout the following year. When you record the current levels of performance, be sure to focus on what Kate *can do,* not what she is unable to perform. For example, if Kate struggles to walk on a line without losing her balance, you would record the following: *Kate is able to walk (insert number of steps) steps on the line independently before losing her balance.* This is much more informative and positive than: *Kate loses her balance easily.* Just telling us Kate will lose her balance doesn't provide sufficient information for the establishment of clear objectives. By telling the IEP team exactly what Kate can do and how she can do it, the TOR can come up with appropriate goal and objectives. (See Figure 3.1 for a complete example of how to write an IEP for Kate).

Ms. Kim: Will I have to change all the activities I do with the class in order to accommodate Kate?

Prof.:   No. Most of the lessons at the grade level you teach will be great for Kate (e.g., balance activities and movements that engage the entire body). What is going to help Kate the most is having a visual model of a new skill, increasing her opportunities to repeat skills, and receiving constructive feedback from a teacher. Some modifications to your lessons may be helpful, but you won't change need to change everything. For example, if your students are kicking a soccer ball to hit moving targets, then Kate might be asked to kick the soccer ball to a stationary target. By providing instructional, environmental, and equipment modifications to your lessons Kate will be able to increase her participation in class. See Figure 3.2 for some examples of modifications for Kate.

Ms. Kim: Is there anything else I should consider?

Prof.:   There is. Some universities offer special movement programs for children with disabilities. An example would be a five-week program that meets once a week where children are paired with university students in both gym and pool settings, and it could be very helpful for Kate (Richards, Wilson, and Eubank 2012).

Ms. Kim: I will consult with Kate's parents and encourage them to have Kate participate in this special opportunity.

Prof.:   I think you are ready to go to help Kate and, in so doing and applying the principles we have discussed, you will be offering pedagogically sound learning opportunities to all your pupils. Good luck!

Present level of performance	Kate is able to perform up to 3 jumping jacks correctly when given a visual model. Katie catches a football thrown to her from 2 feet in 4 out of 10 opportunities. Kate is able to take 3 steps on a line independently before losing her balance. When a ball is kicked to her, Kate is able to stop it with her foot in 1 out of 5 opportunities.
Suggestion for annual PE goal	Kate will increase skill performance and participation in PE by demonstrating 2 of the 3 following objectives independently by (insert time frame).
Suggestions for objectives	– When playing catch, Kate will catch a football thrown to her from a distance of 4 feet in 8 out of 10 opportunities independently. – During PE class or at home, Kate will demonstrate 5 jumping jacks with correct form independently in 8 out of 10 opportunities. – Kate will lead stretches in PE class with a peer in 4 out of 5 opportunities.
Progress measurement	Data collection with event recording
PE accommodations	– seating available when changing clothes for class – extra time for changing clothes – use of pencil grips when writing – written tests taken in resource room – visual modeling when introducing new task

FIGURE 3.1 Sample IEP for Kate: PE components

Instruction modifications	Individualized activities, increased chances for repetition, simple language in instructions, modeling of activities, verbal prompts
Environment modifications	Running on the inside track, shorter throwing distance, simplify patterns, close proximity to teacher
Equipment modifications	Larger/lighter/softer balls, use of tee, velcro mitts and balls, larger targets

FIGURE 3.2 Summary of modification strategies for Kate

Summary

Kate is amongst the small percentage of children in the world with a significant motor impairment – developmental coordination disorder (DCD) – that may characterize her as clumsy or awkward. Fortunately, her parents, together with caring, expert professionals are involved in supporting Kate by analyzing and facilitating her progress towards motor improvement or proficiency. Importantly, Kate's teacher, Ms. Kim, is a professional in PE who has the knowledge, skill, and disposition to work positively in the remediation of DCD through the various strategies or interventions described above. Added to that, Kate is able to engage in a community program where she has an opportunity outside of her school and home to practice various movement forms. Teaching children with disabilities isn't easy, but drawing on the knowledge available in a range of relevant disciplines – in this case motor development, biomechanics, and pedagogy – will help teachers to meet the individual learning needs of Kate and her peers.

Notes

1. These two motor skills tests are examples of commonly used norm-referenced standardized tests that assess children's performance on a variety of gross and fine motor tasks. These tests allow individuals to compare a child's gross and fine motor skills performance to the performance of other children of a similar age.
2. Other Health Impairment is one of the 14 categories of disability in the Individuals with Disabilities Education Act (H.R. 1350, IDEA 2003) in the United States that enables school age-children and youth to receive educational and related services to address their needs.

References

APA (2000) *Diagnostic and statistical manual of mental disorders IV-TR (DSM-IV-TR)*, Washington, D.C.: American Psychiatric Association.

Bruininks, R.H. and Bruininks, B.D. (2005) *Bruininks-Oseretsky Test of Motor Proficiency*, 2nd edn, Minneapolis, MN: Pearson Assessment.

Carlson, S.M. and Moses, L.J. (2001) 'Individual differences in inhibitory control and children's theory of mind', *Child Development*, 72(4): 1032–1054.

Cherng, R.J., Hsu, Y.W., Chen, Y.J. and Chen, J.Y. (2007) 'Standing balance of children with developmental coordination disorder under altered sensory conditions', *Human Movement Science*, 26(6): 913–926.

Cherng, R.J., Liang, L.Y., Chen, Y.J. and Chen, J.Y. (2009) 'The effects of a motor and a cognitive concurrent task on walking in children with developmental coordination disorder', *Gait Posture*, 29(2): 204–207.

Clark, J., Getchell, N., Smiley-Oyen, A. and Whitall, J. (2005) 'Developmental coordination disorder: issues, identification, and intervention', *Journal of Physical Education, Recreation, & Dance*, 76(4): 49–53.

Deconinck, F.J., De Clercq, D., Savelsbergh, G.J., Van Coster, R., Oostra, A., Dewitte, G. and Lenoir, M. (2006a) 'Differences in gait between children with and without developmental coordination disorder', *Motor Control*, 10(2): 125–142.

Deconinck, F.J., De Clercq, D., Savelsbergh, G.J., Van Coster, R., Oostra, A., Dewitte, G. and Lenoir, M. (2006b) 'Visual contribution to walking in children with development coordination disorder, *Child Health Care and Development*, 32(6): 711–722.

Deconinck F.J., Savelsbergh G.J., De Clercq, D. and Lenoir, M. (2010) 'Balance problems during obstacle crossing in children with development coordination disorder', *Gait Posture*, 32(3): 327–331.

Diamond, A. (2000) 'Close interrelation of motor development and cognitive development and of the cerebellum and prefrontal cortex', *Child Development*, 71(1): 44–56.

Fong, S.S., Tsang, W.W. and Ng, G.Y. (2012) 'Taekwondo training improves sensory organization and balance control in children with developmental coordination disorder: a randomized controlled trial', *Research in Developmental Disabilities,* 33(1): 85–95.

Fox, A.M. and Lent, B. (1996) 'Clumsy children: a primer on developmental coordination disorder', *Canadian Family Physician,* 42:1965–1971.

Geuze, R.H. (2005) 'Postural control in children with developmental coordination disorder', *Neural Plasticity,* 12(2–3): 183–196.

Haddad, J.M., Claxton, L.J., Keen, R., Berthier, N., Riccio, G.E., Hamill, J. and Van Emmerik, R. (2012) 'Development of the coordination between posture and manual control', *Journal of Experimental Child Psychology,* 111: 286–298.

Haddad, J.M., Rietdyk, S., Claxton, L.J. and Huber, J.E. (2013) 'Task dependent postural control throughout the lifespan', *Exercise and Sport Science Reviews,* 41(2): 123–132.

Henderson, S.E. and Sugden, D.A. (2007) *Movement Assessment Battery for Children 2.* San Antonio, TX: Psychological Corporation.

Hiller, S. (2007) 'Intervention for children with developmental coordination disorder: a systematic review', *The Internet Journal of Allied Health Sciences and Practice.* 5(3): Nova. Online. Available HTTP: <http://ijahsp.nova.edu> (accessed 21 September 2013).

Hodge, S.R., Lieberman, L.J. and Murata, N.M. (2012) 'Motor delays and developmental coordination disorder', in S.R. Hodge, L.J. Lieberman and N. Murata (eds.) *Essentials of Teaching Adapted Physical Education* (pp. 275–288). Scottsdale, AZ: Holcomb Hathway Publishers.

Hodge, S.R., Murata, N.M., Block, M.E. and Lieberman, L.J. (2003) *Case Studies in Adapted Physical Education: Empowering Critical Thinking,* Scottsdale, AZ: Holcomb Hathaway Publishers.

H.R. 1350–108th United States Congress: Individuals with Disabilities Education Improvement Act of 2004 (2003), in www.GovTrack.us. Online. Available HTTP: <www.govtrack.us/congress/bills/108/hr1350> (accessed 21 September 2013).

Larkin, D. and Hoare, D. (1991) *Out of Step,* Perth: Active Life Foundation.

Laufer, Y., Ashkenazi, T. and Josman, N. (2008) 'The effects of a concurrent cognitive task on the postural control of young children with and without developmental coordination disorder, *Gait and Posture,* 27(2): 347–351.

Lieberman, L.J. and Houston-Wilson, C. (2009) *Strategies for Inclusion: A Handbook for Physical Educators,* Champaign: IL: Human Kinetics.

Lingam, R., Hunt, L., Golding, J., Jongmans, M. and Edmond, D. (2009) 'Prevalence of developmental coordination disorder using the DSM-IV at 7 years of age: a UK population-based study', *Pediatrics,* 123: 693–700.

McCarron, L.T. (1982) *McCarron Assessment of Neuromuscular Development,* Dallas, TX: McCarron-Dial Systems.

Newell, K.M. (1986) 'Constraints on the development of coordination', in M.G. Wade and H.T.A. Whiting (eds.) *Motor Development in Children: Aspects of Coordination and Control* (pp. 341–361). Amsterdam: Nijhoff.

Piek, J.P., Dyck, M.J., Francis, M. and Conwell, A. (2007) 'Working memory, processing speed, and set-shifting in children with developmental coordination disorder and attention-deficit-hyperactivity disorder', *Developmental Medicine and Child Neurology,* 49(9): 678–683.

Piek, J.P., Dyck, M.J., Nieman, A., Anderson, M., Hay, D., Smith, L.M. and Hallmayer, J. (2004) 'The relationship between motor coordination, executive functioning and attention in school aged children', *Archives of Clinical Neuropsychology,* 19(8): 1063–1076.

Pless, M. and Carlsson, M. (2000) 'Effects of motor control intervention on developmental coordination disorder: a meta-analysis', *Adapted Physical Activity Quarterly,* 17: 381–401.

Richards, K., Wilson, W. and Eubank, L. (2012) 'Planning a service-learning program to benefit children with disabilities', *Journal of Physical Education, Recreation, & Dance,* 83(7): 32–38.

Rivilis, I., Hay, J. Cairney, J., Klentrou, P., Liu, J. and Faught, B. E. (2011) 'Physical activity and fitness in children with developmental coordination disorder: a systematic review', *Research in Developmental Disabilities,* 32: 894–910.

Rosengren, K.S., Deconinck, F.J., Diberardino, L.A. III, Polk, J.D., Spencer-Smith, J., De Clercq, D. and Lenoir, M. (2009) 'Differences in gait complexity and variability between children with and without developmental coordination disorder', *Gait Posture,* 29(2): 225–229.

Sigmundsson, H., Pedersen, A.V., Whiting, H.T. and Ingvaldsen R.P. (1998) 'We can cure your child's clumsiness! A review of intervention methods', *Scandinavian Journal of Rehabilitation Medicine,* 30(2): 101–106.

Sugden, D.A. and Chambers, M.E. (1998) 'Intervention approaches and children with developmental coordination disorder', *Pediatric Rehabilitation.* 2(4): 139–147.

Tsiotra, G.D., Flouris, A.D., Koutedakis, Y. *et al.* (2006) 'A comparison of developmental coordination disorder prevalence rates in Canadian and Greek children', *Journal of Adolescent Health,* 39: 125–127.

Utley, A., Steenbergen, B. and Astill, S.L. (2007) 'Ball catching in children with developmental coordination disorder: control of degrees of freedom', *Developmental Medicine and Child Neurology,* 49(1): 34–38.

Watkinson, E., Causgrove Dunn, J., Cavaliere, N., Calzonetti, K., Wilhelm, L. and Dywer, S. (2001) 'Engagement in playground activities as a criterion for diagnosing developmental coordination disorder', *Adapted Physical Activity Quarterly,* 18(1): 18–34.

Welsh, M.C., Pennington, B.F. and Groisser, D.B. (1991) 'A normative-developmental study of executive function: a window on prefrontal function in children', *Developmental Neuropsychology,* 7(2): 131–149.

Whithall, J. and Clark, J. (2012) 'Developmental coordination disorder: biomechanical and neuromuscular considerations', in M. De Ste Croix and T. Korff (eds.) *Paediatric Biomechanics and Motor Control: Theory and Application* (pp. 259–282). London: Routledge.

Wilson, B.N., Kaplan, B.J., Crawford, S.G., Campbell, A. and Dewe, D. (2000) Reliability and validity of a parent questionnaire on childhood motor skills', *The American Journal of Occupational Therapy,* 54: 484–493.

4

PATRICK

Watch, practice, perform, reward: meeting (special) learning needs

Ann MacPhail, Mark Campbell, Ian Kenny, Daniel Tindall and Deborah Tannehill

DEPARTMENT OF PHYSICAL EDUCATION AND SPORT SCIENCES, UNIVERSITY OF LIMERICK, IRELAND

Key words: 7-year-old male, autism, inclusive play programme, bio-psychomotor development, adapted physical education, pedagogy.

Patrick

Patrick is a 7-year-old Irish boy who has autism and the associated behaviours of delayed social and communication skills. Patrick has three older siblings, a sister who is 9 years old and two brothers who are 11 and 13 years old respectively. He has a more engaging relationship with his sister than with his brothers, and his mother believes this is due to his sister being more patient with Patrick favouring the repetition of tasks over and over again. Patrick's father works as an estate agent selling houses in the main town; his mother does not work. Patrick's mother takes him to school every morning and collects him at the end of each day.

Patrick attends the i-PLAY (Inclusive Play and Leisure Activities for Youth) programme at the local university once each week over a ten-week period. This programme is designed for children, youth and young adults with special needs to have an opportunity to play and interact socially with peers. Participants are engaged in a range of physical activities (e.g., dance and games) and each is paired with third year pre-service physical education teachers to ensure the young person can receive individual attention, support and encouragement. The focus of i-PLAY is upon promoting physical activity for young people and incorporating it into their daily lives (i.e., at school, after school, and at home). The programme provides pre-service physical education teachers with the opportunity to gain experience in planning and assisting youth with special needs as it relates to the physical activity setting. Families also benefit from the programme as it offers opportunities to connect with and support each other and their children with special needs.

Patrick attends the i-PLAY programme every week for one hour. The programme is for young children between the ages of six and ten, and it takes place in the multi-purpose sports hall. There are few visible signs that Patrick enjoys being involved in the physical activity opportunities offered. The pre-service teachers facilitate numerous individual physical activity opportunities using different pieces of equipment, but Patrick prefers to rigidly (with no deviation), and repetitively, pace back and forth along two benches that are set out for the participants to sit on during breaks from the activity sections. Patrick is physically capable of undertaking a range of physical activities if he chooses, yet the excitement, colour and noise of the activities happening around him all appear to escape Patrick's attention. Patrick rarely responds to those who call his name.

It is difficult to comment on Patrick's feelings about peer relations. As the programme allows two pre-service teachers to work with each young person, Patrick favours staying with them rather than being integrated into activities that involve working in close proximity with his peers. There is no evidence of a generic problem with physical contact because he happily holds on to the pre-service teachers as he walks along the benches. Instead, it appears that Patrick prefers to work on his own most of the time, suggesting that he is perhaps oblivious, or just uninterested, in what is going on around him.

Given that Patrick has difficulties with language and social communication, including avoiding eye contact, it can be challenging to gauge whether Patrick enjoys participating in the programme. Patrick is, nonetheless, strong-willed, and the determined look on his face reminds us of this. His facial expressions also allow us to determine when he becomes frustrated. Patrick certainly does display a characteristic need for sameness and structure, not only in the activities he undertakes but also in his behaviour. There are instances where Patrick demonstrates a resistance to changing his behaviour (e.g., when the pre-service teachers attempt to stop him from striking them with his hand). His resistance can lead to bouts of out-of-control behaviour before he calms down.

A bio-psychomotor perspective on Patrick as a learner

Patrick has shown four key characteristics stereotypical of people with autism: reduced social interaction, repetitive nature, akinesia muscle rigidity (slowness in the initiation of movement) and bradykinesia (slowness in the execution of movement). The challenge with autistic individuals is to encourage them to engage in physical activity. Coupled with poor motor functioning is low motivation (Koegel, Koegel and McNerney 2001), and successful interventions must target the psychomotor aspect to the problem. Like many people with autism, Patrick displays difficulty in planning and self-monitoring (Hughes, Russell and Robbins 1994; Ozonoff *et al.* 1994). There is no doubt, however, that encouraging Patrick to physically challenge himself and to seek to improve his motor abilities is very desirable. If Patrick can engage in the process, then we expect him to not only improve his physical skills, but also his personal well-being, confidence, motivation to continue and ultimately his social interaction with peers. The key objective is to encourage Patrick to engage in activities with others and to increase confidence and competence. The two sub-sections that follow describe the biomechanical and psychological tools that can be used to help Patrick engage using auditory, visual and motivation techniques.

Classroom tasks – gait and balance games

Persons with autism demonstrate a variety of motor symptoms including: alterations in motor milestone development (Provost, Lopez and Heimerl 2007), hypotonia (i.e., decreased muscle tone), muscle rigidity, akinesia (difficulty with voluntary muscle control), bradykinesia (slow movement)

(Damasio and Maurer 1978; Kohen-Raz, Volkmar and Cohen 1992) and postural control impairments (Kohen-Raz *et al.* 1992; Minshew *et al.* 2004). These motor symptoms can compromise a child's ability to perform common activities of daily living, such as walking, and this is very apparent in Patrick's case. An abnormal walking pattern can lead to pain, fatigue and joint stress which, in turn, may affect a child's functional capabilities resulting in resistance to activity and reduced quality of life. To ensure optimal functionality and independence, and improved quality of life, researchers, clinicians and teachers need to examine and engage both the biomechanical and psychological function of children with autism.

It is recognised that primary-age students with autism demonstrate a restricted range of social communication skills. This is manifest in limited speech, making it difficult to initiate comments, request information from others, listen and respond to others and interact in simple games (VanMeter *et al.* 1997). A promising practice in this regard is the use of videotechnology, which has been used to teach a wide variety of skills to individuals across a range of disabilities and ages. Recently, there has also been interest in the use of treatments such as video and auditory feedback with children with autism (Maione and Mirenda 2006). All the tasks in which Patrick is involved at the i-PLAY programme follow the WPPR principle: WatchPracticePerformReward, and this is illustrated in the examples below.

Task 1: gait – 20 metre gait activity along a balance beam with visual and auditory feedback

Utilising a task with which Patrick feels familiar is key to his engagement. Mimicking his preferred balance tasks (as described in the opening section) setting a progressively difficult and more interactive task can be effective. For example:

1. A 15-centimetre wide, 20-metre strip of white tape is placed along the ground forming a straight walkway. Patrick is tasked with walking at his own pace along the tape without losing balance.
2. Using a metronome with a variable beat, Patrick is tasked with listening to the rhythm of the beat and walking in time along the 20-metre tape without losing balance.
3. The 20-metre tape is transferred to a gym bench (10 cm high) and Patrick is tasked with listening to the rhythm of the beat and walking in time along the 20-metre tape without losing balance: slow for 5 minutes, medium pace for 5 minutes and brisk walking pace for 5 minutes.

Watch = Patrick watches a video projected onto the hall wall of the teacher performing each of the three tasks.

Practice = Patrick practices the task repetitively with support and guidance from the teacher. Patrick is video recorded at each attempt and ten seconds after every walk the software (Siliconcoach Timewarp 2013) relays Patrick's last practice onto the hall wall for Patrick and everyone to see and Patrick to comment on.

Perform = Patrick performs the task to his highest ability competitively alongside the teacher and then other children who perform the task.

Reward = The development of intrinsic motivation is encouraged via a self-monitoring/motivation chart, teacher and attendee support and a celebration for every successful goal reached.

Task 2: balance – Y balance exercise with visual feedback

Continuing the theme of building on Patrick's favourite balance activities, the Y Balance Test (see Figure 4.1) can be used. The reliability of this three-direction Star Excursion Balance Test, or Y Balance Test, has been proven in performing dynamic balance testing, with good intra-rater reliability (ICC: 0.85 to 0.91) and good inter-rater reliability (ICC: 0.99 to 1.00) (Plisky *et al.* 2009). For the test, Patrick balances on one leg and then reaches as far as possible along each of the three white lines, without losing balance. The WPPR test is repeated while balancing on the other leg.

During the i-PLAY programme, Patrick is given 30 minutes each week for 9 weeks to practice and improve his ability on each task. On the tenth week a competition is introduced. Each week the pre-service teacher supporting Patrick assesses his movement ability using Gallahue and Ozmun's (1995) movement development levels checklist. For gait and balance, checklist modules identify three or four key movement characteristics that rate the movement as at an *initial, elementary,* or *mature* stage of development.

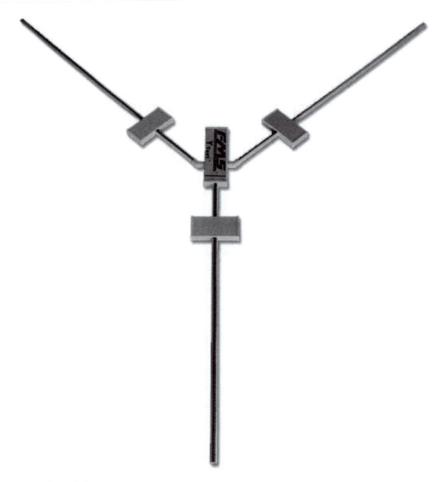

FIGURE 4.1 The Y balance test setup

Supporting adults – in this case pre-service teachers – play an integral role with Patrick during his assessment and intervention. The timing and manner of feedback are key elements in building confidence and competence with all children, and this is magnified in the case of autistic children (Ingersoll, Schreibman and Tran 2003). The pre-service teacher at i-PLAY should encourage Patrick to participate in the gait and balance tasks in a gradual and supportive way. Utilising Gallahue and Ozmun's (1995) developmental level checklist will ensure an appropriate level of difficulty is attempted for the activities. It is also important to ensure there is minimal fear/anxiety linked to the activity and that ultimately there will be an increase in the likelihood of success. Additionally, Patrick's age (7) is usually a time of developing motivational and cognitive readiness (Fry and Duda 1997; Veroff 1969) and supporting adults must look for signs of this readiness during assessments (e.g., signs that Patrick's focus of attention and timing of language are becoming more coordinated). Regarding the feedback for Patrick over the ten weeks, the same WPPR principle can be adopted throughout all activities, and in the sections below we offer a little more detail on these processes.

Watch = As was noted earlier, in addition to Patrick watching the teacher performing the balance test, Patrick will watch himself as he attempts it. This observation is a form of motor imagery training and has been used successfully as an intervention to ameliorate a range of motor clumsiness issues in children (Wilson, Thomas and Maruff 2002). We know from a growing body of literature that when we observe someone performing a motor action, our brains seem to simulate performance of the action we observe (see Moran *et al.* 2012 for a review). Identical areas of the brain activate and function in much the same way as when an action is performed or merely observed, and thus these brain areas (premotor cortex and right superior parietal lobe) have become known as the 'mirror system'. Furthermore, this action observation and simulation has been argued to underpin sophisticated mental functions such as communication (Rizzolatti and Arbib 1998), observational learning (Berger *et al.* 1979) and socialisation (Gallese and Goldman 1998). Interestingly, biomechanically impossible actions have been shown not to activate the mirror system (Stevens *et al.* 2000). Thus, the relatively simple practice of observing an action, particularly ones' own action, is a core part of the intervention with Patrick. Given his autistic traits, Patrick may benefit more from observing himself performing than from observing the teacher but in the intervention described earlier, the decision was taken to show Patrick both types.

Practice = Over the course of the ten weeks Patrick will observe the teacher and himself performing the tasks on a weekly basis. Patrick will be able to monitor his performance gains and see how he has improved each week. Coupled with this will be the pre-service teacher's comments and encouragement. Taken together, this monitoring by self and others should enable significant success and gains to be made. Another aspect to the feedback Patrick will receive will be the auditory feedback. This, coupled with the visual feedback from the video display, will help Patrick to coordinate and synchronise his motor coordination and timing. By utilising a metronome beat at different speeds, depending on the task and the difficulty encountered, it is hoped to maximise the auditory rhythmic entrainment potential of the metronome. For example, we hope to get Patrick to step on the balance test to a slow rhythm initially, and this may enable him to more effectively hold his balance and/or make more balanced steps. Auditory rhythmic entrainment programmes have been shown to have substantial success across a range of domains including: rehabilitation after stroke (Beckelheimer *et al.* 2011), attention deficit hyperactivity disorder (Rice, Marra and Butler 2007) and Parkinson's

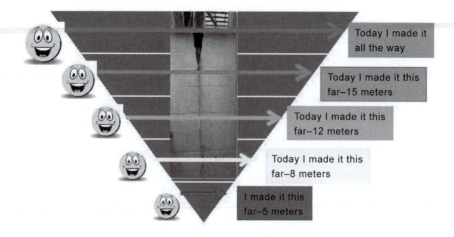

FIGURE 4.2 Self-monitor board example

disease (Dvorsky, Elgelid and Chau 2011). Such programmes offer benefits both as an effective diagnostic tool and a form of treatment for such conditions. It is hoped that either the auditory feedback or the combination of visual and auditory feedback will help Patrick in his balance and gait task competency.

Perform = As mentioned above the pre-service teacher will utilise a self-monitoring board for Patrick. This board (see Figure 4.2 above for an example) will list Patrick's milestones and achievements over the course of the ten weeks, and Patrick will be encouraged to pin smiley faces or gold stars immediately following successful completion of the task. For example, during week 3 of a 10-week programme, the target or goal might be for Patrick to manage 10 metres of the 20-metre balance test without making a mistake. Week four would extend this goal further, and so on. Getting Patrick to see and feel progress will help him to monitor himself and his progress. Using a self-monitoring board has been shown to work successfully in sustaining physical activity programmes with autistic children (Todd and Reid 2006). Given the repetitive nature of behaviours displayed by Patrick and many others with autism, increasing the ability to self-monitor will help Patrick to gauge progress and feel more motivated to refine and improve his task performances. This mastery of the tasks at hand should foster an increase in Patrick's physical competence, his self-perceptions and his psychosocial well-being. Additionally, research literature suggests that an increase in physical activity should decrease Patrick's maladaptive behaviours (Elliott *et al.* 1994; Kern *et al.* 1982; Walton and Ingersoll 2013).

Another important task for the supporting adults in the i-PLAY programme is to observe Patrick every week and complete a social behaviour scale (The teacher or adult observations would be guided by Table 4.1, and Patrick would utilise the monitoring board which is adapted from Pierce-Jordan and Lifter 2005; see Figure 4.3) before, during and after each i-PLAY hour. This scale will enable the pre-service teacher to gauge the development of Patrick's social behaviours and also whether he is engaging in more or fewer maladaptive behaviours (obsession and ritualised behaviours). This log will help the pre-service teacher to provide accurate feedback to Patrick and to adjust the ease or difficulty of the tasks according to his needs.

TABLE 4.1 Social behaviour table (adapted from Pierce-Jordan and Lifter 2005: An example of a Social Behaviour Scale to be utilised with Patrick during i-PLAY.)

Teacher Name:	i-PLAYClass: 5–9 year olds	Week/Date: 10 week programme
Participant Name	*Behaviour Score* Before PA	*Behaviour Score* After PA
Patrick Week 1	1	1
Patrick Week 2	1	1
Patrick Week 3	1	2
Patrick Week 4	2	2

FIGURE 4.3 An example of a picture board

Social behavior scoring key:

1 – *Solitary:* child sits, plays, studies or engages alone in some type of activity; child gazes at the toys in front of him or her or gazes away from the play area (e.g., around the class) without looking at, or interacting with, others.

2 – *On-looking:* child gazes at another person or at a person's actions; child's social status is that of observer, not participant (e.g., child watches another child build a block tower).

3 – *Uncoordinated social:* child's verbal and nonverbal behaviours are socially focused, including talking, sharing objects (e.g., gives object to another child), eye contact or making physical contact (e.g., touch), but the social behaviour is not coordinated with the verbal and nonverbal behaviours of others (e.g., child states, "Look at my tower" and tips block tower before waiting for anyone to look).

4 – *Coordinated social:* child's verbal and nonverbal behaviours are socially focused, including talking, sharing objects (e.g., gives object to another child) or making eye contact or physical contact (e.g., touch), and the behaviour is coordinated with the verbal and nonverbal behaviours of others; that is, the child coordinates his or her focus of attention and timing of language or actions with the focus of attention and timing of language or action of others (e.g., child states "Look at my tower" and tips block tower after obtaining someone's attention).

Reward = On successful completion of the tasks Patrick will be rewarded by getting to pin a smiley face to his monitoring/motivation board. Additionally he will receive praise from the teacher and anyone in attendance.

The ten-week biopsych programme described for Patrick is a combination of research evidence and observations developed over time and incorporated into the i-PLAY programme. The traits and preferences of individual children will always provide a unique teaching environment and in this regard, the teaching of all children should be personalised. The challenge is in identifying what works best for the individual, and Patrick's case illustrates some of the physical activity support needs of one individual child with autism.

An adapted physical education perspective

Research has suggested that most physical education teachers have had limited or no formal training (i.e., courses or workshops) in teaching young people with disabilities (Meegan and MacPhail 2006; Morley *et al.* 2005). The same can be said for pre-service physical education teachers. Initial teacher education (ITE) programmes tend to offer only one course or module to 'prepare' students to plan and teach 'diverse populations', including young people with special educational needs (Hardin 2005). As a result, newly qualified physical education teachers can feel under-qualified to teach young people with disabilities or those with particular special educational needs.

One form of disability of particular concern to physical education teachers is the pervasive developmental disorder of autism, as exhibited by Patrick. Pervasive Developmental Disorders (PDD) is characterized by severe and pervasive impairment in several areas of development: social interaction skills and communication skills, and the presence of stereotyped behaviour, interests, and activities (Auxter *et al.* 2010). The four most common forms of PDD are Autistic Disorder, Asperger's Disorder, Rett's Disorder and PDD-NOS (not otherwise specified). It is the Autistic Disorder, or autism, that is the focus of this case study.

Classic autism, also known as Kanner syndrome, was first described by Dr. Leo Kanner (Kanner 1943). Characteristics of the autistic disorder include significant developmental delays, global and comprehensive language disorders, abnormal and stereotypical behaviour patterns, social isolation and, in some instances, intellectual disabilities. Children with autism, such as Patrick in this case, may exhibit symptoms (in varying degrees of severity) in addition to those mentioned earlier including;

- Inappropriate laughing or giggling
- No real fear of dangers (e.g., running into traffic)
- Apparent insensitivity to pain
- May avoid eye contact or touch (e.g., hugging)
- Uneven verbal or physical skills
- Difficulty in expressing needs (may use gestures)
- Inappropriate attachments to objects
- Echoes words or phrases
- Spins objects or self excessively

Teaching strategies for use with Patrick

Research suggests that daily vigorous, aerobic exercise is beneficial for students with autism (Richardson and Langley 1997; Todd and Reid 2006). It reduces self-stimulatory and off-task behaviour, increases time on academic and vocational tasks, and can help to improve gross motor performance. From a pedagogical perspective, when teaching children such as Patrick, numerous methods or 'systems' have proven to be successful for physical education teachers. There are numerous examples of such methods, including Daily Life Therapy, Treatment and Education for Autistic and Communication-Related Handicapped Children (TEACCH), Applied Behavioural Analysis, and reinforcement strategies such as the Premack Principle.

These are all systems that have proven effective when engaging children with autism in the educational setting and each is explained in more detail below.

Daily Life Therapy (DLT) (Howlin 2005; Quill, Gurry and Larkin 1989) utilises physical regimes to promote independent living and self-esteem with a particular emphasis on vestibular system stimulation (i.e., spatial awareness – body in space, moving, balance etc.). From a physical education perspective, when maturation of the system is delayed, students may demonstrate problems in the following ways:

- Inability to balance on one foot (particularly with the eyes closed)
- Inability to walk a balance beam without watching the feet
- Inability to walk heel-to-toe
- Inefficient walking and running patterns
- Delays in ability to hop and to skip

The TEACCH system (Hume and Odom 2007) is another effective method suitable for Patrick. Due to children with autism demanding consistent and predictable routines as a way to engage with their environment, the TEACCH system requires the identification and implementation of specific routines. The learner and an adult participate in a meaningful activity that requires consistent communication. The system relies on five components to be in place and to be optimal in order for it to be effective: (i) the physical structure of the environment, (ii) the scheduling of the person's overall day and week, (iii) expectations of how the person will work (the work system) during tasks, (iv) routines incorporated within a learning environment, and (v) visual schedules to assist in the actual structure of the learning session. In particular, visual schedules, or picture exchange communication systems, could be very useful for Patrick. They allow him to trade a picture of an item or experience for what he wants to do. Additionally, visual schedules use pictures to help Patrick predict what will occur during the day. For example, each i-PLAY session begins at the picture board so that Patrick and his 'coach' can go over the activities for the day. A typical schedule would include a warm-up game, fitness focus, water break, lesson focus and closing game (see Figure 4.3).

Applied Behaviour Analysis (ABA) (Grey *et al.* 2005) and the Premack Principle (Premack 1959) are more traditional and recognised methods for engaging students with autism. The ABA approach is characterised as a series of trials that involve instruction, a prompt and an opportunity to respond followed by appropriate feedback for the student. The Premack Principle looks to prompt young people with autism to participate usually through a token system of different forms of 'if/then' statements (e.g., "*If* you do two more fitness circuit stations *then* we can shoot baskets for 5 minutes").

An important point to be made about these and other 'systems' is that they have been designed to be progressive and engaging for those children who face some of the biggest challenges to being physically active. They can offer very helpful frameworks for those supporting adults who feel they lack appropriate knowledge and experience.

School physical education progressions for Patrick

Given that Patrick is 7 years old, the emphasis of his primary physical education experience should be upon developing a range of fundamental movement skills. This will include cardiovascular endurance activities, whole body movements and dance and rhythm activities to foster parallel body part identification. Play activities are also important to move Patrick from onlooker, to solitary play and then to parallel play engagement. As Patrick grows older, his physical education experience should continue to focus on cardiovascular endurance activities and also include functional locomotor skills. Such skills might include the use of different surfaces, manoeuvering around a variety of obstacles while carrying objects or pushing objects, rhythm activities and low-organisation games, higher level equilibrium activities and games with very simple rules. As Patrick progresses to post-primary (age 11 onwards) the emphasis of his physical education experience should continue to be upon improving cardiovascular endurance activities. In addition, he should learn about basic leisure, recreation, sport and fitness skills that can be undertaken individually, as relaxation training, and as community-based activities.

Modifications/adaptations/inclusion techniques

Issues relating to Patrick and his level of autism will present challenges for the teacher. Yet, high functioning learners with PDD can be successful in the general physical activity programme when teachers implement appropriate modifications, adaptations and inclusion techniques (Auxter *et al.* 2010). Essentially, teachers must be well organised and provide developmentally appropriate activities for Patrick, emphasising cooperation with appropriate competition. It is equally important that positive behaviour management techniques are used as well as recommended teaching strategies.

Pedagogical perspective

From the outset, it was made apparent that Patrick prefers repetition, sameness and structure in his environment and the activities in which he is engaged. We also note that he does not like change and avoids interacting with others, preferring to work on his own. Comments from the biomechanics, psychology and adapted perspectives all highlight similar goals for Patrick, specifically related to increasing his social interactions and engagement in physical activity. From all three perspectives, it is suggested that progressive task development in these areas, and adaptation to need, are essential if Patrick is to make optimal progress and develop confidence and competence in his skills and abilities.

Based on the evidence from the earlier sections, we conclude that understanding Patrick and his preferences and traits is critical to designing effective learning environments and activities. It is worth remembering, however, that *all* physical education classes are composed of diverse groups of students. Pupils will range from highly skilled boys and girls who are motivated to be successful, to those for whom motor performance is difficult leading to low confidence and desire to participate, and all levels in between. There will be young people who come from physically active families who support and encourage physical activity participation and those whose parents are more concerned with other aspects of school and discourage physical activity involvement. Students will be tall, short, 'skinny' and heavy, racially and ethnically diverse, hail from urban and rural communities, and will – or will not – have apparent or declared disabilities (physical, emotional, behavioural and cognitive). When teaching in these diverse classrooms, and whether teaching students with or without disabilities, physical education teachers and coaches using pedagogically sound strategies will use similar teaching/coaching approaches. Tannehill, van der Mars and MacPhail (in press) argue that effective teachers are active teachers who keep students consistently engaged in learning tasks, use individual, partner, small group and whole-class instruction, and supervise student practice attentively adjusting tasks to meet the needs, abilities and developmental levels of all students. These characteristics are required for all classes of pupils but, as Houston-Wilson, Dunn, van der Mars and McCubbin (1997) suggest, when teaching students with severe disabilities there is likely to be an increased emphasis on adaptations, modifications, and supports.

Learning tasks as content development

Dyson, Griffin and Hastie (2004) consider the role of the teacher as a *facilitator*. They suggest that as students engage in an assigned practice task, the teacher should guide learning based on students' prior knowledge and skill development. As a result of observation of student success, the teacher can then either simplify or challenge through task revision. This is consistent with Rink's (1994; 1996) conceptualisation of learning tasks as essentially comprising content development reflected through a task cycle of refining (focus on improving the quality of task), extending (adaptations to tasks to make them more or less challenging) and applying (tasks that require students to apply skills). Teachers must be able to conduct an analysis of content and then, based on the instructional goal for a lesson, design an appropriate progression that moves each student from a novice (less complex) to advanced (more complex) level appropriate to their individual needs and abilities. The literature is clear that task progressions are 'key' to student learning (Rink, 1996). Research shows, however, that teachers' task development patterns tend to include an 'informing' task followed by an 'application' task, with little attention paid to developing students' quality of performance or practice through more and less *complex* tasks (Hastie and Siedentop 1999). In other words, teachers tend to teach a sport skill then immediately place students in game play without first helping them to refine, extend and locate their skills through an appropriate progression of tasks.

Considering task complexity

After a teacher or coach has analysed the content, learning goal and needs of the students, decisions must be made on how to modify or extend task complexity. Chow and Atencio (2012) propose three categories of potential constraints related to increasing task complexity: *performer,* the *environment,* and the *task* itself. They suggest that these constraints interact with one another and determine whether the student can select appropriate responses and behaviours that will result in success. Performer constraints include structural and functional characteristics of the learner as discussed by the bio-psychological perspective earlier in this chapter. Environmental constraints include both physical and social aspects of the learning context. In Patrick's case, there was an emphasis on cooperative activities in the adaptive physical education strategies. Task constraints include specific activity rules, task goals, and equipment and facilities, and examples of the ways in which these might be adapted for Patrick have been identified.

Physical activity environment

Silverman, Subramaniam and Woods (1998) suggest that in physical activity environments, student skill level is strongly related to the teaching and learning process. They argue that if teachers offer frequent opportunities for low-skilled students to practice tasks, this may result in improved learning outcomes. Whether designing appropriate progressions to meet the needs of all learners, using teaching strategies shown to be effective with different learners, or accessing available instructional aides to facilitate student learning, the 'key' is to focus on the individual learner within a class of diverse students. Patrick may not be as successful as his more physically able peers, and he faces considerable challenges in performance levels in most activities. It is important for teachers and coaches to remember, however, that making adaptations to activities to help children with disabilities is likely to be a helpful strategy for other low-skilled children too. Indeed, at all points on the spectrum of ability in physical education and youth sport, modifying tasks to ensure progression for different learners is a founding principle of professional practice. In other words, an effective teacher or coach will always focus on the student, and modify, adapt and utilise inclusion techniques to meet the needs of all learners.

References

Auxter, D., Pyfer, J., Zittel, L. and Roth, K. (2010) *Principles and methods of adapted physical education and recreation,* 11th edn. New York, NY: McGraw-Hill.

Beckelheimer, S.C., Dalton, A.E., Richter, C.A., Hermann, V. and Page, S.J. (2011) 'Computer based rhythm and timing training in severe stroke induced arm hemiparesis', *American Journal of Occupational Therapy,* 65(1): 96–100.

Berger, S.M., Carli, L.L., Hammersla, K.S., Karshmer, J.F. and Sanchez, M.E. (1979) 'Motoric and symbolic mediation in observational learning', *Journal of Personality & Social Psychology,* 37: 735–746.

Chow, J.Y. and Atencio, M. (2012) 'Complex and nonlinear pedagogy and the implications for physical education', *Sport, Education & Society,* iFirst: 1–21.

Damasio, A.R. and Maurer, R.G. (1978) 'A neurological model for childhood autism', *Archives of Neurology,* 35: 777–786.

Dvorsky, B.P., Elgelid, S. and Chau, C.W. (2011) 'The effectiveness of utilizing a combination of external visual and auditory cues as a gait training strategy in a pharmaceutically untreated patient with Parkinson's disease: a case report', *Physical and Occupational Therapy in Geriatrics,* 29(4): 320–326.

Dyson, B., Griffin, L.L. and Hastie, P. (2004) 'Sport education, tactical games, and cooperative learning: theoretical and pedagogical considerations', *Quest,* 56(2): 226–240.

Elliott, R.R., Dobbin, A.D., Rose, G.V. and Soper, H. (1994) 'Vigorous, aerobic exercise versus general motor training activities: effects on maladaptive and stereotypic behaviors of adults with both autism and mental retardation', *Journal of Autism and Developmental Disorders,* 24(5): 565–576.

Fry, M.D. and Duda, J.L. (1997) 'A developmental examination of children's understanding of effort and ability in the physical and academic domains', *Research Quarterly for Exercise and Sports,* 68(4): 331–344.

Gallahue, D.L. and Ozmun, J.C. (1995) *Understanding motor development: Infants, children, adolescents and adults.* Madison, WI: Brown and Benchmark.

Gallese, G. and Goldman, A (1998) 'Mirror neurons and the simulation theory of mind reading', *Trends in Cognitive Science,* 2: 493–501.

Grey, I.M., Honan, R., McClean, B. and Daly, M. (2005) 'Evaluating the effectiveness of teacher training in applied behaviour analysis', *Journal of Intellectual Disabilities,* 9(3): 209–227.

Hardin, B. (2005) 'Physical education teachers' reflections on preparation for inclusion', *The Physical Educator,* 62(1): 44–56.

Hastie, P. and Siedentop, D. (1999) 'An ecological perspective on physical education', *European Physical Education Review,* 5: 9–29.

Houston-Wilson, C., Dunn, J.M., van der Mars, H. and McCubbin, J. (1997) 'The effect of peer tutors on the motor performance in integrated physical education classes', *Adapted Physical Activity Quarterly,* 14: 298–313.

Howlin, P. (2005) 'The effectiveness of interventions for children with autism', in W.W. Fleischhacker and D.J. Brooks (eds.) *Neurodevelopmental Disorders* (pp. 101–119). New York: Springer Vienna.

Hughes, C., Russell, J. and Robbins, T.W. (1994) 'Evidence for executive dysfunction in Autism', *Neuropsychologia*, 32(4): 477–492.

Hume, K. and Odom, S. (2007) 'Effects of an individual work system on the independent functioning of students with autism', *Journal of Autism and Developmental Disorders*, 37(6): 1166–1180.

Ingersoll, B., Schreibman, L., and Tran, Q. (2003) 'The effect of sensory feedback on immediate object imitation in children with autism', *Journal of Autism and Developmental Disorders*, 33: 673–683.

Kanner, L. (1943) 'Autistic disturbances of affective contact', *Nervous Child*, 2: 217–253.

Kern, L., Koegel, R.L., Dyer, K., Blew, P.A. and Fenton, L.R. (1982) 'The effects of physical exercise on self-stimulation and appropriate responding in autistic children', *Journal of Autism and Developmental Disorders*, 12: 399–419.

Koegel, R.L., Koegel, L.K. and McNerney, E. (2001) 'Pivotal areas in intervention for Autism', *Journal of Clinical Child Psychology*, 30(1): 19–32.

Kohen-Raz, R., Volkmar, F.R. and Cohen, D.J. (1992) 'Postural control in children with Autism', *Journal of Autism and Developmental Disorders*, 22(3): 419–432.

Maione, L. and Mirenda, P. (2006) 'Effects of video modelling and video feedback of peer-directed social language skills of a child with autism', *Journal of Positive Motor Behavior Interventions*, 8: 106–118.

Meegan, S. and MacPhail, A. (2006) 'Irish physical educators' attitude toward teaching students with special educational needs', *European Physical Education Review*, 12(1): 75–97.

Minshew, N.J., Sung, K., Jones, B.L. and Furman, J.M. (2004) 'Underdevelopment of the postural control system in autism', *Neurology*, 63(11): 2056–2061.

Moran, A., Campbell, M., Holmes, P. and MacIntyre, T. (2012) 'Mental imagery, action observation and skill learning', in M. Williams and N. Hodges (eds.) *Skill acquisition in sport- research, theory and practice*, 2nd edn (pp. 94–111). London: Routledge.

Morley, D., Bailey, R., Tan, J. and Cooke, B. (2005) 'Inclusive physical education: Teachers' views of including pupils with special educational needs and/or disabilities in physical education', *European Physical Education Review*, 11(1): 84–107.

Ozonoff, S., Strayer, D.L., McMahon, W.M. and Filloux, F. (1994) 'Executive function abilities in autism and Tourette syndrome: an information processing approach', *Journal of Child Psychology and Psychiatry*, 35: 1015–1032.

Pierce-Jordan, S. and Lifter, K. (2005) 'Interaction of social and play behaviors in preschoolers with and without pervasive developmental disorder', *Topics in Early Childhood Special Education*, 25: 34–47.

Plisky, P.J., Gorman, P.P., Butler, R.J. *et al.* (2009) 'The reliability of an instrumented device for measuring components of the Star Excursion Balance Test', *North American Journal of Sports Physical Therapy*, 4(2): 92–99.

Premack, D. (1959) 'Toward empirical behavior laws: I. Positive reinforcement', *Psychological Review*, 66: 219–233.

Provost, B., Lopez, B.R. and Heimerl, S. (2007) 'A comparison of motor delays in young children: autism spectrum disorder, developmental delay, and developmental concerns', *Journal of Autism and Developmental Disorders*, 37(2): 321–328.

Quill, K., Gurry, S. and Larkin A. (1989) 'Daily Life Therapy: a Japanese model for educating children with autism', *Journal of Autism and Developmental Disorders*, 19(4): 625–635.

Rice, V., Marra, D. and Butler, J. (2007) 'Neuro-cognitive assessment, symptoms of attention deficit and hyperactivity disorder, and soldier performance during 68W advanced individual training'. Army Research Laboratory, ARL-TR-4292, October 2007. Online. Available HTTP: <www.arl.army.mil/arlreports/2007/ARL-TR-4292.pdf> (accessed 23 October 2013).

Richardson, H.C. and Langley, T.A. (1997) 'Research in brief: the potential benefits of daily life therapy for children with autism', *Autism*, 1(2): 236–237.

Rink, J.E. (1994) 'Task presentation in pedagogy', *Quest*, 46: 270–280.

Rink, J.E. (1996) 'Effective instruction in physical education', in S. Silverman and C. Ennis (eds.) *Student learning in physical education: Applying research to enhance instruction*. Champaign, IL: Human Kinetics.

Rizzolatti, G. and Arbib, M.A. (1998) 'Language within our grasp', *Trends in Neuroscience,* 21: 188–194.

Siliconcoach Timewarp (2013) *Timewarp: Immediate Video Analysis.* Online. Available HTTP: <www.siliconcoach.com/products/timewarp/#introduction> (accessed 22 September 2013).

Silverman, S., Subramaniam, P.R. and Woods, A.W. (1998) 'Task structures, student practice, and skill in physical education', *The Journal of Educational Research,* 91(5): 298–307.

Stevens, J.A., Fonlupt, P., Shiffrar, M. and Decety, J. (2000) 'New aspects of motion perception: selective neural encoding of apparent human movements', *Neuroreport,* 11: 109–115.

Tannehill, D., van der Mars, H. and MacPhail, A. (in press) *Building, delivering and sustaining effective physical education programs,* Sudbury, MA: Jones & Bartlett.

Todd, T. and Reid, G. (2006) 'Increasing physical activity in individuals with autism', *Focus on Autism and Other Developmental Disabilities,* 21: 167–176.

VanMeter, L., Fein, D., Morris, R., Waterhouse, L. and Allen, D. (1997) 'Delay versus deviance in autistic social behavior', *Journal of Autism and Developmental Disorders,* 27: 557–569.

Veroff, J. (1969) 'Social comparison and the development of achievement motivation', in C.P. Smith (ed.) *Achievement-related motives in children* (pp. 46–101). New York: Russell Sage Foundation.

Walton, K.M. and Ingersoll B.R. (2013) 'Improving social skills in adolescents and adults with autism and severe to profound intellectual disability: a review of the literature', *Journal of Autism and Developmental Disorders,* 43: 594–615.

Wilson, P.H., Thomas, P.R. and Maruff, P. (2002) 'Motor imagery training ameliorates motor clumsiness in children', *Journal of Child Neurology,* 17: 491–498.

5

DESHANE

Young, gifted and Black . . . and overcoming challenges

Phillip Ward, Jacqueline Goodway, Samuel Hodge and Rick Petosa

KINESIOLOGY, DEPARTMENT OF HUMAN SCIENCES, THE OHIO STATE UNIVERSITY, USA

Key words: 8-year-old male, Black American, overweight, motor development, cultural studies, health promotion, pedagogy.

Deshane

Deshane is an 8-year-old Black American boy. He is a handsome, dark-skinned child, and he has a great smile. Deshane's life is characterized by duality. Like many urban youth, he is constantly confronted with choices and examples of what those choices mean in his family life, his community and at school. He is of above average intelligence, with particular strengths in reading and math. The school nurse at his school, in a required state-mandated assessment of all children in schools, reported that Deshane is overweight (86th percentile of BMI), but not obese.

Deshane lives with his mother and grandmother. Deshane does not know his father, who abandoned his mother and his older brother before he was born. There was a history of domestic violence before his father left and much of it was directed to his brother, the older son. Deshane's brother dropped out of school in grade 10 with a number of cognitive disabilities that the schools and social services did little to address. He was killed crossing the street when Deshane was 5 years old. Deshane's mother did not graduate from high school because she was pregnant with his older brother by the time she was 16. She was a good student in school who was bright and very capable. She has not returned to any form of education, and now works as a maid for a local maid cleaning service during the day and as a waitress at night. She wants Deshane to have what she didn't have: an education through college level. The value of a good education is also a recurring theme for Deshane's grandmother, who views Deshane as the hope of the family.

Deshane's mother rents an apartment in the east side of Columbus, Ohio. His grandmother earns money by babysitting and providing childcare services in their home during the day. As a result, there is not a lot of room inside the apartment for Deshane to play. The apartment complex is 2-stories high with 16 apartments. The building is beside 3 more identical apartment buildings, and there is green space between them running for the length of the apartments and approximately 25 feet wide (7.5 meters). A concrete walkway borders each side of the green space. Neither his mother nor his grandmother will allow Deshane to play outside without supervision due the personal safety issues related to gang activity in the area.

The streets surrounding Deshane's apartment consist of busy three- and four-lane roads. There are few community parks in the area, with the nearest being more than three quarters of a mile away. Getting there involves Deshane crossing several streets and going out of his way to reach safe, traffic light–controlled crossings. His mother and grandmother seldom have the time to take him to the parks other than occasionally on weekends. In any case, the park is not particularly appealing because the playground equipment is usually broken and there is often broken glass around. Deshane feels that his community is familiar because there are a number of people in it who have been there as long as he can remember. There are also a lot of people who seem to come and go over the course of the year.

Deshane lives in a neighborhood that provides mixed messages to him. On the one hand, the church and its members are very supportive of him. They appear to value him as a person, enjoy talking with him and convey a strong belief that he can succeed in school and in life. In contrast, the neighborhood provides very clear examples that others fare less well, offering rather more negative role models. Deshane has relationships with older youth in the neighborhood who are involved with drugs in both passive and active ways, gang activity and prostitution among their peers. Several of these older youths have already dropped out of school. Within his wider family, Deshane has cousins who are middle and high school students, and all claim they want to be elite athletes. Few seem to be on a realistic pathway to such a goal, often making poor decisions and lacking the level of focus that would be required.

There are no grocery stores close to Deshane's family home that would offer easy access to a variety of food, including fruit and vegetables. There are, however, three fast food restaurants and several convenience stores within a mile radius of their home. Family meals tend to be high in fat, carbohydrate and protein, with frozen vegetables that are limited to what everyone will eat – which often comes down to broccoli, peas and carrots. Fruit is rarely available at home because it is too expensive. Once or twice a week, Deshane's mother will grab fast food for dinner on the way home from work because she is simply too tired to cook. There are always plentiful fatty snacks available in the home, and this may partly explain why both Deshane's mother and grandmother are obese and also diabetic. Deshane does qualify for the federal government's free breakfast and lunch program for children from low socioeconomic backgrounds but, sadly, his school bus arrives too late for him to take advantage of the breakfast.

Deshane attends Cowling Elementary School, the local neighborhood public (state) school with an enrolment of 408 students. Of these, 45% are White, 40% are Black, 8% are Hispanic, and the remaining 7% comprise several different races. Male students account for 51% of the student population in the school, and the teacher-student ratio is 29 to 1.[1] Deshane, like most pupils, is bused to school. Deshane is in the 2nd grade and, although he enjoys school, he is often reserved. He likes to talk, but he has become wary because although he is bright, his teacher often acts surprised by his answers, almost as though she didn't expect him to be correct. She is White and has been teaching for over 25 years and, although she has never said anything specific, Deshane feels that she is not as supportive of him as she is of students who are not Black. In fact, if Deshane had attended a school with more resources, his high test results in math and reading might have led to him being assigned to a program for gifted students, but this is not available at Cowling. Deshane has often said to his grandmother that he wants his teacher to know that he likes school and wants to learn.

Physical education classes at Cowling occur once a week for 40 minutes, either in the multipurpose room where lunch is also served or on an asphalt playground approximately the size of five basketball courts. Cowling has no grassed areas and little permanent playground equipment. The physical education teacher, Ms. Flynn, is female, White, and has been teaching in this school for 7 years. She grew up in a small community in rural Ohio that was predominately White and where much of the community attended the same church. In physical education, Deshane likes his teacher and enjoys being outside. He loves sports and enjoys the feeling of moving. Deshane's physical education lesson is typically a fun and active time for him.

A perspective on Deshane's case from motor development

Motor development studies ways in which motor behavior changes over the lifespan and what factors affect these changes (Gallahue, Ozmun and Goodway 2012). In order to help Deshane, teachers and coaches or activity leaders need to understand how motor skills emerge and the kinds of constraints or underlying mechanisms that will influence his developmental trajectory.

Models of motor development

Models of motor development (Clark and Metcalfe 2002; Gallahue *et al.* 2012; Seefeldt 1980) suggest infant reflexes are the foundation of human movement. These reflexes lead to preadapted/rudimentary skills where children learn important motor milestones such as sitting and walking. In Deshane's case, it is possible that he was delayed in the acquisition of key motor milestones due to limited stimulation (Goodway, Robinson and Crowe 2010).

The next most important step recognized across models of motor development is the acquisition of fundamental motor skills (FMS), including locomotorskills (e.g., running) and object control skills (e.g., catching). FMS are the building blocks for future engagement in physical activities and sport, and can be described as the "base camp" of the mountain of motor development providing the basis for later "motor skillfulness" (Clark and Metcalfe 2002: 17). Age-related data in motor development (Gallahue *et al.* 2012) would suggest that by the age of 8, children should have developed competency in FMS. Deshane has not yet developed such competency and, in order to address this delay, Deshane needs a lot of appropriate practice, modeling and feedback on his performance (Gallahue *et al.* 2012). Like many children growing up in poor inner city communities, Deshane's environment does not support timely motor development and the acquisition of FMS (Goodway *et al.* 2010).

It is unfortunate that the only regular physical activity opportunities available to Deshane are 40 minutes of physical education per week at school and some limited time at the Christian Life Center at his church. Deshane's mother cannot afford to pay for youth sports clubs, and the park is both dangerous and far away. Moreover, she works multiple jobs, is obese, and has neither the time nor the energy to play actively with Deshane. While children in more affluent neighborhoods can be active on their streets, Deshane cannot because the streets around his house are unsafe with some areas taken over by gangs and drugs (Goodway and Smith 2005). Deshane's developmental delays in FMS are certainly problematic because such delays prevent him from moving to the next recognized stage of motor development: the performance of specialized, context-specific skills (Clark and Metcalfe 2002; Gallahue *et al.* 2012). In Seefeldt's (1980) words, the FMS delay would act as a "proficiency barrier" to Deshane's ability to successfully engage in sports and lifetime physical activities.

A more recent motor development model connects low motor competence in the early years of life to lower physical activity levels, inadequate fitness, and poor self-perceptions of motor competence (Stodden *et al.* 2008). The interaction between these factors strengthens over time and channels children into a "negative spiral of disengagement" (294) from physical activity placing the child at higher risk of obesity. The early effects of this negative spiral are evident in the case of Deshane, who has low motor competence/fitness and is overweight. Although Deshane enjoys being physically active now, research evidence suggests he will become increasingly inactive as he transitions into adolescence with low perceptions of motor competence (Stodden *et al.* 2008). It is clear from these motor development models, therefore, that developing FMS competence during early childhood is the foundation for lifelong physical activity.

Principles of motor development

Some basic principles of motor development (Gallahue *et al.* 2012) provide a context for understanding Deshane's movement skills and offering effective ways to help him to learn:

- *Change is qualitatively different, sequential and cumulative.* By understanding developmental sequences in FMS (Gallahue *et al.* 2012), Deshane can be helped to shift from inefficient patterns of movement to more mechanically efficient patterns that can be applied across multiple contexts (Clark and Metcalfe 2002). Developmental change is built on previous capabilities/experiences, yet for Deshane, these experiences are limited. Deshane's environment appears to be constraining his motor development trajectory, placing him at high risk of long term negative health consequences.
- *Movement is multi-factorial and a product of the interaction of constraints imposed by the learner, the environment and the task.* Newell's (1984) constraints perspective suggests that changes in motor development are influenced by the interaction of factors from the learner, environment and task. Learner factors, such as being overweight, having delayed FMS and poor fitness will impact Deshane's movement skills negatively. Longer term, lack of motivation to be active will have a devastating influence on Deshane's physical activity levels (Stodden *et al.* 2008). The problems are further compounded by the negative environmental factors surrounding Deshane, such as unsafe environments, limited role models and minimal physical education. The cumulative impact of these constraints will limit Deshane's motor skillfulness, so an understanding of these multiple effects is vital in order to design effective educational interventions.
- *Change is variable between and within children.* The science of learning for Deshane is unique to him, emphasizing the importance of providing personalized instruction. This understanding is central to the definition of sport pedagogy as outlined in the introductory chapter to this book.

Reasons for hope

The research on physical activity and motor development seems to predict a grim future for Deshane, yet the motor intervention literature provides hope for the resiliency of such children who grow up in impoverished circumstances. Motor intervention with disadvantaged and motorically delayed preschoolers has shown significant improvements in their FMS. In most cases, well-designed motor skill instruction can remediate previous developmental delays, and this is an important consideration for pedagogy professionals (Goodway and Branta 2003; Robinson and Goodway 2009; Martin, Rudisill and Hastie 2009). The suggested "dose" to be offered of these remedial programs is ecologically achievable in most cases (30–45 minutes per session for 8–12 weeks with 16–24 lessons), and there are examples of a variety of instructional approaches including direct, mastery, building a motivational climate and using parents as teachers. Most have used Newell's constraints perspective to design instruction by identifying the tasks to be achieved, the individual constraints influencing the ability to achieve the task, and then manipulating environmental constraints to promote success. Overall, these studies suggest when children like Deshane are provided with positive environments in which to learn, they quickly overcome the constraints operating in their environments and remediate the delays they had previously demonstrated.

A perspective from cultural studies

The case narrative describes Deshane as a Black American boy who is the son of a single mother, and who attends a high-poverty urban elementary school. A "high-poverty" school in the US context is in the highest quartile of schools in the state in terms of poverty level (Aud *et al.* 2012). Deshane's life is intersected by his Blackness and maleness within an urban environment as well as a host of mediating variables, such as his overweight status and the family's impoverished socioeconomic status. He is also influenced by cultural norms and has witnessed violence in his home in the past, through his abusive father, and currently in the community through gang and drug-related activities. Furthermore, Deshane has first-hand experience with disability and grief as a result of his late brother's cognitive disabilities and eventual accidental death. Fortunately, Deshane is also influenced by a number of positive mediating variables, which include encouragement and support from his mother and grandmother to receive a good education, and their efforts to ensure that he has a solid spiritual foundation. Given the family's religious beliefs and church connections, it would be usual for praying and the reading of biblical scripts to be practiced routinely. In short, Deshane is positioned in a duality and family-community culture that hosts both negative and positive forces.

Culture, ethnicity and race

Culture comprises beliefs, behaviors, linguistic semantics, practices and traditions. It situates race and ethnic identities and encompasses socioeconomic status, social positioning and family histories. *Ethnicity* is largely reflected in cultural heritage. Ethnicity is constructed through cultural traditions and languages, family ancestries and practices. In other words, ethnicity is *not* distinguishable through biology or genetically determined traits; instead ethnic groups are categories of people considered socially distinct because they share a way of life, which is reflected in cultural norms (e.g., food choices, music) and material possessions that establish a particular way of life (Davis 1992).

In the US, race and ethnicity are separate constructs. The designation of Hispanic or Latino is an ethnicity category, not a race category. The labels used to identify race/ethnic categories are: American Indian/Alaska Native, Asian/Pacific Islander, Black (not Hispanic), Hispanic (not

White), White (not Hispanic) and two or more races (Aud *et al.* 2012). There are no genetic markers to distinguish between different race groups. It is argued therefore that race is a socially constructed invention, not a scientifically valid biological category. Race is generally based on visible human attributes such as skin tone and color (Mukhopadhyay and Henze 2003).

In the logic of Critical Race Theory, Jones (1998), a social psychologist, asserts that *race* is both socially and psychologically constructed from accessible social information. Race, as human creation, takes on defining properties that magnify group differences and contribute to perceptual and behavioral biases. Consequently, individuals from different race groups may have different experiences, and/or different interpretations of their experiences. As such, *race* classifications support, if not contribute to, stereotyping (Jones 1998).

Blackness and maleness

Longstanding stereotypic notions about Black males have depicted them as physically superior while being intellectually inferior to White males (Hodge *et al.* 2008). Such race-based stereotyping has contemporary implications for youth like Deshane, including imposing social and psychological limitations on academic performance. For example, empirical studies confirm the hypothesis that Black students' negative stereotypic beliefs about their intelligence can lead them to lower their expectations in academic arenas (Steele and Aronson 1995). Hodge and colleagues (2008) reported that Black male high school students tend to agree with the stereotypic belief that they are naturally better athletes compared to White athletes. Black males also tend to believe the stereotype that White people are more intelligent than Black and Hispanic people. Educators need to be acutely aware that such stereotypes can influence youth such as Deshane and can encourage them to engage in sport pursuits, sometimes at the expense of their academic progress. This problem is compounded by educational and socioeconomic inequalities.

Educational and socioeconomic inequalities

Research indicates that Black male students, particularly those from impoverished circumstances, are far less likely to graduate from high school than their White peers. Moreover Black students make up an increasing proportion of urban public schools, which are usually the schools with high numbers of pupils from low-income families (Aud *et al.* 2012). Typically, there are significant economic and structural inequalities between urban and suburban schools. For example, urban schools are more likely to have scarce fiscal resources, inadequate facilities, and marginalized physical education programs (Ward and O'Sullivan 2006).

Another concern is that some Black students are likely to feel they must suppress their cultural identity in exchange for focusing on academic success (Fryer and Torelli 2005). This is because Black students can feel that their desire to perform well academically is likely to result in them being thought of as *sell-outs*, or as *acting White* and in conflict with their own cultural identities. The concept *acting White* "describes a set of social interactions in which Black adolescents ridicule other Black adolescents for investing in behaviors characteristic of Whites (having an interest in ballet, raising their hand in class, or making good grades, e.g.)" (Fryer and Torelli 2005: 3). Being labeled as *acting White* can lead Black youth to minimize their academic effort rather than risk the ridicule of peers.

Poor and overweight

According to the National Center for Education Statistics (NCES), Black and Hispanic school-age youth in the US are much more likely than White and Asian youth to live in poverty. The percentage of Black youth living in poverty is about 37% compared to White (12%) and Asian (14%) youth (Aud *et al.* 2012). In addition to educational disparities, the lower socio-economic status of families can have a significant impact on obesity and poor health. Youth who are African American, Hispanic, and American Indian are more likely to be overweight or obese than their White peers (Weschler *et al.* 2004). Deshane is overweight, and this is likely to expose him to negative experiences at school. Research indicates that youth such as Deshane are more likely to be teased and bullied (Carlyle and Steinman 2007). Being the target of "fat jokes" can take a toll on a child. Deshane comforts himself with unhealthy snacks. Poor eating habits combined with low levels of physical activity are likely to result in poor health outcomes for Deshane and his peers in urban schools. In this context, schools can – and should – offer students regular information and appropriate modeling on healthy lifestyles. Modeling good practice is important to ensure the information provided is viewed as authentic and consistent. Schools should certainly model good practice in making healthy dietary choices and ensuring students engage in regular (daily) physical activity.

A perspective from health promotion/public health

It is clear that on a daily basis, Deshane faces many challenges in adopting a healthy lifestyle. Unfortunately, his circumstances are faced by many children living in the United States. Nearly 16 million children in the US live below the federal poverty level. Research has suggested that 45% of children live in low income families that have trouble covering basic needs (Chau 2009). Public health professionals champion the cause of social justice through political engagement. Yet, while social justice may be a noble cause needed for long-term change, Deshane does not have the luxury of time because he is a child requiring education and opportunity now. This health promotion perspective is, therefore, focused on explaining what an immediate action-based approach could offer.

Health Promotion balances educational and environmental approaches in order to promote health practices in the community. While health promotion recognizes the fundamental importance of education, it also recognizes that a supportive social and physical environment is critical to the promotion of health practices among most members of the community. In Deshane's case, he would benefit immensely from an environment that provides supports for physical activity. One physical education class a week falls woefully short of the recommended levels of activity that suggest at least one hour each day (Strong *et al.* 2005).

A first principle of health promotion is the direct engagement of stakeholders in the community (Green *et al.* 1980). Communities are often resistant to outside experts espousing generic solutions. Parents, teachers, school personnel, as well as local churches, charitable organizations, law enforcement and neighborhood businesses are best at articulating the needs and problems of their community. Working together builds teams that help identify resources and develop effective plans of action. Most important, if this approach is taken, the community develops a sense of ownership over the solutions and a feeling of empowerment. What is needed is a catalyst in the form of "program champions". Program champions are those who are willing to bring community members together for a common purpose. In the case of Deshane, potential catalysts could be concerned parents, community mentors, school administrators and school teachers. Bringing stakeholders together can establish networks in which resources (human, physical and fiscal) are identified to meet the challenges facing the community. Personal experience of using this approach in underserved communities has resulted in active outcomes such as schools and churches offering facilities, businesses donating resources and volunteers implementing programs.

The increasing rates of chronic disease among minority populations are a major concern in the US, exacerbated by increasing rates of obesity among minority children. The Center for Disease Control and Prevention has proposed protocols for schools to screen for overweight and obese children. Done correctly, this approach can raise awareness and interest in positive ways (Nihiser *et al.* 2007). Screening without sensitivity, on the other hand, can polarize and anger parents. The key question is whether decision makers believe the community needs to have their awareness raised over an issue or "health problem" or whether they prefer to take a different approach. For the sake of illustration, several key health promotion strategies will be reviewed and stakeholders are encouraged to adopt and adapt the most relevant.

Clearly, the church is a positive and important part of Deshane's neighborhood. Health promotion professionals have often partnered with neighborhood churches to stage programs and interventions (Campbell *et al.* 2007). The case narrative raises the issue of child safety in the neighborhood, yet churches can serve as a safe environment and valuable gateway to community action. For example, the church can offer classes for children and or their families specifically to promote exercise. Another approach is for schools to provide supervised after-school programs for physical activity (Strong *et al.* 2005). At the elementary school level, this is often presented as in the form of specific games including: basketball, kickball, ultimate Frisbee and volleyball, but can also include supervised activity in the form of exercise classes (Smith 2011). The emphasis in these classes is on fun and social development in a safe environment, and working parents certainly appreciate such after school programs.

Peer mentoring has been identified as an effective method for improving the health practices of both mentors and mentees. Smith (2011) has demonstrated the importance of training high school students to serve as health mentors for younger children in the same school system. Student mentors are recruited within the school district and trained locally. This approach encourages professionals to develop mentor training that is realistic and culturally appropriate. Mentors also possess credibility, having lived in the same community as the student mentees. This approach offers student mentors an opportunity to assume responsibility and gain valuable experience as role models/educators/mentors to younger children. The program can also include family level interventions in which parents can receive instruction on improving their children's health related practices. There is evidence that this approach has been effective in increasing physical activity and reducing body fat among children living in poverty in the US (Petosa and Hortz 2009).

Planning to be Active is an evidence-based curriculum designed to increase physical activity among school-age children (Petosa and Hortz 2009). It is particularly effective in promoting moderate intensity activity for sedentary students in neighborhood/home environments. Contemporary school, home and neighborhood environments can make very low physical activity demands on individuals, and this means that there must be an intentional effort to plan daily activity. In this program, students apply concepts of behavioral self-regulation strategies to build exercise self-efficacy. Personal preference is of central importance, meaning that physical activity can be independent of specific sport, competition and performance contexts. This principle is particularly effective for children who are self-conscious and inhibited about engaging in physical activity in school settings. Furthermore, the program encourages children to consider a social approach because they are encouraged to plan activity to be undertaken with friends and family. The program is also experienced-based, meaning that each week students apply and evaluate different approaches to planning activity. At the end of the program, students have designed a personalized program that is tailored to their preferences, abilities and environmental opportunities.

The case of Deshane paints a challenging picture of youth living in poverty. It is unlikely that traditional classroom instruction will be sufficient for most poor children to overcome the numerous barriers to a healthy lifestyle. The health promotion literature presented here suggests that the collective action of schools, families and community agencies is important in promoting physical activity. Time available for formal physical education is very limited, so it is unlikely that it, alone, can ever address the complexities of health/physical activity promotion.

A sport and exercise pedagogy perspective

The commentaries by Professors Goodway from a motor development perspective, Hodge from a cultural perspective and Petosa from a public health/health promotion perspective repeat common and overlapping themes. The themes emphasize an environmental determinism in which Deshane finds himself embedded, and one that is both social and ecological in nature. This environment can be characterized by a litany of statistics that describe the cumulative effects of poverty, disabling family structures, health challenges, violence, and personal and social behaviors that place children like Deshane at-risk (Howard 2013). It is easy to get lost in the statistics and the difficulties that confront Black males in poor urban environments, but it is important to note that the themes framed by Goodway, Hodge, and Petosa describe a different outcome – one where the narrative suggested by the statistics can be rewritten. Where schools and teachers recognize and respond to the social-ecological conditions surrounding Black males, they can provide protective factors as a counter to the many risk-factors in the environment.

In their recent policy report, Casserly *et al.* (2012) summarized the empirical literature on what a school's response should be to the issues confronting Black American males. The report describes necessary supports and practices that schools and teachers need to have in place to help students like Deshane remain on a path toward positive academic, health, socioeconomic and other quality of life outcomes. Among the more important supports identified are those of building trust between teachers and students; establishing high, but achievable goals and achieving them; and establishing a connection between students and role models. Each of these supports is described below, and the implications for teachers (and coaches) are explored.

Building trust

Meaningful relationships between teachers, students and the community lie at the heart of effective urban teaching (Ladson-Billings 2011). Building trust between teachers and students requires an understanding of a student's life context: not just their race and ethnicity, but the circumstances of their lives. It requires active engagement in student learning framed within the context of *caring*. At Ohio State University, one of our assignments for pre-service teachers is to ask them to consider how they might create a climate where students feel safe and respected, and where the physical education teacher is someone to whom students might turn for advice and support. One way to create a supportive climate is to use instructional strategies, particularly for Black males, that have been shown to strengthen caring. These include peer tutoring, cooperative learning and adventure-based learning (Kunjufu 2002). A teacher's engagement with students throughout the school day and beyond, through the creation of extra-curricular activities in before- and after-school physical activity programs, extends the care and safety "bubble" beyond the traditional school hours.

In the health promotion section of this chapter, the identification of a health-promoting community is one strategy used to enlist parent and community involvement in order to extend and integrate further the educational messages and caring support. Physical education teachers also need to find ways to extend the supports beyond schools, and one of the most effective partners in that process for some communities has been found to be the church (Centers for Disease Control 1997). The church is often central in the lives of families in Black communities, in part because of its longstanding role in providing a venue for education and social services, and in part because it offers a safe gathering place. Many churches run before- and after-school programs and, as such, they are willing partners in creating an educative environment for Black males; in short, offering places for the development of social capital (Coleman 1990).

Establishing high but achievable goals and then achieving them

Research on effective teachers of Black students emphasizes, among other things, their tendency to develop a strong positive relationship between expectations and academic achievement (Ladson–Billings 2011). Achievement matters, regardless of whether it is in the classroom or the gymnasium. Many Black males, as noted earlier, view physical activity – and sport in particular – very favorably, and research tells us that Black males often identify with athletes (Hodge *et al.* 2008). From a motor development perspective, it is apparent that Deshane, and students like him, have failed to develop competency in FMS because of limited opportunities in their communities. Since FMS are a precursor to success in physical activities, this represents an important target intervention for physical educators. The good news here is that ready-made and accessible curriculum materials exist to help teachers to teach FMS as long as they can schedule 2 sessions per week that are 45-minutes in length (Goodway and Branta 2003). The problem, of course, is that many physical education programs in the US are scheduled for only one session per week; so this is a good example of where before- and after-school programs and church activities can complement formal physical education.

Role models

Cazers and Curtner-Smith (2013) recently published a life history study of a Black physical education teacher educator: Archie Wade. The paper is framed around mentors at each turning point in Archie's life. The role of mentors, particularly Black male mentors, is widely recognized as an important support for Black male children. For example, many young Black males are taught in schools by White middle class females who may fail to understand them (Kunjufu, 2002). If there are no or few Black males in the school, then inviting Black male role models from outside the school can be helpful. In one local school, children regularly invite a Black role model to their school to talk in a session at the end of the day. The session continues after school where the guest is invited to accompany the children to after school programs.

The above recommendations for supporting Deshane are no different to those that would be considered to be "good" teaching practices that are pedagogically sound for all children. Such practices are based on understanding and differentiating instruction to meet the needs of individual students. It is clear, however, that Black males need a stronger commitment by educators to their support if they are to realize their potential. Two issues distinguish Black males from other minorities. First, "far too many inner-city Black males say they cannot see themselves living beyond the age of 21" (Kafele 2012: 68). Second, regardless of their socioeconomic status, Black males do not perform as well as their Latino, White and Asian counterparts, even when the above education supports are in place (Aud, Fox and Kewal 2010). This is not a problem of race, but rather the effect of a social and educational system that is improving in many ways, but that continues to treat Blacks pejoratively compared to other groups.

It has been argued that it is impossible to understand the plight of Black male Americans without understanding first that their plight is an outcome of racism (Howard 2013). There is also robust evidence demonstrating that regardless of socioeconomic status, Black children and youth, both male and female, *can* achieve the same standards as their non-Black peers (e.g., Slavin *et al.* 2009). This fact places a very high level of responsibility on teachers, and the appropriate response is clear. We know, beyond doubt, that Black males need more support if they are to achieve their potential. As Kunjufu (2002: 48) asks: "Then why not increase your effort, set higher expectations and devote more time on task to circumvent these causes?"

Note

1. Schooling in the United States is typically organized as follows. Ages 5–6 to 10–11 attend kindergarten through grade 5; ages 11–12 to 13–14 attend middle schools in grades 6 through 8, and then ages 14–15 to 17–18 attend high school in grades 9–10.

References

Aud, S., Fox, M.A. and Kewal, R.A. (2010) *Status and Trends in the Education of Racial and Ethnic Groups,* Washington, DC: U.S. Government Printing Office.

Aud, S., Hussar, W., Johnson, F., Kena, G., Roth, E., Manning, E., Wang, X. and Zhang, J. (2012) *The Condition of Education 2012* (NCES 2012–045), Washington, DC: U.S. Department of Education, National Center for Education Statistics. Online. Available HTTP: <http://nces.ed.gov/pubsearch> (accessed 22 September 2013).

Campbell, M., Hudson, M., Resnicow, K., Blakeney, N., Paxton, A. and Baskin, M. (2007) 'Church-based health promotion interventions: evidence and lessons learned', *Annual Review of Public Health,* 28: 213–234.

Carlyle, K.E. and Steinman, K.J. (2007) 'Demographic differences in the prevalence, co-occurrence, and correlates of adolescent bullying at school', *Journal of School Health,* 77: 623–629.

Casserly, M., Lewis, S., Simon, C., Uzzell, R. and Palacios, M. (2012) *A Call for Change: Providing Solutions for Black Male Achievement,* Council of the Great City Schools, Washington, DC. Online. Available HTTP: <www.cgcs.org/cms/lib/DC00001581/Centricity/Domain/87/CGCS%20ebook%20PDF%20FINAL%201213.pdf> (accessed 22 September 2013).

Cazers, G. and Curtner-Smith, M. (2013) 'Legacy of a pioneer African-American educator', *Research Quarterly for Exercise & Sport*, 84: 39–51.

Centers for Disease Control and Prevention (1997) 'Guidelines for school and community programs to promote lifelong physical activity among young people', *Morbidity & Mortality Weekly Report*, 46: 1–36.

Chau, C. (2009) *Low Income Children in the United States: National and State Trend Data*, National Center for Children in Poverty, Mailman School of Public Health, Columbia, University.

Clark, J.E. and Metcalfe, J.S. (2002) 'The mountain of motor development: a metaphor', in J.E. Clark and J.H. Humphrey (eds.) *Motor Development: Research and Review*, Vol. 2, Reston, VA: NASPE Publications, (pp. 163–187).

Coleman, J.S. (1990) *Foundations of Social Theory*. Cambridge: Harvard University Press.

Davis, R.A. (1992) 'Black ethnicity: a case for conceptual and methodological clarity', *The Western Journal of Black Studies*, 16(3): 147–151.

Fryer, R.G., Jr. and Torelli, P. (2005) 'An empirical analysis of 'acting White'', NBER Working Paper No. W11334. Online. Available HTTP: <http://papers.ssrn.com/sol3/papers.cfm?abstract_id=723303> (accessed 22 September 2013).

Gallahue, D.L., Ozmun, J.C. and Goodway, J.D. (2012) *Understanding Motor Development: Infants, Children, Adolescent and Adults*, 7th edn, Boston: McGraw-Hill.

Goodway, J.D. and Branta, C.F. (2003) 'Influence of a motor skill intervention on fundamental motor skill development of disadvantaged preschool children', *Research Quarterly for Exercise & Sport*, 74: 36–47.

Goodway, J.D., Robinson, L.E. and Crowe, H. (2010) 'Developmental delays in fundamental motor skill development of ethnically diverse and disadvantaged preschoolers', *Research Quarterly for Exercise & Sport*, 81: 17–25.

Goodway, J.D. and Smith, D.W. (2005) 'Keeping all children healthy: challenges to leading an active lifestyle for preschool children qualifying for at-risk programs', *Family & Community Health*, 28: 142–155.

Green, L., Kreuter, M., Deeds, S. and Partridge, K. (1980) *Health Education Planning: A Diagnostic Approach*, Mountain View, CA. Mayfield Publishing.

Hodge, S.R., Kozub, F.M., Dixson, A.D., Moore, J.L., III, and Kambon, K. (2008) 'A comparison of high school students' stereotypic beliefs about intelligence and athleticism', *Educational Foundations*, 22(1–2): 99–119.

Howard, T.C. (2013) 'How does it feel to be a problem? Black male students, schools, and learning in enhancing the knowledge base to disrupt deficit frameworks'. *Review of Research in Education*, 37: 54–86.

Jones, J.M. (1998) 'Psychological knowledge and the new American dilemma of Race', *Journal of Social Issues*, 54(4): 641–663.

Kafele, B.K. (2012) 'Empowering Black males', *Educational Leadership*, 20(2): 67–70.

Kunjufu, J. (2002) *Back Students. Middle Class Teachers*, Chicago: African American Images.

Ladson-Billings, G. (2011) 'Boyz to men? Teaching to restore Black boys' childhood', *Race, Ethnicity & Education*, 14: 7–15.

Martin, E.H., Rudisill, M.E. and Hastie, P. (2009) 'The effectiveness of a mastery motivational climate motor skill intervention in a naturalistic physical education setting', *Physical Education & Sport Pedagogy*, 14: 227–240.

Mukhopadhyay, C. and Henze, R.C. (2003) 'How real is race? Using anthropology to make sense of human diversity', *Phi Delta Kappan*, 84(9): 669–678.

Newell, K. (1984). 'Physical constraints on the development of motor skills', in J. Thomas, (ed.) *Motor development during preschool and elementary years* (pp. 105–120). Minneapolis, MN: Burgess.

Nihiser, A.J., Lee, S.M., Wechsler, H., McKenna, M., Odom, E., Reinold, C., Thompson, D. and Grummer-Strawn, L. (2007) 'Body mass index measurement in schools', *Journal of School Health*, 77: 651–671.

Petosa, R. and Hortz, B. (2009) 'Wholistic wellness and exercise among adolescents', in R. Gilman, E. Huebner and M. Furlong (eds.) *Handbook of Positive Psychology in Schools*, New York: Routledge Press (pp. 409–422).

Robinson, L.E. and Goodway, J.D. (2009) 'Instructional climates in preschool children who are at risk. Part I: object control skill development', *Research Quarterly for Exercise & Sport*, 80: 533–542.

Seefeldt, V. (1980) 'Concept of readiness applied to motor skill acquisition', in R.A. Magill, M.J. Ash and F.L. Smoll, (eds.) *Children in Sport,* 2nd edn, Champaign, IL: Human Kinetics Publishers (pp. 31–37).

Slavin, R.E., Madden, N.A., Chambers, B. and Haxby, B. (2009) *2 Million Children: Success for All,* Thousands Oaks, CA: Corwin Press.

Smith, L. (2011) 'Cross-age peer mentoring approach to impact the health outcomes of children and families', *Journal for Specialists in Pediatric Nursing,* 16(3): 220–225.

Steele, C.M. and Aronson, J. (1995) 'Stereotype threat and intellectual test performance of African-Americans', *Journal of Personality & Social Psychology,* 69: 797–811.

Stodden, D.F., Goodway, J.D., Langendorfer, S.J., Roberton, M.A., Rudisill, M.E., Garcia, C. and Garcia, L.E. (2008) 'A developmental perspective on the role of motor skill competence in physical activity: an emergent relationship', *Quest,* 60: 290–306.

Strong, W., Malina, R., Blimkie, C., Dishman, R., Gutin, B., Hergenroeder, A., Must, A., Nixon, P., Pivarnik, J., Rowland, T., Trost, S. and Trudeau, F. (2005) 'Evidence based physical activity for school-age youth', *The Journal of Pediatrics,* 146(6): 732–737.

Ward, P. and O'Sullivan, M. (2006) 'Chapter 1: the contexts of urban settings', *Journal of Teaching in Physical Education,* 25: 348–362.

Weschler, H., McKenna, M.L., Lee, S.M. and Dietz, W.H. (2004) 'Overweight among children and adolescents', *National Association of State Boards of Education,* 5(2): 4–12.

6

TERESA

'Mi vida, mi educación, mi futuro': my life, my education, my future

Gay L. Timken, Hans van der Mars, Margarita Jimenez-Silva, Doris L. Watson and Vicki Ebbeck

WESTERN OREGON UNIVERSITY, ARIZONA STATE UNIVERSITY, UNIVERSITY OF NEVADA-LAS VEGAS, OREGON STATE UNIVERSITY, UNITED STATES OF AMERICA

Key words: 11-year-old female, immigrant, English language learner, multicultural competence, sport and exercise psychology, pedagogy.

Teresa

Sometimes I find myself daydreaming during freshman U.S. history class. Today I am dreaming of my family's *ranchito* in a small rural village of Michoacan, Mexico, with Mamá, four brothers and sisters and other family members who lived with us. For several years, most local farmers' crops failed and many in the village were poor and hungry. Water for people and crops had been diverted, if not stolen, from Mexico for the U.S. Even as a youngster I was well aware of government corruption and how violence was all too common. When we lived in Mexico we waited anxiously every day for news from Papá who worked legally in the U.S. Papá wanted to bring us across the border to the U.S. legally, though we knew friends and family who crossed without papers in search of a better life. Papá promised the U.S. would provide opportunities for a brighter future. We would have an education beyond the 3rd grade, which is all that he had managed to achieve, and maybe even a career. Last year, after eight long years of waiting, Papá told us that he had enough money and sponsorships to bring us across.

So here I am in the U.S. and at school. U.S. history is not my favorite subject, but it is even more intolerable because of the way Miss Ramsey teaches. For a history teacher, she seems to know very little about the contributions of ethnic minorities to the development of the U.S., and Miss Ramsey had never heard of the *Bracero Program*[1]. During World War II, the U.S. government brought Mexicans over the border for agricultural labor while American farmers were at war. My own *bisabeulo* (great-grandfather), who spoke only Spanish, had to sign papers to work until the war ended, but the papers were written only in English. He had to pay much of his earnings to return to Mexico. Even today there are government programs supporting migrant laborers. I tried once in class to discuss this with Miss Ramsey. . . . once! It fell on deaf ears.

Then there's physical education. If my Latina friends don't play, I don't either. We stick together. I like being physically active, but most of the activities are more what guys like. Even many of the white girls talk about it in the locker room. If the school's gym or fields were open after school I would love to bring my siblings and cousins to play. But after school everything is all locked up or the school's athletic teams are using the facilities. The current physical education unit is basketball, which is no different to all the others – I'll sit on the sidelines wasting my time, and never touch the ball even if I am playing. And the boys are allowed to play so aggressively . . . why try? *Que bien* – Oh joy!

I really hate the locker room. Most often we do the 'cover with a towel and get dressed' routine because we're so embarrassed, which drives Ms. Ely *loco*. The other day she yelled at us; "That will be three additional laps for being so slow girls; why won't *you people* ever learn?" What does she mean by 'you people' anyway? If Ms. Ely would just ask, we could explain how we feel.

The typical day in physical education: Read the white board then two laps, stretching, count aloud push-ups and sit-ups. At least I can walk/jog with friends. I don't like to sweat because boys might notice, and I still have half the day to get through, including lunch. Today was more work on dribbling and layups. Great! It feels like we've done these drills for days on end but I'm still not getting any better. And even if I did try, teachers just avoid my girlfriends and me so we rarely improve anyway. My guess is that teachers are uncomfortable with those of us who are still learning English. I wonder if they think Latinas are worth the trouble? My classmates get frustrated waiting for me to chase the ball and throw it back. It doesn't take a rocket scientist (just learned that phrase) to know how to make teachers think I'm practicing: look active when teachers are looking, and stay near the back of the line to avoid layups. That saves me from hearing people laugh and teachers getting so frustrated. At least I have literature and math classes to look forward to afterwards.

I'm an English language learner, and I am picking up English really quickly; at least that's what my favorite teachers, Mr. Sanchez and Ms. McPhail, tell me. I am determined to do well in school, especially because Papá has worked so hard to get us here. Sometimes I feel like we Latino/as aren't welcome. Walking by the teachers' lunchroom one day I overheard a teacher: "Mexicans are a drain on the educational system!" Mr. Sanchez and Ms. McPhail aren't that way though, and because I have a connection with these two teachers, those classes are more enjoyable.

Both Mr. Sanchez and Ms. McPhail have encouraged me to pursue a college education, but they say I need good grades and better attendance. What they don't understand is that I frequently miss school to translate for my family. I'm the oldest child, and since my parents, older brother, and aunt and uncle work long hours in the factory, I must care for my three younger siblings and cousins after school. My physical education teachers talk about the importance of being active in sports after school, but we don't have the money, or the opportunity. The kids want to play but it isn't safe where we live, and we don't have equipment. If only we could play at school, which is just three blocks away from home!

My family and my aunts and uncle live together in a singlewide trailer provided by the factory that employs my parents. Many people here are 'undocumented' workers[2] who have come to the U.S. without permission, and are considered 'cheap' labor. People are afraid to go to the doctor, even when they get sick on the job from the heat. Recently, the factory was raided and many workers, including my Papá, Mamá, brother, aunt and uncle, were detained. It took three days before the police could verify my parents' and brother's legal status so they could come home and help me with all the kids. My aunt and uncle were less fortunate. What does this mean for their children, and what does all this mean for my education, and my future?

An English language learner perspective

There are numerous aspects to consider when working with Teresa and other English language learners (ELLs). Thinking through and addressing the academic needs of ELLs can ease the process as Teresa develops both English language proficiency and specific content knowledge, in this case, concepts and skills related to physical education. Although much of the focus in today's schools is on developing academic English and scaffolding content knowledge for students at various stages of English proficiency, equally important but often overlooked considerations are affective, or socio-emotional, issues. When students experience challenges in school, affective reactions can be counterproductive to their learning processes (Echevarría and Graves 2010).

One commonly cited and influential second language acquisition model developed by Stephen Krashen (1981) includes the idea of an 'affective filter'. He stated that although a language learner, such as Teresa, may understand the language that she is hearing, low self-esteem, anxiety, and other stressors may impact how much of the language is actually processed. Therefore, one major goal when working with ELLs is to "lower" the affective filter in order to allow more language to be processed. This idea has been used to explain why individual students progress differently in their language learning even when presented with the same exposure to English (Wright 2010). Numerous theories about affective issues indicate that students who are in the process of learning English may experience unique school challenges (Cloud 1993; Moll 1988; Torres 2001).

Teresa is attuned to her own learning and understands her strengths as well as the challenges she faces in becoming an engaged and successful student. She likes school, is motivated by gratitude for her father's sacrifices, and is very aware of the "larger picture." Teresa is socio-politically aware, including how a couple of teachers recognize her potential for college, but also recognize challenges commonly confronted by ELLs. Unfortunately, Teresa also knows that not all teachers are comfortable working with students like her (i.e., students who may be undocumented/illegal and/or in the process of learning English). This knowledge is likely to affect Teresa emotionally, creating feelings of discomfort and raising her "affective filter".

It is typical to find that young people from similar backgrounds congregate in groups at school. Teresa comments that she sticks with her Latina friends during physical education and this may provide a space in which she feels safe and comfortable. It is logical behavior in that it provides an opportunity for learning to take place in a low-anxiety environment. Unfortunately, Teresa also comments that she does not try very hard in physical education. She states that this is partly due to her limited time engaging in the activities, many of which she perceives to be boys' activities, and boys' off-putting aggressive play. Even more detrimental to maintaining a low-anxiety environment, however, is the issue of teachers who explicitly or implicitly make it known that they would prefer not to work with Latinas. If Teresa had not heard her physical education teacher yelling at the Latinas for being slow and adding the phrase "why won't *you people* ever learn?" perhaps she would feel confident enough to discuss her concerns about the boys and their aggressive play or her discomfort in the locker room. Physical educators have unique opportunities to scaffold language learning for ELLs (Gómez and Jimenez-Silva 2012) but only when students are comfortable with the teacher.

Among the stressors Teresa faces that originate outside of the school are poor attendance due to family responsibilities and financial struggles. As the oldest daughter, many of these types of tasks will typically fall on Teresa's shoulders. She considers how these challenges impact her grades and ability to be more active with siblings and family members after school. Teresa speaks of finding herself daydreaming of her previous life in Mexico, including her family. Many ELLs live in households that are split with one parent living in the U.S. and one in the native country. This type of separation often leads to disruption in the family structure, financial hardships and, in some cases, family dissolution (Dreby 2012). Teachers must be aware of these possibilities and be sensitive to the fact that many ELLs may go years without any contact with one of their parents. Even in cases where a parent maintains contact with a child via regular phone calls, remittances, or gift giving, children may still develop resentment towards that absent parent (Dreby 2010). Furthermore, as in Teresa's case, many ELLs are aware of the sociopolitical issues such as violence and corruption in their homeland or, in this case, disputes about water rights between Mexico and the U.S. Sadly, Teresa tried to discuss historical events such as the *Bracero Program* that have directly affected her family, but found teachers were uninterested.

Finally, other important considerations are the living conditions and issues of legal status that add a significant amount of stress to Teresa's daily life. Such stress can have serious detrimental effects on students' development and school achievements (Menjívar 2011). Long-term effects include the following: (1) fear of close family members being detained or deported; (2) a constant fear of separation; (3) fear of law enforcement officers; and (4) an association of all immigrants with illegal status regardless of actual status (Dreby 2012). Given past experiences with most of her teachers, it is doubtful that Teresa feels she has a safe place to discuss any of these issues. In order for Teresa to be a successful student, she needs teachers to help her address all aspects, including affective concerns, that impact upon her learning of both English language and specific subject content, and in balancing the demands of home and school. Demonstrating sensitivity to the various issues that impact her daily life can help Teresa to successfully navigate her complex world.

A multicultural competence perspective

The case – *Teresa* – illustrates many relevant issues for immigrant youth in the U.S. Currently, approximately 143,000 people emigrate legally from Mexico to the U.S. each year (Office of Immigration Statistics 2013). The average wait for a permanent resident from Mexico to sponsor a spouse or child under 21 is currently about two years, while the wait time for young adults over 21 is 20 years (U.S. Department of State, Visa Bulletin for January 2013). Indeed, it is *not* common knowledge that many Mexican laborers did participate in the *Bracero Program* during World War II, which facilitated the mass legal migration of Mexican workers as temporary laborers (Portes and Bach 1985). Such policies may have had an impact on the vision of the U.S. as the "promised land" for many living in Mexico. This has contributed to Mexican Americans representing the largest of all Latino/ethnic groups in the U.S. (approximately 59%) (Guzman 2001).

It can be useful to utilize the framework of Pope, Reynolds, and Mueller (2004) when considering our own multicultural competency in reading Teresa's story. *Awareness* addresses an individual's belief that differences are valuable and important to learning. In addition, it includes self-awareness regarding the impact we may have on others. *Knowledge* is an individual's base of information concerning diverse cultures and also includes understanding about privilege and oppression. Lastly, *skill* refers to the development of abilities to work with and in diverse cultures and settings. Having such skill means that we are able to trust and respect, as well as empathize with others from different cultures (Cuyjet, Howard-Hamilton and Cooper 2011). A key to student success is when a teacher's multicultural competence is high and infused into daily practice, thereby ensuring that students realize they matter – that they have *worth*.

Mattering. The need to feel a sense of connectedness – that one belongs – is a fundamental need of all humans. When we feel important to others (i.e., teachers and peers) we feel appreciated and that we matter to others. Rosenberg and McCullough (1981: 163) were among the first researchers to illustrate the concept of *"mattering"* defined as: "Do we believe that we count in other's lives, loom large in their thoughts, or make a difference to them? Are we an object of another's concern, interest or attention?" Clearly, the concept of mattering relates to Maslow's Hierarchy of Needs (McLeod 2012). Once primary needs are satisfied, the need for belonging or socio-emotional connection emerges. "Mattering is related to belonging in that a sense of belonging is necessary to foster feelings of mattering; likewise, greater feelings of mattering may increase a sense of belonging" (France and Finney 2009: 104). Simply belonging to a group, however, is not sufficient to engender feelings of mattering. Rather, it is the *nature* of that belonging that brings about a person's sense that they matter.

Two categories that comprise mattering are proposed by Elliott, Kao, and Grant (2004). The first involves being the focus of another person or persons' *attention*. For example, a teacher might indicate his/her awareness of a student by commenting that she noticed the student was absent from class the day before. To be noticed is more than simply having regular contact with someone, but also includes the idea that the person's presence is important. Certainly, as teachers, we have witnessed the reverse side of awareness. When students act out (behave badly) during class for attention, they are indeed assuring that they matter; it is just being done in a negative manner.

The second category of mattering suggests a relationship between the person and the others to whom one matters. The relationship category of mattering has two additional sub components: *importance* and *reliance*. To take our example above one step further, the teacher might have gone on to state that he or she noticed the student's absence and the absence mattered as they enjoy his/her positive energy in class. This suggests the student is not only noticed (attention), but the relationship is significant (importance) because the teacher enjoys the student's positive attitude (reliance).

Lastly, the concept of *ego-extension* is relevant in this case. This is demonstrated when those around us are excited by our successes and achievements or equally disappointed by our failures or losses (Dixon, Scheidegger and McWhirter 2009). Again, extending the example, the teacher could express facial sadness or concern when the student replies that he/she was absent because there was a death in the family, thus communicating ego-extension. Elliott *et al.* (2004: 342) summarized the components of mattering as ". . . awareness of others that is engendered by some intrinsically captivating characteristic; importance arises out of a sincere concern for the person's welfare; and reliance flows from a sense that others appreciate the resources that one has to offer."

Although a relatively new concept, researchers interested in mattering have reported some very notable findings, particularly in the case of adolescents. For example, mattering correlated negatively with depression and anxiety in adolescents (Dixon *et al.*, 2009; Taylor and Turner, 2001). Likewise, if adolescents feel "mattered" to by their family, they are less likely to use marijuana, and they have a longer life expectancy (Elliott *et al.* 2008). Further, a student's sense of mattering correlates positively to reductions in misconduct in schools. In addition, students who perceive they matter to teachers experience a positive effect in academic achievement (Bloch 2009), as well as a positive association with self-esteem and social support (Elliott *et al.* 2004).

It is the seemingly small things that teachers do that underscore students' perceptions that they matter. These things might include: learning about other cultural practices and customs, making smiling eye contact, patting a student on the back, asking how they are doing, as well as the power of such modeling in encouraging the student to exhibit similar behaviors towards his or her classmates. Thus, such practices can assist teachers in creating bridges between themselves and the ever-increasing number and range of culturally diverse student populations they teach.

A sport and exercise psychology perspective

Teresa's scenario reminds practitioners of the complex and layered circumstances that surround the youth with whom they interact. Moreover, it is evident that Teresa's educational experiences vary as a function of the subject matter, class structure, and teachers themselves, and that these factors influence her level of engagement and likelihood of reaching her full potential. What is encouraging about Teresa's situation is the possibility for positive change. Physical educators have the means to systematically design learning opportunities and foster a class climate that can motivate students such as Teresa. The aim is to help them to eagerly anticipate physical education lessons, apply themselves to class activities, and continue to pursue a physically active lifestyle outside of school. The first important step is to identify the issues that could be addressed to improve Teresa's situation.

Teresa exemplifies a student with low perceived *competence*. Her low level of perceived competence no doubt stems from her ongoing failed attempts at executing basketball skills. The teacher who avoids Teresa and the peers who laugh at, as well as show impatience with, her ineffectual efforts only serve to reinforce her thinking that she lacks any actual ability. The time Teresa spends on the sidelines is in contrast to the maximum participation in developmentally appropriate optimal challenges that could nurture Teresa's perception of competence. In addition, the typical day she describes in physical education is void of any autonomy. Students such as Teresa have no opportunity for choice, input, or self-direction because the teachers control the structure of the entire class and only a single activity is permitted of all students at any given time. Furthermore, there is no clear rationale for why a particular activity was selected, which undermines a sense of volition for students who can feel pressured to behave in a certain way. Finally, the physical education class does not adequately fulfill Teresa's need for *relatedness*. Teresa's involvement with basketball is dependent on her Latina friends playing and a highlight of physical education lessons is when she gets to enjoy the company of her friends. She is not challenged, however, to develop new social relationships, and she clearly does not feel the same connection with her physical education teachers as she does with her English and math teachers. Arguably, the connection with her physical education teachers would be strengthened if they were less punitive, and more respectful and understanding.

The psychological needs for competence, autonomy, and relatedness are central to self-determination theory (Ryan and Deci 2000). According to the theory, experiencing competence, autonomy and relatedness facilitates more self-determined forms of motivation that, by definition, emanate from the self. The more self-determined forms of motivation engender positive outcomes such as commitment, effort, quality performance, and well-being. The key, then, is to create environments or classroom climates that are conducive to fulfilling the three psychological needs. A recent review of the empirical literature revealed growth in the application of self-determination theory in the physical domain (Teixeira, Carraça, Markland, Silva and Ryan 2012). Katartzi and Vlachopoulos (2011) also highlighted the potential of self-determination theory for informing teaching practices in physical education, particularly for children with developmental coordination disorder.

Studies grounded in self-determination theory and conducted within the context of physical education have determined the following:

- Implementation of a teaching style that supports the psychological needs increases the interest-enjoyment and vitality of students yet does not require extensive training of teachers (Mouratidis *et al.* 2011).
- Physical education teachers serve a role of equal importance to parents in supporting adolescents' self-determined motivation and behavior with regard to leisure-time physical activity (McDavid, Cox and Amorose, 2012).
- Higher levels of self-determined motivation for a physical education class were positively associated with higher levels of objectively measured moderate-to-vigorous physical activity as well as student engagement, suggesting the students were more active and more absorbed in the class (Aelterman *et al.* 2012).
- Higher perceptions of needs support from the physical education teacher predicted higher satisfaction of the students' need for competence, autonomy, and relatedness in physical education that, in turn, predicted self-determined motivation, which ultimately accounted for variance in the secondary school students' step count, health-related quality of life, and physical self-concept (Standage *et al.* 2012).

Of note is a recent investigation that determined the psychological needs of competence, autonomy, and relatedness were satisfied by the creation of a caring climate at a university recreation center (Brown 2012). In addition, the perception of a caring climate has been found to influence the psychological well-being of youth sport participants (Fry *et al.* 2012). The notion of a caring climate emanates from the work of Noddings (2005) who characterizes caring in a relational sense, whereby the teachers care for the students and, importantly, the students feel cared for by the teachers. A caring climate would most certainly help Teresa in our case scenario, because she expresses frustration that teachers do not understand, or even try to understand by asking, why, for example, Latinas feel uncomfortable undressing in front of one another in the locker room. In a caring climate described by Noddings, teachers engage students in dialogue, listen to their students, gain the trust of their students, and learn about those aspects of students' needs and interests that should influence the development of lesson plans and the monitoring of individual progress.

The current literature in sport and exercise psychology, therefore, suggests that students such as Teresa would benefit from the creation of a climate in physical education classes that promotes students' sense of competence, autonomy, and relatedness as well as caring relations such that students' psychological needs are met and students know they matter. The results of taking this approach could be gratifying for the teachers as much as the students, because it can lead to the desirable outcome of a vibrant, engaging, and effective learning environment.

A pedagogical perspective

> To a great extent teachers are the curriculum: affect, attitude, and persona have a much
> more powerful impact on classes than do [the subject matter] or the pedagogical techniques
> they employ.
>
> (Marantz Cohen 2002: 534)

Teaching is a human endeavor and, as such, teachers must assume responsibility for developing caring relationships with students. Noddings (2005) argued that teachers who care for and about students do make a difference, and those relationships provide the foundation for academic success, in part because a student's "affective filter" is thereby lowered. Caring teachers send a message of mattering and relevance, trust and respect, as noted in the earlier sections of this chapter. Yet, while this caring relationship is essential for effective support, it does not guarantee competent teaching (Noddings 2005).

Another form of caring that is equally important to student engagement and success is identified by the acronym: CARE (Stuntz and Weiss 2010). From this perspective, it is acknowledged that students want to feel *Competent*, or capable in all that they do. Students long for the opportunity to develop *Autonomy*, or the ability to have individual input and choice, and thoughts and opinions that are viewed as important and relevant by significant adults. *Relationships* matter, in that students want to feel connected with peers and important adults (e.g., caring teachers) in their lives. Finally, students who experience *Enjoyment* in interesting and challenging educational experiences are more likely to stay engaged. In essence, both caring teachers and strategies in CARE form a student's 'psychological safety net'. This can be described as a supportive environment that facilitates the challenge-growth process that is characteristic of learning.

Self-Determination Theory (Ryan and Deci 2000) and the four elements of CARE, provide structure for pedagogical strategies (i.e., those things teachers do from a curriculum/instruction perspective that engage and empower students). Keeping CARE at the center of our thinking, we suggest three curriculum models that offer specific pedagogical strategies that might be helpful in engaging Teresa and her peers in physical education. When implemented faithfully and skillfully, these models support each aspect of CARE; that is, each model must be delivered authentically if students are to experience a model's intended learning outcomes. Taking a models-based approach requires a good deal of knowledge and skill on the part of teachers and coaches if it is to be effective.

Sport education (Siedentop, Hastie and van der Mars 2011)

Competence

Physical education curricula continue to be dominated by competitive team sport at all levels (Fairclough, Stratton and Baldwin 2002; U.S. Department of Health and Human Services 2000). Lower skilled students and females tend to find themselves dominated by pupils with higher-skill levels, resulting in decreased motivation and marginalization (e.g., Carlson 1995; Ennis 2000; McCaughtry, Tischler and Flory 2008). Students who are dominated, marginalized, unchallenged at appropriate levels and, as a result, less motivated, are unlikely to develop competence in physical activity settings.

We would argue that Sport Education 'seasons' are designed to last up to 20 lessons, specifically to allow time for students to improve skill levels. Even within a competition format, the focus in Sport Education remains on mastering the skills (i.e., a mastery motivational climate) and developing an increasingly intimate knowledge of the sport or activity. Students take on specific roles and responsibilities such as captain, coach, statistician, referee, and sports information director, which adds to the learning experience as well as knowledge base. Winning and competition are part of Sport Education, but to win requires much more than simply beating an opponent. Part of the Sport Education structure includes the requirement for adequate completion of roles and responsibilities, and exhibiting fair play. The precise structure of the activity can be co-determined by students and the teacher.

Autonomy

Sport Education is a student-centered approach to physical education. In a developmentally appropriate manner, students gradually take on greater leadership, responsibility and ownership in organizing and managing the sport season. Student captains organize their team with input from team members; student coaches lead practices; and sports councils make league decisions. In essence, students play a significant role in enhancing their own learning experience.

Relationships

Though Siedentop (1994), as the original architect of Sport Education never expressed this intent, when the model is delivered authentically and skillfully, the classroom environment has the potential to transfer into a CARE-ing sporting community (i.e., a place for *all* students to experience success). Sustained 'intact' teams through a season are designed as heterogeneous learning groups with the potential to create a social support network/relationships with peers in which students feel they 'matter' to one another and to team success. Teams find that as they work toward a successful season, even in Sport Education's competitive environment, it is the process of working together that fosters success. To further ensure the development of pro-social behaviors, we recommend using Hellison's (2003) Personal and Social Responsibility model (see Watson and Clocksin 2013 for more specific strategies).

Enjoyment

Increased competence, autonomy and social support impact levels of enjoyment, but it is the festivity surrounding sport and the culminating event of the season that adds to the flavor of the experience. Opening ceremonies, post-season games played in front of a crowd, and team affiliation all serve to increase commitment, interest and excitement beyond that normally found in traditional and disjointed physical education programmes.

Adventure education and outdoor education (Dyson and Brown 2010; Stiehl and Parker 2010)

Competence

Competence in Adventure Education is vastly different from that required in traditional physical education, because the goal is to overcome challenges using 'group think' and problem-solving strategies. While the challenge may be somewhat physical (e.g., avoiding toxic waste or an electric fence), in the end, it is the mental and social processes more than the physical skill that matters. Students who tend to be marginalized in a traditional physical education setting may find their skills highly valued in Adventure Education.

Mastering skills and becoming a more competent mover in activities such as cross country skiing or kayaking are the key aims of Outdoor Education and outdoor pursuits. Though many of these activities can be found in Olympic competition, they are just as easily offered in noncompetitive settings, where an individual pursues skill development simply for the personal challenge rather than to win over others.

Autonomy

In Adventure Education, students are provided with a challenge, and they take an active role in determining their own course of action, albeit within safety considerations. Teachers act as facilitators with very little, if any, direct instruction occurring. Post-activity reflection allows students to share thoughts and derive meaning from their experiences. Voicing opinions about the learning experiences and challenges is important in group problem-solving situations.

The varied nature of activities in Outdoor Education means that students who are sometimes marginalized in traditional physical education can find something that suits their interests. Students can take part in planning a backpacking experience or a safe cycling route, or coordinating a weekend experience with the family. The authentic experience of the outdoors is ripe with possibilities for student input and decision-making.

Relationships

A majority of Adventure Education activities have *inter*dependent and collaborative outcomes based on trust, cooperation, communication, goal setting, risk taking (physical, mental, social and emotional) and problem solving. Being a good listener, sharing ideas, and being a good leader and follower are necessary for groups to achieve a common goal. Challenge by Choice[3] and the Full Value Contract[4] also help establish a safe learning environment where taking risks is a welcome event.

Both Challenge by Choice and the Full Value Contract can be employed in Outdoor Education to increase both physical and emotional/social safety. It may be easier for some teachers and students to create a noncompetitive, mastery motivational climate with novel activities in Outdoor Education than with traditional sports found in physical education.

Enjoyment

The novelty found in both Adventure Education and Outdoor Education may increase the enjoyment factor as much as the focus on individual and/or group development. It is an approach that offers something different to traditional physical education.

Culturally responsive teaching (Timken and Watson 2010)

There can be little doubt that adopting the models described above will be ineffective if teachers themselves are not culturally competent or responsive. First and foremost, teachers must acknowledge their own socio-cultural backgrounds (e.g., 'white' is a race that has cultural implications) and have a level of awareness about their beliefs and values. Without an awareness of personal and professional bias, and how these are enacted in the classroom, neither 'Caring' (as described by Noddings) nor CARE (Stuntz and Weiss 2010), are likely to be effective as approaches. For example, personal beliefs about immigration should be challenged and/or left at the school door, because a professional teacher has a responsibility to teach *all* students. This means that in order to do their jobs, teachers must hold a fundamental affirming belief that all students have inherent value. In so doing, teachers are more likely to embrace varied approaches to knowing and learning; in other words, they teach not from a deficit perspective, but from the unshakeable belief that all students are capable of greatness. This is a value system that will enable teachers to develop strong relationships with students, care for and about students, and implement elements of CARE in their classroom. Further, at the very heart of this value system are teachers who are committed to fighting institutional bias and inequities (i.e., acting as agents of change). What is required within schools are Communities of Practice (Deglau and O'Sullivan 2006) devoted specifically to addressing culturally competent educational practices, as well as individual teachers who are willing to embrace this value system. Without such an approach, teachers will continue to fail to be positive significant adults in the lives of those students who most need them.

Notes

1. *Bracero Program: Bracero* is the Spanish term for *manual laborer*. The *Bracero Program,* implemented by the U.S. government during World War II, facilitated the mass legal migration of Mexican workers as temporary laborers specifically for agricultural production (Portes and Bach 1985).
2. *Undocumented workers:* People who enter a country "illegally", and have thus violated immigration requirements for that country. In most all cases, they find low-wage employment.
3. *Challenge by Choice:* A principle used in Adventure Education activities in which participants are free to *not* engage in an activity should they feel emotional, social, mental and/or physical risk and discomfort. Further, that choice is to be respected by all other participants and instructors.
4. *Full Value Contract:* A mutual social contract among participants in Adventure Education in which each participant vows to be present and attentive, open to outcomes, honest and ensure a safe environment for one another.

References

Aelterman, N., Vansteenkiste, M., Van Keer, H., Van den Berghe, L., De Meyer, J. and Haerens, L. (2012) "Students' objectively measured physical activity levels and engagement as a function of between-class and between-student differences in motivation toward physical education', *Journal of Sport & Exercise Psychology,* 34(4): 457–480.

Bloch, S.S. (2009) 'Mattering in school: Students' perceptions of mattering to teachers and functioning in school', paper presented at the annual meeting of the American Sociological Association, Hilton San Francisco, San Francisco, CA, August 2009. Online. Available HTTP: <www.allacademic.com/meta/p307770_index.html> (accessed 22 September 2013).

Brown, T.C. (2012) 'The effects of an intervention to foster a caring and task-involving climate at a university recreation center', *Dissertation Abstracts International: Section A. Humanities and Social Sciences,* 72(9-A): 3126.

Carlson, T. (1995) 'We hate gym: Student alienation from physical education', *Journal of Teaching in Physical Education,* 14: 467–477.

Cloud, N. (1993) 'Language, culture, and disability: Implications for instruction and teacher preparation', *Teacher Education & Special Education,* 16(1): 60–72.

Cuyjet, M. J., Howard-Hamilton, M.F. and Cooper, D.L. (2011) *Multiculturalism on campus: Theory, models, and practices for understanding diversity and creating inclusion.* Sterling, VA: Stylus.

Deglau, D.A. and O'Sullivan, M. (2006) 'The effects of a long-term professional development program on the beliefs and practices of experienced teachers', *Journal of Teaching in Physical Education,* 25: 379–396.

Dixon, A.L., Scheidegger, C. and McWhirter, J.J. (2009) 'The adolescent mattering experience: Gender variations in perceived mattering, anxiety and depression', *Journal of Counseling & Development,* 87: 302–310.

Dreby, J. (2010) *Divided by borders: Mexican migrants and their children.* Berkeley: University of California Press.

Dreby, J. (2012) *How today's immigration enforcement policies impact children, families, and communities: A view from the ground.* Washington, D.C.: Center for American Progress. Online. Available HTTP: <www.americanprogress.org/wp-content/uploads/2012/08/DrebyImmigrationFamiliesFINAL.pdf> (accessed 25 January 2013).

Dyson, B. and Brown, M. (2010) 'Adventure education in your physical education program', in J. Lund and D. Tannehill (eds.) *Standards-based physical education curriculum development,* 2nd edn, (pp. 218–245). Boston, MA: Jones & Bartlett.

Echevarría, J. and Graves, A. (2010) *Sheltered content instruction: Teaching English language learners with diverse abilities,* 4th edn. Boston, MA: Pearson.

Elliott, G.C., Cunningham, S.M., Becker, L., Reuland, T. and Gelles, R.J. (2008) 'Mattering and subjective life expectancy among adolescents', paper presented at the American Sociological Association, Boston MA, July 2008. Online: Available HTTP: <www.allacademic.com/meta/p240799_index.html> (accessed 22 September 2013).

Elliott, G.C., Kao, S. and Grant, A. (2004) 'Mattering: Empirical validation of a social psychological concept', *Self & Identity,* 3: 339–354.

Ennis, C.D. (2000) 'Canaries in the coal mine: Responding to disengaged students using theme-based curricula', *Quest,* 52(2): 119–130.

Fairclough, S., Stratton, G. and Baldwin, G. (2002) 'The contribution of secondary physical education to lifetime physical activity', *European Physical Education Review,* 8: 69–84.

France, M.K. and Finney, S.J. (2009) 'What matters in the measurement of mattering? Construct validity', *Measurement and Evaluation in Counseling and Development,* 42: 104–120.

Fry, M.D., Guivernau, M., Kim, M., Newton, M., Gano-Overway, L.A. and Magyar, T.M. (2012) 'Youth perceptions of a caring climate, emotional regulation, and psychological well-being', *Sport, Exercise, and Performance Psychology,* 1: 44–57.

Gómez, C. and Jimenez-Silva, M. (2012) 'The physical educator as a language teacher for English language learners', *Strategies: A Journal for Physical and Sports Educators,* 25(4): 14–17.

Guzman, B. (2001) *The Hispanic population: Census 2000 brief.* Online. Available HTTP: <www.census.gov/population/www/cen2000/briefs/index.html> (accessed 4 January 2013).

Hellison, D. (2003) *Teaching responsibility through physical activity,* 3rd edn. Champaign, IL: Human Kinetics.

Katartzi, E.S. and Vlachopoulos, S.P. (2011) 'Motivating children with developmental coordination disorder in school physical education: The self-determination theory approach', *Research in Developmental Disabilities,* 32: 2674–2682.

Krashen, S. (1981) 'Bilingual education and second language acquisition theory', in California State Department of Education (ed.) *Schooling and language minority students: A theoretical framework* (pp. 26–92). Los Angeles: Evaluation, Dissemination and Assessment Center, California State University.

Marantz Cohen, R. (2002) 'Schools our teachers deserve', *Phi Delta Kappan,* 83(7): 532–637.

McCaughtry, N., Tischler, A. and Flory, S. (2008) 'The ecology of the gym: Reconceptualized and extended', *Quest,* 60: 268–289.

McDavid, L., Cox, A.E. and Amorose, A.J. (2012) 'The relative roles of physical education teachers and parents in adolescents' leisure-time physical activity motivation and behavior', *Psychology of Sport and Exercise,* 13: 99–107.

McLeod, S. (2012) *Maslow's Hierarchy of Needs.* Online. Available HTTP: <www.simplypsychology.org/maslow.html> (accessed 22 September 2013).

Menjívar, C. (2011) 'The power of the law: Central Americans' legality and everyday life in Phoenix, Arizona', *Latino Studies,* 9(4): 377–395.

Moll, L. (1988) 'Some key issues in teaching Latino students', *Language Arts,* 65(5): 465–472.

Mouratidis, A. A., Vansteenkiste, M., Sideridis, G. and Lens, W. (2011) 'Vitality and interest-enjoyment as a function of class-to-class variation in need-supportive teaching and pupils' autonomous motivation', *Journal of Educational Psychology,* 103: 353–366.

Noddings, N. (2005) '*Caring in education', The encyclopedia of informal education.* Online. Available HTTP: <www.infed.org/biblio/noddings_caring_in_education.htm> (accessed 22 September 2013).

Office of Immigration Statistics, U.S. Department of Homeland Security, Annual Flow Report, April 2013 at p. 4 (Table 3).

Pope, R.L., Reynolds, A.L. and Mueller, J.A. (2004) *Multicultural competence in student affairs.* San Francisco: Jossey-Bass.

Portes, A. and Bach, R.L. (1985) *Latin journey: Cuban and Mexican immigrants in the United States.* Berkeley: University of California Press.

Rosenberg, M. and McCullough, B.C. (1981) 'Mattering: Inferred significance and mental health among adolescents', *Journal of Research in Community & Mental Health,* 2: 163–182.

Ryan, R.M. and Deci, E.L. (2000) 'Self-determination theory and the facilitation of intrinsic motivation, social development, and well-being', *American Psychologist,* 55(1): 68–78.

Siedentop, D. (1994) *Sport education: Quality PE through positive sport experiences.* Champaign, IL: Human Kinetics.

Siedentop, D., Hastie, P. and van der Mars, H. (2011) *Complete guide to sport education,* 3rd edn. Champaign, IL: Human Kinetics.

Standage, M., Gillison, F.B., Ntoumanis, N. and Treasure, D.C. (2012) 'Predicting students' physical activity and health-related well-being: A prospective cross-domain investigation of motivation across school physical education and exercise settings', *Journal of Sport & Exercise Psychology,* 34(1): 37–60.

Stiehl, J. and Parker, M. (2010) 'Outdoor education', in J. Lund and D. Tannehill (eds.) *Standards-based physical education curriculum development,* 2nd edn (pp. 247–269). Boston, MA: Jones and Bartlett.

Stuntz, C.P. and Weiss, M.R. (2010) 'Motivating children and adolescents to sustain a physically active lifestyle', *American Journal of Lifestyle Medicine,* 4(5): 433–444.

Taylor, J. and Turner, R.J. (2001) 'A longitudinal study of the role and significance of mattering to others for depressive symptoms', *Journal of Health and Social Behavior,* 42: 310–325.

Teixeira, P.J., Carraça, E.V., Markland, D., Silva, M.N. and Ryan, R.M. (2012) 'Exercise, physical activity, and self-determination theory: A systematic review', *International Journal of Behavioral Nutrition & Physical Activity,* 9: 78. Online. Available HTTP: <www.ijbnpa.org/content/9/1/78> (accessed 22 September 2013).

Timken, G.L. and Watson, D. (2010) 'Teaching all kids: Valuing students through culturally responsive and inclusive practice, in J. Lund and D. Tannehill (eds.), *Standards-based physical education curriculum development,* 2nd edn (pp. 122–153). Boston, MA: Jones and Bartlett.

Torres, M. (2001) 'Teacher-researchers entering into the world of limited-English proficiency (LEP) students: Three case studies', *Urban Education,* 36(2): 256–289.

U.S. Department of Health and Human Services. (2000) *Healthy people 2010.* Washington, DC: U.S. Gov. Printing Office.

U.S. Department of State, Bureau of Consular Affairs. (2013) 'Visa Bulletin: Immigrant numbers for January 2013', 9(52): 1–6. Online. Available HTTP: <http://travel.state.gov/visa/bulletin/bulletin_5834.html> (accessed 22 September 2013).

Watson, D.L. and Clocksin, B.D. (2013) *Using physical activity and sport to teach personal and social responsibility.* Champaign, IL. Human Kinetics.

Wright, W. (2010) *Foundations for teaching English language learners. Research, theory, policy, and practice.* Philadelphia, PA: Caslon.

7

ROB

Talent in ice hockey: age, neighborhood, and training

Jean Côté, David J. Hancock, Steven L. Fischer and Brendon J. Gurd

SCHOOL OF KINESIOLOGY AND HEALTH STUDIES, QUEEN'S UNIVERSITY, CANADA

Key words: 11-year-old male, elite sport, motivation, contextual perspective, psychology, biomechanics, exercise physiology, pedagogy.

Rob

Rob Burton, an 11-year-old boy, was recently selected to an elite ice hockey team in Canada. Rob was born and resides in Sydenham, Ontario, a small village of approximately 5000 habitants. Sydenham is a 30 minute drive from Kingston (a city of 120,000 citizens) and within a two-and-a-half drive from three major Canadian cities – Toronto, Montréal, and Ottawa. Rob's parents are Brian (age 44) and Barbara (age 40) and he has an older brother, Frank (age 14), and a younger sister, Liz (age 9). Brian is a high-level civil servant who works in Kingston and Barbara is a part-time nurse also working in Kingston at the General Hospital. Their combined income in 2012 was $110,000 Canadian dollars. The Burton family has two cars and a house with 20 years remaining on the mortgage. Their disposable monthly income is approximately $5,000 Canadian dollars.

Rob's father, Brian, is originally from Toronto and grew up playing ice hockey. He played at the highest amateur level in Canada, Major Junior, but was never drafted by a professional team. He retired from competitive ice hockey at age 20. Brian still plays ice hockey for fun with friends two or three times a week. The other members of the family are not involved in organized ice hockey, however, Barbara, Frank, and Liz all enjoy skating on the outdoor rink in their village and play outdoor pick-up ice hockey[1] in the winter with family and friends. Indeed, Rob was first introduced to ice hockey on an outdoor rink in Sydenham at age 3 with his father, mother, and older brother. From ages 3 to 7, Rob played ice hockey outside four or five times a week from December to March with his dad, family, and friends. In the summers, starting at age 6, Rob spent his days playing baseball, soccer, and basketball with friends as well as swimming in the nearby lake. He got involved in organized ice hockey, basketball, and baseball at age 7 while continuing to play sports for fun with friends. These organized sport leagues took place in Kingston and involved one practice and one game per week from October to March for ice hockey, November to April for basketball, and June to September for baseball.

At age 9, Rob's ice hockey coach told him that he should try out for the Kingston all-star ice hockey team (a travelling team). Rob discussed this with his parents and decided to try out. Rob did not have the skating skills of some players but because of his larger size he was selected to the team. Rob played the entire season at age 9 and age 10 on the Atom[2] all-star team. At age 11, Rob was again selected to the all-star team, this time at the next age level, Peewee. His involvement on the all-star teams from ages 9 to 11 required a commitment of four practices and two games per week from September to April, totalling approximately 10 hours of ice hockey engagement per week. Ten hours of ice hockey participation, however, resulted in a commitment of about 25–30 hours per week when accounting for travelling to and from practices and games. During the ice hockey season from ages 9–11, Rob stopped playing organized basketball, but in the summer he kept playing baseball. His time spent playing sports for fun with his family and friends was reduced significantly during these years.

Rob was born on January 5. Canada has a cut-off date of January 1 for selecting players in a specific age group in youth ice hockey. Therefore, a child born on January 5, like Rob, is almost one year older than a child born on December 30 of the same year. These two players would, however, play ice hockey together in the same age group. Given his older relative age compared to his peers, Rob has always been more physically mature than his teammates in organized ice hockey. In fact, his growth and maturation measures have always been in the 90th percentile of his ice hockey teammates. At age 11, Rob measured 153 cm and weighed 48 kg, and he is the biggest player on his team. Rob's physiological characteristics are also above the 90th percentile when compared with peers from his age group: body fat of 11%, resting heart rate of 60 beats per minute (bpm), and a VO_2 max of 56 ml/kg-min. Rob enjoys the physical play in ice hockey and always manages to use his body to gain an advantage over an opponent. He is an intelligent player who can read the play well and position himself effectively on the ice. Rob is not, however, a very fast player, and his skating skills are below average.

To improve his skating Rob's all-star coach asked him to attend a power skating clinic for five hours a week during the summer. His coach also suggested an off-ice training program (5 hours a week year-round) to strengthen his lower body. Rob loves playing ice hockey but does not like off-ice training and other non-ice hockey related training. Rob's dad, Brian, would also like to see his son invest more time in non-ice hockey activities to improve his strength and his skating skills. Brian recently talked to Rob's coach and they both agree that Rob should be more serious about his training if he wants to keep playing at an elite level and have a chance at a professional career. Rob is more interested in playing ice hockey and other sports for fun with his friends than investing solely in ice hockey training.

A contextual perspective

Rob has birth advantages and family advantages that, if capitalized upon, could lead to elite athletic success. The following paragraphs will describe these advantages and how to capitalize on them.

Birth advantages

Two types of birth advantages are relative age and birthplace. Relative age effects refer to athletes of different ages in a one-year cohort who have participation or performance advantages (Musch and Grondin 2001). Typically, relatively older athletes are over-represented on elite sport teams, and this effect is particularly evident in male, team sports (Cobley *et al.* 2009). Rob (born on January 5) took advantage of his age, as the Hockey Canada selection year runs from January 1 to December 31. Quite often, relatively older athletes have growth advantages, as is indeed the case with Rob, who measures 153 cm and 48 kg, making him the largest on his team. However, these physical advantages do not automatically translate to being a more talented ice hockey player. As witnessed, Rob does not have the same skating ability as some players, but was selected to teams anyway – probably due to his size. Thus, Rob has an opportunity to become more talented, but he must capitalize on this through dedicated training.

Another birth advantage is birthplace. There are athletic advantages associated with an individual's birthplace (Côté *et al.* 2006). Specifically, Canadian ice hockey players who make the National Hockey League (NHL) tend to come from cities with populations between 1,000 and 500,000, while players from larger cities (> 500,000) are under-represented in the NHL. These advantages are similar for developmental ice hockey players in Canada also (Turnnidge, Hancock and Côté, in press). Born in Sydenham (village of approximately 5,000 people), Rob has the advantages of coming from a small town that include open spaces, opportunities for play, and a connection to community. Living within 30 minutes of a larger city (Kingston, 120,000 citizens), Rob also has the advantages of bigger cities: access to facilities, coaching, and training. In fact, looking at Rob's past shows how advantageous each environment has been for him. In Sydenham he had the opportunity to learn to skate and play ice hockey on an outdoor rink. He also played many sports growing up, but was able to play with the same group of friends, which likely increased his connection to sport, as well as his passion and motivation (Balish and Côté 2013). In Kingston, Rob was able to join organized sport teams and joined an all-star ice hockey team (a travelling team). In this manner, Rob's birthplace resulted in several advantages, contributing to his early sporting success.

Family influences

In order to witness prolonged engagement in sport, and possibly elite success, it is important to have a supportive family (Côté, 1999). Parents, for example, provide children with opportunities for playing sport (e.g., enrolling them in sport), as well as offering tangible support (e.g., money or transport), and emotional support (e.g., caring or comfort). Rob's background exemplifies a family that values sport and physical activity. His parents and siblings are all active, even though they do not all play competitive sport. This probably increased Rob's opportunities to play sport, be active, and participate in informal games or activities, which facilitated his passion for sport. As Rob's parents have two vehicles and an above-average household income, it is likely that they can offer Rob tangible support for sport, particularly if he decides later in life to pursue elite sport. Finally, Rob's family has the opportunity to provide him with emotional support. The literature is clear on this point: his family should support his wishes rather than pressure him in into sport (Côté 1999). Ultimately this will lead to increased sport satisfaction in the "sampling years" (ages 6–12), after which, peers and coaches will have a larger influence on Rob's development (Côté and Abernethy 2012).

Developmental activities

Rob's coach and father want him to increase his skating training and begin an off-ice training program – essentially investing more time in ice hockey than in other activities. However, the adults should consider Rob's wishes at this stage. Rob has indicated that he would rather keep playing ice hockey and other sports for fun. If the coach and father pressure Rob too much, he might drop out of ice hockey. Instead, it is recommended that Rob is developed along the lines suggested in the Developmental Model of Sport Participation (DMSP; Côté and Abernethy 2012). The DMSP is a model that can be used to guide talent development in sport, is based on evidence from retrospective interviews with professional athletes, and describes two main pathways to expertise: early specialization and early diversification.

The DMSP is a general guideline and, as with all such guidelines, must be adapted to the individual by a knowledgeable teacher or coach. The DMSP is, however, evidence-based, and it states that children from 6 to 12 years old should be *sampling* sports. Sampling means that these children should have high amounts of deliberate play (i.e., free play with friends and little involvement from adults), low amounts of deliberate practice (i.e., practice centred on skill acquisition and repetition, which is not inherently enjoyable), and be involved in several sports. At ages 13–15, youths enter the *specializing* years where play and practice should be balanced, and the number of sports reduced. Finally, at age 16 and older, youth begin the *investment* years, which are characterized by high levels of deliberate practice in one sport.

Based on the DMSP and Rob's evident resistance to increasing training, the next two seasons (ages 11 and 12) should be focused on having fun in a wide range of sports with a slow transition toward increasing training activities specifically to improve ice hockey performance. If Rob is to be involved in sport for 20 hours per week, we might expect 5 hours of deliberate practice, but 15 hours of playing games and deliberate play. At age 13, Rob will be better equipped mentally and physically to increase deliberate practice (e.g., 10 hours of play and practice per week), meaning that skating practice and off-ice training could then be increased (Côté and Fraser-Thomas 2008).

Summary

Rob has many advantages that could lead to elite success. The biggest recommendation now is that the key adults need to allow Rob to be a child, and enjoy sport without focusing on deliberate practice. At age 13, he would then be prepared for more deliberate practice where he could capitalize on his age, birthplace, and family advantages.

A biomechanics perspective

Rob's coach would like him to improve his skating ability in the off-season. He has recommended power-skating and off-ice strength and conditioning program to help strengthen his lower body. This section will describe a biomechanically relevant approach to training that could be applied to improve Rob's skating ability while remaining cognizant of Rob's current physical abilities and desire to enjoy the training process.

The task of skating

Skating is a biomechanically complex task. The skating stride is a bilateral-biphasic continuous motion consisting of support (propulsion) and swing (recovery) phases (Pearsall, Turcotte and Murphy 2000; Upjohn *et al.* 2008). During the propulsion phase, Rob applies a "push-off" force by abducting and extending his leg to increase forward momentum. Once the leg has extended and abducted through the propulsion phase, Rob transitions into the swing phase. During the swing phase, Rob begins to flex and adduct at the hip, flex the knee, and dorsiflex at the ankle to pull the leg back out in front of the body, and then again extend at the knee in preparation for the next propulsion phase. These phases are repeated bilaterally, where the ability to repeatedly complete this sequence of movements in a powerful and effective way will dictate Rob's skating proficiency.

The biomechanical concepts of momentum and impulse are relevant to understanding and improving skating ability. Momentum is the product of mass and velocity (Zatsiorsky 2002). When skating, the maximum momentum Rob can generate is a product of his body mass and top skating speed. Given Rob's enhanced physical maturity, if he can develop similar on-ice speeds to his competitors, his increased mass will give him considerably more momentum, providing him with a distinct on-ice advantage. However, in order to increase on-ice speed he must increase the impulse that he can apply to the ice surface. Impulse is the amount of force applied over a given time interval (Zatsiorsky 2002). When skating, the impulse is determined by the amount of force applied through the duration of each stride (Stidwell et al. 2009). Impulse and momentum share a distinct relationship, where the impulse is equal to the change in momentum. So to enhance Rob's momentum, allowing him to benefit from his enhanced maturity, his training must focus on increasing the amount of impulse he can apply.

Increasing Rob's impulse in the target direction can be achieved in two complimentary ways. Rob's power-skating training can help him focus on technique, where targeted instructions can help Rob improve how effectively he coordinates his movements to push into the ice, at the appropriate angle, propelling him forward. Second, Rob's off-ice strength and conditioning can be structured to help him improve his strength, or more precisely his power or speed-strength to allow him to push into the ice quickly and effectively, with more force.

Improving technique

Improving Rob's skating technique is essential to enable Rob to maximize the benefits of his enhanced physical maturity. With the support of a power-skating instructor Rob can learn how to more effectively apply horizontal propelling forces into the ice to increase skating speed. Conceptually, with each stride Rob pushes his skate blade into the surface applying a force to the ice, where the ice applies an equal and opposite force back onto Rob's skate blade. This reaction force is referred to as the ground reaction force (GRF). The net direction of this GRF dictates the size and direction of the impulse, which ultimately determines Rob's direction and rate of travel. Indeed, McPherson and colleagues (2004) reported that developmentally aged skaters who can apply more horizontal impulse to the ice, particularly those with more mass, are often more likely to skate at higher speeds. For example, a power skating instructor can help Rob learn to apply more horizontal impulse by helping him to outwardly rotate his thigh, coinciding with an initial extension/abduction of the hip and extension of the knee (Pearsall et al. 2000) as he transitions through the propulsion phase of his stride. Further, the relationship between extension and abduction has been shown to differentiate high- and low-calibre skaters (Upjohn et al. 2008), so an initial focus on this aspect of technique will likely yield near-term tangible gains. Through targeted focussed instruction, Rob can learn to apply more horizontal impulse, increasing his on ice momentum.

Off-ice training

Rob's skating can also be improved through off-ice training targeted to develop the ability to produce a greater impulse. Principally, training should improve Rob's ability to develop more force, through a greater range of motion at a faster rate, particularly in the lower limbs (McPherson *et al.* 2004; Upjohn *et al.* 2008). Developing more force at a quicker rate (power or speed-strength) is often achieved through plyometric-based training (Siff 2003). For instance, it is common to see television highlights of professional ice hockey players leaping onto boxes or overtop of hurdles, challenging their bodies plyometrically to improve their power. While plyometric-based exercises can be advantageous when training youth (Behm *et al.* 2008), it is important to consider Rob's stage of development before prescribing this intense off-ice regimen. Rob should be encouraged to play and continue sampling different activities, rather than focusing too much on deliberate practice and training. To balance his desire for play with the need to develop a foundation of strength and power, Rob could be encouraged to participate in other activities and games; particularly where they include strength and plyometric components. For example, rather than training each week by jumping over boxes and hurdles, Rob could be encouraged to participate in basketball, or volleyball where he would jump hundreds of times during the course of the activity. While this may not be the best form of training to directly improve his power for skating, it is perhaps more beneficial taking into account Rob's needs for fun, play, and enjoyment.

An exercise physiology perspective

Rob Burton represents an interesting case study of a young athlete who, primarily because of his relative age, size, and early maturation, is experiencing early success as an ice hockey player. However, there are warning signs that his success may not continue as the size gap between Rob and his peers begins to shrink. Specifically, Rob is a relatively slow skater, and this has been highlighted by his coach as an area requiring significant attention. This section of the case study will focus on the physiological determinants of skating speed, and discuss a variety of different approaches that Rob might take in an attempt to improve his skating ability.

Physiology of speed

Skating speed appears to result from a combination of aerobic fitness, leg strength, and anaerobic power. The first of these factors, aerobic fitness, appears to be the least tightly correlated with skating speed and while a relationship between fitness and skating speed has been observed in females, aerobic fitness appears not to predict skating speed in males (Gilenstam, Thorsen and Henriksson-Larsen 2011). While not predictive of skating speed, an analysis of NCAA Division I ice hockey players revealed that an individual's aerobic fitness was predictive of total net scoring opportunities (difference between scoring chances for and against while a player is on the ice) (Green *et al.* 2006). This suggests that while aerobic fitness may not predict skating speed, it does appear to predict in-game success, and thus should remain a focus for ice hockey specific training programs.

Unlike aerobic fitness, both leg strength and anaerobic power are predictive of skating speed. There is a positive association between off-ice performance of strength and power tasks (sprinting and jumping) and on-ice measures of skating speed (Farlinger, Kruisselbrink and Fowles 2007). In addition, peak levels of anaerobic power generated over brief, all-out efforts (e.g., during a 30-second cycling Wingate test) are also predictive of skating speed (Potteiger *et al.* 2010). Interestingly, in an analysis of 853 elite ice hockey players participating in the NHL entry draft combine, there was a relationship between individuals with high peak anaerobic power and the likelihood of an early draft selection (Burr *et al.* 2008).

These results highlight both anaerobic power and leg strength as critical targets for training programs aimed at improving skating speed. For Rob, any training program being considered should, therefore, have a primary focus on improving both leg strength and anaerobic power. While aerobic fitness should remain an important component of any ice hockey-specific training program, Rob's already high levels of aerobic fitness make this a lower priority at present.

Training for improved speed: on-ice or off?

Rob's coach has recommended both on-ice power skating and off-ice training as means of improving Rob's skating speed. Interestingly, there is controversy regarding whether or not on-ice training improves aerobic fitness, leg strength, power, and ultimately skating speed; indeed, decreases in fitness have been reported across the course of a competitive ice hockey season (Durocher, Leetun and Carter 2008). There is some evidence that anaerobic power may be increased by on-ice activities (Green and Houston 1975), but it is unclear if this adaptation is associated with improved skating speed. The reasons for the apparent lack of change in fitness following on-ice training are undoubtedly complex, but may be related to relatively high amounts of on-ice time (both practice and games) spent on non-skating activities. Further, in-season practices typically do not emphasise improving skating and fitness, but rather tend to focus on skill development (e.g., shooting and passing) and game strategies.

In a particularly applicable study, changes in top skating speed and acceleration were compared in a group of Bantam ice hockey players (~13–14 years) participating in either off-ice, ice hockey specific training, or a summer ice hockey league (Greer *et al.* 1992). Improvements in both top speed and acceleration were observed in the group who completed off-ice training, but not the group that participated in summer league ice hockey. Consistent with these results, improvements in leg strength and power, and skating speed have repeatedly been observed following off-ice training (Reyment *et al.* 2006). These studies utilize body weight bearing, plyometric exercises (squats, lunges, jumps etc.), and resistance training to improve leg strength and power (for detailed description of an ice hockey-specific off-ice training program, see Reyment *et al.* 2006). Given Rob's dislike of non-ice hockey training, adherence and enjoyment of either power-skating or off-ice training will represent a challenge. Nonetheless, evidence of uncertain results derived from on-ice training suggests that the best use of time and effort may be to focus on off-ice training. It is of course important to remember that ice hockey-specific training programs utilized in the studies above are easily adapted to group settings. If Rob were to be offered this form of training in a group setting, it may enhance motivation and help distract him from the fact that this type of activity is most certainly training rather than play.

Summary

At 11 years old, and if sustained elite performance is the aspiration, Rob may benefit from being allowed to mature and grow while participating in activities that he enjoys and that are characterised by play rather than dedicating himself to training. There is certainly evidence to suggest that regular participation in running sports that involve repeated sprinting, like basketball and soccer, can improve aerobic fitness, leg power, and repeated sprint ability. Participation in these sports is likely to infer some of the expected benefits from ice hockey-specific training while allowing Rob to participate in activities that he will enjoy.

If it is decided that Rob does indeed need to dedicate himself to training it is recommended that he participate in ice hockey-specific, off-ice training, at least two times per week and in an enjoyable group setting. This training will provide Rob with the best chances of improving leg strength, anaerobic power, and skating speed.

Pedagogical perspective

Rob and his family are facing a dilemma that is becoming more and more frequent in youth sport: should Rob specialize in ice hockey and invest in specialized training during childhood? The social pressure to specialize and acquire ice hockey-specific skills that will give Rob an advantage over his peers at age 11 is attractive and can be compelling for ambitious parents and coaches. The perspective provided by the experts in sport psychology, biomechanics, and exercise physiology, however, does not necessarily support this view. Instead, it is argued that the pre-adolescence developmental needs of Rob need to be considered.

The long-term outcomes that could be achieved by getting involved in more specialized training have to be weighed against the short-term costs of fun and/or injury that are involved with extreme specialization during childhood. It is clear from our experts in sport psychology, biomechanics, and exercise physiology, that Rob should retain his level of involvement in sport. The key question is whether during the next two years, Rob's involvement should include increases in serious training (i.e., deliberate practice) and the answer is that this is debatable from a talent development perspective. Retrospective studies of ice hockey players show that successful professional players did not specialize early and were involved in more hours of deliberate play than deliberate practice during childhood (Soberlak and Côté 2003). Furthermore, a study comparing dropout and elite adolescent players showed that dropout players started off-ice training at an earlier age and invested more in deliberate practice type activities than elite players (Wall and Côté 2007). In other words, the dropout cost of early specialization is real and is well documented in the youth sport literature.

Parcels (2002) calculated the odds of becoming a professional ice hockey player in Canada and showed that the success rate from youth sport participation to elite level performance in ice hockey is extremely low. As an example, 30,000 males born in 1975 began their ice hockey careers by registering with the Ontario Minor Hockey Association, probably with a glimmer of hope that they would play in the NHL. Of the 30,000 original players, only 48 (0.15%) were drafted by an NHL team; 32 (0.09%) played one NHL game; 15 (0.04%) played more than one full NHL season; and just six of the 30,000 (0.01%) played enough NHL games (400) to qualify for the NHL Player's Pension. It is important to keep these odds in mind when evaluating Rob's chance of developing a sustainable professional career in ice hockey.

A fact worth highlighting, and it is central to this case, is that sport performance in childhood is a poor predictor of adult performance (Vaeyens *et al.* 2009). It is important, therefore, that Rob keeps his passion for ice hockey and takes a long-term approach to developing his skills. In the short-term it may mean that Rob will not maximize his skating potential and his physical capacity. As suggested by our biomechanics and exercise physiology experts, Rob could be encouraged to participate in other sports such as basketball and volleyball to improve his strength, power, and anaerobic capacity. The most important aspects of Rob's participation in ice hockey and other sports at this point in time is that he is provided with choices and has the ability to make his own decisions about his involvement. This approach to talent development in sport is consistent with a developmental perspective. From this perspective, talent is understood as an entity that is inherently multidimensional, is difficult to assess during childhood and, for its realization, needs input from a wide range of personal and social variables over a long period of time (Côté and Lidor 2013).

Rob grew up in an environment where there was little pressure on performance outcomes and he had limited prescribed learning from adults. His passion for ice hockey emerged from a context that favored child-led activities such as play as well as interactions with peers and adults that were determined flexibly. There is very little support from research on expert performance in team sports that would suggest that this context needs to drastically change before adolescence. In fact, the high degree of unpredictability and flexibility present in deliberate play, and participation in multiple sports, has allowed Rob to experiment with new skills and behaviors in safe and stimulating environments. By being involved in various types of child-led and adult-led activities, Rob had the opportunity to "learn how to learn." A drastic transition to an adult-prescribed model of learning (e.g., 5 hours per week of power skating) will thwart Rob's creativity, adaptability, and flexibility in learning, which might hinder his motivation to keep investing time and energy in ice hockey. Although there are definite benefits to getting involved in power skating and off-ice training, this involvement should occur gradually and not become the dominant focus of Rob's involvement in sport at age 11. There are emerging bodies of literature in sport pedagogy, such as implicit motor learning, non-linear pedagogy, and games for understanding, that are helpful in considering Rob's optimal involvement in sport in the next few years.

The concept of implicit motor learning suggests that many motor skills in children's sport can be learned without formal instruction or adult involvement. According to Masters (1992), implicit motor learning involves a set of conditions for the acquisition of a motor skill that does not include the explicit knowledge associated with the execution of that skill. Implicit learning avoids taxing the cognitive capacity of the child when learning a motor skill and changes the role that adults play in this learning environment. In an implicit learning context, the adults (coaches and parents) become facilitators and developers of opportunities for the child to play sport instead of consistently providing instructions on "how to do" something. The concept of implicit learning offers innovative perspectives about the role of unstructured practice and play activities in the design of effective learning environments. Specific to this case, Rob was immersed in play activities during childhood that mainly focused on implicit learning, a context that likely facilitated his current development and is appropriate over the next few years of his life (Masters, van der Kamp and Capio 2013). In other words, simply providing opportunities for Rob to continue playing hockey for fun with his dad and kids of different ages will help develop his skills.

Non-linear pedagogy is a framework that can be used to adapt the principles of play and implicit learning in the more structured sport settings in which Rob is involved. This framework accounts for the complex and dynamic situation that occurs in different learning situations in sport. Non-linear pedagogy is based on principles derived from dynamic systems theory and provides guidelines for designing games in sport that maximize time on task and the potential for youth sport participants to learn new skills. Chow and colleagues (2013) propose practical suggestions to align the dynamics of a learning environment with the individual needs of the participants. Their main recommendations relate to adjusting the intensity of a practice or a game by controlling the time and space that players have to execute skills. The number of players on the playing surface, size of the playing area, and rules of the game are the main variables that can be tailored to increase or decrease the intensity and maximize the learning experiences of young players. These variables can be changed, depending on the context, to create modified games (see Griffin and Butler 2005, for a review) that then provide enjoyable learning environments. Rob's parents should evaluate the experience and skills of the coaches with whom Rob will work over the next few years. Ideally, creative coaches that integrate the principles of non-linear pedagogy and use modified games as learning tasks in their practices should be favored.

From these different research perspectives, there is further support for the value of concepts in learning such as creativity, cross training, implicit learning, and play. These are regarded as sound pedagogical methods to structure the learning environment of children in sport (see Côté and Lidor 2013, for a review of this literature). Accordingly, the informal learning environment in which Rob grew up allowed him to develop his ice hockey skills with limited instructions or corrections from adults. At age 11, Rob's coach and father have suggested that he get involved in more "rational learning" activities that are prescribed and monitored by adults. Instead of applying an immediate switch to this type of "adult" mode of learning, it would be beneficial for Rob's development to integrate some learning guidelines that incorporate the unique characteristics of being a child in sport.

Summary

Considering the suggestions made by our experts in sport psychology, biomechanics, and exercise physiology, it will be beneficial in the next few years for Rob to increase his commitment to ice hockey, improve his skating techniques, and enhance his physical capacity. The challenge is to achieve these objectives without suppressing the inherent enjoyment that Rob is currently demonstrating in ice hockey. The research on children's talent development in sport steers us away from prescribing a more regimented training environment until Rob is ready to make a full commitment to this environment. Because of his birth advantages, Rob is not in danger of falling too far behind his peers in terms of skills; thus, a slower developmental pace should not hinder his long-term ice hockey achievements.

Rob and his parents need to be aware of the importance of finding coaches (including a new power skating coach) who understand the *long-term* impact of their interventions and their relationships with Rob. As he matures in the next couple of years, Rob will realize and start to understand the effect that certain types of training have on his development as an ice hockey player. The evidence suggests that if the adults around Rob are able to keep things in perspective and consider him as a child first, Rob will mature as a strong individual and will decide for himself to increase his training intensity. It will be important for coaches who interact with Rob to understand that his development as a person is as important as the development of his ice hockey skills. For these reasons, it is important to avoid prescribing a training regime that ignores the elements that make Rob passionate about sport. Here are some suggestions that might be discussed with Rob and other children facing similar decisions:

1. Get involved in power skating for one hour per week with a coach who takes a non-linear pedagogy approach with a strong emphasis on learning skills through playful activities and modified games.
2. Encourage Rob to try other sports in the off-season that have a cross training effect for ice hockey, such as basketball or volleyball.
3. Inform Rob's parents that they need to be diligent in ensuring that Rob's needs are being met by the social agents in his life (e.g., his power skating coach).

By following these guidelines, we believe that Rob will have optimal opportunities to see growth in his ice hockey skills and, within a few years, he might cultivate the initiative and drive necessary to engage in deliberate practice and sustained ice hockey specialization.

Notes

1. Pick-up ice hockey is a low-organization game often played by children. Typically, children arrive at an outdoor rink, decide the teams amongst themselves, and often alter rules to make the game more enjoyable or fair. This would be similar to low-organizational games for basketball or soccer.
2. In Canadian ice hockey, age divisions are labeled as follows: Novice (7–8 years), Atom (9–10 years), Peewee (11–12 years), Bantam (13–14 years), and Midget (15–17 years). In each age division, there are multiple competitive levels ranging from House League (the most recreational) to AAA (the most elite).

References

Balish, S. and Côté, J. (2013) 'The influence of community on athletic development: An integrated case study', *Qualitative Research in Sport, Exercise and Health*: DOI:10.1080/2159676X.2013.766815.

Behm, D.G., Faigenbaum, A.D., Falk, B. and Klentrou, P. (2008) 'Canadian Society of Exercise Physiology position paper: Resistance training in children and adolescents', *Applied Physiology, Nutrition & Metabolism*, 33: 547–561.

Burr, J.F., Jamnik, R.K., Baker, J., Macpherson, A., Gledhill, N. and McGuire, E.J. (2008) 'Relationship of physical fitness test results and hockey playing potential in elite-level ice hockey players', *Journal of Strength & Conditioning Research*, 22: 1535–1543.

Chow, J.Y., Davids, K., Renshaw, I. and Button, C. (2013) 'The acquisition of movement skill in children through non-linear pedagogy', in J. Côté and R. Lidor (eds.) *Condition of children's talent development in sport* (pp. 41–60). Morgantown, WV: Fitness Information Technology.

Cobley, S., Baker, J., Wattie, N. and McKenna, J. (2009) 'Annual age-grouping and athlete development: A meta-analytical review of relative age effects in sport', *Sports Medicine*, 39: 235–256.

Côté, J. (1999) 'The influence of the family in the development of talent in sport', *The Sport Psychologist*, 13: 395–417.

Côté, J. and Abernethy, B. (2012) 'A developmental approach to sport expertise', in S.M. Murphy (ed.) *The Oxford handbook of sport and performance psychology* (pp. 435–447). Oxford, UK: Oxford University Press.

Côté, J. and Fraser-Thomas, J. (2008) 'Play, practice, and athlete development', in D. Farrow, J. Baker and C. MacMahon (eds.) *Developing elite sport performance: Lessons from theory and practice* (pp. 17–28). New York, NY: Routledge.

Côté, J. and Lidor, R. (2013) *Condition of children's talent development in sport*. Morgantown, WV: Fitness Information Technology.

Côté, J., MacDonald, D.J., Baker, J. and Abernethy, B. (2006) 'When "where" is more important than "when": Birthplace and birthdate effects on the achievement of sporting expertise', *Journal of Sports Sciences*, 24: 1065–1073.

Durocher, J.J., Leetun, D.T. and Carter, J.R. (2008) 'Sport-specific assessment of lactate threshold and aerobic capacity throughout a collegiate hockey season', *Applied Physiology, Nutrition & Metabolism,* 33: 1165–1171.

Farlinger, C.M., Kruisselbrink, L.D. and Fowles, J.R. (2007) 'Relationships to skating performance in competitive hockey players', *Journal of Strength & Conditioning Research,* 21: 915–922.

Gilenstam, K.M., Thorsen, K. and Henriksson-Larsen, K.B. (2011) 'Physiological correlates of skating performance in women's and men's ice hockey', *Journal of Strength & Conditioning Research,* 25: 2133–2142.

Green, H.J. and Houston, M.E. (1975) 'Effect of a season of ice hockey on energy capacities and associated functions', *Medicine & Science in Sports & Exercise,* 7: 299–303.

Green, M.R., Pivarnik, J.M., Carrier, D.P. and Womack, C.J. (2006) 'Relationship between physiological profiles and on-ice performance of a National Collegiate Athletic Association Division I hockey team', *Journal of Strength & Conditioning Research,* 20: 43–46.

Greer, N., Serfass, R., Picconatto, W. and Blatherwick, J. (1992) 'The effects of a hockey-specific training program on performance of Bantam players', *Canadian Journal of Sport Science,* 17: 65–69.

Griffin, L.L. and Butler, J.I. (2005) *Teaching games for understanding: Theory research and practice.* Champaign, IL: Human Kinetics.

Masters, R.S.W. (1992) 'Knowledge, nerves, and know-how: The role of explicit versus implicit knowledge in the breakdown of a complex motor skill under pressure', *British Journal of Psychology,* 83: 343–358.

Masters, R.S.W., van der Kamp, J. and Capio, C. (2013) 'Implicit motor learning by children', in J. Côté and R. Lidor (eds.) *Condition of children's talent development in sport* (pp. 21–40). Morgantown, WV: Fitness Information Technology.

McPherson, M.N., Montelpare, W.J, Wrigley A. and Purves N. (2004) 'Analyzing kinematic variables: A structural equation model application for the assessment of skating in developmental and elite ice hockey players', *Proceedings of the XXII International Symposium of Biomechanics in Sports.* Ottawa (ON).

Musch, J. and Grondin, S. (2001) 'Unequal competition as an impediment to personal development: A review of the relative age effect in sport', *Developmental Review,* 21: 147–167.

Parcels, J. (2002) 'Chances of making it in pro hockey', *Ontario Minor Hockey Association.* Online. Available HTTP: <www.nepeanhockey.on.ca/Docs/General/MakingIt.pdf> (accessed 7 January 2013).

Pearsall, D.J., Turcotte, R.A. and Murphy, S. (2000) 'Biomechanics of ice hockey', in W.E. Garrett and D.T. Kirkendall (eds.) *Exercise and sport science* (pp. 675–692). Philadelphia, PA: Lippincott Williams & Wilkins.

Potteiger, J.A., Smith, D.L., Maier, M.L. and Foster, T.S. (2010) 'Relationship between body composition, leg strength, anaerobic power, and on-ice skating performance in Division I men's hockey athletes', *Journal of Strength & Conditioning Research,* 24: 1755–1762.

Reyment, C.M., Bonis, M.E., Lundquist, J.C. and Tice, B.S. (2006) 'Effects of a four week plyometric training program on measurements of power in male collegiate hockey players', *Journal of Undergraduate Kinesiology Research,* 1: 44–62.

Siff, M.C. (2003) *Supertraining.* Denver, CO: Supertraining LLC.

Soberlak, P. and Côté, J. (2003) 'The developmental activities of elite ice hockey players', *Journal of Applied Sport Psychology,* 15: 41–49.

Stidwell, T.J., Turcotte, R.A., Dixon, P. and Pearsall, D.J. (2009) 'Force transducer system for measurement of ice hockey skating force', *Sports Engineering,* 12: 63–68.

Turnnidge, J., Hancock, D.J. and Côté, J. (in press) 'The influence of birth date and place of development on youth sport participation', *Scandinavian Journal of Medicine & Science in Sports.*

Upjohn, T., Turcotte, R.A., Pearsall, D.J. and Loh, J. (2008) 'Three-dimensional kinematics of the lower limbs during forward ice hockey skating', *Sports Biomechanics,* 7: 206–221.

Vaeyens, R., Güllich, A., Warr, C.R. and Philippaerts, R. (2009) 'Talent identification and promotion programmes of Olympic athletes', *Journal of Sports Sciences,* 27: 1367–1380.

Wall, M. and Côté, J. (2007) 'Developmental activities that lead to dropout and investment in sport', *Physical Education & Sport Pedagogy,* 12: 77–87.

Zatsiorsky, V.M. (2002) *Kinetics of human motion.* Champaign, IL: Human Kinetics.

8

YASMIN

Learning about unacceptable sexual behaviour in a sport setting

Kristine De Martelaer, Tine Vertommen, Caroline Andries, Johnny Maeschalck and Lore Vandevivere

DEPARTMENT OF PHYSICAL EDUCATION AND PHYSIOTHERAPY, UNIVERSITEIT BRUSSEL, BELGIUM, INTERNATIONAL CENTRE FOR ETHICS IN SPORT (ICES)

Key words: 11-year-old female, early maturing, sexual behaviour, child development, sport ethics/policy, legislation/law, pedagogy.

Yasmin

Yasmin is a timid 11-year-old girl who plays korfball in a sports club at local level in Flanders. She is relatively early maturing, and is the only one in her age group with signs of an adolescent body (growth of body hair, breasts, menstruation). At a sport technical level, Yasmin is one of the average performers in the team. She is not a top scorer but she does possess good basic skills at the level of the competition in which she is participating.

Yasmin's team traditionally celebrates a winning game with a group hug (see Figure 8.1). During one of these celebrations, where all team members have intense body contact, Joe (14 years) touched Yasmin's breasts. It was not the first time this had happened. Yasmin dislikes Joe touching her breasts but she has always felt too ashamed and shy to tell him or anybody else. Her facial expression, however, makes her feelings very clear. All of Yasmin's teammates are aware of Joe's physically uninhibited behaviour but they ignore it – and Yasmin's feelings – and instead find it rather amusing. Victor is one of the 18 years old in the club who competes in the adult korfball team. He enjoyed watching the group hug, and took a picture of the incident. Later that evening, when he arrived home, he published the photograph on Facebook and zoomed in on Yasmin's breasts. The position of Joe's hand was clearly visible, and Victor marked it with a huge red circle (see Figure 8.2).

In a text comment, Victor wrote *"Big friends . . . big boobs"*. Other club members reacted immediately with *"porn baby"*, *"fucking chick"*, *"wow!"*, *"Take every chance in your life with both hands"*. From then on, Yasmin was teased regularly during training sessions and competition. Moreover, in just two weeks, the reactions snowballed, and several peer athletes had added growing numbers of comments to Facebook.

FIGURE 8.1 The group hug

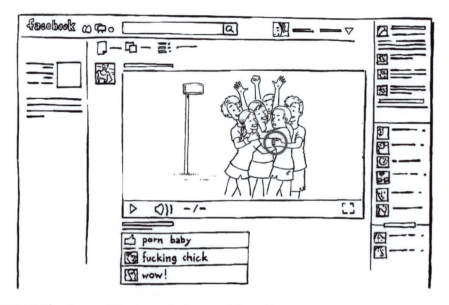

FIGURE 8.2 The picture of Yasmin on the internet followed by comments

Yasmin felt lonely and sad about the comments and the teasing, and there was nobody she felt she could trust enough to discuss her distress. Her motivation to stay in the club decreased, and she felt too ashamed to attend training sessions in the weeks following this incident. Yasmin hoped that perhaps someone would react and interfere to stop the physical and verbal harassment but, after two months, the bullying had not stopped so Yasmin decided to end her involvement with the club and the sport. Yasmin's parents did not understand why she had dropped out because they knew nothing about the incident and the subsequent Facebook problem. They were much more concerned about Yasmin's technical capacities and the importance of being active in leisure time. One day, however, Yasmin's mother noticed that her daughter had left her Facebook page open on her computer, and she finally discovered what had happened. She realized why Yasmin had been acting so differently in recent weeks, and was concerned that Yasmin had not reported her experience in the korfball team. By the time the problem was revealed, Yasmin had already decided to quit the team, and she had stopped playing korfball immediately.

Yasmin's parent complained to the club and asked a board member what had gone wrong and, importantly, who was responsible. His response was rather dismissive, suggesting that youngsters at that age often have feelings of shame about their physical development, that teasing among peers is common and even that such experiences could be seen as positive in order to make youngsters resilient to such comments. No action was undertaken in the sports club.

One year later, and Yasmin is still not engaged in sport or any other leisure activity. At school she has changed noticeably, and has become increasingly shy and introverted. Joe is still popular in the club, and he continues to intimidate other young girls with his behaviour. Victor, the older boy who took the photograph, has become an instructor for the youngest age group (6–8 years), and he was given the opportunity to attend a course for volunteer coaches. The content and teaching methods of the course focus on technical, tactical and some pedagogical advice. There is, however, no training on ethics, sexually appropriate behaviour or conflict resolution.

A child development perspective

In a chronological approach to developmental psychology, sexual development is generally discussed along with puberty and adolescence, while in a topical approach, sexual development is mostly situated under the gender issue. These different viewpoints indicate that sexuality is a broad concept related to the basic domains of development (physical, cognitive and social-emotional). Although these domains are mostly described separately, they are interdependent and development should be seen as a holistic process. So it is with sexuality and sexual development.

Most research on adolescent sexuality focuses on problem behaviour outcomes, such as infections and unwanted pregnancy, resulting in a narrow perspective on the sexual lives of adolescents (Halpern 2010; O'Sullivan et al. 2006). Recently, researchers have been challenged to take a broader perspective of sexual development and to characterize the array of normative physical, psychological and social changes that are fundamental to a developing sense of self (O'Sullivan et al. 2006). According to Halpern (2010: 6) more research should:

> approach sexuality as a developmental process that intersects with other facets of developmental change (e.g. identity, moral development and interpersonal skills) taking into account the product of multiple types or levels of interacting factors (e.g. biological, psychosocial and cultural-contextual factors) that may have bi-directional influences.

This approach will require interdisciplinary collaboration.

Yasmin is an 11-year-old girl whose physical development is ahead of her female peers. Early maturation in girls is detected as a risk factor for emotional and behavioural problems during adolescence and early adulthood. In their review article Mendle, Turkheimer and Emery (2007) provide a synthesis of the negative psychological results of early pubertal maturation compared with on-time or late maturation. Early maturing girls have a greater chance of displaying depressive symptoms, anxiety problems and of reporting psychosomatic symptoms. These girls are more likely to report body dissatisfaction and are more vulnerable to developing disturbed eating patterns. Concerning psychosocial functioning, young women who are earlier maturers report poorer quality of relationships with family and friends, a smaller social network, and lower life satisfaction than on-time maturers (Graber *et al.* 2004). Early maturing girls are, of course, more attractive to boys and are more likely to engage in dating and romantic relationships. As a result, they tend to have an earlier initiation in sexual activity. Friendships with an older peer group can also explain the occurrence of earlier and more substance (mis-)use among these girls. All this may result in poorer academic achievement as they spend less time than others on schoolwork. So, in these cases, problems with academic achievement are not a matter of cognitive difference but instead a psychosocial mechanism. Psychosocial theory suggests that affiliation with older adolescents can explain engagement in delinquent behaviours. The research findings on boys and the effects of timing of puberty are less consistent. Early puberty in boys was traditionally and widely described as advantageous (Moore and Rosenthal 2006). More recent studies (Mendle and Ferrero 2012) conclude that for boys too, the evidence suggests that early puberty predicts negative outcomes.

Beside individual differences in pubertal timing, there are substantial differences between boys and girls. On average, puberty and growth spurt occur one and a half to two years earlier for girls than for boys (Berk 2013). Based on general material from developmental psychology (Berk 2013; Santrock 2008; Siegler, Deloache and Eisenberg 2006) we can analyse the case narrative. The spectacular bodily changes taking place in a relatively short time in adolescence are accompanied by psychological and behavioural changes, such as increasing sexual interest. Focusing on the two boys in the case, each is situated in a different phase of adolescence: Joe (14 years old) is at the beginning of middle adolescence, whereas 18-year-old Victor is starting late adolescence. When teenagers are 14–15 years old, their social relationships become increasingly oriented towards peers, and they become more interested in developing romantic relationships. Middle adolescence is a period of experimentation: engagement in risk behaviour peaks, prevalence of tobacco, alcohol and cannabis use increases sharply and exploring sexuality is a major concern (Hibell *et al.* 2012; Sensoa 2011). Joe's use of the celebration as an opportunity to touch a girl's breasts can be explained by his sexual curiosity. It is important to explain to Joe that his behaviour is unacceptable, but he also needs to be reassured that his sexual interest is normal. Concerning Victor, his harassment can be categorized as anti-social behaviour, and an intervention by the club is required.

The process of physical growth and sexual maturity during adolescence does not take place in a vacuum of time or context. Physical development starts at birth, or even earlier at conception, while gender identity – the awareness of being a boy or a girl – develops during preschool years (Berk 2013). Gender is a broader term than sex and "refers to the attitudes, feelings and behaviours that a given culture associates with a person's biological sex" (American Psychological Association 2011: 1). Gender role is the reflection of cultural stereotypes of gender in everyday behaviour: clothing, hairstyle, psychological characteristics, and behaviour. Gender identity and gender role are further developed during adolescence and play an important role in sexual relationships. The cause of psychological gender differences is not the result of biological dispositions (only). Social and cognitive theories also explain how gender roles develop (Carroll 2013). Social learning theory suggests that gender roles are learned like other social roles by operant conditioning. Cognitive theories, e.g. the gender schema theory of Sandra Bem (1981), explains that gender stereotypical views and behaviours are due to gender schema, a cognitive mechanism that organizes our knowledge about a certain concept. Society plays an important role in determining what is seen as typically 'feminine' and 'masculine'. Both parents and educators are responsible for guiding youngsters through their sexuality and gender development (Shtarkshall, Santelli and Hirsh 2007). The series of events recorded in Yasmin's case suggest there may be some further work to do in sports clubs.

A perspective from sport ethics and sport policy

Sexual harassment and abuse occur in every sector of society, including sports. What follows below is contextual information about the nature and extent of sexual harassment and abuse, and definitions and sport policy actions in Flanders.

Youth sport is a setting that is vulnerable to sexually transgressive behaviours as it is characterised by values and norms that can lead to abuse; for example:

- *Intimate coach-athlete relationships* based on trust, loyalty, inequality and dependence;
- *Pressure* to perform;
- Repeatedly pushing *personal boundaries* on physical and emotional levels;
- Extensive *physical contact*. Instruction-related touching is often a necessary part of sport practice, and non-instruction-related behaviours, such as hugging, have always been part of the sport culture. Physical rituals when celebrating a victory are also seen as 'part of the game' and are, therefore, seldom questioned;
- *Initiating rites* (e.g. hazing) are common in some parts of the world and in certain sports, and often have a sexual content. The link between such practices and sexual harassment has not yet been addressed (Kirby and Wintrup, 2002);
- The *dome of silence:* a term used by Kirby *et al.* (2000) to describe the systematic barriers in place in sport, which ensure that athletes who experience abuse in sport do not speak up about it.

Researching sexual harassment and abuse in youth sport is complicated by the lack of definitional consensus. In order to create international awareness and stimulate prevention policy, the International Olympic Committee (IOC) introduced the Consensus Statement on Sexual Harassment and Abuse in Sport. The statement includes the following definitions:

> Sexual harassment refers to behaviour towards an individual or group that involves sexualised verbal, non-verbal or physical behaviour, whether intended or unintended, legal or illegal, that is based upon an abuse of power and trust and that is considered by the victim or a bystander to be unwanted or coerced. Sexual abuse involves any sexual activity where consent is not or cannot be given.
>
> (International Olympic Committee 2007: 3)

Taking into account the 'grey zone' between sexual harassment and abuse, Brackenridge (2001) has proposed a *sexual exploitation continuum*. It displays different types and degrees of unwanted sexual experiences, making the important point that despite *objective* definitions of such behaviours, they are experienced *subjectively* (see Figure 8.3).

Estimates of the prevalence of sexual harassment and abuse in sport vary between two and 44 per cent (Chroni *et al.* 2012). Because of the predominant research focus on female victims and authority perpetrators, those numbers do not give us an insight in the prevalence of sexually transgressive behaviour between peers. Given that previous sexual harassment and abuse in sport research do not cover peer-to-peer sexual harassment, prevalence rates of these behaviours can only be estimated.

Up until now, researchers in sport have mainly focussed on the existence of sexual harassment and abuse by authority figures, such as the coach. Recent studies in other settings, however, indicate that large numbers of perpetrators are peers (e.g. Radford *et al.* 2011). Very little is known about peer-to-peer sexual harassment or abuse among young athletes. Alexander *et al.*

SEX DISCRIMINATION →

SEXUAL & GENDER HARASSMENT →

HAZING & SEXUAL ABUSE →

INSTITUTIONAL...PERSONAL

"the chilly climate"	*"unwanted attention"*	*"groomed or coerced"*
vertical & horizontal job segregation	written or verbal abuse or threats	exchange of reward or privilege for sexual favours
lack of harassment policy and/or officer or reporting channels	sexually oriented comments jokes, lewd comments or sexual innuendoes, taunts about body, dress, marital situation or sexuality	groping
lack of counselling or mentoring systems	ridiculing of performance	indecent exposure
		forced sexual activity
differential pay or rewards or promotion prospects on the basis of sex	sexual or homophobic graffiti	sexual assault
	practical jokes based on sex	
poorly/unsafely designed or lit venues	intimidating sexual remarks, propositions, invitations or familiarity	
absence of basic security	domination of meetings, play space or equipment	physical/sexual violence
	condescending or patronising behaviour undermining self-respect or work performance	rape
	physical contact, fondling, pinching or kissing	incest
	vandalism on the basis of sex	
	offensive phone calls or photos	
	stalking	
	bullying based on sex	

FIGURE 8.3 The sexual exploitation continuum (Brackenridge 1997)

(2011) surveyed 6,062 young people between the ages of 18 and 22 about their experiences in sport up to the age of 16. The study revealed that sexual harassment was the second most common form of harm (after emotional harm). It was reported by 29 per cent of respondents who had at least one experience with one of the behaviours defined as verbal, physical or non-physical sexual harassment. Around two thirds of these respondents said that a team mate or peer was involved, compared to 21 per cent saying that a coach was involved (Alexander *et al.* 2011). Sexually abusive behaviour was experienced by three per cent of respondents. Somewhat surprisingly perhaps, young men were more likely than girls to have experienced sexually abusive behaviour (5% versus 2%). The most common form of sexual harm experienced was being 'flashed at' (80% of those reporting sexual abuse). Twenty-two per cent of those reporting sexual abuse indicate being touched against their will, as in the case of Yasmin. Eighty-eight per cent of those who reported sexual abuse indicated that teammates were responsible. In the coming years, researchers of sexual harassment in sport will shift their attention in order to investigate these new insights.

Other (inter-) national sport organisations[1] developed prevention strategies on sexual harassment and abuse in sport in the late 1990s or early 2000s. It was only recently, however, that the Flemish authorities, responsible for sports in Flanders, took action. In February 2012, the Flemish Ministers of Sport, Youth, Education and Welfare signed a declaration of commitment on protecting children's physical and sexual integrity (Flemish Minister of Sport 2012). In addition, the entire Flemish sports sector co-signed this declaration, affirming their willingness to create a positive and safe sport environment for children and young people. Since then, different prevention initiatives have been implemented in Flemish sports. A framework on sexual and physical integrity was introduced, consisting of different instruments at different policy levels (quality, prevention and reaction). These included: guidelines for sport organisations to initiate prevention policies; an action protocol; a 'contact person integrity' profile (a first contact person and referral point based in sport federations and clubs); a competence checklist for coaches; a code of conduct; a signals list; a sport-specific flag system; and an overview of various organisations for advice, assistance and reporting. The flag system encourages clubs to think about rules of behaviour for athletes, to develop a code of conduct for trainers and to write agreements around changing rooms and shower use. In addition, the flag system attempts to make sport coaches aware of the need to respect the personal integrity of each individual.

A legislation and law perspective

From a judicial point of view, there are several 'theoretical possibilities' for Yasmin's case, taking into account criminal law as well as civil rights. The United Nations (UN) Convention on the Rights of the Child (UNCRC 1989), is by far the most widely agreed international treaty, ratified by 192 governments in the world (including Belgium). Ratification means that governments undertake action to implement the UNCRC in law, policy and practice and to report regularly to the UN Committee on the Rights of the Child on their progress in so doing. These regular government documents are published on the UNICEF website. The UNCRC's formally agreed standards include three partly overlapping kinds of rights: provision, protection and participation rights (Alderson 2008). Children's rights are based on the UN Convention of Human Rights from 1948, ratified by Belgium in 1990 and implemented in 1992. A child is defined as every young person under the age of 18. Relevant in this case of Yasmin in a sport context is the *right to play,* the *right of protection* and the *right of privacy.* In a sport context, the social conduct of all members and for sport leaders is often specified in a code of conduct. Each of the participants involved in Yasmin's case will be described separately.

Joe (age 14 years)

In Belgium, minors are not included in the general **criminal law** and thus are subject to exception law. The possibility for repressive measures starts at the age of 18, as described in article 36, al.[2] 1§4 of the juvenile protection law. Therefore Joe holds criminal law immunity. Concerning **civil rights,** Joe can be called to the juvenile court, but the question in this case is: who will file a complaint? Yasmin herself, being a minor, can go to the police but not to a judge without the assistance of an adult. For minors who have committed a 'crime', and who come to the juvenile court, the judge has numerous measures available focussing on the person behind the behaviour (although it is debatable that the incident in Yasmin's case constitutes a crime). The measures are educative and oriented towards a rehabilitation process. Civil rights sanctions are, however, still possible, based on article 1384, lid 2 B.W.,[3] and available to the parents. In this case, there is a responsibility upon the club, because they know about Joe's uninhibited behaviour and its regularity.

Victor (age 18 years)

From the perspective of *criminal law,* Victor can be accused of 'violation of decency' (respectability) because he is considered (judicially) as an adult. 'Violation of decency' is a broad term and is defined in article 372 of the penal (criminal) code, and refers to behaviour that harms an individual's sexual integrity. The interpretation of how damage to sexual integrity can be defined is developing over time and in case law. Justice assumes that the violation of decency only exists when the actions have a certain degree of weightiness, consistent with the collective consciousness of a society at a certain moment (Cass [2nd chamber] A.R. P95.1312 N, 7 January 1997, A.J.T., 1998–99, 172 with annotation). Publication and dissemination of books, press, films, radio, television or other methods such as texts, drawings, photos, images or sound fragments, where the identity of the victim is made apparent, are forbidden, unless there is written consent by the victim (article 378bis S.W.[4]). On the basis of these articles, a prosecution is possible in Yasmin's case, especially because Yasmin is a minor (11 years old) and thus cannot give permission for actions harming her sexual integrity. The phrase 'age of consent' rarely appears in legal statutes when used in relation to sexual activity (Waits 2005) but it refers to the minimum age at which a person is considered to be legally competent to consent to sexual acts. The age of consent for sexual activity in Belgium is 16 years old. Laws vary widely in different countries, and while most jurisdictions set the age of consent in the range 14 to 18, worldwide ages of consent are recorded as low as 12 and as high as 21 (http://en.wikipedia.org/wiki/Age_of_consent).

   The earlier question arises again: who will take the initiative to complain when the victim is younger than the minimum age? Victor can be approached, based on article 1382 of the civil code. The three conditions for civil responsibility in causing damage are: mistake, causal relationship, and damage. He can also be accused of ignoring Yasmin's right over her own image(s). It is obvious she never agreed to the taking of pictures, and certainly not to their publication.

Making pictures disappear from the Internet is no sinecure. The sports club can possibly also be approached based on the following:

> People are responsible, not only for the damage they cause themselves but also for the harm that is effected by the actions of individuals for whom they are responsible or for matters they take charges of.
>
> (article 1384, lid1 B.W.)

A disciplinary charge seems most adequate in this case.

To conclude, the approaches or juridical possibilities as described above are predicated on the word *possibly* and so are very provisional. In 'theory' there are different possibilities but the experience of practice teaches us that in most cases, very little is actually done in cases such as Yasmin's.

The International Centre for Ethics in Sport (ICES) has been appointed by the Department of Culture, Youth, Sports and Media (in Flanders) to carry out a new project: To provide expertise in the domain of ethics in sports, including issues with regard to integrity, sexual abuse and violence. This project consists of translating scientific research into practice. ICES is expected to play a guiding and supporting role in the sports world. In order to reach these goals, ICES is cooperating with four universities and with other partners related to the Flemish sports landscape. There is a growing awareness that several sectors, including sport, have to take greater responsibility for clear agreements, trust and respect in order to prevent feelings of powerlessness and confusion involving physical and sexual harassment and abuse. One of the tasks of this interdisciplinary group is to give advice for the decree (law) on medically and ethically sound sport in Flanders. (Doping is being considered separately.) In 2013, the aim is for new policies to stimulate ethically sound sport participation, and these policies will add a clear judicial element to the organised sport sector.

A sport pedagogy perspective

It is obvious that Yasmin has had negative experiences in the sports club. The incident started with Joe's sexual harassment during the group hug, and was exacerbated by the picture taken by Victor and circulated on the Internet, and the numerous remarks made by peers. This case can be split into two phases: (a) the incident of physically uninhibited behaviour on the playing field and (b) the cyber-bullying that followed. In both cases, there is fundamental problem of failing to respect Yasmin's integrity and/or violation of her boundaries and, thus, her personal safety. When reflecting on this case and the various pedagogical responsibilities, the following actors are involved: Yasmin's peers or teammates (same age and older), parents, coach(es), and club board members.

In Flanders, a didactical tool has been created to help individuals in the assessment of different situations of physical or sexual behaviour in sport settings. A general version of the tool was developed (Frans and Franck 2010) and it has recently been adapted for the specific context of youth work (Neyens et al. 2012) and one year later for sport (Vandevivere et al. 2013). The *flag system*[5] is based on six assessment criteria (Table 8.1). Rather than judging an action 'right' or 'wrong', the system allocates a score (OK/not OK/not applicable) for the six criteria. In addition, a global score is allocated, consisting of a coloured flag (ranging through

TABLE 8.1 Six criteria and four flags in the flag system to reflect on physical and sexual behaviour (Frans and Franck 2012)

Criterion	Green flag	Yellow flag	Red flag	Black flag
Mutual agreement	Clear mutual agreement (all parties derive pleasure from it)	Unclear mutual agreement	One-off (unique) lack of mutual agreement	Repeated lack of mutual agreement
Free will	Voluntary (no coercion)	Light coercion or pressure	One-off (unique) use of manipulation, blackmail (position of) power	Repeated use of manipulation, blackmail (position of) power, aggression, violence or threats to that effect
Equality	Equal partners	Slight inequality in terms of maturity, age, intelligence etc.	One-off bigger inequality in terms of maturity age, intelligence etc.	Repeated, large inequality in terms of maturity, age, intelligence etc.
Appropriate for age	At least 20% of children and young people display this behaviour	Behaviour of somewhat younger or somewhat older children or young people	Behaviour of children or young people with a greater age difference	Behaviour of children or young people with a major age difference
Appropriate for context	Behaviour disturbs nobody; privacy is respected	Given the context, the one-off behaviour is slightly offensive (impolite)	Behaviour is more offensive (hurtful or insulting) and no longer suited to the context at all	The repeated behaviour is severely offensive (shocking) – public violation of morality
Self-respect	Sufficient self-respect (there is respect of personal integrity)	Behaviour can be self-harming	Behaviour has physical, emotional or psychological damage as a consequence	Behaviour has serious physical, emotional or psychological damage as a consequence

green, yellow, red and black) to assess situations whereby the sexual integrity of children might be violated. The diagram above (Table 8.1) functions as a guideline and serves as a structure for a more extensive, normative list. This is based on the literature on sexual development, including examples of age appropriate behaviour. The pale grey zones in Table 8.1 correspond with sexual harassment, while the dark grey cells with sexual abuse.

In Yasmin's case, the situation corresponds with a red flag because of following assessment on each of the six criteria:

- mutual agreement: not OK
- free will: not OK
- equality: not OK
- appropriate for age: OK
- appropriate for context: not OK
- self-respect: not OK

TABLE 8.2 Pedagogical guidelines to react depending on the flag (Frans 2010)

Green flag	Yellow flag	Red flag	Black flag
Examine	Examine	Examine/listen	Examine/listen
Listen	Listen	Name/confront	Name
Confirm	Limit/divert	Forbid	Forbid
Explain	Explain	Explain	Explain
	Observe	Observe more	Punish/refer on
			Observe more

Each flag colour reflects a different degree of seriousness of the situation, and requires appropriate action towards the victim, the offender and sometimes bystanders.

In the case of Yasmin, the touching of her breasts is not accidental; and Joe has a reputation for behaving in sexually inappropriate ways. In this case, therefore, the *coach* as well as the *athletes* should observe and confront him when he behaves inappropriately. Yasmin did not give permission for the touching, and she feels unhappy with the situation. She can/should be taught that she can give clear signals (verbal and non-verbal) to Joe to convey her feelings. Coaches or other adults responsible in the club who find themselves as *bystanders* in such a situation could react to Joe as follows:

> Joe, it is normal that you like the group hug and at your age you show interest in girls. But I saw you touching the Yasmin's breast, and this is not OK because it is in public and it was obvious she did not like that! I want you to apologize to her. If this happens again, be sure sanctions will follow. Such behaviour is damaging to both your and Yasmin's self-respect.

If the inappropriate behaviour is also a problem amongst other group members, the message should be given to the group. If not, as in this case, it is pedagogically better to choose an individual approach.

An appropriate reaction to Yasmin could be:

> Yasmin, we could see you did not like the group hug because Joe was touching your breast. Try to find a way to tell him you do not want this anymore. If this happens again, please make sure you tell somebody about it. We will undertake actions, and we will keep an eye on him!

Slater and Tiggeman (2011) found that girls reported significantly higher overall levels of teasing experiences in sport participation and physical activity. Small to moderate positive correlations were observed between teasing experience and the different body image variables (self-objectification, self-surveillance, body shame, appearance anxiety and disordered eating) for boys and girls. This relationship between being teased and having a low body image seemed to be stronger among girls when the focus was on the level of anxiety. It is important, therefore, to tell Yasmin that the club is committed to ensuring that everyone is happy and that if any young person finds herself in an uncomfortable situation she should talk about what is happening.

Yasmin's dropout from the club and sport more generally is largely the result of the cyber-bullying. It was sustained and had a widespread, public effect due to the nature of the Internet. Victims of bullying perceive themselves as less socially accepted than others, and they report increased anxiety and depressive symptoms, and a lower self-worth (Bouman *et al.* 2012). Traditional and cyber-bullying have similar psychological, emotional, and social effects on victims (Hemphill *et al.* 2012). In addition, cyber-bullying can negatively impact young people's dating, peer and parental relationships, and also friendships (Ortega *et al.* 2012; Spears *et al.* 2009).

Recently, experts in cyber-bullying identified two additional criteria to the three traditional bullying criteria of intentionality, repetition, and imbalance of power. These new criteria are anonymity and public versus private. The strongest criterion seems to be 'imbalance of power', with severe consequences for the victim who is upset and does not know how to defend him/herself (Menesini *et al.* 2012). Based on interviews with young people, Parris and colleagues (2012) describe several coping strategies at two levels (Figure 8.4).

There is generally a lack of attention to *peer* group influences on bullying attitudes and behaviours, although encouraging bystanders to create a more positive climate through intervening is relevant (Espelage, Green and Polanin 2011). Notwithstanding the fact that most recommendations from research on bullying come from the school context, actions like reporting an incident and confronting the bully apply equally to sports clubs. Youngsters are more likely to intervene if they believe their friends expect them to support victims (Rigby and Johnson 2006). Thus, friends' attitudes and peer influences play an important role in prevention

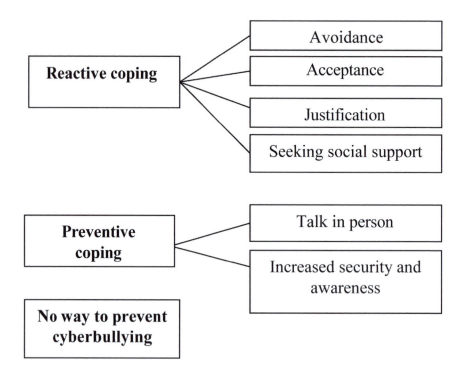

FIGURE 8.4 Coping strategies for cyber-bullying (Parris *et al.* 2012: 291)

programs that can alter bystander behaviour and increase interventions in bullying situations (Polanin, Espelage and Pigott 2012). Establishing clear peer norms for bullying, including in-group and out-group norms, can be helpful (Espelage *et al.* 2011).

The literature (Shtarkshall *et al.* 2007; Walsh and Brandon 2012) indicates that *parents* usually feel uncomfortable approaching their children about sexual matters, and many adolescents find it difficult to talk to their parents about sex-related topics. These authors support collaboration between home and school, therefore, in educating adolescents to become sexually healthy adults. While there is a consensus that parents and schools are the primary sex educators, sexual socialisation also takes place outside home and school environments (Shtarkshall *et al.* 2007). Children and adolescents observe community norms, consume mass media, and participate in cultural and (sometimes) religious activities. It is necessary that parents are aware of the messages youngsters are exposed to and of (in)appropriate physical contact with peers and adults in sport. In addition, the development of social skills, to support young people to be able to react to situations such as the harassment by Joe, is central to sex education and socialization. This signals the broader – and essential – roles for parents and educators/coaches in fostering sexual literacy and sexual health. Parents' strengths should lie in a focus on boosting children's self-esteem and empowering their children, building trusting relationships, and monitoring their safety (Walsh and Brandon 2012). Among parents there is often some debate about the need for protection on the one hand, and wariness of over-protection on the other hand (Walsh and Brandon 2012). The younger the child, the more the balance should tend towards protection. As puberty arrives, the balance inclines towards freedom in order to liberate the young person to allow him or her to explore boundaries. It is desirable, therefore, to develop joint statements of principles, or codes of conduct, in combination with establishing a positive climate of respect and trust. In this climate, open dialogue and collaboration between coaches and parents would be possible.

A crucial part of the *coach-athlete relationship* is the quality of communication as this is the basis of building a close and trusting relationship (LaVoi 2007; Sand *et al.* 2011). Usually coaching requires interactions with young athletes in a wide range of situations and settings, and will therefore involve both democratic and authoritarian behaviours (Sand *et al.* 2011). 'Power' is a crucial aspect in the interactions during coaching because of the power relations and power differences inherent in the situation. Sand *et al.* (2011) make a distinction between 'power to' – referring to a person's ability (knowledge, intellect, resources . . .) – and 'power over' – to dominate and impose one's will on other individuals or groups (often associated with force and treat). In the (male) coach's 'power capital', four main types can play an essential role: positional, expert, physical and gender power. According to Lyle (2002) unbalanced power distribution embodies a potential ethical dilemma (Sand *et al.* 2011). In potential ethical dilemmas, the challenge for the coach is to focus on the individual needs of young athletes and, therefore, a holistic approach to coaching should be emphasized (Sand *et al.* 2011). In the case of Yasmin, there was no power problem between the athlete and the coach but instead the problem was between peers. The older club member, Victor, who took the picture and published it on Facebook, should be punished by the members of the club Board. Suspension for a period of time would signal that the club takes bullying seriously. If Victor is to become a coach, a deep and serious conversation and follow up will be necessary. In addition, a coach mentoring system (as described by Griffiths 2011) could be a solution if Victor changes his behaviour and perseveres in his dream to become a coach.

Conclusion

The case of Yasmin emphasises the importance of being aware of the risk of sexual harassment and (cyber)bullying in sports clubs. There are dangers for the individual victim (Yasmin), but also for the self-esteem and reputation of the perpetrator(s) (Joe and Victor) and finally for the learning climate of the sports club. Reflection can be identified as a key component of pedagogy (Pollard 2010). Parents and coaches are sometimes unfamiliar with the process of critical reflection in a sports club context, and with ethical dilemmas related to harassment. It must be recognised that the criteria used to judge and estimate the consequences of such behaviours (or non-behaviours) are complex and until recently were largely unknown to the broader public.

Notes

1. Some examples: Development of the prevention project on sexual harassment in sport by NOC*NSF, the Dutch Olympic Committee and sports confederation, in 1998; the adoption of guidelines to prevent sexual harassment in sports by the Norwegian Olympic and Paralympic Committee and Confederation of Sports (NIF) in 2001; Installation of the Child Protection in Sport Unit in the UK, as a part of the NSPCC, in 2001; the IOC Consensus Statement in 2007.
2. al. = abbreviation of alinea = paragraph
3. lid = clause; B.W. = Burgelijk Wetboek = Civil Code
4. S.W. = Strafwetboek = Penal Code
5. More information on the flag system can be downloaded at www.seksuelevorming.be/download/pub/pub_6_english.html.

References

Alderson, P. (2008) *Young children's rights. Exploring beliefs, principles and practice.* London: Jessica Kingsley Publishers.

Alexander K., Stafford, A. and Lewis R. (2011) *The experiences of children participating in organised sport in the UK,* London: NSPCC.

American Psychological Association (2011) *Guidelines for Psychological Practice with Lesbian, Gay, and Bisexual Clients.* Online. Available HTTP: <www.apa.org/pi/lgbt/resources/guidelines.aspx> (accessed 21 December 2012).

Bem, S. (1981) 'Gender Schema Theory – A cognitive account of sex typing', *Psychological Review,* 88: 354–364.

Berk, L.E. (2013) *Child development.* Boston: Pearson.

Bouman, T., van der Meulen, M., Goossens, F.A., Olthof, T., Vermande, M.M. and Aleva, E.A. (2012) 'Peer and self-reports of victimization and bullying: Their differential association with internalizing problems and social adjustment', *Journal of Social Psychology,* 50: 759–774.

Brackenridge, C.H. (1997) '"He owned me basically . . ." Women's experience of sexual abuse in sport', *International Review for the Sociology of Sport,* 32: 115–130.

Brackenridge, C.H. (2001) *Spoilsports: Understanding and preventing sexual exploitation in sport,* London: Routledge.

Carroll, J.L. (2013) *Sexuality now: Embracing diversity,* Pacific Grove, CA: Wadsworth – Cengage Learning Publishers.

Chroni, S., Fasting, K., Hartill, M., Knorre, N., Martin, M., Papaefstathiou, M., Rhind, D., Rulofs, B., Tofregaard Støckel, J., Vertommen, T. and Zurc, J. (2012) *Prevention of sexual and gender harassment and abuse in sports. Initiatives in Europe and beyond.* Frankfurt: Deutsche Sportjugend in Deutschen Olympischen Sportbund. Online. Available HTTP: <www.dsj.de/childprotection> (accessed 22 September 2013).

Espelage, D.L., Green, H. and Polanin, J. (2011) 'Willingness to intervene in bullying episodes among middle school students: Individual and peer group influences', *Journal of Early Adolescence,* 32(6): 776–801.

Flemish Minister of Sport (2012) *Declaration of Commitment for the protection of minors' sexual integrity in the sports sector,* Brussels: Department of Culture, Youth, Sport and Media.

Frans, E. (2010) 'Seksueel gedrag van kinderen bespreekbaar stellen. Het vlaggensysteem als pedagogische interventie'. *Lief & Leed* 4: 118–122.

Frans, E. and Franck, T. (2010) *Flag system: Talking with children and young people about sex and unacceptable sexual behavior.* Antwerpen: Sensoa & Garant.

Frans, E. and Franck, T. (2012) *(N)iets is mee?! Omgaan met seksueel getinte situaties met het vlaggensysteem. Speciaal voor het jeugdwerk.* Antwerpen: Sensoa & Garant.

Graber, J.A., Seeley, J.R., Brooks-Gunn, J. and Lewinsohn, P.M. (2004) 'Is pubertal timing associated with psychopathology in young adulthood?', *Journal of the American Academy of Child and Adolescent Psychiatry,* 43(6): 718–726.

Griffiths, M. (2011) 'Mentoring as a professional learning strategy', in. K. Armour (ed.) *Sport Pedagogy: An introduction for teaching and coaching* (pp. 299–309). Boston: Pearson Education Limited.

Halpern, C.T. (2010) 'Sexual and reproductive health: Priorities for the next decade. Reframing research on adolescent sexuality: Healthy sexual development as part of the Life Course, Roundtable', *Perspectives on Sexual and Reproductive Health,* 42(1): 6–7.

Hemphill, S.A., Kotevski, A., Tollit, M., Smith, R., Herrenkohl, T.I., Toumbourou, J.W. and Catalano, R.F. (2012) 'Longitudinal predictors of cyber and traditional bullying perpetration in Australian secondary school students', *Journal of Adolescent Health,* 51(1): 59–65.

Hibell, B., Guttormsson, U., Ahlström, S., Balakireva, O., Bjarnason, T., Kokkevi, A. and Kraus, L. (2012) *The 2011 ESPAD report: Substance use among students in 36 European countries,* Stockholm: CAN.

International Olympic Committee (2007) *Consensus statement on sexual harassment and abuse in sport,* Lausanne: IOC.

Kirby, S., Graves, L. and Hankivsky, O. (2000) The Dome of Silence. Sexual harassment and abuse in sport. Halifax: Fernwood Publishing.

Kirby, S. and Wintrup (2002) Running the gauntlet: An examination of initiation/hazing and sexual abuse in sport. *Journal of Sexual Aggression,* 8(2): 49–68.

LaVoi, N.M. (2007) 'Expanding the interpersonal dimension, Closeness in the coach-athlete relationship', *International Journal of Sport Science and Coaching,* 2(4): 497–512.

Lyle, J. (2002) *Sport coaching concepts: A framework for coaches' behaviour,* London: Routledge.

Mendle, J. and Ferrero, J. (2012) 'Detrimental psychological outcomes associated with pubertal timing in adolescent boys', *Developmental Review,* 32: 49–66

Mendle, J., Turkheimer, E. and Emery R.E. (2007) 'Detrimental psychological outcomes associated with early pubertal timing in adolescent girls', *Developmental Review,* 27: 151–171.

Menesini, E., Nocentini, A., Palladino, B.E., Frisén, A., Sofia Berne, S., Ortega-Ruiz, R., Calmaestra, J., Scheithauer, H., Schultze-Krumbholz, A., Luik, P., Naruskov, K., Blaya, C., Berthaud, J. and Smith. P.K. (2012) 'Cyberbullying definition among adolescents: A comparison across six European countries', *Cyberpsychology, Behavior, and Social Networking,* 15(9): 455–463.

Moore, S. and Rosenthal, D. (2006) *Sexuality in adolescence: Current trends.* Hove, East Sussex: Routledge.

O'Sullivan, L.F., Meyer-Bahlburg, H.L. and McKeague, I.W. (2006) 'The development of the sexual self-concept inventory for early adolescent girls', *Psychology of Women Quarterly,* 30: 139–149.

Ortega, R., Elipe, P., Mora-Merchan, Luisa Genta, M., Brighi, A., Guarini, A., Smith, P.K., Thompson, F. and Tippett, N. (2012). 'The emotional impact of bullying and cyberbullying on victims: A European cross-national study', *Aggressive Behavior,* 38: 342–356.

Parris, L., Varjas, K., Meyers, J. and Cutts, H. (2012) 'High school students' perceptions of coping with cyberbullying', *Youth & Society,* 44(2): 285–306.

Polanin, J.R., Espelage, D.L. and Pigott, T.D. (2012) 'A meta-analysis of school-based bullying prevention programs' effect on bystander intervention behavior', *School Psychology Review,* 41(1): 47–65.

Pollard, A. (2010). *Professionalism and pedagogy: A contemporary opportunity. A commentary by TLRP and GTCE,* London: Teaching and Learning Research Programme Publications.

Radford, L., Corral, S. and Bradley, C. (2011) *Child cruelty in the UK 2011,* London: NSPCC.

Rigby, K. and Johnson, B. (2006) 'Expressed readiness of Australian schoolchildren to act as bystanders in support of children who are being bullied', *Educational Psychology,* 26(3): 425–440.

Sand, T.S., Fasting, K., Chroni, S. and Knorre, N. (2011) 'Coaching behaviour: Any consequences for the prevalence of sexual harassment?', *International Journal of Sports Science & Coaching,* 6(2): 229–241.

Santrock, J.W. (2008) *Life-span development,* Boston: McGraw-Hill

Sensoa (2011) *Feiten en Cijfers: Jongeren en seksualiteit,* Antwerpen-Gent: Digitaal rapport.

Shtarkshall, R.A., Santelli, S. and Hirsh, J.S. (2007) 'Sex education and sexual socialization: Roles for educators and parents', *Perspectives on Sexual and Reproductive Health,* 39(2): 116–119.

Siegler, R., Deloache, J. and Eisenberg, N. (2006) *How children develop,* New York: Worth Publishers.

Slater, A. and Tiggeman, M. (2011) 'Gender differences in adolescent sport participation, teasing, self-objectification and body image concerns', *Journal of Adolescence,* 34: 455–463.

Spears, B., Slee, P., Owens, L. and Johnson, B. (2009) 'Behind the scenes and screens: Insights into the human dimension of covert and cyberbullying', *Journal of Psychology,* 217: 189–196.

United Nations (UN) Convention on the Rights of the Child (UNCRC 1989): Online. Available HTTP: <www.unicef.org/crc/>

Vandevivere, L., Frans E., Vertommen, T., Vandenhoudt, J., De Martelaer, K., Cools, S. and Geenen, M. (2013). *Sport, een spel met grenzen. Omgaan met lichamelijk of seksueel grensoverschrijdend gedrag via het vlaggensysteem.* Sensoa/ICES

Waites, M. (2005) *The Age of Consent: Young People, Sexuality, and Citizenship.* New York: Palgrave Macmillan

Walsh, K. and Brandon, L. (2012) 'Their children's first educators: Parents' views about child sexual abuse prevention education', *Journal of Child and Family Studies,* 21: 734–746.

9

GRETA

Weaving strands to allow Greta to flourish as Greta

Tania Cassidy, Anne-Marie Jackson, Motohide Miyahara and Jon Shemmell

SCHOOL OF PHYSICAL EDUCATION, SPORT AND EXERCISE SCIENCES, UNIVERSITY OF OTAGO, NEW ZEALAND

Key words: 13-year-old female, Māori, talented, Māori culture, motor learning, development, pedagogy.

Greta

Introduction: teacher's comment

I am a sports co-ordinator in a secondary school in New Zealand, and, as such, I am the first "port of call" when it comes to sport in the school. My broad job description is to oversee the organization and administration of the 150 school sports teams. This job requires me to ensure the following: teams are registered with their respective associations; teams have coaches and managers; umpires and referees are supplied when required; teams are informed as to where and when they are playing; and, teams have transport to get to and from games.

School sport, as we know it, only exists because of the voluntary work undertaken by the coaches and managers. If we had to pay people to coach and manage the teams there would be no school sport. While I enjoy my job, the hardest part is dealing with some of the coaches, especially those who see themselves as "traditionalists". Unfortunately, many of the traditional coaches do not agree with the position of Sport New Zealand[1] (and the school) that coaching should be athlete-centred. Some of these coaches continue to adopt the attitude, "it is my way or the highway". This causes tension as I am often asked by the coaches to reprimand a student, for example, when he/she has been absent from training and/or games. It is not my style to reprimand without first trying to understand the student's perspective. Recently, at the end of the winter term, the coach of the girls' 1st XV rugby team complained to me about the lack of commitment displayed by the team over the season. He was particularly disappointed with the commitment of Greta, a new member of the team who, despite only being in Year 9,[2] showed huge promise. While I agreed to have a chat, I didn't want to reprimand her, rather I wanted to get to know more about her. So I decided to try something new. My flatmate happened to be Greta's Year 9 English teacher, so between us we designed a task for the whole class. The task was to write a creative piece about the "highs and lows" of becoming a member of our high school community, particularly what it was like to join a sports team or club in their new school. This is what Greta wrote.

Greta's comment

Finally, the winter term is over and there is only one more term to go before the school year for 2012 is finished and I can't wait for it to end. This year has been a "biggie"! Not only have I started a new school, I have also shifted off the farm and now live in town, ok maybe not right in town, we still have a 5-acre[3] block, but I miss the farm. Thankfully, we still live in the same district so all my old friends from my primary school go to my new school and my aunties and grandparents still live close. I thought I would really enjoy high school because my big brother was already there so I thought I knew what to expect but it hasn't been that easy. Don't get me wrong, there have been some really good bits, like going on the school ski trip. But even that wasn't straightforward because going on that trip got me into trouble with my rugby coach who made me hold the tackle bags for two practices just because I couldn't play on the weekend I went skiing. It wasn't as if I didn't give him plenty of warning, I told him months in advance I was going to be away!

I used to love playing rugby. At my primary school there weren't very many kids and hardly any girls so if I wanted to play on the fields at playtime or during lunch I had to play rugby with the boys. I didn't mind, I was used to playing rugby, and with boys, because at home when the whānau[4] gets together, which is often, we always play "touch".[5] We even have a whānau team in the local senior competition, and even though I have just turned 13 I get quite a bit of game time because I am fit and fast and they say I am a good "dummy half". Also once a year we all travel "up north" to attend the marae[6] tournament.

When I came to high school I was looking forward to joining a girls' rugby team. At primary school we had to play rugby on Saturday for the club and usually I was the only girl playing in either team. I knew at high school that girls could play rugby in an all girls' team and I was looking forward to that. What I didn't realize was that at high school there was only one girls' team (impressively called the 1st XV). That meant, even though I was in Year 9, I was often playing with or against girls who were in Year 13 and some of them were big girls!!! Thankfully I am beginning to grow too, although that has had its pluses and minuses. I am still fast and fit but my boobs have got big and believe it or not that has really played havoc with my passing. When grandad watched me play at the start of the season he said he had never realized how much boobs could get in the way. I am really going to have to rethink how I pass if I want to keep getting better. But I am not sure if I want to keep playing rugby. I did get asked to trial for the provincial Secondary School girls' rugby team this year but I didn't end up going because grandad died on the Friday before the trial and I had to go up north for his tangi[7]. That was another time I got into trouble with my coach because he said I had wasted an opportunity to play for my province, which would have made my grandad proud.

One of the good things about coming to high school is that there is so much to do. I hardly go straight home these days because I am always being invited to go back to girls' places to hang out. I was never able to do that when I lived on the farm. Not all my new friends are sporty girls either. I met some of my new friends when I joined a social basketball team, and others are in my music class. When I am with my music friends we talk about playing in a band because I play the guitar and can sing ok and one of my friends plays the keyboard and another one plays the drums. I love Boh Runga because she is the lead singer and guitarist in her very own band called "Stellar". I have been invited to lots of parties since I have been at high school. My family joke that I must be the "rent a friend" who people invite when they want more people at their party. I don't always go to the parties because while I am flattered that people invite me, sometimes I like going home and hanging out with the animals or just kicking a ball around with my brother.

Teacher's response

When I read what Greta wrote I was flabbergasted. This was obviously a very talented and interesting young girl. How could I, and the school, best support her to develop, first as a person and secondly, as a sportswoman? Maybe the experts at the local university could provide some insight on what we could do to support her and possibly other young people who face such challenges in our school. I could get in touch with Tania Cassidy, who I know teaches a course on sports coaching at the university, and ask her to see what she and her colleagues (Anne-Marie, Jon and Motohide) think about what Greta wrote.

A Māori perspective from Anne-Marie

Well, Tania . . . Greta's case raises a number of interesting points. I take it that Greta is Māori? And that she is a *rangatahi*? *Rangatahi* is the Māori word for youth. How I think about rangatahi is to look at the word. The word *rangatahi* comes from a combination of two words, the first being *raranga* which means to weave and the second being *tahi* which means one. Thus, I conceptualise rangatahi as follows: each young person has at their fingertips their individual talents, gifts, skills and *taonga,* interests, *whānau*, cultural heritage, identity and all of these strands are woven together – as *raranga,* and this is what makes them – them, or *tahi* – one. Each rangatahi with whom we come into contact will be informed by their particular context, which reflects the above strands. So maybe one of the roles of a coach is to weave together those strands to support the development of rangatahi. Rather than compartmentalising the various strands or components individually, each operates together to support the development of the rangatahi.

For me, from a Māori perspective I would be trying to understand and bring to light those strands that make Greta unique. This, however, may not be as simple as it sounds. The broader context in which Greta is situated is one where Māori youth have poor educational achievement, multiple health issues and come from low socio-economic backgrounds (Ministry of Health 2010; Ministry of Youth Development 2008; NZQA 2012; Statistics New Zealand 2007). I believe that these issues are not the fault of rangatahi like Greta; the problem – or deficit – does not lie with Greta. The heart of the problem is rooted in structural issues such as colonisation, role of government in the oppression of Māori and the shredding of the social fabric of Māori society (Reid and Robson 2006). What we see today are the multiple ways in which these structural issues impact upon rangatahi, such as through a loss of cultural identity, and some of those impacts are being seen in poor educational achievement.

So, with that mind when considering Greta's case, one of the first things I thought about was that Greta is Māori. For rangatahi, "being Māori" can be difficult because in many aspects of their lives, such as those I've described, being Māori is associated with negative stereotypes. I would advise coaches and teachers to allow Greta to flourish first as being Māori. This is the anchor point that will connect the other strands of her being that will be developed. Some of our cultural reference points as Māori are *pepeha* and *whakapapa*. This means understanding where Greta is from, not where she was born or the town she lives in, but her Māori home. Growing up in the South Island of New Zealand, she may be Ngāi Tahu or perhaps, like many Māori, she lives outside of her *iwi* (tribal) or *hapū* (sub-tribal area). My guesses are, based on what you have described, that she has grown up outside of her tribal area because she heads back "up north" to play touch rugby with her whānau and also for her grandfather's tangi. Understanding where Greta is from will assist educators to understand her anchor point in the world. Māori are not a homogeneous group of people and each iwi, hapū and in some cases whānau has particular ways of viewing the world. So, being cognisant of where Greta is from, and the cultural practices of that place, will impact on how Greta can be Māori.

The second point I would make is about how educators can enable the strands that make Greta "Greta", and thereby to flourish. This process of "flourishment" can be achieved through fostering her *wairua*. *Wairua* is a hard word to describe, and it has multiple meanings, such as spirit, and spiritual aspects. For me, wairua is about finding ways to capture Greta's heart and mind and allow for a mind-set shift to occur from within, while still being part of something much larger. We can foster Greta's wairua through positive reinforcement, a collective approach and through providing hope. These actions can be fostered through Māori-specific pedagogies. Some of those pedagogies include: the use of the Māori social structure, such as the whānau; or *ako* which describes the process of teaching and learning, and *tuakana/teina*. The following *whakatauki* (proverb) describes the tuakana/teina process:

> *Ma te tuakana ka totika te teina, ma te teina ka totika te tuakana.* From the older sibling the younger one learns the right way to do things, and from the younger sibling the older one learns to be tolerant.

One of the troubling aspects of what Greta has written is her statement about what happened when she attended her grandfather's tangi. In my view, no matter what ethnicity the rangatahi is, this type of negative behaviour by the coach is unacceptable. From my perspective, as Māori, death has a series of *tikanga* or customs that safeguard the living world and the spiritual world. On my *marae,* tangi takes precedence over all other activities; thus, for Greta to be reprimanded for her cultural practices, her right to "be Māori", is unequivocally wrong. This is an example of the pervasiveness of colonisation. Colonisation is the replacement of one set of worldviews, values, practices, landscapes, language and power with another (Reid and Robson 2006). The example provided in Greta's narrative may seem insignificant, or something not to be taken "seriously". For many people colonisation is something that existed in the 1800s and consisted of white men with wigs wielding muskets over Māori as the "noble savage"[8] adorned in his tribal clothing like a museum artefact trapped behind a glass wall. Yet, what may seem to be nothing more than a small act of punishing a teenager for attending a tangi is, in fact, part of the process that, piece by piece, shreds Māori identity by the replacement of Māori values with another set of values. Colonisation in its various forms has consequences and those consequences act to form – layer upon layer – negative stereotypes for rangatahi, contributing to their poor educational achievement, ill-health and the low socio-economic status. For Greta to learn effectively as Māori she must be enabled to flourish and thrive as Māori.

A motor learning perspective from Jon

Greta is in the middle of a major transition with respect to her athletic performance and understandings of the role she sees sport playing in her future. She is experiencing significant changes in her body, and those changes are affecting the way she plays rugby and, no doubt, have implications for all physical activities in which she engages. In this section I discuss the rapid bodily growth that takes place during puberty and the relationship between that growth and motor performance and learning. I approach this issue directly by first investigating the effect of changing body size on the movement control centre – the brain – before addressing two other important issues for Greta that speak to the wider context of her daily life. The first is her interest in pursuing activities other than rugby, either as organized activities or just for fun, and the pressure she is facing to ignore these pursuits in the interest of her rugby "career". I will make the counter case for the potential benefits of performing movement in a variety of contexts, especially during periods of rapid growth. The second issue is that of scheduling practice times for different activities such that learning is maximised. This represents fine tuning of the practice process but, if Greta is to be involved in multiple activities, it is an idea that could avoid unnecessary delays in adapting to her changing body shape and size. Taken together, our current understanding of motor control and learning processes can guide us towards practice schedules that help teenagers to learn how their changing bodies behave physically. I will provide some suggestions for practice that may help Greta to adapt to her physical development and therefore continue to enjoy taking part in sport and exercise.

As Greta's limbs grow, the mechanical system (the body) that she needs to control and coordinate during movement is changing. This change brings with it all of the difficulties of learning to interact with an unfamiliar object. For example, modern tennis racquets are extremely light and stiff compared to older, wooden racquets. This is no problem if we only use one type of racquet, but switching quickly from an older racquet to a new one produces tremendous problems for the brain. We must learn that our familiar tennis technique will not work with the new racquet, since the same level of muscle force will now move the racquet further. The same difficulties are produced by a rapid change in the length and weight of our body segments, and it is this control problem that is primarily responsible for the deterioration of limb coordination that is common to teenagers going through puberty.

The manner in which we humans adapt to novel mechanics has received considerable research attention in the last few decades, and we now understand a great deal about how these adaptations take place. As we develop in childhood, our sensory system provides us with a rich source of information about the movements we make. Importantly, we are able to compare our sensation of movement with the motor commands that we originally used to produce the movements. By performing this comparison we develop a detailed, and entirely subconscious, understanding of the ways in which our limbs respond to any motor command. In the research literature, this understanding has been termed an 'internal model' because our brain forms a model of our limb behaviour that it can use to predict the effects of any command it produces (Imamizu and Kawato 2010; Wolpert, Miall and Kawato 1998). While we grow, we are constantly updating these internal models to accurately reflect the properties of our limbs, but this updating process takes time (Shadmehr and Mussa-Ivaldi 1994). It takes many repetitions of the same movement to accumulate enough sensory evidence to force a change to these models and, for this reason, rapid periods of growth such as the one Greta is experiencing do not allow sufficient time to be spent practicing with any specific version of her body. Her body is changing too rapidly for her to maintain an accurate internal body model. In this context, it is unsurprising that when our brain thinks of our body as being small when it is actually large, the commands created by the brain to produce movement are also inaccurate, and uncharacteristic uncoordinated movements may result.

A few interesting characteristics of internal models may help Greta's parents, teachers and rugby coach understand the coordinative benefits conferred by each activity in which she is involved. First, internal models developed during practice of one skill (e.g., passing in rugby) are subject to interference from practice of a second skill (e.g., swinging a golf club) if the two skills are practiced within a few hours of each other (Muellbacher *et al.* 2002; Shadmehr, Brashers-Krug and Mussa-Ivaldi 1995; Richardson *et al.* 2006). The interference effect reduces the benefits gained in practicing the first skill. Second, the development of accurate internal models benefits from performance feedback that emphasises movement errors (Emken and Reinkensmeyer 2005). Third, given the role they play in developing a representation of body dynamics, internal models contain elements that are not specific to the skill being learned (Goodbody and Wolpert 1998; Kadiallah, Franklin and Burdet 2012). That is, when we practice a skill, some learned information is specific to that skill and some information adds to the accuracy of our general body model. The generalizable information about our body can therefore be obtained in many movement contexts and, likewise, can provide coordination benefits for many different movement skills. Using this information in Greta's situation provides us with an interesting framework to decide which activities are preferable if her goal is to continue to become proficient in rugby.

The idea that our internal body model can be made less accurate as well as more accurate, depending on the relative timing of practice sessions, suggests that when learning skills that require very specific patterns of limb coordination (e.g., goal kicking), Greta might be well advised to avoid practicing other skills for a few hours afterward. Since making mistakes is actually beneficial for improving her internal body model, practice activities in which success is measured very precisely could help her internal model keep pace with her physical development. Performing movements in unstable environments like snow and ice would also amplify the effects of movement errors. So instead of regarding her skiing trip as a waste of time, it would be worthwhile for the rugby coach to consider the advantages of having access to snow for a period of time and to give her some planned activities to try out. In the same way, the fact that internal models are somewhat generalizable, means that coordinative improvements will result not just from practising rugby, but from skiing, playing the guitar and many other activities. Far from being encouraged to spend all her time on rugby, Greta should be encouraged to try many different types of unfamiliar movement skills. The vast amount of sensory information and error correction that takes place when she tries new movements will enhance the accuracy of her body model and therefore improve her performance in all movements. By trying a range of activities she might even have fun and rediscover the fun she had playing rugby.

A developmental perspective from Motohide

The sports co-ordinator may already know what I have to say as a consequence of being involved in youth sports. Greta is obviously in the midst of adolescence, and the theoretical knowledge on adolescence stems from group data, thus such knowledge may not necessarily be applicable to Greta's individual context. Nonetheless, it may still be useful to recognize what a majority of adolescents typically go through, and what their developmental trajectories would be (depending on their personal experiences) during this critical period. With this recognition, the sports co-ordinator may be able to offer better informed advice when she next interacts with the rugby coach.

According to Erik Erikson's classic theory of psychosocial development (Erikson 1959), adolescence is a stage of potential crisis of identity vs. role confusion. The problem, as perceived by the coach, is Greta's lack of commitment to rugby and her spending time exploring alternatives (e.g., basketball, music band, parties). One explanation as to why Greta is not fully committed to playing rugby is that she is experiencing an identity *moratorium* (Marcia 1966), a status that explains her desire to explore alternatives. The perceived problem arises because the coach does not share the same identity status as Greta.

As the saying goes, Rome was not built in a day. While asserting the importance of informing young people about the value of *serious leisure,* Stebbins (1999: 5) specified that leisure educators, like the sports co-ordinator and the rugby coach can 'help individual youth discover and get started in the types [of leisure that] they *find most interesting*'. The important point here is that a leisure activity to which people commit themselves seriously must be – primarily – of personal interest. According to Greta's essay, her enthusiasm for rugby seems to be waning which means that rugby is unlikely to be her serious leisure activity at present.

The rugby coach may argue that it is not possible to decide whether an activity is interesting or not, unless Greta fully immerses herself in the activity. To encourage Greta's total engagement, however, it is neither effective nor 'educationally sound to have beneficial physical activities, [e.g., hold the tackle bags for two practices][9], become unpleasant because they have been used as punishment' (Smoll and Smith 1987: 241). Evidence suggests that a negative approach such as this may contribute, in the long run, to negative images of the body and physical activity (Maliha 2004) as well as a lack of enjoyment and withdrawal (Richardson, Rosenthal and Burak 2012). The coach clearly needs to learn about the benefits of adopting a positive approach to coaching, communicating, understanding, and relating with young players.

It may be reassuring for teachers and coaches to know that it is acceptable for young people to be *indecisive* about different physical activities. Indeed, Elkind (1967), a renowned developmental psychologist, listed this as one of the characteristics of a normal course of development for adolescents. The time pressure to make commitment emanates from the values and inflexibility of society. It is interesting to note, for example, that some societies don't even recognize the concepts of "adolescence" or "leisure time". In contemporary Aotearoa[10] (New Zealand), Year 9 students are generally allowed to explore various areas of self identity, and the freedom and responsibility associated with this have consequences that Greta is learning to live with.

More recently, Erikson's identity theory and Marcia's four phase model have been criticized as being too independence- and achievement-oriented. For example, some women (Gilligan 1982), people in Māori culture (Penetito 2000) and the Pacific ethnicities in New Zealand (Tupuola 2004) do not necessarily establish such a clear-cut, static self identity or go through linear phase transitions. Instead, it has been argued that there are many examples where people would rather form temporary flexible identities through a labyrinth of personal relationships by considering all complex contemporary sociocultural variables. This sort of flexible identity formation, or *diasporic* as Tupuola (2004) called it, may be relevant to Greta. Not only does she fall into at least one of the socio-demographic categories listed above, but she also seems capable of deftly relating to a diverse network of people in different contexts. Indeed, many people – female or male, young or old, of any ethnic origin, seem able to form a diaspora identity in the contemporary world.

I now shift my focus from Greta's psychosocial development to her *movement skill development, physical growth and maturity.* The coach evaluates Greta's rugby skills, presumably coupled with her growing body, as showing "huge promise". Anthropometric and physical performance measures of male and female rugby players indicate that players at the higher levels are larger in size and perform better on physical tests than players at lower levels (Quarrie *et al.* 1995). According to Greta and the coach, her physical size and performance sound auspicious, and thus Greta's *body scale*[11] (Newell, Scully, Tenenbaum and Hardiman 1989) appears favorable for playing rugby. However, her illustration of breast development, which increasingly interferes with her passing movements, adds a new subjective voice 'on a subject that has been given little visibility within mainstream academia' (Lee 1997: 460). It is interesting to note that breast development has not been openly discussed in a functional context in sports. To date, female breast development has been objectively categorized into five stages in relation to the timing of menarche (e.g., Christensen *et al.* 2010). Moreover, the timing of menarche has been associated with psychosocial events (Romans, Martin, Gendall and Herbison 2003; Boden, Fergusson and Norwood 2011). For this reason, Greta's physical maturation status is of interest as it illustrates the interactions between the physical and psychosocial domains. Given the fact that the mean age of menarche in Aotearoa (New Zealand) women is slightly under 13 years of age (Ministry of Health 2002), and that there is no mention of her romantic interaction with boys or girls, Greta might or might not have reached menarche. When she hits "full blown" puberty, she may develop more interest in romantic interactions, which may further change her interest in all girls' rugby.

To sum up, it may be useful to remind the coach that the exploration of alternatives and indecisiveness are significant developmental characteristics of adolescence. To encourage Greta's further participation – and that of others like her – a developmental perspective suggests that it would be helpful to avoid punitive exercise and, instead, to employ positive coaching strategies.

A pedagogical perspective from Tania

The purpose of this section is to draw on the literature, as well as the expert commentaries presented above, to identify pedagogically sound practices that coaches could reflect upon and consider when designing and delivering their coaching sessions. The discussion is framed around three concepts, which can be thought of as the "3 Rs": risk, resilience and resourcefulness; and it is within this framework that the possible implications for coaches will be identified.

Risk

At the beginning of the chapter, the sports co-ordinator was described as wanting to "support" Greta to develop as a young (sports)woman and, in his own way, the coach also wanted to support Greta to become a good rugby player. The desire to support young people can be viewed as reflecting a humanitarian discourse which, according to Withers and Batten, is 'grounded in concerns about *harm, danger, care* and *support,* for those young people who might be at-Risk' (in Kelly 1998: 27, [*italics in original*]). Drawing on the work of Rose, Kelly pointed out that the power of this discourse is illustrated by the number of interventions that have been constructed in an 'attempt to regulate the young people's behaviours and dispositions' (p. 26). A number of interventions have used sport as a vehicle by which to change behaviours (for examples see Hellison and Martinek 2006). It is, therefore, useful to reflect on why participation in sport is promoted as a positive activity. There are numerous examples of programmes that are based on the assumption that participation in sport can reduce the possibility of young people becoming involved in "at-Risk" behaviours. Yet, one of the criticisms of the youth at-risk literature is that the young people being labelled as "at-Risk" are often those 'whose appearance, language, culture, values, home communities, and family structures . . . do not match those of the dominant culture' (Howard, Dryden and Johnson 1999: 308). Drawing on the work of Goodlad and Keating, Howard *et al.* (1999: 308) suggested that this tendency illustrates the ways in which 'ideological factors may be implicated in the construction or application of the concept of risk'.

Ideological factors may have persuaded Greta's coach to consider her to be "at-Risk" of not achieving her "potential", despite identifying her as a player who showed "huge promise". Did the coach label Greta as being "at-Risk" because she was a young, female and Māori and missed a provincial trial to attend her grandfather's tangi? That Greta "got into trouble" with the coach because she attended her grandfather's tangi is unconscionable but highlights what Anne-Marie, in her expert commentary above, called the pervasiveness of colonisation and how "being Māori" can be difficult because of the associated negative stereotypes. Added to that, being a 13-year old female in some cultures is – of itself – associated with being "at-Risk" because of the observed rates of young females "dropping out" of sport around this age and the reported "difficulties" associated with "becoming a teenager". Kelly (1998: 33 [*italics in original*]) problematized this negative view of "becoming" by highlighting that it is informed by a youth at-Risk discourse, which 'mobilises a form of probabilistic thinking, about certain *preferred,* or *ideal* Adult futures and present behaviours and dispositions of Youth'. He also pointed out that the youth at-Risk discourse 'rests on identifying and quantifying a range of factors which place at-Risk those "teenagers" unable to "effect" a 'secure transition to adulthood' (p. 34). Both Jon and Motohide, in their expert commentaries earlier in this chapter, viewed Greta as being in a transitory period, which has possible implications for her movement patterns and involvement in physical activities; and this is another manifestation of the pervasiveness of the at-Risk discourse. Probabilistic thinking is also apparent in the sport talent identification and development literature. Even those who recognise that 'the determinants of [senior] performance and the determinants of potential during adolescence are likely to be disparate' (Button 2011: 20) still advocate for a set of procedures that see:

> development coaches pay most attention to those factors that are likely to impact on the capacity of a young athlete to translate early potential into successful performances at the senior level, rather than those that aid their current achievement.
>
> (p. 20)

Resilience

The stated goal of many Western governments is to increase opportunities for young people to be involved in physical activities and to participate across their lifespan. In order to achieve this goal, it may be useful for coaches to shift away from thinking probabilistically. In response to the critiques of the at-Risk discourses, a paradigm shift has emerged which has resulted in the discussion moving from *risk* to *resilience* (Howard *et al.* 1999). While there are many definitions of resilience, one that reflects a commonly held interpretation is that resilience is 'the process of, capacity for, or outcome of successful adaptation despite challenging or threatening circumstances' (p. 307). Resilience, which focuses on an individual's *strength,* has been emphasised in the current New Zealand Health and Physical Education curriculum, (http://nzcurriculum.tki.org.nz/Curriculum-documents/ The-New-Zealand-Curriculum/Learning-areas/Health-and-physical-education), specifically in the Mental Health Key Area of Learning of the curriculum and subsequent resources (http:// health.tki.org.nz/Key-collections/Curriculum-in-action/Making-Meaning).

The concept of resilience has also emerged in the sporting context. In summarizing and cri-tiquing the literature on the orthodox conception of talent identification, which is dominated by performance or physique-based models, Button (2011: 19) made the claim that '[ir]respective of physical make-up, unless athletes actively interact with the environment and have the resilience to cope with the challenges and set backs they encounter as they strive to develop, they will fail to excel'. In 2009, the *International Society of Sport Psychology* published a position statement on early specialization and sampling. It stated that a 'comprehensive approach to sport expertise should consider the entire situation that is comprised of the person, the task, the environment, and the complex interplay of these components' (Côté, Lidor and Hackfort 2009: 7). The *Society* went on to make seven claims 'regarding the role that sampling and deliberate play, as opposed to special-ization and deliberate practice, can have during childhood in promoting continued participation and elite performance in sport' (p. 7). The position statement is consistent with Jon's expert comment above about the importance of coaches, parents and teachers being open minded enough to consider the characteristics of internal models and to 'understand the coordinative benefits conferred by *each* activity' in which Greta is involved.

Despite Jon advocating the benefits of being involved in a broad programme of physical activity, he did suggest that it would be useful for coaches to give consideration to the timing of various practice sessions so that the learning of specific motor patterns was not compromised. Being open-minded is one attribute that Dewey (1916) suggested is necessary in order to be able to reflect on a practice. If members of a coaching community were willing to reflect criti-cally upon their practices and be open minded to new evidence, they may be more enthusiastic to support Motohide's expert comment above that coaches should adopt a 'positive approach to coaching' and examine the relationships they develop with the young players with whom they are working.

Many questions still remain regarding the resilience of athletes to cope with unstable periods in their development. In an attempt to answer some of these questions, Button (2011: 19) proposed that it would be useful to view development as 'a construct that evolves as a result of active interactions between an individual and his/her environment, and that this evolu-tion is facilitated through the application of psychological behaviours'. This view could link into broader cultural-historical and ecological perspectives on development, e.g., Vygotsky, Bronfenbrenner and Māori perspectives (Drewery and Bird 2004) that also recognise youth development as multi-faceted, complex and dynamic. The assumptions underpinning these broad perspectives on development are consistent with some interpretations of sport pedagogy, specifically those which consider there to be an interaction between how one learns, how one teaches, what is being taught and the context in which it is being taught (Cassidy 2000; Cassidy, Jones and Potrac 2009; Jones, Armour and Potrac 2004). This approach leads to ques-tions, not only about the resilience of athletes to cope, but also about the concept of resilience itself. For example: are the variables associated with resilience just antonyms of the variables previously populating the at-Risk literature? Is resilience a distinct quality that people could possess? Can resilience be distilled into a few global aggregates? (Rutter in Howard *et al.* 1999). Others have pointed out that we can be more, or less, resilient at various points in our lives depending on the accumulation of experience and the interactions we have with individuals and the environment (Masten, Best and Garmezy 1990). More recently MacKinnon and Derickson (2012: 2) argued that the concept of resilience is conservative because it 'privileges established social structures, which are often shaped by unequal power relations and injustice' and the onus is placed on individuals 'to become more resilient and adaptable to a range of external threats'.

Resourcefulness

If coaches design programmes or have expectations that are, implicitly or explicitly, informed by at-Risk and/or resilience discourses, it is possible their practices will not resonate with the beliefs or experiences of young people. If a discord does occur, it is possible this is because the young people are not using the same criteria as adults to make judgments regarding what constitutes risk and resilience (Howard *et al.* 1999). To overcome this dissonance, coaches could reflect on what they are doing to support the athlete to become resourceful. MacKinnon and Derickson (2012: 15) identify the value of resourcefulness as the ability to foster 'self-determination through local skills and "folk" knowledge'. Moreover, resourcefulness is conceptualized as a process 'rather than as a clearly identifiable condition amenable to empirical measurement or quantification' (p. 12). When resourcefulness is interpreted in this way, coaches have an opportunity to acknowledge and integrate characteristics that are specific to the athlete and their context. This view supports Anne-Marie's comment above that it would be useful for coaches, when working with young people, to acknowledge and assist with incorporating – or weaving – the various strands or elements in the young person's life together, rather than viewing the strands as operating individually and possibly in competition with one another. As Motohide pointed out above, Greta already appears to be very adept at relating to a 'diverse network of people in different contexts'; so the question becomes: What can the coach do to build on this? Enabling Greta to continue to flourish may put the coach in a situation where he will be required to demonstrate his own resourcefulness. Time will tell how resourceful coaches can become.

Notes

1. *Sport New Zealand* (*Sport NZ*) is the new name for the government organisation responsible for sport and recreation.
2. Year 9 is the first year of secondary school, which usually equates to 13 years old.
3. 5 acres is approximately 2 hectares.
4. A New Zealand Māori word that can mean *family*.
5. An abbreviation term used for *touch rugby*. Touch rugby is an adapted 7-a-side version of the 15-a-side game of rugby.
6. A New Zealand Māori word that means *tribal meeting ground*.
7. A New Zealand Māori word that literally means *to mourn or to cry*, but it is also used to refer to a Māori funeral rite.
8. The term coined by Rousseau (Hokowhitu 2003).
9. The original examples are running laps or doing push-ups.
10. Māori name for New Zealand, meaning *the land of the long white cloud*.
11. To date, the tasks for body scale have been limited to hand prehension and locomotion following Newell *et al.* (1989), and jumping over an object (Kluwe *et al.* 2012).

References

Boden, J.M., Fergusson, D.M. and Norwood, L.J. (2011) 'Age of menarche and psychosocial outcomes in a New Zealand birth cohort', *Journal of the American Academy of Child and Adolescent Psychiatry,* 50: 132–140.

Button, A. (2011) 'Aims, principles and methodologies in talent identification and development', in D. Collins, A. Button, and H. Richards (eds) *Performance Psychology. A Practitioner's Guide* (pp. 9–29). Edinburgh: Elsevier.

Cassidy, T. (2000) Investigating the pedagogical process in physical education teacher education. Unpublished doctoral dissertation, Deakin University, Australia.

Cassidy, T., Jones, R. and Potrac, P. (2009) *Understanding Sports Coaching: The Social, Cultural and Pedagogical Foundations of Coaching Practice,* 2nd edn, London: Routledge.

Christensen, K.Y., Maisonet, M., Rubin, C., Holmes, A., Flanders, W.D., Heron, J., Ness, A., Drews-Botsch, C., Dominguez, C., McGeehin, M.A. and Marcus, M. (2010) 'Progression through puberty in girls enrolled in a contemporary British cohort', *Journal of Adolescent Health,* 47: 282–289.

Côté, J., Lidor, R. and Hackfort, D. (2009) 'ISSP position stand: To sample or to specialize? Seven postulates about youth sport activities that lead to continued participation and elite performance', *International Journal of Sport & Exercise Psychology,* 7(1): 7–17.

Dewey, J. (1916) *Democracy and Education: An Introduction to the Philosophy of Education.* New York: Macmillan.

Drewery, W. and Bird, L. (2004) *Human Development in Aotearoa. A Journey Through Life,* 2nd edn, Sydney: McGraw Hill.

Elkind, D. (1967) 'Egocentrism in adolescence', *Child Development,* 13: 1025–1034.

Emken, J.L. and Reinkensmeyer, D.J. (2005) 'Robot-enhanced motor learning: Accelerating internal model formation during locomotion by transient dynamic amplification', *IEEE Transactions on Neural Systems and Rehabilitation Engineering,* 13(1): 33–39.

Erikson, E.H. (1959) *Identity and the Life Cycle. Selected Papers.* New York: International Universities Press.

Gilligan, C. (1982) *In a Different Voice: Psychological Theory and Women's Development.* Cambridge, MA: Harvard University Press.

Goodbody, S.J. and Wolpert, D.M. (1998) 'Temporal and amplitude generalization in motor learning', *Journal of Neurophysiology,* 79(4): 1825–1838.

Hellison, D. and Martinek, T. (2006) 'Social and individual responsibility programs', in D. Kirk, D. Macdonald and M. O'Sullivan (eds) *The Handbook of Physical Education* (pp. 610–626). Thousand Oaks: Sage.

Hokowhitu, B. (2003) '"Physical beings": Stereotypes, sport and the "physical education" of New Zealand Māori', *Culture, Sport, Society,* 6(2–3): 192–218.

Howard, S., Dryden, J. and Johnson, B. (1999) 'Childhood resilience: Review and critique of literature', *Oxford Review of Education,* 25(3): 307–323.

Imamizu, H. and Kawato, M. (2010) 'Cerebellar internal models: Implications for the dexterous use of tools', *The Cerebellum,* 11(2): 325–335.

Jones, R.L., Armour, K.A. and Potrac, P.A. (2004) *Sports Coaching Cultures: From Practice to Theory.* London: Routledge.

Kadiallah, A., Franklin, D.W. and Burdet, E. (2012) 'Generalization in adaptation to stable and unstable dynamics', *PLoS ONE,* 7(10): e45075.

Kelly, P. (1998) Risk and the regulation of youth(ful) identities in an age of manufactured uncertainty. Unpublished doctoral thesis, Deakin University, Australia.

Kluwe, M., Miyahara, M. and Heveldt, K. (2012) 'A case study to evaluate balance training with movement test items and through teaching observation: Beyond specificity and transfer of learning', *Physical Education & Sport Pedagogy,* 17: 463–475.

Lee, J. (1997) 'Never innocent: Breasted experiences in women's bodily narratives of puberty', *Feminism & Psychology,* 7: 453–474.

MacKinnon, D. and Derickson, K. (2012) 'From resilience to resourcefulness: A critique of resilience policy and activism', *Progress in Human Geography:* August, 1–18.

Maliha, K. (2004) 'Body image and physical activity', *Visions Journal,* 2: 37–38.

Marcia, J.E. (1966) 'Development and validation of ego-identity status', *Journal of Personality & Social Psychology,* 3: 551–558.

Masten, A., Best, K. & Garmezy, N. (1990). 'Resilience and development: Contributions from the study of children who overcome adversity', *Development and Psychopathology,* 2: 425–444.

Ministry of Health (2002) *New Zealand Youth Health Status Report.* Wellington: Ministry of Health.

Ministry of Health (2010) *Tatau Kahukura. Māori Health Chart Book 2010.* Wellington: Ministry of Health.

Ministry of Youth Development (2008) *Suicide.* Online. Available HTTP: <www.youthstats.myd.govt.nz/indicator/healthy/suicide/index.html> (accessed 30 September, 2013).

Muellbacher, W., Ziemann, U., Wissel, J., Dang, N., Kofler, M., Facchini, S., Boroojerdi, B., Poewe, W. and Hallett, M. (2002) 'Early consolidation in human primary motor cortex', *Nature,* 415(6872): 640–644.

Newell, K.M., Scully, D.M., Tenenbaum, F. and Hardiman, S. (1989) 'Body scale and the development of prehension', *Developmental Psychobiology,* 22: 1–13.

NZQA (2012) *Annual Report on NCEA and New Zealand Scholarship Data and Statistics (2011).* Wellington: New Zealand Qualifications Authority.

Penetito, W. (2000) 'The social construction of Māori identity: The role of tastes and preferences', in L. B. W. Drewery (ed.) *Human Development in Aotearoa* (pp. 52–65). Sydney: McGraw-Hill.

Quarrie, K.L., Handcock, P., Waller, A.E., Chalmers, D.J., Toomey, M.J. and Wilson, B.D. (1995) 'The New Zealand rugby injury and performance project: Anthropometric and physical performance characteristics of players', *British Journal of Sports Medicine,* 29: 263–270.

Reid, P. and Robson, B. (2006) 'The state of Māori health', in M. Mulholland (ed.) *State of the Māori Nation. Twenty-first Century Issues in Aotearoa* (pp. 17–31). Auckland: Reed Publishing Limited.

Richardson, A.G., Overduin, S.A., Valero-Cabre, A., Padoa-Schioppa, C., Pascual Leone, A., Bizzi, E. and Press, D.Z. (2006) 'Disruption of primary motor cortex before learning impairs memory of movement dynamics', *Journal of Neuroscience,* 26(48): 12466–12470.

Richardson, K., Rosenthal, M. and Burak, L. (2012) 'Exercise as punishment: An application of theory of planned behaviour', *American Journal of Health Education,* 43: 356–365.

Romans, S.E., Martin, J.M., Gendall, K. and Herbison, G.P. (2003) 'Age of menarche: the role of some psychosocial factors', *Psychological Medicine,* 33: 933–939.

Shadmehr, R., Brashers-Krug, T. and Mussa-Ivaldi, F. (1995) 'Interference in learning internal models of inverse dynamics in humans', *Advances in Neural Information Processing Systems,* 7: 1117–1124.

Shadmehr, R. and Mussa-Ivaldi, F.A. (1994) 'Adaptive representation of dynamics during learning of a motor task', *The Journal of Neuroscience,* 14(5): 3208–3224.

Smoll, F.L. and Smith, R.E. (1987) 'Principles of effective coach-athletic interactions', in V. Seefeldt (ed.) *Handbook for Youth Sports Coaches.* Washington, D.C.: American Alliance for Health, Physical Education, Recreation, and Dance.

Statistics New Zealand (2007) *QuickStats About Māori.* Wellington: Statistics New Zealand.

Stebbins, R.A. (1999) 'Serious leisure, leisure education and wayward youth', paper presented at the conference on Leisure, Education and Youth at Risk, Monterrey, Mexico: Universidad Mexicana del Noreste.

Tupuola, A. (2004) 'Pasifika edgewalkers: Complicating the achieved identity status in youth research', *Journal of Intercultural Studies,* 25: 87–100.

Wolpert, D.M., Miall, R.C. and Kawato, M. (1998) 'Internal models in the cerebellum', *Trends in Cognitive Sciences,* 2(9): 338–347.

10

ONNI

A lucky adolescent in Finland

Pilvikki Heikinaro-Johansson, Terhi Huovinen, Eileen McEvoy, Arja Piirainen and Raili Välimaa

DEPARTMENT OF SPORT SCIENCES, DEPARTMENT OF HEALTH SCIENCES, UNIVERSITY OF JYVÄSKYLÄ, FINLAND

Key words: 13-year-old male, computers, physically inactive, physical education, health education, home-school partnerships, physiotherapy, pedagogy.

Onni

Onni (meaning "luck") is a 13-year-old Finnish boy. An only child, he lives with his parents in a second-floor apartment in a middle-class, suburban neighbourhood in Jyväskylä, the city in which he was born. Onni's father, a consultant in the field of information technology, and his mother, an entrepreneur, both work long hours and struggle to maintain the balance between work and home life. When his parents are away on business, as is often the case, Onni is cared for by his grandparents who live nearby. Due to the amount of time he spends alone, Onni has developed a particularly independent spirit.

Onni begins seventh grade today, which means he has completed elementary school and is now in middle school. He is woken by his mother as she leaves for work: "Wake up my sleepy-head or you will be late for school. Breakfast is on the table. Don't forget your schoolbag and PE outfit. Love you."

Onni is anxious about beginning in this new school, especially as most of his classmates attended different elementary schools and he will not know many of them. Onni does not usually have any close friends at school and sometimes feels lonely. This feeling of loneliness is not unique to Onni; according to a recent Health Behaviour among School-aged Children (HSBC) study, 8% of boys and 15% of girls in the seventh grade in Finland feel lonely either very often or quite often (Kämppi *et al.* 2012). Onni is a quiet boy, small for his age. This is compounded by the fact that, as he was born in December, some of his classmates are almost one year older than Onni.

An imaginative child, Onni can draw very well and is highly proficient at various computer programs. In the evenings, he spends a lot of time on his computer playing video games, communicating with virtual friends and exploring software programmes. This is not unusual for children in Finland. A recent study shows that approximately 15% of nine- to ten-year-old Finnish children are technologically skilled, producing and sharing their own material online through, for example, blogs and videos. Onni is often tired during the school day because he stays up late, sometimes playing video games or editing videos until dawn. He often suffers from neck problems and backaches but, like many boys of his age (Välimaa 2000), he prefers not to complain.

Physical activity has not played a significant role in Onni's life. He has never belonged to any sports club and is not physically active during his leisure time. Like most pupils in his school, Onni travels to school either by bicycle or on foot. According to the results of a recent national evaluation study, approximately 75% of 15-year-old pupils in Finland, whose home is located less than five kilometres from school, actively commute to school throughout the year (Palomäki and Heikinaro-Johansson 2011). Although he enjoys being outdoors, his active commute to school is the only regular physical activity in which Onni participates.

Onni's new school is a typical Finnish middle school with almost 400 pupils. It is mid-August and the first day of the school year is not for pupils, it is a dedicated planning day for staff. This planning day is a statutory requirement but it is also an important opportunity for staff to consider the priorities for the coming academic year. In Finland, education has been identified as an essential part of the development of the nation and national identity. High-quality professional development is a strategic imperative in efforts to maximise learning outcomes. Teachers have always played an important and respected role in society (Sahlberg 2011) and are seen as highly educated, pedagogical experts (Jakku-Sihvonen *et al.* 2012; Sahlberg 2011; Välijärvi *et al.* 2007; Westbury *et al.* 2005).

During the planning day, the principal and other teachers agree to use the School Wellbeing Profile as a tool for measuring and enhancing the school's overall wellbeing. The Profile is based on the School Wellbeing Model (Konu and Rimpelä 2002). According to this model (Figure 10.1), wellbeing is associated with teaching and education on one hand, and with

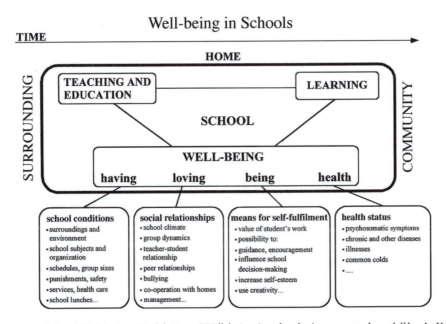

FIGURE 10.1 School Well-being Model. From 'Well-being in schools: A conceptual model' by A. Konu and M. Rimpelä, 2002, *Health Promotion International,* 17(1), p. 83.

learning and achievements on the other. Wellbeing is assessed under four categories: (i) school conditions, (ii) social relationships, (iii) means for self-fulfilment, and (iv) health status. The importance of the influence on wellbeing of the home, school, community and surroundings is also an important feature of the model. This tool is important both in assessing how well the school is supporting the wellbeing of its pupils and also in validating the health promotion efforts undertaken by staff.

After much discussion, it is decided that this year the focus will be on pupils' health and wellbeing, with the central objectives (i) to foster co-operation between classmates, and (ii) to enhance and consolidate home-school partnerships. The interaction between home and school is a key focus in the National Core Curriculum for Basic Education (NCCBE 2004). Each class is assigned a homeroom teacher who will bear responsibility for the educational care of the relevant class group. Homeroom teachers are expected to monitor pupils' studies, assess their needs, and relay pertinent information to parents and guardians.

Onni's homeroom teacher is Mikael, a 40-year-old teacher with 15 years teaching experience in basic education. Mikael is one of four physical education teachers in the school. He and the other three teachers (one male, two female), like most physical education teachers in Finland, graduated from the University of Jyväskylä and teach health education as their second subject. A qualified physical education teacher is expected to be an expert in physical wellbeing and, as such, he or she must be able to incorporate the content of several basic disciplines, from biology to social sciences and their paradigms, as the need arises (Klemola, Heikinaro-Johansson and O'Sullivan 2012; Palomäki and Heikinaro-Johansson 2008). In Finland, the status of a physical education teacher is equal to that of other teachers and as a profession it is very popular. Finnish teachers are afforded a great deal of autonomy and independence (Jakku-Sihvonen and Niemi 2006).

Mikael will be Onni's homeroom teacher, physical education teacher and health education teacher. The National Core Curriculum requires that seventh grade pupils receive 90 minutes (two lessons) of compulsory physical education and, on average, one 45-minute lesson of health education per week. So Mikael will be seeing a lot of Onni.

On the second day of the semester Onni, along with the other pupils in the school, begin lessons. It is on this day that Onni and his classmates meet Mikael. The day starts with some teambuilding activities. The intention is to strengthen group cohesion, encourage friendship between pupils and allow the teacher to get a first impression of the individual pupils and their needs. Onni seems to enjoy the activities. Mikael perceives Onni to be a quiet little boy. "It is a positive thing that Onni did not join the disruptive behaviour of some of his classmates. He did not interrupt the lesson or try to speak over the other children. Nice boy!" thought Mikael after the first school day.

Onni's physical education lessons

Mikael spends the first physical education lesson planning, together with the pupils, the physical education program for the year. The concept of active participation by pupils is a central tenet of the collaborative school system (NCCBE 2004). Mikael wants to take into account the individuality of each of his pupils and allow them to be part of the planning and decision-making process. To this end, he decides to have the pupils fill in a questionnaire outlining their hobbies, physical activity preferences, health issues and hopes for the physical education lessons.

Onni described his health, habits and preferences:

> *My favourite hobby is playing computer games; one of my favourites is called Batman Arkham City.*
> *I also like to develop programmes of my own, and drawing is fun. In physical education, I hope that*
> *we don't just play football or ice hockey. I'd like to try something new. And I prefer to practice by*
> *myself, not with a group or team. My health? Well, sometimes I have problems with my neck, and*
> *a pain in my lower back also. I am not sure if I will always be able to take part in PE.*

Mikael wants all his pupils to be motivated and have fun during physical education lessons. The fundamental goal in his teaching is to promote physical literacy. Pupils should feel confident about their potential for progress and success, and a key to this is the development of physical competence. They need to be able to process information and reach understanding in order to create the knowledge that they can rely on to maintain a healthy pattern of physical activity as they grow older. This has clear implications for teaching-learning approaches. In order to develop physical literacy, pupils need to experience a range of activities, challenges and opportunities. The climate in which this development takes place is also crucial. All lessons should evolve in an atmosphere where each pupil feels valued and experiences success at his/her own level so that each child is optimally motivated, irrespective of the activity or setting. Teaching two different subjects gives Mikael the opportunity to get to know his pupils well. Often pupils behave and express themselves differently in different teaching contexts, whether in the classroom, in the gym, or outdoors.

During the physical education lesson, Mikael observes that Onni does not participate very actively. He often withdraws from activities to stand or sit near the wall. While other pupils are eagerly waiting for their turn, Onni usually goes to the end of the line. Mikael notices that Onni even tries to give his place to a classmate in order to avoid performing a task. Bigger boys in the class laugh at Onni's attempts to catch a ball or perform other tasks. Mikael notes that Onni is a timid child, and he does not have very diverse motor skills.

While ballgames lessons often take place in single gender classes in Finland (Heikinaro-Johansson, Palomäki and Kurppa 2011), dance lessons are usually organized in mixed gender groups. When Onni's class have a dance lesson, none of the girls are interested in being his partner. "He is too tiny to be my dance partner" a girl from his class argues. Onni does not show up at the next dance lesson.

Onni's health education lessons

Health education, as a school subject, provides an opportunity to allow pupils to understand and live through their own developmental challenges. As with physical education, Mikael begins his health education lessons by planning, in collaboration with the pupils, the programme for the year. Mikael uses a triangle-method for the planning lesson. The pupils first think about the topic individually (*what does health mean to you?*), then they discuss in pairs (*what is important for the health of young people of your age?*), and finally they form groups of four to ponder what they would like to learn at school about health and wellbeing. Mikael collects these ideas and attempts to match them to the national curriculum and the school's own curriculum. As is usually the case, Mikael finds that, while the pupils' wish-list begins with sex education and alcohol, the individual answers which pupils give directly to the teacher reveal that many pupils want to learn about other issues such as emotions, quarrels at home and with friends, sleep and growing up.

Seventh-grade health education lessons typically include themes that are related to young people's self-knowledge, social skills, emotional skills, and daily rhythms (concerning sleep, nutrition and physical activity). Health education is a pupil- and action-oriented subject which aims to enhance pupils' knowledge and skills concerning understanding, managing and enhancing their own health and wellbeing and to increase pupils' capacity to take care of the health and wellbeing of others (NCCBE 2004). The subject also aims to increase pupils' skills to critically observe and analyze contemporary health-related phenomenon (e.g. consumer culture, media messages related to body-images).

Teachers have the authority to concentrate on themes or issues that are interesting to the specific pupils, even if they are not in the curriculum for the grade in question. Time pressure is a stress factor encountered in school that is connected to pupils' psychosomatic symptoms and thus also negatively impacts on pupils' wellbeing and mental health (Konu and Rimpelä 2002). For this reason, Mikael chooses to concentrate on only a few themes and organize the teaching and learning of health education around them.

In line with the school's key aim, to support every child's health and wellbeing, Mikael always tries to differentiate his teaching (the extent, depth, and progress of learning) to suit each of his pupils. The teacher's orientation towards pupils' active participation makes health education lessons a little difficult for Onni but the use Mikael makes of multiple teaching methods gradually relieves this tension.

Based on international studies, the national School Health Promotion Study in which their school participated, and the answers to the questionnaire pupils completed during their physical education lesson, Mikael knows that many pupils in his class have several subjective health complaints. Research indicates that approximately one in four Finnish boys experience headaches on a weekly basis, one in five regularly experience neck/shoulder pain, and lower back pain regularly affects one in six. The figure is even higher for girls with more than one third experiencing weekly headaches and/or neck/shoulder pain and almost one fifth suffering from regular lower back pain (School Health Promotion Study 2010/2011). As children age, health complaints become more common (World Health Organization 2012), as does the practice of medicating to combat these symptoms (Gobina *et al.* 2011).

Health education provides an opportunity to teach school-aged children to correctly interpret their bodily feelings and to respond appropriately to these feelings. To make his pupils more aware of their health, Mikael suggests that pupils keep a diary of their own wellbeing for one week. In the diary they record information such as physical activity participation, eating habits and sleeping habits.

The participatory methods employed by the teacher enhance the pupils' learning of social skills and self-awareness. The social skills theme is one which continues throughout the year in health education. Social relationships at school strongly influence the subjective health and wellbeing of children (Konu and Rimpelä 2002, Currie *et al.* 2004, Danielsen *et al.* 2009). Self-awareness is another central theme of health education and is the key to the diary task pupils are given in their first lesson.

In health education, boys and girls are taught together. Mikael observes that Onni is quiet, self-effacing, but theoretically knowledgeable. However, he appears to have trouble finding partners when tasks require group work. Both the boys and girls of his class avoid him. It also becomes clear that Onni is often tired, and he has difficulty concentrating on work and study. Schoolchildren's daily rhythms are critical for their wellbeing and academic achievement. Wolfson and Carskadon (2003) in their review of research, found that self-reported shortened total sleep time, erratic sleeping patterns, late bed and rise times, and poor sleep quality are negatively associated with the academic performance of adolescents. "I wonder if he has slept at all last night!" Mikael thought after Monday morning's health education lesson.

Maximising the school-home partnership

Throughout the first few weeks in school, Mikael gained an insight into Onni's needs through careful observation during health education and physical education lessons. Mikael had concerns regarding this small boy, and many of his colleagues shared similar concerns. As Onni's homeroom teacher, Mikael decided to contact Onni's parents using Wilma, the nationwide web interface for pupil administration. Wilma allows pupils to register for courses, check grades, read announcements and communicate with teachers. In addition, teachers can grade pupils, register absences and update pupil profiles. Teachers can also communicate directly with pupils and guardians. Guardians can see and approve absences, communicate with teachers and other guardians, view pupil profiles, and read announcements.

When Mikael made contact through Wilma, Onni's parents requested that he call them. It was Onni's mother, Johanna, who answered when he called. Mikael explained that Onni had not participated in the dance lesson the previous week and was very tired in the mornings. The conversation continued as follows:

Mikael: I'm concerned, in case he is ill or something.

Johanna: Not to my knowledge, no. I don't think he is ill. At least he has not said so. And I'm very surprised to hear that he was absent from the dance lesson. I thought that he was attending lessons as normal. But I'm not sure. I had to leave home early that day, as I had a business trip to London. And his father was attending an international information technology conference in Sydney. We thought that Onni was responsible enough to go to school by himself . . .

Mikael: I see. Was he home alone for a long time?

Johanna: No, of course not. His grandmother came in the afternoon to take care of him.

Mikael: Have you noticed that Onni is often quite tired?

Johanna: Not really. You know, right now I'm very busy at work. A lot of things going on at the same time . . . I know that he loves to play those computer games late at night but, still, I thought that he was getting enough sleep.

Mikael: I have noticed that Onni has no friends at school. Does he have friends in the neighbourhood?

Johanna: I have no idea. You know, he is 13 years old – not very eager to speak about such things with his mum.

The conversation continued at length. Johanna voiced concern about having difficulty communicating with Onni. She also explained that she and Onni's father had very demanding jobs, and Onni spends many afternoons after school at home alone. Onni's parents realize that this is not very good for a developing child, but they feel quite unable to change the situation. This conversation echoes an ongoing national debate in Finland concerning the balance between work, family and leisure in everyday life. Studies show that, although family and leisure time is more highly valued, work takes up a lot of time, resulting in feelings of guilt and inadequacy (Moisio and Huuhtanen 2007).

Johanna also brought up the issue of Onni's recurring lower-back and neck/shoulder pain. According to a Finnish Basic Education Act (National Board of Education 2010) "pupils participating in education are entitled to receive sufficient support for growth and learning immediately when the need for support becomes apparent." With this in mind, Mikael and Onni's mother agreed that, together with school health care personnel and pupil welfare services, they would begin to plan support services that would help Onni to participate in physical education and other school subjects more fully. They also agreed, in light of Onni's apparent musculoskeletal problems, to consult the school physiotherapist and monitor Onni's physical activity levels.

A visit to the physiotherapist

Onni went with his mother to meet the school physiotherapist in the local health care centre. The physiotherapist, Anne, observed Onni's sitting position as he played a computer game, carried out a gait analysis and assessed the functioning of Onni's spinal column. Anne noted that Onni's sitting position was rotated, he had a tendency to keep his right shoulder slightly elevated while on the computer, and his right step was longer than his left. The combination of these observations led Anne to conclude that Onni had functional rotation in his lower thoracic column (middle back) that causes muscles to be overworked when moving, or sitting for long periods.

Anne noted that due to his limited functional rotation, resulting in muscular imbalance and an uneven walking rhythm, Onni could sometimes appear clumsy. This muscular imbalance was not overtly apparent to Onni when he was sitting, but manifested itself in head and back pain. Onni had poor body awareness. Body awareness concerns the relation between one's own body and feelings, and the perception of the body as "me". It is dependent on the capacity to perceive and integrate information coming from all the senses (Dragesund *et al.* 2010). Onni needed to improve his body awareness by strengthening the connection between his body and mind, thus improving his body consciousness, body management and body experience (Kvåle and Ljunggren 2007). Anne guided Onni through some exercises aimed at strengthening his muscles. She also gave him instructions on how to use a mirror as a tool to improve the balance of his sitting position at his desk at home.

Anne advised Onni's mother and Mikael how they could help Onni to become more aware of his body, and how to guide him in his daily exercises, both at home and at school. A final suggestion from Anne was that Onni and his father should participate together in the local Father and Son Exercise Club, which is organized in co-operation with the school, health services and sports services of the city (City of Jyväskylä, 2012). The club meets at the school every second Thursday at 3 pm. This would give Onni an extra opportunity to practice his new exercises and also, in accordance with the aim of the initiative, support the social interaction between Onni and his father. The club also aims to challenge fathers to be better role models in the area of sport and physical activity. Research suggests that parents play a critical role in determining whether their children get involved in sport programs. Furthermore, it has been found that the same-sex parent has a stronger influence on the child's behaviour than the cross-sex parent (Brophy 1987; Lewko and Ewing 1981; Ruddel and Shinew 2006). Onni's participation in this club with his father is very important, as inactivity tends to track from youth to adulthood. Also, such physical activity reinforcement is especially necessary in periods of transition, such as the beginning of middle school.

Mikael invited Anne to his health education lesson to teach the pupils how to determine the best way to adjust their furniture and sitting position to avoid physical impairments. Research shows strong correlations between inappropriate school furniture and pupils' neck and back pain (Milanese and Grimmer 2004; Murphy, Buckle and Stubbs 2007; Trevelyan and Legg 2011) and between inappropriate sitting positions and instances of lower back pain (Trevelyan and Legg 2006). Tables and chairs are often too high (Panagiotopoulou *et al.* 2004; Gouvali and Boudolos 2006; Molenbroek, Kroon-Ramaerkers and Snijders 2003), especially for a small child like Onni.

Anne discussed Onni's ergonomic demands with his mother and they planned together how to assemble a suitable workstation which would cater for Onni's physical, cognitive, technical and social needs, so that both Onni and his friends could be seated appropriately in his home (Hakala, Rimpelä, Salminen, Virtanen and Rimpelä 2002; Hakala, Saarni, Ketola, Rahkola, Salminen and Rimpelä 2010). Onni had a follow-up appointment with the physiotherapist two weeks later, at which she assessed how well he had managed to become aware of his body and perform the exercises he was given at school and at home. Anne also attended Onni's health education lesson one more time to discuss body awareness with the whole class.

Supporting Onni's learning and development

Differentiation of instruction is a primary means of taking the needs of the teaching group and the diversity of pupils into account. Every pupil must be given an opportunity to succeed in learning. (National Board of Education 2010). Over the course of the school year Mikael noticed that if he differentiated his teaching by giving students the freedom to choose activities, all pupils, irrespective of ability, were more active than in lessons where a more teacher-centred approach was taken. Careful planning and anticipation helped Mikael to meet the needs of children with limited motor skills. This included choosing proper equipment, planning pupil groupings and pupil-appropriate tasks, and using a suitable location and suitable instructions for activities. He also used active supervision involving high rates of interaction with the pupils and offered feedback, encouragement and manual support to pupils, especially those, like Onni, who required specific attention.

Mikael found that his active supervision was a key factor in supporting the children in their psychomotor learning. He noticed how easily methods such as verbalizing movements, repeating the rhythm, using visual and manual tips, and encouraging each child, could become part of all physical education lessons. These teaching methods helped Onni to develop his body awareness and to learn new skills. Due to the success he experienced in adopting new ball game skills, Onni's self-esteem gradually improved.

Mikael knew from experience that activation of reasoning is important in physical education, both for those who process instructions quickly and for those who need more time. Some techniques help those who need additional time to understand instructions (e.g. using pictures or bridging), and some focus on keeping learners, such as Onni, who pick up on cues quickly, interested in the task (e.g. cognitive cues or tasks with special responsibility). Through the use of these techniques, Mikael helped all pupils to become cognitively active in physical education. He noticed that activation of reasoning techniques seemed to have an effect not only on pupil motivation and concentration, but also on the socio-emotional climate of the lesson.

As fostering co-operation between classmates was one of the core objectives agreed by the teaching staff at the beginning of the school year, Mikael was especially concerned with supporting his pupils' socio-emotional learning. He found that this was very important in Onni's class as there was some evidence that children were bullying each other and were not able to co-operate. Mikael's strategy was to support pupils' self-esteem and build trust between the teacher and class, and also between pupils. Noticing, listening, accepting, trusting and appreciating the pupils were all techniques used to increase pupils' self-esteem. Discussions, humour and empathy were important in building trust in lessons. Also, Mikael's willingness to give his time to the children (and sometimes also to their parents) was essential in building a trusting emotional climate.

School-based physical activity

Regular physical activity during childhood and adolescence is associated with improvements in numerous physiological and psychological variables. Health-enhancing physical activity is also promoted as a means of disease prevention (WHO 2012) and research evidence suggests that regular physical activity participation is correlated with high academic achievement (Syväoja *et al.* 2012). A considerable challenge worldwide is the growing number of children and adolescents who are inactive during their leisure time. In line with this general trend, about 20% of Finnish school-aged children, like Onni, are physically inactive during their leisure time (Heikinaro-Johansson, Varstala and Lyyra 2008; Huisman 2004; Huotari 2012; Laakso *et al.* 2006; Laakso *et al.* 2008). This has drawn growing attention from policymakers and stakeholders. Supporting physical education, physical activity and youth sports has become a priority area for the Finnish Ministry of Education and Culture. During recent years, several initiatives have been implemented to promote school-based, and leisure-time, physical activity among children and adolescents. In addition, as in many other countries, physical activity recommendations have been developed (Tammelin and Karvinen 2008). According to these recommendations, those aged from 7 to 18 should be physically active for at least one to two hours daily. It is also recommended that young people avoid sitting periods of more than two hours, and use of entertainment media (TV, computer games etc.) should be limited to a maximum of two hours per day.

From the viewpoint of young people, and their parents or guardians, as well as teachers, the beginning of middle school is an eventful time. Seventh grade sees the daily rhythms and lifestyles of pupils begin to change as they seek more independence and wish to be seen as older than their years. The amount of sleep often decreases (Gradisar, Gardner and Dohnt 2010) and food habits and contexts for eating change (Ojala 2012). Physical activity patterns can also be altered significantly as pupils' territories become broadened, and their lives become more friend-oriented than previously (Wilkinson 2004).

For children such as Onni, who do not participate in physical activity during their leisure time, the importance of the amount and variety of physical activity offered through school is amplified. Mikael and the school principal are aware of the importance of ensuring that, in addition to effective physical education lessons, pupils are offered a variety of opportunities to be active during school breaks and through after-school activity initiatives. Bearing this in mind, the school principal successfully applied for funding from a national physical activity project: "Schools on the Move".[1] This project provides funding to schools for suitable physical activity promotion projects, with the objective of supporting efforts to ensure all children and adolescents adhere to the national physical activity guidelines. The grant received by Onni's school made it possible to reconstruct the school yard. Teachers and pupils were invited to make suggestions regarding what kind of activities should be offered in the yard and how the space could be best utilised. Onni's computer skills, especially in programming and editing films, became useful as his class discussed how to maximise the potential of the school yard. Onni created a virtual platform where his classmates could upload pictures of built environments, playgrounds, and youth spaces, which could then be discussed in the context of their own school yard. The pupils also shared ideas for what kind of activities to facilitate in the space. Onni was eager to take photos with his smart phone to upload for his classmates to see. The project provided Onni with the opportunity to co-operate with his classmates in an area in which he was comfortable. This experience improved Onni's self-esteem and made it easier for him to take part in other group activities.

Through the time spent together working on this project, the pupils developed a sense of group cohesion and began to also spend more time together outside of school. Over the course of seventh grade, Onni developed friendships, spent more time outdoors with other youths and also improved his body awareness and motor skills. Onni continued to take photographs, as he had done with the school yard project, often finding himself climbing structures to get the right angle for a shot. He soon discovered that he had good balance and co-ordination and enjoyed moving dynamically in space. This inspired him to join the local Parkour club with his new friend, Toivo.

Onni's parents have limited the time he is allowed to spend playing computer games at home. This restriction was not met with many objections because Onni has found that he is too busy outdoors with his friends these days to spend much time in the virtual world.

Conclusion

In the home, supporting young peoples' development is often a balancing act between catering for the young person's dependency and satisfying his/her need for autonomy. Parents are often in need of the broader perspectives that schoolteachers, as the experts of the whole age-group, can offer. The advantages of the amalgamation of school and home influences to support the development of the child were clearly evident in Onni's case. However, the success of such collaboration depends on a number of factors. Teacher education needs to emphasise the various influences acting on children as they progress through school so that pre-service teachers gain an understanding of how to harness these influences for the child's benefit. A supportive school ethos which prioritises the collaboration between school and home is also important. In addition, sufficient resources must be available to allow teachers the time to maintain contact with parents or guardians and to ensure that the processes involved are efficient and case sensitive. Onni needed a combination of interventions in order to ensure his educational, psychosocial, and physiological needs were met. This was only possible because effective systems and procedures were in place, reinforced by resources and policy, to allow his teacher to attend to his individual circumstances and facilitate adjustments where necessary.

We saw in Onni's case that Mikael began the school year by determining the health, physical activity habits and activity preferences of each of his pupils. The level of a teacher's knowledge about each pupil's individual needs and abilities is crucial to maximising learning outcomes and reinforcing student wellbeing. Such knowledge is enhanced by the observation of pupils' actions in different learning situations, and by the teacher's positive attitude and his/her ability to notice each child individually. Active participation, which was a focus in Mikael's lessons, is encouraged by establishing an inspiring learning environment, using pupil-centred teaching methods, giving clear instructions, allocating concrete tasks and supporting everything with positive teacher feedback (Huovinen and Heikinaro-Johansson 2006; Siutla *et al.* 2012).

Although the Finnish core curriculum emphasises collaboration between schools and home, research has highlighted barriers to such collaboration such as inadequate school resources, insufficient expertise, rigidity of structures, and poor attitudinal climate. Home-school collaboration can, in some cases, remain a one-way endeavour with the involvement of parents in the school community remaining low, but active initiation from the school (as seen in Onni's case) can encourage parents and improve the quality of co-operation (Sormunen 2012).

Mulvihill, Rivers and Aggleton (2000) emphasise that the determinants of physical activity in young people are complex and that there is a need for flexible and differentiated approaches. As learners, young people also have individual needs which manifest themselves in varying levels of motivation and participation. Onni was a child who did not love physical activity and was very attached to the virtual world. Through careful collaboration between the adults in his life, the utilisation of innovative techniques and, crucially, the involvement of Onni in decision-making regarding his learning and physical activity options, it was possible to overcome the social, physiological and psychological barriers he experienced.

Note

1. See www.liikkuvakoulu.fi.

References

Basic Education Act (2010) 24.6.2010/642.

Brophy, J.E. (1987) 'Synthesis of research on strategies for motivating students to learn', *Educational Leadership*, 45(2): 40–48.

City of Jyväskylä (2012) Official website of sport services in Jyväskylä. Online. Available HTTP: <www.jyvaskyla.fi/liikunta/en/sports_and_recreation/activities> (accessed 17 October 2013).

Currie, C., Roberts, C., Morgan, A., Smith, R., Settertobulte, W., Saamdal, O. and Barnekow Rasmussen, V. (2004) *Young people's health in context: International report from the HBSC 2001/02 survey.* (Health Policy for Children and Adolescents, No. 4). Copenhagen: WHO Regional Office for Europe.

Danielsen, A.G., Samdal, O., Hetland, J. and Wold, B. (2009) 'School-related social support and students' perceived life satisfaction', *Journal of Educational Research,* 102(4): 303–318.

Dragesund, T., Ljunggren, A.E., Kvåle, A. and Strand, L.I. (2010) 'Body Awareness Rating Questionnaire – Development of a self-administered questionnaire for patients with long-lasting musculoskeletal and psychomatic disorders', *Advanced In Physiotherapy,* 12: 87–94.

Gobina, I., Välimaa, R., Tynjälä, J., Villberg, J., Villerusa, A., Iannotti, R.I., Godeau, E., NicGabhainn, S., Andersen, A., Holstein, B.E. and the HBSC Medicine Use Writing Group (2011) 'Medicine use and corresponding subjective health complaints among adolescents, a cross-national survey', *Pharmacoepidemiology and Drug Safety,* 20: 424–431.

Gouvali, M.K. and Boudolos, K. (2006) 'Match between school furniture dimensions and children's anthropometry', *Applied Ergonomics,* 37: 65–773.

Gradisar, M., Gardner, G. and Dohnt, H. (2010) 'Recent worldwide sleep patterns and problems during adolescence: A review and meta-analysis of age, region, and sleep', *Sleep Medicine,* 12(2): 110–118.

Hakala, P., Rimpelä, A., Salminen, J.J., Virtanen, S.M. and Rimpelä, M. (2002) 'Back, neck, and shoulder pain in Finnish adolescents: National cross sectional surveys', *British Medical Journal,* 325: 743–745.

Hakala, P., Saarni, L., Ketola R., Rahkola, E., Salminen J.J. and Rimpelä, A. (2010) 'Computer associated health complaints and sources of ergonomic instructions in computer related issues among Finnish adolescents: A cross-sectional study', *BMC Public Health,* 10: 11. Online. Available HTTP: <http://biomedcentral.com/1471-2458/10/11> (accessed 23 September 2013).

Heikinaro-Johansson, P., Palomäki, S. and Kurppa, J. (2011) 'Koululiikunnassa viihtyminen – yhdeksäsluokkalaisten mielipiteitä liikunnanopetuksen mieluisuudesta ja sekaryhmäopetuksesta. [How students like PE – Ninth graders' opinions about PE and mixed gender groups]', in S. Laitinen and A. Hilmola (eds) *Taito- ja taideaineiden oppimistulokset – asiantuntijoiden arviointia* [Results of the evaluation studies in skill and art subjects] (pp. 249–258). Report No. 11. Helsinki, Finland: National Board of Education.

Heikinaro-Johansson, P., Varstala, V. and Lyyra, M. (2008) 'Yläkoululaisten kiinnostus koululiikuntaan ja kiinnostuksen yhteydet vapaa-ajan liikunnan harrastamiseen. [Middle school students' individual interest in physical education and the relationship between individual interest and leisure-time physical activity]', *Liikunta & Tiede [Sport and Science],* 45(6): 24–30.

Huisman, T. (2004) *Liikunnan Arviointi Peruskoulussa 2003.* [National Evaluation Study of Physical Education Learning Outcomes in Basic Education in 2003]. Helsinki, Finland: Finnish National Board of Education.

Huotari, P. (2012) *Physical fitness and leisure-time physical activity in adolescence and in adulthood – A 25-year secular trend and follow-up study.* Research Reports on Sport and Health 255. Jyväskylä: LIKES Research Center in Sport and Health Sciences.

Huovinen, T. and Heikinaro-Johansson, P. (2006) 'Liikunnanopetuksen yksilöllistäminen esiopetuksen heterogeenisessa ryhmässä. [Individualizing physical education in a heterogeneous preschool group]', *Liikunta & Tiede [Sport and Science],* 43(6): 33–39.

Jakku-Sihvonen, R. and Niemi, H. (2006) 'Research-based teacher education', in R. Jakku-Sihvonen and H. Niemi (eds) *Research-based teacher education in Finland: Reflections of Finnish teacher educators* (pp. 31–50). Research in Educational Studies 25. Turku: Finnish Educational Research Association.

Jakku-Sihvonen, R., Tissari, V., Ots, A. and Uusiautti, S. (2012) 'Teacher education curricula after the Bologna Process – A comparative analysis of written curricula in Finland and Estonia', *Scandinavian Journal of Educational Research,* 56(3): 261–275.

Kämppi, K., Välimaa, R., Ojala, K., Tynjälä, J., Haapasalo, I., Villberg, J. and Kannas L. (2012) *Koulukokemusten kansainvälistä vertailua 2010 sekä muutokset Suomessa ja Pohjoismaissa 1994–20. WHO-Koululaistutkimus (HBSC-Study).* [School perceptions in international perspective in 2010, and the trends in Finland and Northern Countries during 1994–2010. HBSC Study.] Koulutuksenseurantaraportit 2012:8. Helsinki, Finland: Finnish National Board of Education.

Klemola, U., Heikinaro-Johansson, P. and O'Sullivan, M. (2012) 'Physical education student teachers' perceptions of applying knowledge and skills about emotional understanding studied in PETE in a one-year teaching practicum', *Physical Education & Sport Pedagogy.* Advance online publication doi:10.1080/17408989.2011.630999

Konu, A. and Rimpelä, M. (2002) 'Well-being in schools: A conceptual model', *Health Promotion International,* 17(1): 79–87.

Kvåle, A. and Ljunggren A. E. (2007) 'Body awareness therapies', in R.F. Schmidt and W.D. Willis (eds) *Encyclopedia of pain* (pp. 167–169). Berlin: Springer Verlag.

Laakso, L., Nupponen, H., Rimpelä, A. and Telama, R. (2006) 'Suomalaisten nuorten liikunta-aktiivisuus, katsaus nykytilaan, trendeihin ja ennusteisiin. [Physical activity of Finnish youth: A review on current status, trends and predictions]', *LiikuntajaTiede [Sport and Science],* 43(1): 4–13.

Laakso, L., Telama, R., Nupponen, H., Rimpelä, A. and Pere L. (2008) 'Trends in leisure-time physical activity among young people in Finland, 1977–2007', *European Physical Education Review,14*(2): 139–155.

Lewko, J.H. and Ewing, M.E. (1981) 'Sex differences and parental influence in the sport involvement of children', *Journal of Sport Psychology,* 2: 62–68.

Milanese, S. and Grimmer, K. (2004) 'School furniture and the user population: An anthropometric perspective', *Ergonomics* 47(4): 416–426

Moisio, E. and Huuhtanen, H. (2007) *Got your everyday life together? Finnish expert views on work, family and leisure time in 2015. Results from the Delphi panel.* Helsinki, Finland: Finnish Institute of Occupational Health. Research Report 31. Online. Available HTTP: <www.ttl.fi/fi/tyo_ja_ihminen/Documents/ Tutkimusraportti_31.pdf [t]> (accessed 10 December, 2012).

Molenbroek, J., Kroon-Ramaekers, Y.M.T. and Snijders, C.J. (2003) 'Revision of the design of a standard for the dimensions of school furniture', *Ergonomics,* 46: 681–694.

Mulvihill, C., River, K. and Aggleton, P. (2000) 'Views of young people towards physical activity: Determinants and barriers to involvement', *Health Education,* 100(5): 190–199.

Murphy, S., Buckle, P. and Stubbs, D. (2007) 'A cross-sectional study of self-reported back and neck pain among English schoolchildren and associated physical and psychological risk factors', *Applied Ergonomics,* 38(6): 797–804.

National Board of Education (2010) 'Amendments and additions to the National Core Curriculum for Basic Education'. Online. Available HTTP: <www.oph.fi/download/132551_amendments_and_ additions_to_national_core_curriculum_basic_education.pdf> (accessed 23 September 2013).

National Core Curriculum for Basic Education (2004) (NCCBE 2004) Helsinki, Finland: Finnish National Board of Education.

Ojala, K. (2012) *Nuorten painon kokeminen ja laihduttaminen.* [Adolescents' self-perceived weight and weight reduction behaviour – Health Behaviour in School-aged Children (HBSC) study, a WHO Cross-National Survey.] *Studies in Sport, Physical Education and Health,* 167. Jyväskylä: University of Jyväskylä.

Palomäki, S. and Heikinaro-Johansson, P. (2008) 'Opettajan pedagogisen ajattelun kehittyminen liikunnanopettajakoulutuksen aikana. [The influence of teacher education on the pedagogical thinking of physical education pre-service teachers]', *Liikunta & Tiede [Sport and Science],* Tutkimusartikkelit [Research Articles], 45(6): 24–30.

Palomäki, S. and Heikinaro-Johansson, P. (2011) *Liikunnan Oppimistulosten Seuranta-Arviointi Perusopetuksessa.* [National Evaluation Study of Physical Education Learning Outcomes in Basic Education in 2010]. Helsinki, Finland: Finnish National Board of Education.

Panagiotopoulou, G., Christoulas, K., Panagiotopoulou, A. and Mandroukas, K. (2004) 'Classroom furniture dimensions and anthropometric measures in primary school', *Applied Ergonomics,* 35: 121–128.

Ruddel, J.L. and Shinew, K.J. (2006) 'The socialization process for women with physical disabilities: The impact of agents and agencies in the introduction to an elite sport', *Journal of Leisure Research,* 38(3): 421–444.

Sahlberg, P. (2011) 'Lessons from Finland', *American Educator,* July 2011.

School Health Promotion Study (2010/2011) Online. Available HTTP: <www.thl.fi/fi_FI/web/fi/tilastot/ vaestotutkimukset/kouluterveyskysely/tulokset/aiheittain/terveys> (accessed 17 October 2013).

Siutla, H., Huovinen, T., Partanen, A. and Hirvensalo, M. (2012) 'Opetusviestintä heterogeenisen kolmannen luokan liikuntatunneilla. [Instructional communication in teaching a heterogeneous 3rd grade physical education group]', *LiikuntajaTiede [Sport and Science],* 49(1), 59–66. Online. Available HTTP: <https://jyx.jyu.fi/dspace/handle/123456789/38269> (accessed 23 September 2013).

Sormunen, M. (2012) *Toward a home-school health partnership. A participatory action research study, 2008– 2010.* Publications of the University of Eastern Finland. Dissertation in Health Sciences. University of Eastern Finland.

Syväoja, H., Kantomaa, M., Laine, K., Jaakkola, T., Pyhältö K. and Tammelin T. (2012) *Liikunta ja oppiminen.* Tilannekatsaus – Lokakuu 2012. [Physical activity and learning. The state of art in October 2012.] Muistiot 2012:5. Helsinki: Opetushallitus. [Finnish National Board of Education].

Tammelin, T. and Karvinen, J. (eds) (2008) *Fyysisen aktiivisuuden suositus kouluikäisille 7–18-vuotiaille.* [Physical activity recommendations for school-aged children]. Helsinki, Finland: Ministry of Education and Culture and the Young Finland Association. [Opetusministeriö ja Nuori Suomi].

Trevelyan, F.C. and Legg, S.J. (2006) 'Back pain in school children – where to from here?', *Applied Ergonomics, Special Issue: Fundamental Reviews,* 37(1): 45–54.

Trevelyan, F.C. and Legg, S.J. (2011) 'Risk factors associated with back pain in school children', *Ergonomics,* 54(3): 257–262.

Välijärvi, J., Kupari, P., Linnakylä, P., Reinikainen, P., Sulkunen, S., Törnroos, J. and Arffman, I. (2007) *Finnish success in PISA and some reasons behind it.* Jyväskylä: University of Jyväskylä.

Välimaa, R. (2000) *Nuorten koettu terveys kyselyaineistojen ja ryhmähaastattelujen valossa.* [Adolescents' perceived health based on surveys and focus group discussions.] *Studies in Sport, Physical Education and Health,* 68. Jyväskylä: University of Jyväskylä.

Westbury, I., Hansen, S.-E., Kansanen, P. and Björkvist, O. (2005) 'Teacher education for research-based practice in expanded roles: Finland's experience', *Scandinavian Journal of Educational Research,* 49(5): 475–485.

Wilkinson, R.B. (2004) 'The role of parental and peer attachment in the psychological health and self-esteem of adolescents', *Journal of Youth Adolescence,* 33: 479–93.

Wolfson, A.R. and Carskadon, M.A. (2003) 'Understanding adolescents' sleep patterns and school performance: A critical appraisal', *Sleep Medicine Reviews* 7(6): 491–506.

World Health Organization (2012) *Social determinants of health and well-being among young people: Health Behavior in School-Aged Children (HBSC) study: International report from the 2009/2010 survey.* Copenhagen, WHO Regional Office for Europe (Health Policy for Children and Adolescents, No. 6).

11

JENNY

Specialist needs for the specialising phase

Stephen Harvey, Stacey Pope, Iain Fletcher and Charlotte Kerner

INSTITUTE OF SPORT AND PHYSICAL ACTIVITY RESEARCH, UNIVERSITY OF BEDFORDSHIRE, UK

Key words: 13-year-old female, early maturing, talented, physiology, sociology, psychology, pedagogy.

Jenny

Jenny is a 13-year-old field hockey player from Nottingham in England, which is an area with a population of over 600,000 people. Her parents are White-British and they both work full-time, sometimes including the weekends. Together they earn around £30,000 per annum, which puts them in the category of below average earners in England.[1] Jenny has one brother who trains at a well known football club's academy for talented young players. Her mother and father spend much of their spare time supporting him by providing transport to training sessions and, where possible, accompanying him to matches at weekends. Jenny's parents are wholly supportive of her brother's aspirations to be a professional football player, but they are less certain about Jenny's ambitions to play elite level hockey as it does not offer the same financial incentive.

Jenny attends an English 'Academy' school with a specialism in languages[2] which additionally offers an 'extended schools' programme for sport, including field hockey, outside of normal school hours. Jenny participates in field hockey once per week after school with a qualified coach. The school does not, however, have a viable team to play in matches as there is no teacher willing to take on this commitment. While Jenny is very keen to improve her skills, she is unable to access the pitch for extra practice at lunchtimes and after school. No teachers are available to supervise field hockey practice sessions, and young people (mainly males) enjoying an informal football *kickabout* often dominate the unsupervised playing areas. Many of Jenny's close friends have begun to drop out of playing sport so this leaves her feeling rather isolated.

A local hockey club bases its training at Jenny's school where they practice once each week. There is a qualified coach with the team, and Jenny attends these sessions with her best friend as the school is only a short 10-minute walk from her home. The club plays regular matches and Jenny sometimes watches, hoping that when she is older she can break into one of the adult teams to further develop her game. Jenny also plays for the under-16 team at the club. They have matches about once per month on Sundays.

Once every week, Jenny has attended the local field hockey development group (the Junior Development Centre) and this is also based at her school. She pays £5.00 for each session but it seems worth it as she was selected to attend the Junior Academy Centre. This centre is based at another local school and costs £8.00 for each session, but she is able to finance much of this cost through her part time job as a leaflet distributor. Transport to the Academy might have been a problem but her best friend was also selected so they have been able to travel with her parents.

Jenny is delighted that her efforts seem to be paying off. She has been selected to attend the regional development group (the Junior Regional Performance Centre), and this is a particularly noteworthy achievement given that she is a year younger than most other players. The problem is that the Performance Centre sessions take place at a location 30 miles away from Jenny's home. Her parents have only one car and with the extensive demands of her brother's football commitments, it is not possible for them to offer transport. Her best friend was not selected for the Performance Centre, so that alternative form of transport is no longer an option. There is a bus route to the training sessions, but Jenny's parents are concerned about allowing her to travel alone, especially when they are away with her brother and/or working at weekends.

Jenny is keen to continue to improve her skills. She has been told by many of her coaches that she is *talented* but Jenny is restricted by her current circumstances, and she is concerned that she may be left behind if she does not continue her development as a player. Jenny would like to change schools and attend the private school that is also close to her home. The school places a strong emphasis on field hockey – playing every day – but Jenny's parents cannot possibly afford the fees.

Jenny is considered to have matured physically a lot earlier than many of her peers. She is not only taller than her peers but, due to her early transition into puberty, she also has a comparatively higher body fat percentage. Jenny constantly compares the size and shape of her body with peers and media images of high profile athletes. She is often highly critical of her performance and believes that in order to become a better player, she should reduce her body fat. Jenny is conscious about the food she eats and often becomes frustrated as she feels that her parents do not provide her with healthy options. She sometimes skips meals, and will often throw away her lunch at school preferring, instead, to engage in physical activity.

Jenny is an athlete with clear talent, but the opportunities to achieve her full potential appear limited. In terms of the Developmental Model for Sport Participation (DMSP) proposed by Côté and Hay (2002) Jenny is at the crossroads marking the beginning of her *specialising years,* where competition becomes increasingly important. She has almost reached the end of her peak height velocity window, where accelerated adaptations to strength, speed and agility fitness components can be vital to determining her final level of achievement. She is also at a stage where she may be at increased risk of injury, particularly Anterior Cruciate Ligament (ACL) problems. Jenny is not, however, receiving the necessary skill/technical coaching or the physical preparation to fulfil her physical and skill potential and limit the risk of injury. Consequently, she is in danger of becoming a talented player at a local club, when potentially she could play at a much higher level.

A physiological perspective

Attempts to model the process of talent development and maximise sporting achievement have often been linked to Long-Term Athlete Development (LTAD) systems. Many National Governing Bodies (NGBs) of sport have adopted these systems, including the field hockey NGB in England. This implementation has been almost universal in England and the rest of the UK despite a lack of any long term evidence of the model's efficacy and its very narrow focus, based around skill, speed, suppleness, stamina and strength (Ford *et al.* 2011). Despite these shortcomings, the LTAD model highlights *Windows of Opportunity,* where training gains can be maximised but also can lead to limitations in an athlete's potential development if they are not fully utilised (Balyi and Hamilton 2004). Jenny is involved in hockey's LTAD strategy. She is currently at the *training to train* phase of her development and, at the age of 15, she will move into the *training to compete* phase. She has been identified as *talented* and is involved with her Junior Academy and Regional Performance Centres. As a 13-year old she has already missed her first training window (ages 5–9) and is now in her adolescent growth spurt. This is considered to be the second training window and is linked to her Peak Height Velocity (PHV) and Peak Weight Velocity (PWV) (Balyi and Hamilton 2004). According to the LTAD model, it may already be too late for Jenny to achieve her full genetic potential as a hockey player. On the other hand, research has shown that later specialisation may actually be the key to adult sporting success (Moesch *et al.* 2011). Increasing training load in the mid-teenage years could, therefore, be the key to progression to an elite level.

Jenny is an early developer, and has learned many of the fundamental movement skills that should be ingrained (Higgs *et al.* 2008). These are needed to perform the wide and varied movements of sporting actions including stability (balancing, twisting, turning), locomotion (walking, running, hopping) and object manipulation (throwing, catching, kicking, hitting). In order to progress and to master more complex motor skills in her later adolescent years, she will need to continually reinforce and progress earlier learnt movements to prevent detraining taking place (Gallahue and Donnelly 2003).

The basic components of fitness linked to hockey performance have varied recommendations in terms of optimal trainability, and luckily for Jenny all seem to still be within her reach. Aerobic endurance can be actively developed throughout childhood and adolescence (Baquet, Van Praagh and Berthoin 2003), while plyometric and then strength training optimises speed during PHV (Rumpf *et al.* 2012). There is no definitive *window* identified for the development of muscular power, which is vital for high-level performance in actions such as jumping, agility and acceleration. It is known, however, that increases are possible pre and post adolescence (Branta, Haubenstricker and Seefeldt 1984) though the mechanisms behind these changes are likely to shift from neural adaptation into more structural changes, linked to hormonal maturation in adolescence.

It seems Jenny is at a crossroads in her development. She is in the middle of her adolescent growth spurt and needs to address her physical training patterns quickly or she may fail in her ambition to become an elite hockey player. Jenny is attending 3–4 hockey sessions per week under the guidance of a qualified coach, but could be missing vital aspects of physical training during a sensitive time in her development. Without specialised training, adolescent girls show little improvement in strength, power and balance during/after puberty, and they have a heightened risk of non-contact ACL injury (Hewett *et al.* 2010).

With this in mind, of particular concern is Jenny's lack of a resistance training background. Ford *et al.* (2010) indicate that musculoskeletal growth among females during puberty, with no concurrent modification to the neuromuscular system, can result in abnormal joint mechanics with an increased risk of injury. Resistance training during maturation provides opportunities to promote safer movement mechanics, particularly with regard to posterior chain strength (Ford, Myer and Hewett 2011). This has a high correlation to hamstring and ACL injury (Myer *et al.* 2009) and seems almost endemic in female field-based sports performers. The evidence suggests, therefore, that resistance training is essential for adolescent athletes (Emery and Meeuwisse

2010). The type of resistance training performed during adolescence is vital. The focus of any program should be on strength and movement skill, not on increases in muscle mass (Lloyd and Oliver 2012). Free weight exercises are recommended over machine-based actions because of the greater crossover to the dynamic athletic qualities required in sport (Granacher *et al.* 2011).

Another vital aspect to Jenny's development as a player involves her ability to efficiently use stretch shortening cycle (SSC) actions involving control of her body mass. This is linked to her ability to land efficiently, absorb landing forces quickly, balance during ground contact, and enhance her proprioception before producing a rapid forceful take off. This action is integral to most movements linked to hockey performance. If her SSC actions are performed correctly, not only can performance increases be observed, but injury occurrence is also decreased (Escamilla *et al.* 2009). Plyometric training is a way of systematically overloading the SSC and has been shown to increase strength, power, joint stability and increase performance (Matavulj *et al.* 2001), while helping prevent injury (Lephart *et al.* 2005) in adolescent athletes.

A sociological perspective

Sport is sometimes perceived as meritocratic activity that offers everyone the opportunity to compete on a level playing field. From this idealistic point of view, the most talented and successful athletes will, quite naturally and inevitably, 'rise to the top'. As Coakley and Pike (2009: 349) put it, people do like to believe that 'sports transcend issues of money, power and economic inequalities'. Yet, this viewpoint overlooks the financial requirements that are necessary in order to participate and succeed in sport. In Jenny's case, for example, it is impossible to ignore the impact of her relatively low socio-economic background. Wilson (2002) has found that those rich in 'economic capital' are most likely to be most involved in sports because such capital makes it possible to afford the 'cost' of participation in terms of both time and money. If Jenny were able to attend the local independent school, which offers team games such as hockey, she would have access to extensive opportunities to increase the role that field hockey could play in her life (Tozer 2012). However, the reality for Jenny is that her parents are unable to afford private school fees[3] and the state-funded school that Jenny attends is unable to offer sufficient high quality coaching to support her to reach the elite levels for which she appears to have the potential.

Jenny's experiences are illustrative of wider problems of social stratification in British society. For example, Paton (2012) reports recent research findings which showed that 37 per cent of British medallists at the London 2012 Olympic Games attended fee paying schools, despite these schools educating only 7 per cent of the school population. Their success was attributed to the time allocated for sport at private schools, the range and quality of sporting facilities available and the availability of highly qualified coaches. Jenny and her friends have to look beyond school for opportunities to develop their game. Added to that, Jenny has to fund the cost of attendance at the development and academy centres by undertaking part-time work. This means that Jenny has to balance her passion for playing field hockey with the competing demands of work and school commitments. Contrast her situation with those from wealthier backgrounds who are more likely to be able to focus on their sport without having to make major financial sacrifices (Coakley and Pike 2009).

Collins (2008: 80–81) reports research findings that show how those with 'higher incomes, higher educational attainment, their own cars (often personal rather than one shared by the household) and a wide-ranging social network – spend more on sport and leisure'. Jenny's parents are unable to offer adequate financial support for her involvement in sport. They have already chosen to use their shared family car to support Jenny's brother who is training at a leading football club's youth academy. Moreover, her family does not have an extensive social or support network, so Jenny has been required to utilise her own contacts to organize lifts to field hockey centres. As noted earlier, however, now that she has reached the regional level, new problems have been created as she is no longer able to share transport.

Jenny's parents are concerned that a career as an elite level hockey player does not offer the same attraction as the possibility (for her brother) of becoming a professional football player. There is no doubt that women – as athletes – are under-represented in the media (Eastman and Billings 2000; Messner, Duncan and Cooky 2003), with women's sport making up a fraction of total sport media coverage in the United Kingdom (Topping 2012). As a result, women's hockey does not have the same status and prestige as those traditionally 'male' team sports such as football and cricket. This lack of media exposure has made it difficult for Jenny's parents to take their daughter's involvement in hockey as seriously as they might.

Income and other aspects of social class interconnect with a range of structural forms of inequality and this includes gender issues. Kay and Jeanes (2008) argue that parents will often transmit gendered values to their children, and these help to reproduce gendered stereotypes. The close association between sport and masculinity can result in sport being placed in direct opposition to gendered notions of 'femininity'. Pope and Kirk (2012), in research on the formative experiences of female football fans, found that parents can play a crucial role in channelling young females into or away from sport. Although Pope and Kirk report that some parents took active measures to prevent their daughter's involvement in sport, there was also evidence of male family members playing a vital role in nurturing sporting interests. Jenny's parents, however, have not demonstrated the same level of interest or support in her sporting aspirations as they have in her brother's.

Jenny's age is another important factor to consider in analysing her potential sporting career. Many of Jenny's friends have 'dropped out' of sport, and the evidence suggests that she, too, will come under pressure from peers (Pope and Kirk 2012). During adolescence in particular, females may experience tensions between femininity and athleticism. These components of female identity are often regarded as incompatible, and young females are pressured to cement their identity with either masculinity or femininity (Welford and Kay 2007). Whereas for boys, playing sport can serve to affirm heterosexual masculinities, for girls the case is different and playing sport can be perceived as 'unfeminine' (Kay and Jeanes 2008).

Jenny's experiences of lunchtime sport are further evidence of the gender separation that peaks at early adolescence (Thorne 1993). There is wider evidence to show that the lunchtime playing areas in schools are usually dominated by young males having a 'kickabout' which excludes many girls and also non-footballing boys (Clark and Paechter 2007). Moreover, Gorely, Holroyd and Kirk (2003) have commented that showing physical prowess through sport is not perceived as a means for heterosexual females to attract males. Hence, rather than making attempts to reclaim playground space by playing sport, Jenny's friends tend to be more preoccupied with feminine ideals of body image. Coaches and teachers need to be alert, therefore, to these and other structural forms of inequality and their intersection if they are to maximise opportunities for Jenny and others like her to achieve their sporting potential. Finally, in a wider sense, Jenny also resides in a town that is outside of the reported optimum size (i.e. between 1,000 and 500,000 population) associated with the achievement of elite sporting status. It has been suggested these towns are conducive to supporting the development of elite athletes because young people have greater access to facilities at low or no cost, as well as opportunities to develop physical strength and a strong work ethic (see MacDonald and Baker 2013).

A psychological perspective

Examining Jenny's case study from a psychological perspective highlights a number of factors that may be dysfunctional for her athletic achievement and that may need to be considered by coaches. First, the case study presents a number of issues in relation to how Jenny's views her body. It is acknowledged that adolescence and the transition into adolescence present issues with regard to how young people feel about and perceive their bodies. The physical changes associated with this transition period lead to an enhanced focus on and evaluation of the physical construction of the self. It is estimated, for example, that between 50 per cent and 80 per cent of adolescent girls have a desire to become thinner (Levine and Smolak 2002).

This period of enhanced body focus is particularly relevant given the sporting context in which Jenny finds herself. The sporting environment can enhance social pressures to adopt a lean physique. This is done through a number of mechanisms such as pressures from peers and coaches, the competitive environment, or perceived performance advantages. Research in the field of exercise and health psychology suggests that young athletes pay more attention than others to body image and diet, sometimes viewing their bodies in a distorted manner and displaying maladaptive eating behaviours (Pruneti *et al.* 2010). It has also been established that as young athletes progress to elite status, the prevalence of eating disorders is significantly higher than would be found in the general population (Sundgot-Borgen and Tortveit 2004). It is already apparent in some of Jenny's behaviours (such as skipping meals) that she may be engaging in some of the behavioural strategies identified by Pruneti *et al.* (2010). Although sport participation is a potential risk factor for the adoption of such behaviours, it must also be acknowledged that it is only one risk factor in a complex mix of factors that can lead to the development of body image and diet problems.

Another point to be considered is that Jenny identifies herself as different to many of her peers. Her relatively early progression into puberty has meant that her body has undergone the physical changes of maturation before many of her friends and teammates. The increase in fat mass associated with girls' transitions into puberty can result in a rapid shift away from the 'ideal' slim female body portrayed in the media and still retained by many of Jenny's prepubescent peers. This discrepancy between an ideal self and the current self can heighten body dissatisfaction during this period. This is significant for Jenny because body image concerns and dissatisfaction have been linked to negative eating behaviours (Levine and Piran 2004), low self esteem (McCabe and Ricciardelli 2003), depressive mood (Paxton *et al.* 2006) and a number of other negative health related behaviours and psychological well-being factors. Jenny's tendency to compare her body to media images of athletes is also problematic. Media images often present idealised images of physical attractiveness and associated performance qualities (McCabe and Ricciardelli 2001). Jenny's comparison of her own body to these idealised images only serves to emphasise the discrepancy between current and ideal perceptions of the body.

The concerns that Jenny displays about body image, and the consequent eating behaviours, are particularly significant given that we know Jenny is an overcritical performer who is rarely satisfied with her performance. It appears that Jenny views her body as the main route to successful performance accomplishment and thus may be developing a preoccupation with obtaining the 'perfect' body to meet this objective. Flett and Hewitt (2005) consider the ways in which perfectionistic individuals can become concerned with bodily perfection. It is certainly clear that there are established links between perfectionist performers, body image concerns and eating disorders (Haase, Prapavessis and Owens 2002). Perfectionism, therefore, may be the underlying cause of Jenny's preoccupation with her body and perceived associated performance benefits.

A pedagogical understanding of Jenny as a learner

Pedagogy has been defined as 'the interdependence and irreducibility of subject matter, learning, instruction and context' (Kirk 2011: 167) and includes four interrelated elements: teachers/ coaches, learners, knowledge and learning environment (Armour 2004). Given the brevity of the synopsis required for this pedagogical case, it is not possible to overview all four of these elements in detail. Therefore, we have chosen one element to focus our discussion; that is, coaches and coaching and, more specifically, the problems that Jenny is having in accessing good coaching.

From a theoretical standpoint, Vygotsky's (1978) Zone of Proximal Development (ZPD) is a useful way of theorising about Jenny's current situation and why good quality coaching could provide the necessary *scaffolding* Jenny requires to exploit her ZPD. The ZPD has been defined as the difference between 'actual developmental level as determined by independent problem solving' and the higher level of 'potential development as determined through problem solving under adult guidance or in collaboration with more capable peers' (Vygotsky 1978: 86). In other words, if Jenny continues on her current path and continues to conduct her own training sessions – be these fitness sessions, skill development, or pick-up game sessions in the playground at lunchtime – she may only reach a certain level of her potential. We will demonstrate in the final part of this chapter, however, the *value added* benefit that Jenny would gain from the scaffolding associated with access to good quality coaching.

Developing game performance

At the specialising phase within the Developmental Model of Sports Participation, Côté and Hay (2002) identify positive experiences in sport that can lead children to specialise in that sport. These experiences include having a good relationship with a coach and having positive early experiences (MacPhail and Kirk 2006). Jenny is therefore in a critical phase of her holistic development where a move into the specialising phase can involve 'the construction of a slightly different sense of self' (Kirk and MacPhail 2003: 32). Indeed, MacPhail and Kirk (2006) noted several essential characteristics of the specialising phase including: a reduction in the number of sport and leisure activities being pursed; enjoyment and success; the notion of deliberate practice; and family, school and club support. All of these factors could have a critical impact on Jenny's continued participation in field hockey.

While Jenny has chosen to specialise and reduce the number of sports she is playing, the coach must take what Côté and Gilbert (2009) cited 'as the "holistic" approach to coaching' (310) in order to encourage her long-term development. Indeed, Gould *et al.* (1982) found that those coaches who adopted an autocratic approach tended to expect too much of their performers, lacked empathy, and were more likely to have performers who dropped out. Recent research (Partington and Cushion 2013) has shown that coaches often lack self-awareness about the coaching behaviours they use in practice sessions and their impact on young athletes. A useful thing to do when beginning to plan sessions would be for the coach to plan his or her use of coaching behaviours alongside the content to be taught. This would ensure more congruence between coaching objectives, practice type, coaching behaviours and the needs of the performers (Côté and Gilbert 2009). Moreover, videotaping coaching sessions would also stimulate coaches to engage in introspection and reflection (Côté and Gilbert 2009). This process could be a helpful form of continuing professional development, and could signal a move away from 'folk pedagogies' (Armour 2004) towards evidenced-based coaching practice (Williams and Hodges 2005).

Attempting to gain access to the Junior Regional Performance Centre is critical to Jenny's development both physically and in game play. In the Junior Regional Performance Centre, for example, Jenny would have access to coaches with greater *professional knowledge* (Côté and Gilbert 2009) than in her local area. This would include knowledge of the sport and its techniques and tactics, as well as pedagogical knowledge gained through experience and higher levels of formal coach education and certification. Access to this expertise is required now because at her age and stage of development, Jenny is clearly in the specialising phase of player development.

One way that coaches might advance Jenny's sport-specific and procedural knowledge of the game would be to plan game-situated practice. This form of practice includes a 'focus on both the technique to be improved and the tactic to be understood' (Slade 2011: 23). The field hockey NGB in England has promoted the use of game-situated practice, which has been shown to be useful in developing not only on-the-ball skills, but also off-the-ball skills (Harvey *et al.* 2010). Research by Vickers *et al.* (1999) has shown that practice with a greater degree of *contextual interference* (akin to game-situated practice) is more useful for longer-term *learning and development* as well as performance for individuals at Jenny's stage of learning and development. This is because it provides a competitive, game-intense environment in which there is a greater likelihood of positive transfer to match play (Harvey 2009). Game-situated practice may also be considered ideal in the specialising phase as it is based on a 'hands-off' coaching style, where the coach steps back (Light 2004) and facilitates learning through the use of appropriate feedback and questioning. This is arguably a more *positive* pedagogical approach that focuses *less* on what a player is doing wrong, and *more* on what she can do to improve her game performance (Light 2013) and has been found to be effective in fostering intrinsic motivation (Renshaw, Oldham and Bawden 2012).

As game-situated practice requires collaboration with peers during dialogue and reflection *on action,* it has been shown to help develop teamwork and communication (Harvey 2009). The social element of this type of practice should also offer Jenny opportunities to feel a sense of affiliation and belonging, which is critical to this specialising phase (Light, Harvey and Memmert 2013). The opportunity to socialise and make friends has also been identified as an important factor in reducing dropout from sport (Fraser-Thomas, Côté and Deakin 2008). This would seem to be especially important in Jenny's case given that many of her close female friends have now 'dropped out' of active involvement in sport.

A suggested way forward for coaches to support Jenny's physical development is to take a holistic approach to training. This would involve the integration of a wide range of fundamental movements and plyometric actions *within* her current hockey training sessions. A well-structured warm-up, involving varied movements to promote physical robustness and core strength, is particularly important. This activity would address many issues within Jenny's movement competence, such as balance, co-ordination and posture. Developing core strength and robustness is important for all UK children as research reports that there has been a significant decrease in strength in recent years (Cohen *et al.* 2011). Strength is especially pertinent for Jenny who has aspirations to become an elite athlete. Indeed, injury has been shown to be a common reason for dropping out of sport (Enoksen 2011) and has also been linked to negative psychosocial effects, such as feelings of loss and frustration (Tracey 2003).

As coaching is a system of social interaction (Côté and Gilbert 2009), Jenny could access new opportunities by being fully involved in the field hockey coaching *system*. She could do this by continuing to play club hockey as well as attending the Junior Regional Performance Centre training and, as a result, gaining access to new coaches and new social networks in the game. The benefits gained could be further supported if Jenny could gain access to facilities at school at lunchtimes, which could be provided at no financial cost. Access to specialist facilities is important to enable Jenny to continue to practice skills learned at the regional performance centre in her own time and to further support her on-going development (MacDonald and Baker 2013).

In order to try to find a way to allow Jenny to take up her place at the Junior Regional Performance Centre, she could consider contacting the centre administrator to find out whether there are other travel options. Jenny could also be encouraged to apply for a travel grant from an organisation such as Sport England. Access to such funds does require the support of coaches, club and parents, but it is one avenue for young performers who show potential.

Conclusion

Jenny's case mirrors that of many young sports performers who have ambitions to develop to a good – even elite – level of high level of play. The intersection of the factors outlined in each section of this chapter offers a framework for considering the needs of a player such as Jenny. As she enters her specialising years, she needs access to high quality coaching in order to succeed. Appropriate scaffolding of her learning will result in a *value added* experience that can help Jenny to overcome the unique blend of physiological, psychological and social challenges she faces. Her case also highlights common themes that are faced by other talented young people in similar situations.

Notes

1. The average income for a British family with two adults working is £40,000 in 2011 (Cronin 2011) while two parents are said to need to earn at least £18,400 each to support themselves and two children (Davis, Hirsch, Smith, Beckhelling and Padley, 2012).
2. An 'Academy' is a school funded directly from central government and therefore independent of local government control. Each Academy has a specialism (e.g. languages, technology, the arts, sport etc.). The Specialist Schools Program began in 1995 as a way of boosting academic achievement.
3. Average day fees for private schools are now £13,800, and £26,000 for boarders (Stanford 2012). These figures are said to be almost beyond the reach of even middle class families.

References

Armour, K.M. (2004) 'Coaching pedagogy', in R.L. Jones, K.M. Armour and P. Potrac (eds.) *Sports coaching cultures: from practice to theory* (pp. 94–115). London: Routledge.

Balyi, I. and Hamilton, A. (2004) 'Long-term athlete development: trainability in childhood and adolescence, windows of opportunity, optimal trainability'. Victoria, Canada: National Coaching Institute British Columbia & Advanced Training and Performance.

Baquet, G., Van Praagh, E. and Berthoin, S. (2003) 'Endurance training and aerobic fitness in young people', *Sports Medicine,* 33: 1127–1143.

Branta, C., Haubenstricker, J. and Seefeldt, V. (1984) 'Age changes in motor skills during childhood and adolescence', *Exercise and Sport Science Review,* 12: 467–520.

Clark, S. and Paechter, C. (2007) '"Why can't girls play football?" Gender dynamics and the playground', *Sport, Education and Society,* 12(3): 261–76.

Coakley, J. and Pike, E. (2009) *Sports in Society: Issues and Controversies.* London: McGraw-Hill.

Cohen, D.D., Voss, C., Taylor, M.J.D., Delextrat, A., Ogunleye, A.A. and Sandercock, G.R.H. (2011) 'Ten-year secular changes in muscular fitness in English children', *ActaPaediatrica,* 100: 175–177.

Collins, M. (2008) 'Social exclusion from sport and leisure', in B. Houlihan (ed.) *Sport and society,* 2nd edn, (pp. 77–105). London: Sage.

Côté J. and Gilbert, W. (2009) 'An integrative definition of coaching effectiveness and expertise', *International Journal of Sports Science & Coaching,* 4(3): 307–323.

Côté, J. and Hay, J. (2002) 'Children's involvement in sport: a developmental perspective', in J. M. Silver and D. Stevens (eds.) *Psychological foundations of sport* (pp. 484–502). Boston, MA: Allyn & Bacon.

Cronin, F. (2011) 'Is £40,000 really a liveable income for families in the UK?' *BBC News.* Online. Available HTTP: <www.bbc.co.uk/news/magazine-15197860> (accessed 5 October 2013).

Davis, A., Hirsch, D., Smith, N., Beckhelling, J. and Padley, M. (2012) 'A minimum income standard for the UK in 2012'. *Joseph Rowntree Foundation.* Online. Available HTTP: <www.jrf.org.uk/publications/MIS-2012> (accessed 5 October 2013).

Eastman, S. and Billings, A. (2000) 'Sportscasting and sports reporting: the power of gender bias', *Journal of Sport & Social Issues,* 24(2): 192–213.

Emery, C.A. and Meeuwisse, W. (2010) 'The effectiveness of a neuromuscular prevention strategy to reduce injuries in youth soccer: a cluster-randomised controlled trial', *British Journal of Sports Medicine,* 44: 555–562.

Enoksen, E. (2011) 'Drop-out rate and drop-out reasons among promising Norwegian track and field athletes: a 25 year study', *Scandinavian Sport Studies Forum,* 2: 19–43.

Escamilla, R.F., Fleisig, G.S., DeRenne, C., Taylor, M.K., Moorman, C.T., Imamura, R., Barakatt, E. and Andrews, J.R. (2009) 'A comparison of age level on baseball hitting kinematics', *Journal of Applied Biomechanics,* 25: 210–218.

Flett, G.L., and Hewitt, P.L. (2005) 'The perils of perfectionism in sports and exercise', *Current Directions in Psychological Science,* 14(1): 14–17.

Ford, K.R., Myer, G.D. and Hewett, T.E. (2011) 'Longitudinally decreased knee abduction and increased hamstrings strength in females with self-reported resistance training', *Proceedings of the American College of Sports Medicine Annual Meeting.* Denver, Colorado.

Ford, K.R., Shapiro, R., Myer, G.D., Van Den Bogert, A.J. and Hewwett, T.E. (2010) 'Longitudinal sex differences during landing in knee abduction in young athletes', *Medicine & Science in Sports & Exercise,* 42: 1923–1931.

Ford, P., De Ste Croix, M., Lloyd, R., Meyers, R., Moosavi, M., Oliver, J., Till, K. and Williams, C. (2011) 'The long-term athlete development model: physiological evidence and application', *Journal of Sports Science,* 29: 389–402.

Fraser-Thomas, J.L., Côté, J. and Deakin, J. (2008) 'Examining adolescent sport dropout and prolonged engagement from a developmental perspective', *Journal of Applied Sport Psychology,* 20: 318–333.

Gallahue, D. and Donnelly, F. (2003) *Development of Physical Education for All Children,* 4th edn, Champaign, IL: Human Kinetics.

Gorely, T., Holroyd, R. and Kirk, D. (2003) 'Muscularity, the habitus and the social construction of gender: towards a gender-relevant physical education', *British Journal of Sociology of Education,* 24(4): 429–48.

Gould, D., Feltz, D., Horn, T. and Weiss, M. (1982) 'Reasons for attrition in competitive youth swimming', *Journal of Sports Behavior,* 5: 155–165.

Granacher, U., Goeseles, A., Roggo, K., Wischer, T., Fischer, S., Zuerney, C., Gollhofers, A. and Kriemler, S. (2011) 'Effects and mechanisms of strength training in children'. *International Journal of Sports Medicine,* 32: 357–364.

Haase, A.M., Prapavessis, H. and Owens, R.G. (2002) 'Perfectionism, social physique anxiety and disordered eating: a comparison of male and female elite athletes', *Psychology of Sport and Exercise,* 3(3): 209–222.

Harvey, S. (2009) 'A study of interscholastic soccer players perceptions of learning with Game Sense', *Asian Journal of Exercise & Sports Science,* 6(1): 1–10.

Harvey, S., Cushion, C., Wegis, H. and Massa-Gonzalez, A. (2010) 'Teaching Games for Understanding in American high-school soccer: a quantitative data analysis using the Game Performance Assessment Instrument'. *Physical Education & Sport Pedagogy,* 15(1): 29–54.

Hewett, T., Ford, K., Hoogenboom, B. and Myer, G. (2010) 'Understanding and preventing ACL injuries: current biomechanical and epidemiological considerations – update 2010', *North American Journal of Sports Physical Therapy,* 5: 234–251.

Higgs, C., Balyi, I., Way, R., Cardinal, C., Norris, S. and Bluechardt, M. (2008) *Developing Physical Literacy: A Guide for Parents and Children Aged 0 to 12.* Vancouver, BC: Canadian Sports Centres.

Kay, T. and Jeanes, R. (2008) 'Women, sport and gender inequity', in B. Houlihan (ed.) *Sport and society,* 2nd edn, (pp. 130–154). London: Sage.

Kirk, D. (2011) 'Towards a socio-pedagogy of sports coaching', in J. Lyle and C. Cushion (eds.) *Sports coaching: professionalism and practice* (pp. 165–176). London: Elsevier.

Kirk, D. and MacPhail, A. (2003) 'Social positioning and the construction of a youth sports club', *International Review for the Sociology of Sport,* 38(1): 23–44.

Lephart, S.M., Abt, J.P., Ferris, C.M., Sell, T.C., Nagai, T., Myers, J.B. and Irrgang, J.J. (2005) 'Neuromuscular and biomechanical characteristic changes in high school athletes: a plyometric versus basic resistance programme', *British Journal of Sports Medicine,* 39: 932–938.

Levine, M.P. and Piran, N. (2004) 'The role of body image in the prevention of eating disorders', *Body Image,* 1(1): 57–70.

Levine, M.P. and Smolak, L. (2002) 'Body image development in adolescence', in T.F. Cash and T. Pruzinsky (eds.) *Body Image: A handbook of theory research and clinical practice,* (pp. 74–82). New York: Guilford.

Light, R. (2004) 'Coaches' experiences of Games Sense: opportunities and challenges', *Physical Education & Sport Pedagogy,* 9(2): 115–131.

Light, R. (2013) *Game Sense: Pedagogy for Performance, Participation and Enjoyment.* London: Routledge.

Light, R.L., Harvey, S. and Memmert, D. (2013) 'Why children join and stay in sports clubs: case studies in Australian, French and German swimming clubs', *Sport, Education & Society,* 18(4): 550–566.

Lloyd, R.S. and Oliver, J.L. (2012) 'The youth physical development model: a new approach to long-term athletic development', *Strength & Conditioning Journal,* 34: 61–72.

MacDonald, D.J. and Baker, J. (2013) 'Circumstantial development: birthdate and birthplace effects on athlete development', in J. Côté and R. Lidor (eds.) *Conditions of children's talent development in sport* (pp. 197–208). Morgantown, WV: Fitness Information Technology.

MacPhail, A. and Kirk, D. (2006) 'Young people's socialisation into sport: experiencing the specializing phase', *Leisure Studies,* 25(1): 57–74.

Matavulj, D., Kukolj, M., Ugarkovich, D., Tihanyi, J. and Jaric, S. (2001) 'Effects of plyometric training on jumping performance in junior basketball players', *Journal of Sports Medicine & Physical Fitness,* 41: 159–164.

McCabe, M.P. and Ricciardelli, L.A. (2001) 'Parent, peer, and media influences on body image and strategies to both increase and decrease body size among adolescent boys and girls', *Adolescence,* 36(142): 225–240.

McCabe, M.P. and Ricciardelli, L.A. (2003) 'Body image and strategies to lose weight and increase muscle among boys and girls'. *Health Psychology,* 22(1): 39–46.

Messner, M. Duncan, M. and Cooky, C. (2003) 'Silence, sports bras, and wrestling porn: women in televised sports news and highlights shows', *Journal of Sport and Social Issues,* 27(1): 38–51.

Moesch, K., Elbe, A.M., Hauge, M.L. and Wikman, J.M. (2011) 'Late specialization: the key to success in centimetres, grams, or seconds (cgs) sports', *Scandinavian Journal of Medicine & Sciences in Sports,* 21: 282–290.

Myer, G.D., Ford, K.R., Barber Foss, K.D., Liu, C., Nick, T.G. and Hewett, T.E. (2009) 'The relationship of hamstrings and quadriceps strength to anterior cruciate ligament injury in female athletes'. *Clinical Journal of Sports Medicine,* 19: 3–8.

Partington, M. and Cushion, C. (2013) 'An investigation of the practice activities and coaching behaviors of professional top-level youth soccer coaches', *Scandinavian Journal of Medicine & Science in Sports,* 23(3): 374–382.

Paton, G. (2012) 'London Olympics 2012: four-in-ten Team GB medallists "educated privately"', *The Telegraph,* 14 August. Online. Available HTTP: <www.telegraph.co.uk/sport/olympics/news/9473344/London-Olympics-2012-four-in-10-Team-GB-medallists-educated-privately.html> (accessed 23 September 2013).

Paxton, S.J., Neumark-Sztainer, D., Hannan, P.J. and Eisenberg, M.E. (2006) 'Body dissatisfaction prospectively predicts depressive mood and low self esteem in adolescent boys and girls', *Journal of Clinical Child and Adolescent Psychology,* 35(4): 539–549.

Pope, S. and Kirk, D. (2012) 'The role of physical education and other formative experiences of three generations of female football fans', *Sport, Education & Society,* iFirst Article, 1–18, doi.10.1080/13573322.2011.646982:1–18

Pruneti, C.A., Montecucco, M., Fontana, F., Fante, C., Morese, R. and Lento, R.M. (2010) 'Eating behaviour and body image in a simple of young athletes', *ActaBiomedica,* 81(3): 171–184.

Renshaw, I., Oldham. A.R. and Bawden, M. (2012) 'Non-linear pedagogy underpins intrinsic motivation in sports coaching', *The Open Sports Sciences Journal,* 5: 1–12.

Rumpf, M.C., Cronin, J.B., Oliver, J.L. and Hughes, M.G. (2012) 'Effect of different training methods on running sprint times in male youth', *Paediatric Exercise Science,* 24: 170–186.

Slade, D. (2011) 'Teaching field hockey for understanding using constraining games in a TGfU model of instruction', *Active and Healthy Magazine,* 18(2): 23–27.

Stanford, P. (2012) 'Private education: what price is excellence?' *The Telegraph.* Online. Available HTTP: <www.telegraph.co.uk/education/9228953/Private-education-what-price-excellence.html> (accessed 5 October 2013).

Sundgot-Borgen, J. and Tortveit, M.K. (2004) 'Prevalence of eating disorders in elite athletes is higher than the general population', *Clinical Journal of Sports Medicine,* 14(1):25–32.

Thorne, B. (1993) *Gender Play.* New Brunswick, NJ: Rutgers University Press.

Topping, A. (2012) 'Women's sport is underfunded and ignored, charity claims'. Online. Available HTTP: <www.theguardian.com/lifeandstyle/2012/oct/24/womens-sport-underfunded-ignored-charity-claims> (accessed 21 October 2013).

Tozer, M. (2012) 'State pupils do have the mettle for medals', *The Times Educational Supplement.* Online. Available HTTP: <www.tes.co.uk/article.aspx?storycode=6265691> (accessed 7 January 2012).

Tracey, J. (2003) 'The emotional response to the injury and rehabilitation process', *Journal of Applied Psychology,* 15(4): 279–293.

Vickers, J.N., Livingston, L.F., Umeris-Bohnert, S. and Holden, D. (1999) 'Decision training: the effects of complex instruction, variable practice and reduced delayed feedback on the acquisition and transfer of a motor skill', *Journal of Sport Sciences,* 17(5): 357–367.

Vygotsky, L.S. (1978) *Mind in Society: The Development of Higher Psychological Processes,* Cambridge, MA: Harvard University Press.

Welford, J. and Kay, T. (2007) 'Negotiating barriers to entering and participating in football: strategies employed by female footballers in the United Kingdom', in J. Magee, J. Caudwell, K. Liston and S. Scraton (eds.) *Women, Football and Europe* (pp. 151–171). Oxford: Meyer and Meyer Sport.

Williams, A.M., and Hodges, N.J. (2005) 'Practice, instruction and skill acquisition in soccer: challenging tradition', *Journal of Sport Sciences,* 23(6): 637–650.

Wilson, T. (2002) 'The paradox of social class and sports involvement: the roles of cultural and economic capital', *International Review for the Sociology of Sport,* 37(1): 5–16.

12

TONY

In search of meaning and relevance in physical education

Kyriaki Makopoulou, Nikos Ntoumanis, Mark Griffiths and Francois-Xavier Li

SCHOOL OF SPORT, EXERCISE & REHABILITATION SCIENCES, UNIVERSITY OF BIRMINGHAM, ENGLAND

Key words: 14-year-old male, poor body image, physically inactive, psychology, sociocultural studies, motor control, pedagogy.

Tony

A group of researchers visited a 'typical' secondary mainstream secondary school in England (1,100 pupils aged 11–18). The purpose was to examine physical education (PE) teachers' professional development needs and also collect some evidence on pupils' experiences of PE. Following the visit, the researchers intended to use the evidence to design and deliver a new Continuing Professional Development (CPD) intervention specifically for this school, and to measure the impact of the personalised, school-based approach it involved. As part of the project, researchers asked pupils to complete learning blogs at different points in time (before and after the CPD intervention) to capture any changes in their perspectives on or engagement in PE lessons.

One of the pupils, Tony, had a lot to say about his PE experiences in his first 'learning blog' (prior to the teachers' CPD programme). Tony is a 14-year-old boy who is new to the school having recently moved into the local area. His thoughts about PE were expressed eloquently, and the researchers were struck by the insights his comments gave into the way he perceived himself and his body within and beyond the PE context:

My PE lessons

I am fat and I am terrible in sport. My PE lessons are good. I cannot blame my teachers (not the teachers in this school – I just moved in this area). My PE teachers want me to be active because it is good for my health. I know that. I am clever. But I cannot exercise and I cannot explain this.

My learning in PE

Do I learn in PE? I don't feel that I learn anything. I learn about things that I cannot use in my life because I do not exercise. I am no good at it. I don't feel that I progress . . . maybe sometimes I can do something more or better than the previous lesson but it doesn't matter . . . I don't want to participate really.

The project in which the researchers were engaged was all about (i) understanding the diversity and range of different students' experiences and thoughts; (ii) analysing PE teachers' existing pedagogies; and (iii) designing a CPD programme in a way that could support the PE teachers to improve pupils' experiences and engagement in lessons. Tony's blog entries were fascinating.

The researchers were keen to unpack some of the meanings behind these blog comments, and Tony agreed to participate in an individual interview:

Interviewer:	You write in your blog that you just moved into the area. So, would you like to tell us a bit more about yourself?
Tony:	Ok . . . erm . . . I live with my parents and brother and sister. We moved here a couple of months ago because of my father's job. He is very important . . . what else would you like to know?
Interviewer:	What would you like to tell us about your family that you think affects your thoughts and feelings about PE?
Tony:	My family, they are very active. . . . You wouldn't expect that, would you? My father used to be a bodybuilder champion, many years ago, but he still exercises. My mum perhaps less so . . . she is a bit chubby. I think I got the gene from her [laughs]. I would like to exercise, if that makes sense . . . but maybe PE hasn't helped a lot. My brother and my sister have their sport hobbies. My brother plays rugby and my sister likes dancing, netball and volleyball. I like walking. I love swimming but not in school. I like doing weights. I don't like doing things that I'm not good at . . . I don't know many people in this school. Some seem nice, some not. I prefer to be invisible sometimes.
Interviewer:	Those are interesting thoughts, Tony. You said that you would like to exercise but that PE hasn't helped a lot. I would like to understand a bit more about your PE experiences.
Tony:	Not much to say about PE. In my previous school, they [PE teachers] kept talking about being fit and losing weight . . . I mean my teachers wanted me to be healthy but their system didn't work for me. I didn't like to run around and be last. I didn't want to do much and I didn't understand why I had to run around or learn how to play football. I was always rubbish! Not good at all. Anyway, I don't believe that they [PE teachers] valued me much anyway.
Interviewer:	What do you mean?
Tony:	Well, I feel that I was visible when I shouldn't be and I was invisible when I should. . . .
Interviewer:	Can you give me an example?
Tony:	It was obvious who was the worst football player and I was more or less ignored during the lesson. Or other students got mad at me. I didn't matter [to the teachers]. I didn't want to learn and that must have put my teachers off as well. So, I was invisible to them. And then, they [PE teachers] had this system, with group fitness tests . . . like groups of five and we did group bleep tests. Everyone had to complete at least ten runs but I was put first because I guess I was the slowest and the faster ones were after me. And everyone could see me and I don't look good when I run. And others ran past me . . . hmm . . . I hated it. I didn't want to take part again.

Interviewer:	What about this school?
Tony:	More or less the same? I don't know really. They [PE teachers] seem nice. We didn't have to do the fitness test a few weeks ago [at the beginning of the school year]. So I am happy about that [laughs]. They do ask me what I like and what I don't like. They always try to promote their clubs. I think they seem worried about me, about my state [laughs].

The PE department in Tony's 'new' school consists of seven full time PE teachers (four male and three female). Paul, the head of the department, is an experienced and committed teacher with almost 25 years of teaching experience. In interviews, Paul expressed a number of views that are relevant to Tony's comments. For example, Paul has recently persuaded his colleagues (but not without resistance) to abandon fitness tests. Echoing research findings (Cale and Harris 2009), he described fitness testing as 'an inaccurate measure of children's fitness' that runs counter to the department's primary goal of engaging all pupils in 30 minutes of physical activity in each lesson. As he commented:

> For some students, a bleep test might last for two-three minutes. So I do not find administering such a test a productive use of time.

Paul still has to battle, however, with his colleagues' diverse views about the importance of fitness testing. Some believe that fitness tests should remain in the curriculum in order to show pupils how much they can improve if they commit to regular exercise. Others feel that pupils could 'build a strong(er) character and their persistence' by 'trying hard' to complete a challenging physical activity.

Beyond the issue of fitness testing, Paul believes that some traditional pedagogies and practices are still far too prevalent in his department and that these are not helping pupil engagement. In particular, Paul feels there is an urgent need to get better at 'motivating obese children to participate in PE'. In an email exchange with one of the researchers, he wrote:

> When I heard about this scheme, where we could work with researchers I was very interested because we have many students, like Tony, who do not seem to value PE or they lack the confidence and competence to participate. Tony, in particular, is a clever boy; for example, if you ask him to evaluate other students' performances, he understands the criteria and is able to analyse the situation and offer valid suggestions. I am, however, concerned about his engagement in physical activity. Our main goal here is to support our students to be physically active for a minimum of thirty minutes. We use two strategies to engage overweight or obese students in PE lessons: we try to emphasise personal improvement and we make links with real life scenarios; for example, lessons where students learn about calorie intake; for example how many calories they consume when they eat a cheese burger and what forms of exercise – and how much – they need to do to burn off a cheese burger. My colleague believes that these links to real life motivate her pupils, particularly the girls. Another colleague suggested creating clubs that target students like Tony so they exercise in a 'safe' environment, but to be honest, we still need to learn a lot about motivation for obese students like Tony. We do not 'reach' them and sometimes we are uncertain about what is 'safe' for students given their size or ability, and also whether our groupings (organised into ability and gender) are appropriate, especially as there is still a lot of variation within each group. We are struggling to get this right.

Paul's comments raise many issues, and the researchers realized that he and his team needed help if they were to support Tony, safely and effectively, as a learner. For example, there is helpful published research available on decision-making, effective learning environments, the influence of contexts, the role of PE in addressing obesity, the physiological implications of obesity and exercise, and much, much more. It became apparent to the researchers therefore, that the CPD intervention they needed to develop had to offer knowledge from a range of perspectives to inform new pedagogies and practices. The researchers selected three disciplinary perspectives that seemed to be particularly appropriate in considering Tony's experiences of PE.

A psychological perspective

There are a number of issues that PE teachers need to consider if they are to support Tony, and other children with similar views, to have positive PE experiences. The evidence we collected from Tony and his teacher shows that Tony is amotivated; that is, he lacks intrinsic or extrinsic motivation to participate in PE. Empirical evidence (e.g., Ntoumanis 2002) suggests that although average levels of amotivation in British PE are relatively low, there is a significant minority of children who can be described as highly amotivated towards the subject, but nevertheless have to participate in PE lessons. When PE teachers encounter these children in their classes, they need to first look at the various reasons that might explain why children – in this case Tony – are amotivated in PE. This should form a key part of the discussion in the CPD intervention. A qualitative investigation into amotivated children in British PE (Ntoumanis *et al.* 2004) identified a number of personal and contextual antecedents of amotivation (and recommendations for tackling it). This research is discussed in relation to Tony's comments and experiences.

It is likely that Tony is experiencing social physique anxiety; that is, he becomes anxious when others observe or evaluate his physique (Hart, Leary and Rejeski 1989). Such body image-related concerns become increasingly salient during adolescence and can become a barrier to physical activity engagement (Sabiston *et al.* 2007). Due to rules and arrangements regarding clothing, changing and showering, Tony might feel that his body is 'on display' when he has to participate in PE. Such concerns can be partly addressed by teachers reconsidering these routine procedures and offering Tony (and other children with similar body image concerns) flexible rules regarding clothing options and changing routines.

It is also apparent that Tony avoids exerting effort in lessons because he does not value PE. He does however seem to value, to some extent, physical activity. In Tony's case, it is possible that the devaluation of PE, and the associated reduction in effort, is due to previous unsuccessful experiences. His actions, therefore, can be regarded as strategic decisions known as self-handicapping (Standage *et al.* 2007) that aim to protect his self-worth in case of failure. A review by Puhl and Heuer (2009) indicated that overweight and obese pupils are sometimes stigmatized by both teachers and peers, and this could induce self-handicapping tendencies and hinder the educational achievement of these pupils. In PE, Greenleaf and Weiller (2005) have shown that teachers have moderate levels of anti-fat attitudes and hold lower expectations for achievement for overweight versus normal weight pupils. Unfortunately, teacher expectations often result in self-fulfilling prophecies that influence pupil engagement and achievement (Trouilloud *et al.* 2006). Tony also dislikes competitive situations in PE as these highlight differences in normative ability across children. In a study by Carlson (1995) amotivated children reported that the competitive nature of PE classes was a deterrent to their participation and enjoyment.

Poor or inappropriate motivational strategies used by PE teachers can also undermine pupil motivation (Treasure 2001). It is possible (but we cannot know for sure) that Tony's previous PE teachers used a controlling instructional style (Bartholomew, Ntoumanis and Thøgersen-Ntoumani 2009) characterized by yelling, humiliating or belittling Tony, dismissing his opinion or feelings, being impatient, and failing to offer a clear rationale for the lesson activities. It is also likely that PE teachers have created an ego-involving climate (Ames 1992; Treasure 2001) by giving attention and praise only to the most competent children in the class and ignoring pupils with poor physical competencies. Such teacher behaviours will serve to undermine a child's basic psychological needs.

According to self-determination theory (Deci and Ryan 2000), amotivation is the result of lack of satisfaction of three innate psychological needs, namely autonomy, relatedness, and competence.

Autonomy

In relation to autonomy, past research has shown that lack of personal volition is associated with dissatisfaction and amotivation in PE (e.g., Chen 2001; Ntoumanis 2002). Reeve (2009) suggested that autonomy supportive teacher environments can support all three psychological needs and promote more self-determined motivation (i.e., motivation reflecting enjoyment or personal value of an activity). For example, with regard to fostering the need for autonomy, Tony's teacher could increase the range of activities on offer (within curricula and practical constraints) to include those that do not have a strong competitive element (e.g., dancing). This action could increase task choice and feelings of enjoyment, and could enhance Tony's intrinsic motivation. Tony should be also offered opportunities to volunteer his ideas and become more involved in the lessons. Moreover, his teacher could offer a rationale for task engagement and the need for rules. Pupils are more likely to be motivated when they are offered explanations that are clear, truthful, and meaningful as opposed to when they are treated with a "it's my way or the highway" attitude.

Relatedness

With regard to relatedness, Carlson (1995) reported that amotivated children in PE have a strong sense of separation from their peers. Such feelings of alienation from the peer group could be attributed to the fact that amotivated children often have poor physical competencies. In Tony's case, it is also plausible that his peers are sometimes judgmental about his physique, making inappropriate comments. To tackle amotivation resulting from lack of relatedness with fellow pupils, PE teachers should promote a task-involving motivational climate which encourages student cooperation and teamwork (Ames 1992; Treasure 2001). Feelings of relatedness between Tony and his PE teacher could also be fostered if the teacher shows personal interest, is empathetic, and acknowledges Tony's difficulties or negative feelings. There is evidence from the case narrative that some of these practices exist already, but an analysis of the literature would undoubtedly reveal new strategies.

Competence

In order for Tony to develop feelings of competence, he should be given opportunities to achieve success. This could be achieved by offering him tasks and challenges that match his ability levels; for example, by modifying existing drills or developing new ones. Amotivated pupils tend to like to work in groups of similar ability levels so that intra-group differences in ability are less salient. However, such homogeneous ability groupings can be problematic because they accentuate inter-group differences and marginalize less competent students (Ames 1992). Hence, it is important that Tony works in groups with heterogeneity in terms of physical ability and weight status, with the emphasis in these groups being on cooperative tasks. In a task-involving teaching environment (Ames 1992) amotivated pupils such as Tony can be supported if their PE teachers evaluate competence on the basis of self-referenced as opposed to normatively referenced criteria. Paul, the head of PE seems to be aware that Tony could become more self-determined to participate in PE lessons if teachers reward him for effort, individual improvement and skill development. It would appear that Paul needs support to ensure that all teachers in the department embed these strategies in their practices.

A sociocultural perspective

A sociocultural perspective views individual behaviour, in part, as the product of experiences in multiple contexts (e.g., school, family, work, leisure time, and sports clubs). Drawing on the work of Vygotsky (1978), a sociocultural approach offers a lens through which to examine *how* individuals learn in different contexts, and *how* the culture of different environments influence their choices and dispositions. It is worth remembering that culture is defined as symbolic forms of meaning through which individuals experience any situation (Swidler 1986). In PE, symbolic forms of meaning are present in activities, traditions, clothing, language and stories.

In the context of the case narrative and Tony's experiences, it is clear that his perceptions of PE are shaped by individual interpretation and also influenced by wider contexts of social practice; e.g., *'My family, they are very active . . . my mom perhaps less so . . . she is a bit chubby. I think I got the gene from her [laughs]'*. These acts of interpretation have influenced what Tony views as important. Moreover, other comments are illustrative of the range of influences: *'I learn about things that I cannot use'*, *'my PE teachers want me to be active because it's good for my health'*, and *'I did not understand why I have to run around or learn how to play football'*. From a sociocultural perspective, three concepts that appear to mediate Tony's amotivation towards PE are: authenticity, constructed meaning, and facilitating cultural (individual and organizational) change. These concepts could be of interest to PE teachers who are struggling to make sense of Tony's views on PE.

Authenticity

In seeking to facilitate Tony's engagement in PE, an alignment should be established between activities inside school and activities outside school. As Paul, the head of PE recognised, Tony needs to see the relevance of what is being delivered in school to his wider lifestyle activities. The critical point, as Gard, Hickey-Moodey and Enright (2013: 100) note, is that, 'the problem is not what physical education is, the problem is what it *means*' (emphasis in original). In examining Tony's act of interpretation, it is useful, therefore, to draw on the work of French sociologist Pierre Bourdieu and his use of the term 'habitus' (Bourdieu 1990).

For Bourdieu, habitus is seen as product of a cultural socialisation process through which individuals perceive, produce and evaluate new encounters. Habitus represents the absorption of certain actions, knowledge and feelings within different social settings. As described previously,

Tony belongs to multiple settings, each one influencing his habitus and, moreover, because it is acquired through personal experiences, habitus is unique to individuals. Addressing individual differences in PE is not new. Of note, however, is that an emphasis on habitus draws attention to the *sources* of individual differences. In the context of Tony's story, previous experiences act as a form of social legacy that filters new experiences, thereby influencing Tony's learning dispositions towards PE. For Kirk (2006), the role of PE pedagogy is to challenge Tony's habitus in terms of how he filters, selects, accepts and rejects new situations. This is a difficult task, yet it is critical in pursuit of an authentic curriculum 'attuned to youth voices' (Gard *et al.* 2013: 104).

Constructed meaning

It was apparent in Tony's comments that health had been used as a justification for participation in PE and physical activity. Teachers also used health promotion as a rationale for the practices in which they believed. The logic of this argument is questionable. Policy makers, teachers, and the general public have increasingly located PE within a health-related exercise (HRE) domain and have argued that PE can make a significant contribution to children's health (Kirk 2006). In a PE curriculum guide in England, Harris defined HRE as, "the teaching of knowledge, understanding, physical competence and behavioural skills, and the creation of positive attitudes and confidence associated with current and lifelong participation in physical activity" (2000: 2). Research evidence suggests that PE teachers are making efforts to include a 'health' component in the PE curriculum (Cale 2000; OFSTED 2009). Yet, numerous concerns have been expressed about confusion and variability in the delivering of HRE (Cale and Harris 2009); and the (negative) impact of some prevailing HRE practices (e.g., fitness testing, drills) upon pupils has been highlighted (Corbin 2002; Trost 2004).

The head of PE has begun to challenge some established practices regarding the use of fitness testing, but clearly other teachers in the department need more persuasion if they are to question the health discourses that appear to underpin their practices. For example, the prevailing biomedical discourse of the so-called obesity 'epidemic' has been described as a 'cultural toxin, a powerful influence . . . on the mindset of teachers in schools' (Evans, Evans and Rich 2003). It is, therefore, crucial for PE teachers to engage with this body of literature and to critically analyse the messages they send (implicitly and explicitly) to their students.

A sociocultural perspective acknowledges health behaviours as an outcome of the interaction between environments (e.g., family), organisation (e.g., school) and individual features (e.g., habitus). If we accept that one of the aims of school PE is to encourage lifelong engagement in physical activity, it might be more effective to design a PE curriculum that engenders critical thinking, critical inquiry and problem-solving (Wright 2004). This approach highlights the educative purpose of PE, and recognises that young people learn about health across multiple learning situations beyond school. Tony's comments remind us that school PE needs personal and social relevance if pupils are to progress towards goals they care about.

Cultural (individual and organizational) change

It is interesting to consider what an authentic/relevant PE curriculum might look like for Tony. Green (2008) noted trends in school PE that suggest there is declining interest in traditional sport and competitive games, and a shift towards lifestyle sports/activities such as kabbadi, bmx, skateboarding, urban gymnastics (Parkour), and exergames (Nintendo Wii). Interestingly, the UK Government's Department for Children, Schools and Families Survey of PE and School Sport in 2009 found that between 2004 and 2009, golf participation increased from 14% to 42%, cycling from 21% to 50%, and boxing from 0% to 9%. For Green (2008) such evidence suggests that pupils are attracted to more informal and individualised activities that resonate with activities outside school. The challenge for policy makers and teachers, therefore, is to understand how young people consume and apply physical activity in their lives.

For Tony, and other young people who dread 'traditional' PE, an alternative curriculum might be built around a process-driven model (as opposed to a product-driven model) that embraces physical, social, affective *and* cognitive development. Such an approach would involve activities that encourage evaluating, analysing, exploring, communicating, identifying and creating. This leads to participation that is 'emotionally transcendent' (Gard *et al.* 2013: 111). Such an approach would require schools, teachers and young people to be receptive to cultural change (individually and organizationally), as young people's voices become louder in constructing a school experience which has personal significance.

A motor control perspective

Amotivation, lack of confidence and lack of exercise result in a vicious circle which is pushing Tony to be progressively less active. From motor control, biomechanical and physiological perspectives, there are short term and long term consequences arising from the lack of physical activity reported by Tony.

Biomechanics (weight impact)

The most obvious effect of the extraneous adipose tissue carried by Tony is on his weight. Mechanically, this translates into increased inertia, making starting, rotating and stopping more difficult (Hills *et al.* 2002). Whilst running, Tony's joints would be subject to higher level of forces and torques compared to other teenagers, and this means that Tony has an increased risk of injury. The relative impact of extra weight depends on the activity. Non-weight bearing activities such as cycling on the flat or swimming (which Tony seems to prefer) are less affected than weight-bearing activities such as running. Activities requiring a lot of weight-bearing rotations, such as football or basketball, will expose Tony's knees to extremely high torques (Bartlett 2007), and his teachers should certainly be aware of this.

Musculo-skeletal system

Muscles strength is the result of contraction, eccentric and concentric, at high intensity (Powers and Howley 2008). Counter to intuition perhaps, Tony is, in absolute terms, comparatively strong because each time he moves he has to counteract high levels of mechanical constraint due to his weight. The ratio between his weight and his power is low, however, and this limits his ability to perform in an explosive event such as sprinting. Changing the weight-power ratio is key to helping Tony to move faster (Regensteiner 2009), so weight loss is the most efficient way to achieve this objective. Yet, Tony's strength is not uniformly spread because the limited spectrum of activities in which he is involved reduces the range of muscles he mobilises. For instance, Tony's quadriceps are likely to be strong, but his core muscles are not. The accumulation of adipose tissue limits also the range of motion that Tony can afford (Park *et al.* 2010). In addition, low level of engagement in physical activity negatively impacts conjunctive tissues, in particular tendons and ligaments (Wearing *et al.* 2006). What is needed is regular, progressive increase in the level of stress imposed to increase or maintain the length of tendons. Any reduction in tendon length due to lack of mobilisation means that the range of motion declines, and this will impact negatively on Tony's ability to move.

Coordination

Lack of engagement in physical activity over a sustained period has resulted in poor coordination. Movement coordination occurs during the crucial phases of childhood and adolescence (Haywood and Getchell 2009). The interaction between perception and action is essential to create a strong perception–action coupling which will facilitate efficient and smooth movements. For instance, when children switch from one type of movement to another, e.g., crawling to walking, it is essential that they experience the changes of action capability in order to link their perception of the environment and the execution of their movement (Adolf 2000). This process is repeated at adolescence when rapid morphological changes occur that lead to a reduction in coordination, making this another critical developmental phase. Lack of coordination leads to poor movement efficiency, which can be defined as a higher energy cost for a given action (Chen *et al.* 2004). Poor coordination also leads to a reduced self-confidence (see earlier analysis from a psychological perspective). Finally there is some evidence that overweight children are more likely than others to have Developmental Coordination Disorder (DCD) (Cairney *et al.* 2005) which is a motor performance impairment.

Cardio-vascular deficiency

Tony is not used to exercising regularly, and this means that he is unlikely to have developed his aerobic system optimally (Sothern 2001). Correcting this is a long-term process. This deficiency puts Tony at a disadvantage when performing endurance-based activities, reinforcing his desire to avoid them. In addition, Tony faces a greatly increased risk of developing diabetes (Hypponen *et al.* 2000).

Potential solutions for Tony

Tony clearly lacks confidence, and he is also objectively limited in some sports. The first step, therefore, is to find activities where his weight constitutes a lesser disadvantage. As mentioned earlier, non-weight bearing activities such as cycling are likely to be better for Tony. They can be tuned to a higher intensity to provoke anaerobic changes, but also undertaken at a lower intensity to improve the aerobic system. Both levels of intensity will increase overall energy output, therefore contributing to a weight-loss programme. A single activity cannot, however, address all the challenges that Tony is facing, so this means that offering a wide range of exercises is likely to be more effective. Special attention needs to be given to the potential risks of injury linked to the high level of forces Tony experiences.

Tony needs to experience a wide range of situations in which he can improve the control of his body and his perception of changes in the environment. This might include the approach of a ball. At the same time, it is important to contain the effect of other limitations, such as lack of relative explosive power. For instance, for someone like Tony, a mid-field football environment would be less favourable than a defence position. Engagement in a range of movement situations is also essential to challenge Tony's core muscle system. Weight lifting could be a particularly good activity for Tony as this would capitalise on his absolute strength and may improve his self esteem. It is vitally important, however, that Tony is prescribed a comprehensive weight lifting programme to help him to improve overall strength. Without this, the risk is that Tony would work only the muscle groups where he is already strong, without challenging the weaker ones. Teachers should be aware that this would serve to increase his muscular imbalance and potentially lead to further injuries.

A pedagogical perspective

So, based on Tony's blog, Paul's interview, and the input of experts in psychology, sociocultural studies and motor control, what should the CPD intervention for the teachers in this school look like? It is important first to clarify that in England the link between PE and physical activity/health has historical roots. Curriculum, medical, and policy (e.g., Department for Education and Skills and Department of Health 2005) authorities reinforce the view that PE and School Sport (PESS) is a key vehicle for reaching all pupils and promoting participation in physical activity. The development of 'confident individuals', who 'value active lifestyles' and 'make informed choices about lifelong physical activity' (Qualifications and Curriculum Authority 2007: 3) is one of the most important missions of PESS. Thus, teachers in England and Wales have, unquestionably, a statutory obligation to promote healthy, active lifestyles. But, how can the pedagogies and practices of these teachers be better informed such that they can meet the needs of Tony and other pupils who share one or more of his characteristics, experiences and challenges? As the research team started to consider the CPD intervention, they were struck by a number of issues that both helped and hindered them in their deliberations.

Perhaps the first thing to point out is that Tony is not alone. Recent statistics in England point that around three in ten (30%) boys (aged 2 to 15) are classed as either overweight or obese (Public Health England 2012). Nor is England alone; World Health Organisation (WHO) statistics tell us that childhood obesity is on the rise (WHO 2013). What this means is that developing informed pedagogies and practices for Tony could offer insights for the many PE teachers around the world facing similar challenges.

The starting point for this CPD intervention should be that all learners are fundamentally different. They are all, however, entitled to meaningful PE experiences. There was no evidence to suggest that Tony felt he was an active member of this school community and/or PE lessons. In the area of PE and health, there are multiple and diverse perspectives on what teachers actually need to know (Corbin 2002; Evans 2003; Kirk 2006). It could be argued, therefore, that teachers need opportunities to consider and debate these perspectives; for example: studies examining health-related school interventions (e.g., Verstraete et al. 2007); established (e.g., SPARK – McKenzie et al. 2004; EPEC – Martin, Anderson and Hodges 2004) and recently developed (Haerens et al. 2011) instructional/pedagogical models; and research from the fields of exercise psychology and body pedagogies (e.g., Evans and Rich 2011).

The motor control perspective presented earlier highlighted that Tony needs opportunities to experience a wide range of activities in which he can improve the control of his body. A broad and balanced curriculum is therefore more appropriate than an exclusive focus on activities such as walking or swimming that Tony favours. Essentially, PE teachers need to explore ways to highlight, utilise and build upon Tony's strengths in order to engage him and facilitate his wider learning. For example, Tony appears capable of analysing the performances of others. The Sport Education curriculum model (Hastie, Martinez de Ojeda and Luquin 2011) encourages students to take different roles and responsibilities within the sports context. Tony could spend some time as a coach with responsibilities to analyse the team's performance and provide constructive feedback and guidance to peers. Cross-curriculum links to other subject areas (e.g., maths through the need to do statistical analysis) and broader learning outcomes (e.g., cognitive development) could also be emphasised. There is certainly evidence to suggest that PE has educational value beyond the development of sports skills (e.g., cognitive ability, social skills, creativity) (Bailey *et al.* 2009). The English National Curriculum also emphasizes that all pupils should progress not only in their ability to perform skills but also to analyse, evaluate and improve their own and others' performances. This form of engagement and opportunities to become affiliated with a team is often valued by pupils (Hastie *et al.* 2011) and could provide a good starting point for developing Tony's sense of belonging and engagement in PE lessons.

Supporting Tony to develop his physical competence is also paramount. In order to do so, PE teachers need to understand how to set up 'task-oriented' activities (both in team games and other activities) to ensure that Tony feels valued and has opportunities to learn and progress (physically) in a non-threatening environment. Ideas from other curriculum approaches, such as Catherine Ennis and colleagues' (1999) 'Sport for Peace' could be debated, adapted, and contextualised with the purpose of contesting any traces of 'fat phobia' (Sykes and McPhail 2008) evident in PE lessons. It is also crucial to enable PE teachers to discuss the contradictory messages pupils receive in relation to the competitive nature of PE. For example, despite conflicting research evidence about the effect of competitive team games (Singleton 2003), the draft National Curriculum in England (currently under consultation) underlines that all pupils should be 'inspired to succeed and excel in competitive sport and other physically-demanding activities' (Department for Education 2013: 179). Similarly, the Youth Sport Strategy (DCMS 2012) in England focuses on encouraging children and young people to participate in competitive school sport, which should be a 'vibrant part of the ethos of all schools' (Bardens *et al.* 2012, p. 5), in order to 'create a sporting habit . . . that will last a lifetime' (DCMS 2012, p. 3). The discourse of competitive sport in PE in England reflects earlier historical debates about the purpose of PE in schools: is it about nurturing elite sporting talent in major sports or providing a variety of sport, exercise and movement opportunities for all children and young people? To some extent, such debates persist in the PE profession, and PE teachers need to examine their own philosophies on this matter, and the evidence of impact on pupils.

The decision to teach PE in single-sex, ability-set groups can also be questioned. Research findings are mixed and contradictory on the benefits of different forms of grouping. Early research showed positive effects of ability grouping for high achievers and negative effects for low achievers (e.g., Kerckhoff 1986), but other studies found no effects for either of these groups or even negative effects for both groups (Braddock and Slavin 1992; Ireson, Hallamm and Hurley 2005; Slavin 1990). Primary children (up to the age of eleven) of all levels of attainment appear to do better when taught in mixed ability classes (Whitburn 2001).

There is a growing body of research, with mixed findings, focusing on the design and effects of physical activity (PA) interventions for children. For example, a recent qualitative study in England (Hester, McKenna and Gately 2010) examined obese young people's experiences of a residential 'weight-loss' camp. Findings showed that, although these young people had positive experiences whilst attending camp, there was a need for sustained and on-going support after the end of the intervention if they were to sustain lifestyle changes. A systematic review of school-based PA interventions found that the outcomes/result of such interventions are 'inconsistent and short term' (Brown and Summerbell 2009: 110). The issue of high drop-out rates has been also highlighted (Alberga *et al.* 2013). Whilst some of these studies offer valuable knowledge about what can be done (highlighting also some of the challenges encountered in the process), important questions remain about how such interventions can work for obese children in and beyond school. The PE profession needs to engage with these debates, examining all such interventions from a critical perspective, to ensure that they are not, without realizing it, viewing PE as a 'corrective agency' with a primary aim to address the 'obesity epidemic' (Evans *et al.* 2003: 220) and contributing to a 'cult of slenderness' (Kirk 2006).

In the broader educational context in England, guidance on developing a pedagogy of personalised learning has been offered and this could also be useful to PE teachers. In practice, personalising learning means that a PE teacher is able to identify and support a pupil or a group of pupils who have limited understanding of certain aspects of a lesson, e.g., a skill, while supporting others to achieve at different levels. Within each group of pupils, and for individuals, variations in levels of achievement, motivation, interest, attitudes and understanding would be recognised by the teacher in the planning process. This type of *detailed, refined* and *tailored* planning and provision assumes that teachers are able and willing to recognise or – borrowing from medical terminology – 'diagnose' pupils' diverse learning needs (Armour, Chambers and Makopoulou 2010). Diagnosing needs (and identifying subsequent learning objectives) is the first step in developing personalised pedagogies. Tony's narrative illustrates vividly why this is an important step to take.

Conclusion

The issues discussed in this chapter are complex and diverse, as are Tony's experiences. In order to support Tony as a learner and improve his enjoyment of PE, teachers need to be aware of the broader research evidence that is available to support their own learning. Looking back on the case narrative and the expert evidence, therefore, it can be argued that the CPD intervention should aim to engage PE teachers as critical, reflective, inquiry-based learners, and 'curriculum makers' (Clandinin and Connelly 1996). Such an approach would stimulate critical analysis of existing perceptions and pedagogies as a basis for developing innovative and effective ways of teaching that are tailored to pupils' needs and specific contexts.

References

Adolph, K.E. (2000). Specificity of learning: why infants fall over a veritable cliff. *Psychological Science,* 11(4), 290–295.

Alberga, A.S., Medd, E.R., Adamo, K.B., Goldfield, G.S., Prudhomme, D., Kenny, G.P. and Sigal, R.J. (2013) 'Top 10 practical lessons learned from physical activity interventions in overweight and obese children and adolescents', *Applied Physiology, Nutrition, & Metabolism*, 38(3): 249–258.

Ames, C. (1992) 'Classrooms: goals, structures, and student motivation', *Journal of Educational Psychology,* 84: 261–271.

Armour, K.M., Chambers, F. and Makopoulou, K. (2010) '"Diagnosis" as the foundation of teachers' professional learning in physical education: a conceptual conversation', paper presented at the *annual meeting of the American Educational Research Association,* Brisbane, September 2010.

Bailey, R., Armour, K., Kirk, D., Jess, M., Pickup, I. and Sandford, R. (2009) 'The educational benefits claimed for physical education and school sport: an academic review', *Research Paper in Education,* 24(1): 1–27.

Bardens, J., Long, R. and Gillie, C. (2012) *School Sport.* London: House of Commons Library.

Bartholomew, K., Ntoumanis, N. and Thøgersen-Ntoumani, C. (2009) 'A review of controlling motivational strategies from a Self-Determination Theory perspective: implications for sports coaches', *International Review of Sport and Exercise Psychology,* 2: 215–233.

Bartlett, R. (2007) *Introduction to Sports Biomechanics,* 2nd edn, London: Routledge.

Bourdieu, P. (1990) *The Logic of Practice,* Cambridge: Blackwell Publishers.

Braddock, J.H. and Slavin, R.E. (1992) 'Why ability grouping must end: achieving excellence and equity in American education', paper presented at the Common Destiny Conference, Baltimore, September 1992.

Brown, T. and Summerbell, C. (2009) 'Systematic review of school-based interventions that focus on changing dietary intake and physical activity levels to prevent childhood obesity: an update to the obesity guidance produced by the National Institute for Health and Clinical Excellence', *Obesity Reviews,* 10: 110–141.

Cairney, J., Hay, J.A., Faught, B.E. and Hawes, R. (2005) 'Developmental coordination disorder and over-weight and obesity in children aged 9–14 years', *International Journal of Obesity,* 29: 369–372.

Cale, L. (2000) 'Physical activity promotion in schools – PE teachers' views', *European Journal of Physical Education,* 5(2): 158–167.

Cale, L. and Harris, J. (2009) 'Fitness testing in physical education – a misdirected effort in promoting healthy lifestyles and physical activity?', *Physical Education & Sport Pedagogy,* 14(1): 89–108.

Carlson, T.B. (1995) 'We hate gym: student alienation from physical education', *Journal of Teaching in Physical Education,* 14: 467–477.

Chen, A. (2001) 'A theoretical conceptualization for motivation research in physical education: an integrated perspective', *Quest,* 53: 35–58.

Chen, K., Acra, S., Donahue, C., Sun, M. and Buchowski1, M.S. (2004) 'Efficiency of walking and stepping: relationship to body fatness', *Obesity Research,* 12(6): 982–989.

Clandinin, D.L. and Connelly, F.M. (1996) 'Teachers' professional knowledge landscapes: teacher stories – stories of teachers – school stories – stories of schools', *Educational Researcher,* 25(3): 24–30.

Corbin, C.B. (2002) 'Physical activity for everyone: what every physical educators should know about promoting lifelong physical activity', *Journal of Teaching in Physical Education,* 21: 128–144.

DCMS (2012) *Creating a Sporting Habit for Life: A New Youth Sport Strategy.* London: Department for Culture, Media and Sport.

Deci, E.L. and Ryan, R.M. (2000) 'The "what" and "why" of goal pursuits: human needs and the self-determination of behavior', *Psychological Inquiry,* 11: 227–268.

Department for Education (2013) *The National Curriculum in England: Framework Document for Consultation.* Online. Available HTTP: <http://media.education.gov.uk/assets/files/pdf/n/national%20curriculum%20consultation%20-%20framework%20document.pdf> (accessed 23 September 2013).

Department for Education and Skills and Department of Health (2005) *National Healthy School Status. A Guide for Schools.* London: author.

Ennis, C.D., Solmon, M.A., Satina, Loftus, S.J., Mensch, J. and McCauley, M.T. (1999) 'Creating a sense of family in urban schools using the "Sport for Peace" Curriculum', *Research Quarterly for Exercise & Sport,* 70: 273–285.

Evans, J. (2003) 'Physical education and health: a polemic or "let them eat cake"', *European Physical Education Review,* 9(1): 87–101.

Evans, J., Evans, B. and Rich, E. (2003) '"The only problem is, children will like their chips": education and the discursive production of ill-health', *Pedagogy, Culture & Society,* 11(2): 215–240.

Evans, J. and Rich, E. (2011) 'Body policies and body pedagogies: every child matters in totally pedago-gised schools?' *Journal of Education Policy,* 26(3): 361–379.

Gard, M., Hickey-Moodey, A. and Enright, E. (2013) 'Youth culture, physical education and the question of relevance: after 20 years, a reply to Tinning and Fitzclarence', *Sport, Education & Society,* 18(1): 97–114.

Green, K. (2008) *Understanding Physical Education.* London: Sage.

Greenleaf, C. and Weiller, K. (2005) 'Perceptions of youth obesity among physical educators', *Social Psychology of Education,* 8: 407–423.

Haerens, L., Kirk, D., Cardon, G. and de Bourdeaudhuij, I. (2011) 'Towards the development of a pedagogical model for health-based physical education', *Quest,* 63(3): 321–338.

Harris, J. (2000) *Health-Related Exercise in the National Curriculum: Key Stages 1 to 4.* London: Human Kinetics Publishers.

Hart, E.A., Leary, M.R. and Rejeski, W.J. (1989) 'The measurement of social physique anxiety', *Journal of Sport & Exercise Psychology,* 11: 94–104.

Hastie, P.A., Martinez de Ojeda, D. and Luquin, C. (2011) 'A review of research on sport education: 2004 to the present', *Physical Education & Sport Pedagogy,* 16(2): 103–132.

Haywood, K.M. and Getchell, N. (2009) *Life Span Motor Development,* 5th edn. London: Human Kinetics.

Hester, J.R., McKenna, J. and Gately, P.J. (2010) 'Obese young people's accounts of intervention impact', *Patient Education & Counseling,* 79(3): 306–314.

Hills, A.P., Hennig, E.M., Byrne N.M. and Steele J.R. (2002) 'The biomechanics of adiposity – structural and functional limitations of obesity and implications for movement', *Obesity Reviews,* 3: 35–43.

Hypponen, E., Virtanen, S., Kenward, M., G., Mikaelknip, M.D. and Akerblom, H. (2000) 'Obesity, increased linear growth, and risk of Type 1 diabetes in children', *Diabetes Care,* 23(12): 1755–1760.

Ireson, J., Hallamm, S. and Hurley, C. (2005) 'What are the effects of ability grouping on GCSE attainment?', *British Educational Research Journal,* 31(4): 443–458.

Kerckhoff, A.C. (1986) 'Effects of ability grouping in British secondary schools', *American Sociological Review,* 51(6): 842–858.

Kirk, D. (2006) 'The "obesity crisis" and school physical education', *Sport, Education & Society,* 11(2): 121–133.

Martin, J.J., Anderson, S.R. and Hodges, P. (2004) 'The influence of EPEC professional development training on curricular efficacy', paper presented at the *Annual meeting of the American Alliance for Health, Physical Education, Recreation and Dance,* New Orleans, LA, March 2004.

McKenzie T.L., Sallis, J.F., Prochaska, J.J., Conway, T.L., Marshall, S.J. and Rosengard, P. (2004) 'Evaluation of a two-year middle school physical education intervention: M-SPAN', *Medicine & Science in Sports & Exercise,* 36: 1382–1388.

Ntoumanis, N. (2002) 'Motivational clusters in a sample of British physical education classes', *Psychology of Sport & Exercise,* 3: 177–194.

Ntoumanis, N., Pensgaard, A.M., Martin, C. and Pipe, K. (2004) 'An ideographic analysis of amotivation in compulsory school physical education', *Journal of Sport & Exercise Psychology,* 26: 197–214.

OFSTED (2009) *Physical Education in schools 2005/8.* London: The Office for Standards in Education, Children's Services and Skills (Ofsted).

Park, W., Ramachandran, J., Weisman, P. and Jung, E.S. (2010) 'Obesity effect on Male active joint range of motion', *Ergonomics,* 53(1): 102–108.

Powers, S.K. and Howley, E.T. (2008) *Exercise Physiology,* 7th edn, New York: McGraw Hill.

Public Health England (2012) *Statistics on obesity, physical activity and diet: England, 2012.* Online. Available HTTP: <www.noo.org.uk/news.php?nid=1850> (accessed on 23 September 2013).

Puhl, R.M. and Heuer, C.A. (2009) 'The stigma of obesity: a review and update', *Obesity,* 17: 941–964.

Qualifications and Curriculum Authority (2007) *Physical Education: Programme of Study for Key Stage 3 and Attainment Target.* London: Qualification and Curriculum Authority.

Reeve, J. (2009) 'Why teachers adopt a controlling motivating style toward students and how they can become more autonomy supportive', *Educational Psychologist,* 44: 159–175.

Regensteiner, J.G. (2009) *Contemporary Diabetes: Diabetes and Exercise,* Boston: Humana Press.

Sabiston, C.M., Sedgwick, W.A., Crocker, P.R.E., Kowalski, K.C. and Mack, D.E. (2007) 'Social physique anxiety in adolescence: an exploration of influences, coping strategies, and health behaviors', *Journal of Adolescent Research,* 22: 78–101.

Singleton, E. (2003) 'Rules? Relationships? A feminist analysis of competition and fair play in physical education', *Quest,* 55: 193–209.

Slavin, R.E. (1990) 'Achievement effects of ability grouping in secondary schools: a best-evidence synthesis', *Review of Educational Research,* 60(3): 471–499.

Sothern, M. (2001) 'Exercise as a modality in the treatment of childhood obesity', *Pediatric Clinics of North America,* 48(4): 995–1015.

Standage, M., Treasure, D.C., Hooper, K. and Kuczka, K. (2007) 'Self-handicapping in school physical education: the influence of the motivational climate', *British Journal of Educational Psychology,* 77: 81–99.

Swidler, A. (1986) 'Culture in action: symbols and strategies', *American Sociological Review,* 51(2): 273–286.

Sykes, H. and McPhail, D. (2008) 'Unbearable lessons: contesting fat phobia in physical education', *Sociology of Sport Journal,* 25: 66–96.

Treasure, D. (2001) 'Enhancing young people's motivation in youth sport: an achievement goal perspective', in G.C. Roberts (ed.) *Advances in Motivation in Sport and Exercise,* 2nd edn, (pp. 79–100). Champaign, IL: Human Kinetics.

Trost, S.G. (2004) 'School physical education in the post-report era: an analysis from public health', *Journal of Teaching in Physical Education,* 23: 318–337.

Trouilloud, D., Sarrazin, P., Bressoux, P. and Bois, J. (2006) 'Relation between teachers' early expectations and students' later perceived competence in physical education classes: autonomy-supportive climate as a moderator', *Journal of Educational Psychology,* 98: 75–86.

Verstraete, S.J., Cardon, G.M., De Clercq, D.L.R. and De Bourdeaudhuij, I.M.M. (2007) 'Effectiveness of a two-year health-related physical education intervention in elementary schools', *Journal of Teaching in Physical Education,* 26: 20–34.

Vygotsky, L.S. (1978) *Mind and Society: The Development of Higher Mental Processes.* Cambridge, MA: Harvard University Press.

Wearing, S.C., Hennig, E.M., Byrne, N.M., Steele, J.R. and Hills, A.P. (2006) 'The impact of childhood obesity on musculoskeletal form', *Obesity Reviews,* 7(2): 209–218.

Whitburn, J. (2001) 'Effective classroom organization in primary schools: mathematics', *Oxford Review of Education,* 27(3): 411–428.

World Health Organisation (2013) *Obesity and overweight.* Online. Available HTTP: <www.who.int/mediacentre/factsheets/fs311/en/index.html> (accessed 23 September 2013).

Wright, J. (2004) 'Critical inquiry and problem-solving in physical education', in J. Wright, D. Macdonald and L. Burrows (eds.) *Critical Inquiry and Problem-Solving in Physical Education,* Routledge: London.

13

MARIA[1]

Italian, female, and pursuing dreams of elite soccer success in Switzerland

Dean Barker, Natalie Barker-Ruchti, Markus Gerber and Uwe Pühse

DEPARTMENT FOR FOOD AND NUTRITION, AND SPORT SCIENCE, UNIVERSITY OF GOTHENBURG, SWEDEN;
INSTITUTE OF EXERCISE AND HEALTH SCIENCES, UNIVERSITY OF BASEL, SWITZERLAND

Key words: 14-year-old female, migration background, keen football player, critical ethnicity, gender studies, psychology, pedagogy.

Maria

Switzerland, Sunday 8.20pm: Maria is standing half way up the terrace staircase beside a large group of chanting football fans. The game is going on behind her back because she is concentrating on selling ice creams and cold drinks. This is frustrating for Maria since she is an avid fan and devoted football player. But for the diminutive 14 year old of Italian migration background, it is still preferable to working in the seated areas where the "fans" barely cheer or shout. The terraces are where the action takes place, where the atmosphere is created.

When the game finishes Maria leaves, satisfied that the money she has earned will go to her own football club. She takes the bus home and is soon outside her apartment block. Maria lives with her mother, brother and two sisters. Her dad moved out of the family home when she was 4 years old, and he now lives in a small one bedroom apartment nearby. As she climbs the stairs to her home, Maria remembers that several days ago she decided not to speak to her family following a disagreement over household chores with her younger sister, Chiara. Maria resolves to continue the stand-off, turns the key in the lock and enters the apartment. Maria's mother is watching the news on one of the Italian channels but looks up and greets Maria. Maria does not respond but instead makes herself some muesli and fruit and goes up to the room in the attic. She considers calling her boyfriend but settles for watching football and listening to music before going to bed.

Monday 6.45am: Maria is awoken by her phone alarm and starts to get ready for school. She would like to put on her track suit but several teachers have spoken to her class about appropriate clothing. The teachers argue that although the students may be in a sport class,[2] this does not mean that they can dress for recreation when they come to school. Instead, they argue, school is about preparing for a vocation, and students should dress accordingly. Maria ponders this as she finishes a nectarine: "_As if I didn't know the difference between dressing for school_ *and dressing for work. And besides, professional footballers do wear track suits to work*". She wonders how the teachers would react if she turned up at school like her sister and many other girls: dressed in a very short mini skirt and covered in thick make-up. They probably wouldn't even recognize her.

Monday 7.25am: Maria's first lesson is mathematics. It is not her strongest subject and, to make matters worse, her teacher, Herr Schmocker, is absent. Maria respects Herr Schmocker. He is tall, blond and Swiss; he is also good at sports and seems to understand what it is that Maria and her classmates like so much about sports. She wonders why he might be absent and then remembers that he mentioned a knee operation. *"That's what happens when you get old"* she thinks. She returns to her textbook and works through the first set of questions. Maria knows she needs to work hard in mathematics if she wants a good school report but still she finds it difficult. The activities make her tired, numb almost. Her mind wanders to Cristiano Ronaldo and his goal against Milan on Saturday and then to her trip back to Sicily two weeks ago where she played football with some local boys. Her brother introduced them, and they were so surprised because Italian boys had never seen a girl play football. With some effort Maria brings herself back to the lesson, giving the clock a quick glance.

Monday 2.20pm: It is mid-afternoon and Maria and her classmates are just finishing their French lesson. Maria has just come top of the class in a vocabulary test, and she is feeling good. The students leave the building and disperse. Other classes have at least one more lesson to complete before finishing and the schoolyard is empty. Maria's training does not start for another two and a half hours so she has time to spare. She decides to stop by the shopping mall to see if her cousin is working at the sports shop.

After helping a customer, Mario finds Maria in the shoe section of the shop.

"Ciao, Bella! How are you?" Mario asks.

"Good."

"What are you doing here? Why aren't you at football training?" says Mario with a slight frown.

"It's not till later." responds Maria.

"Good. Good. How's it going? Who did you play on Saturday?"

"Yverdon. Two-one. I got both our goals." Maria attempts modesty but it is obvious she is very proud.

"Bravo." says Mario, genuinely pleased for his younger cousin.

"There was a guy there. Talked to my coach. Asked who I was and how old I am. He thought I was 16. He asked me if I had a Swiss passport. I said no."

"What did he say then?"

"He just said, 'Go and get it as quick as possible'. He said that I could only come when I was 15 anyway. But he said that he thought I would get into the national squad."

"Hey, wow! That's the big time! You gotta get training. How's that left foot coming along – you know they'll be checking that out."

"Yeah."

"Hey, I gotta get that customer over there but I'll see you on Sunday. We're coming over for lunch. You can tell me more then."

"Yeah, ok. Bye"

"Ciao."

As Maria walks away, she remembers that she will miss the afternoon with her cousins because she will be at a soccer training camp for the whole weekend.

Monday 4.20pm: Maria arrives forty minutes too early for training. She takes her time putting on her football clothes and boots, and once she's ready she begins her warm-up routine. She jogs, skips, side-steps, jogs backwards, and stretches and does some sit-ups. She will be repeating these activities later but that's okay. She reasons that the more training she does, the better player she will be and the more valuable she will be to her team when she's older. She is resting after her fifth set of sit ups when her friend Valentina arrives and calls out. Valentina, like Maria, lives near the football ground and does not need to take public transport to get to training. Maria and Valentina have played together for several years and often talk nostalgically about when they played football on the boys' team. Both feel that they would learn more if they were still playing with the boys. Valentina has a ball in her bag that she takes out and drop-kicks forcefully to Maria. Maria deflects the ball with the outside of her right foot taking most of the power out of the kick. She turns gracefully and follows after the ball as it runs away from her. For the first time that day, Maria feels alive and free.

A critical ethnicity perspective

There is a growing body of literature that examines race and ethnicity as it relates to sport and pedagogy (Chappell 2002; Azzarito 2009; Azzarito and Solmon 2006; Barker *et al.* 2011). In the face of globalization and increasing cultural heterogeneity, researchers have examined racism (Carrington 2011; Hylton 2011), inclusion and exclusion (Dagkas, Benn and Jawad 2011; Elling and Claringbould 2005), and identity construction (Burdsey 2007; Walseth 2006). Our intention here is not to provide a summary of this literature; rather it is to select key ideas that are relevant to Maria's case and that could be important for teachers and coaches working with groups of young people.

The idea of *capital* has proven useful for thinking through the social relevance of sport participation (Coalter 2007). For Bourdieu (1991), cultural capital relates to knowing how to act in certain circumstances and is related to status. In sport, it has been claimed that individuals with migration backgrounds sometimes have less cultural capital in sport settings (knowledge about training and competition, dress, work ethic and so forth) and therefore they navigate these environments less successfully than others (Burdsey 2004). To an outsider, Maria does not appear to lack cultural capital. She probably dresses in the "right way" by eschewing make-up and traditionally feminine clothes, and she has fan knowledge. In addition, she shows commitment by arriving early to training, and she is a skilled player.

At the same time, it is worth considering a second kind of capital, which refers to knowing people, or being connected (Putnam 2000). Burdsey (2004) suggests that to succeed in the world of youth football, personal contacts are vital. Scouting procedures, for example, have typically revolved around established networks of parents, teachers, club managers and regional selectors. Having an existing contact within the game is a significant advantage but young people with migration backgrounds rarely have these contacts. Maria has a cousin who works in a sports shop but this is quite different from having a cousin that has played professional football or a father who is friendly with the under-19 national coach. Her own coach, then, becomes a crucial person in connecting Maria to people who will facilitate her movement into networks that exist in higher levels of the sport.

It is important to note here that ethnic difference should not be equated with problems. Some social scientific critiques of sport have been based on the notion of individuals being "caught between cultures" (Carroll and Hollinshead 1993). This work has concentrated on risks and deficits, and the "inevitable tensions" that occur in culturally heterogeneous settings. It would be relatively easy to apply this thinking to Maria and to consider the kinds of conflict her south Italian background might cause as she interacts with Swiss culture. An obvious example would be how Maria might find herself pulled between, say, a traditional culture that discourages female sport participation and a culture that is more open to female involvement.

Recently though, the idea of "caught between cultures" has received critique (Knez 2010). First, it supports the notion of monolithic, distinct cultures. Yet, commentators have argued that national cultures are imagined and instead are always made up of a myriad of sub-cultures (Müller, Van Zoonen and De Roode 2008). To say that Maria's Italian heritage discourages sport participation would be to miss the variety of ways there are to be Italian (and Swiss). This leads to a second critique: the culture gap thesis overlooks cultural interaction and hybridization. Maria does not have to be seen as *either/or,* or even *both* Italian and Swiss. It is quite possible to see Maria in her particular circumstances as someone forming a new personal way of being that will change according to context. Finally, the idea of "caught between" tends to portray individuals as disoriented and confused (Brah 1996). This ignores the ways in which individuals are actively involved in creating hybrid and "hyphenated" identities.

There has been some interest in how young, non-white individuals invest (or do not invest – see Barker *et al.* 2011) in sporting identities and how this investment relates to success in other areas of life, such as school (Brooks 2011). It would be possible to read Maria's case from this kind of transactional perspective, where soccer takes time away from schooling and diminishes personal resources that will prove useful later for employment. From this point of view, a teacher or coach might be tempted to encourage Maria to reduce the amount of sport she does, an idea to which we will return. First though, we are going to consider a second reading of Maria's case based on gender.

A gender perspective

In social theory, gender is seen as socially constructed and *performed*. Many feminist researchers have analyzed social phenomena including media representations of athletes (e.g. Markula 2009), sporting organizations (e.g. Shaw and Slack 2002), women coaches (e.g. Norman 2010) and athletes' sporting experiences (e.g. Barker-Ruchti 2011). A gender approach has also been used to understand how individuals challenge and re-construct masculine and feminine ideals. Such research has provided insights into how dominant gender ideologies can be reformulated by those involved in sport (e.g. Pringle 2008; Theberge 2003). In what follows, we employ this perspective to develop interpretations on how Maria (re-)constructs and performs gender.

Before presenting our interpretations, it is worth considering the Swiss and Italian contexts of women's soccer. In both countries, traditional gender stereotypes shape women's soccer. Historically, this has meant that men have organized, played and watched soccer on the "center stage", while the women's game has taken place on the margins. Although women's clubs have been founded since the beginning of the 20th century and despite the current popularity of women's soccer, the social perception of women players, the media coverage that games receive, and the financial support that flows to female teams, are still starkly unequal to that of men (Matteucci 2012; Meier, 2004).

Within this context, Maria's narrative gains significance. How did Maria come to participate in soccer within this resistant context? How did Maria develop her passion and commitment for this sport? These questions are puzzling given that girls, and in particular girls with immigration backgrounds, have been found to face opposition regarding their choices of sports (Kleindienst-Cachay 2007). Maria's case did not reveal instances of overt resistance and, at this point in time, her continued participation in soccer seems assured, even without additional backing from her club or coach.

Answers to the questions of how Maria was able to develop passion and commitment despite social reservations can help those involved in soccer understand how gender ideals become redefined. Sobiech (2012) suggests that exceptional stories have the potential to re-construct traditional gender ideologies. By choosing soccer and striving to become an international player, we would suggest that Maria challenges the popular assumption that women are not suited to team sports traditionally played by men. By playing soccer, which involves actions typically associated with men (e.g. aggressive tackling, explosive shooting), Maria redefines corporeal ideals. While Maria's passion and commitment for soccer are highly valued in the communities in which she is integrated, she may face negative reactions from members of other communities, particularly as she approaches adulthood. Lesbian prejudices, in particular, have been attached to women soccer players (Degele and Janz 2012).

Maria's narrative also points to ways in which she maintains traditional ideals of femininity. She reminisces with her team player Valentina, for instance, about playing with boys because they believe that through such contact they could become (even) better soccer players. This points to assumptions made by Valentina and Maria that boys not only play a different game, but also a *better* one. From a social justice perspective, a biological deterministic account of men's and women's sporting abilities has been criticized widely (e.g. Hargreaves 1994) largely because it suggests that oppression of women by men is natural. But even from a performance perspective, this deficit-approach to women's performance might be counter-productive because women come to believe that they cannot play as well as men.

A further way that Maria can be seen to embody traditional ideals of femininity is her dependence on her cousin and the talent scout she meets at the tournament in Yverdon. Women's submissiveness and dependence on others, often male coaches, have been found in numerous situations in sport (e.g. Barker-Ruchti 2008; Barker *et al.* in press). Maria seems to have developed a close relationship with her male cousin, mainly because he understands and supports her passion and enthusiasm for soccer. While relying on scouts to identify talent may be a common way for soccer careers to progress, this dependence has been problematized (e.g. Unnithan *et al.* 2012). No research has examined the male scout-female player relationship, but gender discourses, particularly in relation to passivity, may put players in disadvantageous positions. In Maria's situation, her non-Swiss citizenship may also increase this disadvantage.

An acculturation psychology and self-determination perspective

Immigrants who reside in culturally plural societies have different strategies for tackling the process of acculturation. Following Berry (2006), such strategies relate to attitudes (preferences) and behaviors (actual practices), which can be recognized in day-to-day intercultural encounters. Examples of such encounters include what a person values, what a person eats and drinks, what language a person uses, and in what environment a person feels most comfortable.

While ethnic majority populations often think that assimilation is the best way to integrate into the host society (Makarova 2008), it is important to note that not all immigrants seek contact with the dominant group, nor are all immigrants willing to abandon their minority culture in favor of the culture of the mainstream society. Given this notion, acculturation psychology (Sam 2006) generally distinguishes four prototypical acculturation strategies:

> *Biculturalism* (relationships sought among groups, interest in maintaining the heritage culture and identity),
>
> *Separation* (no interest in intercultural contacts, focus on maintenance of heritage culture and identity),
>
> *Assimilation* (relationships sought among groups, willingness to abandon own heritage culture and identity), and
>
> *Marginalization* (no interest in intercultural contacts and maintenance of heritage culture).

In Maria's case, we see a girl who is willing to adopt an integrative approach towards acculturation. While it is obvious that she still values her Italian heritage culture (evidenced by the frequent "code switching" between Italian and German and the importance of family activities), she seeks contact with the Swiss culture by choosing a sport that is uncommon among girls in her home place (Sicily). In addition, Maria is an ardent fan of the local football team, and is proud to be a volunteer who earns money for her own football club.

In some respects, Maria can be considered as a relatively atypical Italian girl. Recent surveys show that South-European girls are less physically active than their Swiss female counterparts, and that South-European girls are notoriously underrepresented in organized sports (Lamprecht, Fischer and Stamm 2008). On the other hand, studies also show that biculturalism is an important route towards integration for many youngsters with migration backgrounds. In recent studies with Swiss adolescents, the two dominant acculturation strategies were biculturalism and separation, whereas few youngsters opted for an assimilatory approach (Makarova, 2008; Gerber *et al.* in preparation). This finding is corroborated in other European countries (Phinney *et al.* 2006). Given this knowledge, the question arises about how participation in youth sports can increase the likelihood that immigrant youth choose a bicultural attitude towards acculturation. In the following paragraphs, self-determination theory (Deci and Ryan 2000) will be used to explain how Maria's engagement in a bicultural sport setting strengthens her bicultural identity.

As a starting point, bicultural identities do not appear automatically. Rather, becoming bicultural is an active process that needs *motivation* from both the immigrant and the members of the host society. Deci and Ryan (2000) posited that motivation should be regarded as a continuum with varying degrees of self-determination. *Intrinsic regulation* generally represents the highest level of self-determination. In this form, integration into the host society is sought for its own sake, because biculturalism and contact with people of the host society enrich one's daily life. *Identified regulation* is the next level, where integration is sought because the consequences are valued and endorsed (e.g. intercultural contacts can be used as a door opener). The two forms of non-self-determined motivation (self-discordance) include: *introjected regulation* where a person seeks intercultural contacts because otherwise she/he would feel guilty; and *external regulation* where intercultural contacts are only sought because other people want it (e.g. the parents would punish him/her otherwise).

Deci and Ryan (2000) further posited that intrinsic motivation is promoted if a certain behavior contributes to the satisfaction of basic psychological needs such as *autonomy, competence* and *relatedness*. Recent research supports this idea across various types of behaviors including physical activity engagement (Teixeira *et al.* 2012). We assume, therefore, that participation in bicultural sport-settings can bolster youngsters' motivation to adopt a bicultural attitude if these basic psychological needs are satisfied through regular intercultural contacts.

For Maria, football contributes to her development as an autonomous young person. It gives her life meaning, and thus helps her to cope with school pressure and family conflict. The decision to engage in football was taken freely (despite possible cultural gender role conflicts as noted above), and it is up to Maria alone to plan her future career as a football player. Maria likes the training in her mixed-ethnic football club because she is a respected person and can be herself *despite* her Italian background. Moreover, participation in mixed-ethnic football makes an important contribution to Maria's need for competence. Being recognized as a talented player by a Swiss scout makes Maria happy and proud; and the prospect of playing in the Swiss national team is a strong incentive to become further integrated in Swiss society. Finally, being a football player and being part of a football team helps Maria to feel related to other Swiss youngsters and adults. Practicing regularly during training sessions and training camps provides her with the opportunity for continued intercultural contacts and for building enduring friendships with Swiss peers. How much she values these contacts is illustrated through Maria's wish to support her team through excellent performances on the pitch. Finally, Maria's attitudes towards her training clearly illustrate that she has adopted values that correspond with accepted Swiss work ethics.

In summary, Maria's case illustrates how positive experiences in youth sport can reinforce youngsters' motivation to adopt biculturalism as an acceptable strategy towards acculturation. The other side of the coin, however, is that mixed-ethnic youth sports may hinder integration if they fail to support adolescents' need for autonomy, and feelings of mastery, and do not actively foster mutual respect and acceptance. A final remark seems necessary regarding the potential of participation in mono-ethnic sport settings. Although such settings do not have the same potential to strengthen intrinsic motivation towards biculturalism, they are valuable in other ways so cannot be dismissed. For example, they may be well suited to satisfying basic psychological needs within minority communities. In addition to that, regular participation in mono-ethnic sports may help to address some of the health disparities that still exist in many European societies (Rommel, Weilandt and Eckert 2006).

A pedagogical perspective

For coaches of young performance athletes, Maria's case offers several key learning points. These points are centred on the following themes: (i) capital; (ii) (non)problematization of difference, (iii) identity construction; (iv) consideration of context; (v) changing narratives; (vi) promotion of independence; (vii) player adaptation; and (viii) basic psychological needs in terms of autonomy, competence and relatedness.

Player capital

Both the wider literature and Maria's case suggest that it is necessary to be cognizant of ways in which players' personal histories provide them with different levels of sporting cultural capital, i.e. implicit knowledge of how to act, dress, talk etc. within the sport (Burdsey 2004). Some players will both appear and feel more natural and "at home" than others in sporting contexts. They will, essentially, look and feel as if they belong. This appearance of belonging may – or may not – be related to ethnicity. (For example, some ethnic minorities [stereotypically] may look as if they are naturally suited to certain sports – i.e. African-Americans in basketball – see Brooks [2011] for a discussion). To ensure that selection processes are fair, coaches should recognize different ways that athletes can display cultural capital and how these might afford players different opportunities. When players do not have the "right look", coaches have at least two options. They could attempt to teach these players "how things are done" perhaps by providing buddies, or more experienced players as mentors, who can show these new individuals what is expected of them and how to handle particular situations. Alternatively – or in combination – coaches might attempt to promote the value of performance behaviors such as work ethic, tactical thinking and motoric excellence while limiting the emphasis and value assigned to other factors that are not directly related to performance (e.g. clothing, ways of talking, and hairstyle).

(Non)problematization of difference

Current theorizing suggests that cultural differences do not necessarily lead to problems (Knez 2010). Indeed, athletes themselves may feel that sport is an arena in which cultural differences matter little or not at all. Addressing cultural difference, then, is something that should be done with care and in recognition of the fact that it is often challenging. One factor that creates difficulties is that many of the ways we have for talking about cultural difference are grounded in deficit thinking. Accordingly, being different implies being somehow less capable. Coaches should certainly attempt to avoid enacting deficit models as these could further alienate athletes.

Other identities

Recent literature suggests that athletes should be given opportunities to create other non-sporting identities (Coakley 2007). There is also some literature reporting that athletes from minority groups are less likely to develop multiple identities and that academic development frequently suffers as a result of intense sporting involvement (Brooks 2011). The solution appears to be relatively simple: ensure that athletes have interests beyond sport and encourage them to work on other aspects of education while they are developing a sporting career. While intuitively appealing, this solution is probably easier said than done in many settings as elite athletes face increasing pressure to specialize (Rishe 2003). Further, we might ask whether simply freeing up time for academic study will actually improve academic performance. In Maria's case, decreasing involvement in sport might not necessarily mean that she will develop a passion for another activity. It is also conceivable that her sporting involvement complements her academic life and that her educational performance would suffer if she reduced her involvement in sport. It should be recognized that while Maria's intense sport participation *might* negatively affect her chances of social mobility, it also improves her general sense of well-being. So whereas there is evidence to suggest that young athletes should be encouraged to develop other aspects of their capabilities, this is a complex issue. Who would be brave enough to state, with certainty, that achieving better academic grades will make Maria a more successful/happier/more fulfilled person?

Context

Consideration of context, or culture, emerged as an important factor from all three interpretations in this case. There is agreement that it is useful to reflect on the contexts in which sporting practices take place and consider the kinds of taken for granted assumptions that predominate. It may be beneficial to think, for example, about how particular common sense assumptions define what it means to be an athlete, female, and/or have a particular cultural heritage. It may also be productive to think about where such assumptions might shape an athlete's behavior in negative or positive ways. This kind of reflective understanding of context could result in a greater appreciation of the choices made by individual athletes. This would seem to be particularly advantageous in cases where athletes' backgrounds and experiences differ markedly from those of their coaches.

Changing narratives

As a girl from an Italian family – or indeed any family – Maria is doing something rather unusual (see Meier and Hürlimann 2012, for participation figures). She might encounter difficulties as she challenges established understandings and constructs new ways of being. Coaches should appreciate the effort it can take for athletes to "re-reformulate" (Pringle 2008; Theberge 2003) "acceptable" stories. Consider, for example, the small but significant number of women aged 25 and over who are still competing in elite gymnastics despite the prevailing story of success being the preserve of very young gymnasts. New stories encourage us, as teachers, coaches and policy makers, to have a degree of flexibility concerning athletes and be open to the possibility that people with a wide range of characteristics can be successful. Clearly this idea represents a challenge to some traditional understandings of talent identification (Unnithan *et al.* 2012) where certain attributes are thought to be necessary for success. The intention here is not to refute this contention totally, but rather to suggest that athletes might have the capacity to write different success stories from those that we expect and that without our support, they are less likely to do this. In other words, being open to new narratives could have positive outcomes for all parties.

Independence

Some research shows that athletes, and female athletes in particular, assume a relatively passive stance towards their sport participation (Barker-Ruchti 2008). They can become submissive, relying on their coaches to tell them how and when to train. Athletes justify this level of submission because they believe it is essential for success. Yet, it is difficult to support any claim that passive athletes are more successful; to our knowledge, there are no large scale projects that investigate this claim. There are however, emerging findings that suggest that submissive behavior on the part of athletes results in a greater potential for athlete abuse (Barker-Ruchti 2011) and that submissive athletes may experience increased difficulties when they leave sport (Barker *et al.* in press). For these reasons alone, it would seem prudent to encourage athletes to make decisions and take responsibility for their athletic careers. From a pedagogical perspective, of course, growing learner independence from an instructor is a cornerstone of effective practice.

Player adaptation

It is important for youth sport providers to ensure that regardless of cultural background, adolescents feel valued and accepted in sport situations. Furthermore, it is important to provide equal opportunities for youth with and without migration backgrounds. Creating caring and safe learning climates is central to supporting player adaptation. Young people with different ethnic backgrounds need to feel they can communicate on equal terms, thus facilitating the development of intercultural links.

Basic psychological needs

The classic psychology literature suggests that it is important to promote intrinsic motivation (Deci and Ryan 2000). To do this, behaviors should contribute to the satisfaction of an individual's basic psychological needs such as autonomy, competence and relatedness (Teixeira *et al.* 2012). Autonomy is similar to independence (described above) and refers to an individual's sense of control over a situation. Feelings of competence can be supported by designing tasks that athletes find challenging yet achievable. Relatedness is about generating a sense of belonging and might signal athletes feeling connected to other athletes and to the club/activity. This final aspect can be enhanced by various strategies including the provision of non-sporting activities such as cooking and eating together where sporting performance is not the focus. Opportunities for athletes to demonstrate skills from other areas of their lives may also be useful in increasing self-esteem and mutual respect.

Summary

Research from the fields of critical ethnicity, gender, and acculturation psychology/self determination theory provide different concepts with which we can think about Maria in a pedagogical context. We have identified what we see as some of the main points from three sub-disciplinary perspectives, that could be relevant to teachers and coaches who are responsible for structuring an effective learning environment for Maria and other young people who share some of her characteristics and experiences. We recognize, of course, that others using the same broad perspectives could draw different conclusions, and we have indicated where there are areas of disagreement in the literature. Our interpretations, therefore, are presented as evidence-based ideas to "play with" rather than as rigid guidelines. As ever, in a youth sport setting, theories and concepts should be considered and adapted to reflect individual situations and circumstances.

Notes

1. This case is a grounded-fictional account (Alvesson, 2002) based on data collected within the project "Social integration of youths with migration background through sport". The project was conducted in Basel, Switzerland and was funded by the Swiss National Science Foundation (grant number 100017–120380).
2. A number of schools in Switzerland have "sport classes". These classes contain students that have substantial sport commitments, and lessons are organized so that students can balance their sporting and academic endeavors.

References

Alvesson, M. (2002) *Postmodernism and social research*. Buckingham: Open University Press.

Azzarito, L. (2009) 'The Panopticon of physical education: Pretty, active and ideally white', *Physical Education & Sport Pedagogy,* 14: 19–39.

Azzarito, L. and Solmon, M.A. (2006) 'A post-structural analysis of high school students' gendered and racialized body meanings', *Journal of Teaching in Physical Education,* 25: 75–98.

Barker, D., Barker-Ruchti, N., Rynne, S. and Lee, J. (in press) 'Moving out of sports: A sociocultural examination of athletic career transitions, *International Journal of Sport Science and Coaching.*

Barker, D.M., Barker-Ruchti, N., Gerber, M., Gerlach, E., Sattler, S. and Pühse, U. (2011) 'Youths with migration backgrounds and their experiences of physical education: An examination of three cases', *Sport, Education & Society,* iFirst article.

Barker-Ruchti, N. (2008) '"They *must* be working hard": An (auto-)ethnographic account of women's artistic gymnastics', *Cultural Studies – Critical Methodologies,* 8: 372–380.

Barker-Ruchti, N. (2011) *Women's artistic gymnastics: An (auto-)ethnographic journey.* Basel: Edition gesowip.

Berry, J.W. (2006) 'Contexts of acculturation', in D.L. Sam, and J.W. Berry (eds.) *The Cambridge Handbook of Acculturation Psychology* (27–42). Cambridge: University of Cambridge Press.

Bourdieu, P. (1991) *Language and symbolic power.* Cambridge, MA: Harvard University Press.

Brah, A. (1996) *Cartographies of diaspora: Contesting identities.* London: Routledge.

Brooks, S.N. (2011) 'Just a dream? Structure, power and agency in basketball', in J. Long and K. Spracklen (eds.) *Sport and Challenges to Racism* (143–149). Basingstoke, Hampshire: Palgrave Macmillan.

Burdsey, D. (2004) '"One of the lads"? Dual ethnicity and assimilated ethnicities in the careers of British Asian footballers', *Ethnic & Racial Studies,* 27: 757–779.

Burdsey, D. (2007) 'Role with the punches: The construction and representation of Amir Khan as a role model for multiethnic Britain', *The Sociological Review,* 55: 611–631.

Carrington, B. (2011) '"What I said was racist – but I'm not a racist": Anti-racism and the white sports/media complex', in J. Long and K. Spracklen (eds.) *Sport and Challenges to Racism* (83–89). Basingstoke, Hampshire: Palgrave Macmillan.

Carroll, B. and Hollinshead, G. (1993) 'Ethnicity and conflict in physical education', *British Educational Research Journal,* 19: 59–76.

Chappell, B. (2002) 'Race, ethnicity and sport', in A. Laker (ed.) *The Sociology of Sport and Physical Education* (92–109). Abingdon, Oxon: Routledge.

Coakley, J. (2007) *Sport and society: Issues and controversies.* Boston: McGraw Hill.

Coalter, F. (2007) 'Sports clubs, social capital and social regeneration: Ill-defined interventions with hard to follow outcomes', *Sport in Society,* 10: 537–559.

Dagkas, S., Benn, T. and Jawad, H. (2011) 'Multiple voices: Improving participation of Muslim girls in physical education and school sport', *Sport, Education & Society,* 16: 223–239.

Deci, E.L. and Ryan, R.M. (2000) 'The "what" and "why" of goal pursuits: Human needs and the self-determination of behaviour', *Psychological Inquiry,* 11: 227–268.

Degele, N. and Janz, C. (2012) 'Homosexualität im Fussball – Zur Konstruktion von Normalität und Abweichung', in G. Sobiech and A. Ochsner (eds.) *Spielen Frauen ein anderes Spiel? Geschichte,*

Organisation, Repräsentationen und kulturelle Praxen im Frauenfussball [Do women play another game? History, organisation, representations and cultural practices in women's football] (195–214). Wiesbaden: Springer VS.

Elling, A. and Claringbould, I. (2005) 'Mechanisms of inclusion and exclusion in Dutch sports landscape: Who can and wants to belong?' *Sociology of Sport Journal*, 22: 498–515.

Gerber, M., Mäder, U., Bergman, M. and Pühse, U. (eds.) (in preparation). *Soziale Integration, Migration und Sport. Eine empirische Studie zur Bedeutung des Sports vor dem Hin-tergrund aktueller Migrationsent-wicklungen und Integrations-theorien* [Social integration, migration and sport: An empirical study on the meaning of sport against a background of current migration developments and integration theory]. Zürich: Seismo.

Hargreaves, J. (1994) *Sporting females: Critical issues in the history and sociology of women's sports*, London: Routledge.

Hylton, K. (2011) 'Too radical? Critical race theory and sport against racism in Ireland', in J. Long and K. Spracklen (eds.) *Sport and Challenges to Racism* (229–246). Basingstoke, Hampshire: Palgrave Macmillan.

Kleindienst-Cachay, C. (2007) *Mädchen und Frauen mit Migrationshintergrund im organisierten Sport: Ergebnisse zur Sportsozialisation – Analyse ausgewählter Maßnahmen zur Integration in den Sport* [Girls and women with migration backgrounds in organised sport: Results from a sport-socialisation analysis of selected measures for integration into the sport]. Hohenbgehren: Schneider Verlag.

Knez, K. (2010) 'Being Muslim and being female: Negotiating physical activity and a gendered body', in J. Wright and D. MacDonald (eds.) *Young people, physical activity and the everyday* (104–117). London: Routledge.

Lamprecht, M., Fischer, M. and Stamm, M. (2008) *Sport Schweiz 2008. Kinder- und Jugendbericht* [Sport Switzerland 2008: Report on children and youth]. Magglingen: BASPO.

Makarova, E. (2008) *Akkulturation und kulturelle Identität. Eine empirische Studie bei Jugendlichen mit und ohne Migrationshintergrund in der Schweiz* [Acculturation and cultural identity: An empirical study with youths with and without migration backgrounds in Switzerland]. Ber: Haupt Verlag.

Markula, P. (2009) *Olympic women and the media: International perspectives.* New York: Palgrave.

Matteucci, I. (2012) 'Sport as a cultural model: Italian women's soccer over the past ten years', *International Journal of the History of Sport*, 29: 353–373.

Meier, M. (2004) *'Zarte Füsschen am harten Leder . . .': Frauenfussball in der Schweiz 1970–1999* ['Soft little feet on hard leather . . .' Women's football in Switzerland 1970–1999]. Frauenfeld: Verlag Huber.

Meier, M. and Hürlimann, H. (2012) 'Pfeifendamen, Stauffacherinnen und Champions: Geschichte und aktueller Stand des Schweizer Frauenfußballs' [Whistle women, Stauffacher women and champions: History and the current situation of Swiss women's football], in G. Sobiech and A. Ochsner (eds.) *Spielen Frauen ein anderes Spiel? Geschichte, Organisation, Repräsentationen und kulturelle Praxen im Frauenfußball* [Do women play another game? History, organisation, representations and cultural practices in women's football] (21–39). Wiesbaden: Springer VS.

Müller, F., Van Zoonen, L. and De Roode (2008) 'The integrative power of sport: Imagined and real effects of sport events on multicultural integration', *Sociology of Sport Journal*, 25: 387–401.

Norman, L. (2010) 'Feeling second best: Elite women coaches' experiences', *Sociology of Sport Journal*, 27: 89–104.

Phinney, J.S., Berry, J.W., Vedder, P. & Liebkind, K. (2006) 'The acculturation experience: Attitudes, identities, and behaviors of immigrant youth', in J.W. Berry, J.S. Phinney, D.L. Sam and P. Vedder (eds.) *Immigrant youth in cultural transition* (71–116). Mahwah, NJ: Lawrence Erlbaum Associates.

Pringle, R. (2008) '"No rugby – no fear": Collective stories, masculinities and transformative possibilities in schools', *Sport, Education & Society*, 13: 215–237.

Putnam, R.D. (2000) *Bowling alone: The collapse and revival of American community.* New York, NY: Simon & Schuster.

Rishe, P.J. (2003) 'A re-examination of how athletic success impacts graduation rates: Comparing student-athletes to all other undergraduates', *American Journal of Economics and Sociology*, 62: 407–427.

Rommel, A., Weilandt, C. and Eckert, J. (2006) *Gesundheitsmonitoring der schweizerischen Migrationsbevölkerung, Endbericht* [Health monitoring of the Swiss migration population: End report]. Bonn: Bundesamt für Migration.

Sam, D.L. (2006) *The Cambridge handbook of acculturation psychology*. Cambridge: University of Cambridge Press.

Shaw, S. and Slack, T. (2002) '"It's been like that for donkey's years": The construction of gender relations and the cultures of sport organizations', *Culture, Sport, Society*, 5: 86–106.

Sobiech, G. (2012) 'Die Logik der Praxis: Frauenfussball zwischen symbolischer Emanzipation und männlicher Herrschaft' [The logic of practice: Women's soccer between symbolic emancipation and masculine domination], in G. Sobiech and A. Ochsner (eds.) *Spielen Frauen ein anderes Spiel? Geschichte, Organisation, Repräsentationen und kulturelle Praxen im Frauenfussball* [Do women play another game? History, organisation, representations and cultural practices in women's football]. Wiesbaden: Springer VS.

Teixeira, P.J., Carraca, E.V., Markland, D., Silva, M.N. and Ryan, R.M. (2012) 'Exercise, physical activity, and self-determination theory: A systematic review'. *International Journal of Behavioural Nutrition & Physical Activity*, 9: doi:10.1186/1479-5868-9-78.

Theberge, N. (2003) '"No fear comes": Adolescent girls, ice hockey, and the embodiment of gender', *Youth & Society*, 34: 497–516.

Unnithan, V., White, J., Georgiou, A., Iga, J. and Drust, B. (2012) 'Talent identification in youth soccer', *Journal of Sports Sciences*, 30(15): 1–8.

Walseth, K. (2006) 'Young Muslim women and sport: The impact of identity work', *Leisure Studies*, 25: 75–94.

14

WILLIAM

A 15-year-old sport-crazy Millennial in Ireland

*Fiona Chambers, Niamh Murphy, Yvonne Nolan
and Orla Murphy*

SPORTS STUDIES AND PHYSICAL EDUCATION, SCHOOL OF EDUCATION, UNIVERSITY COLLEGE CORK, IRELAND

Key words: 15-year-old male, Millennial, sport-crazy, food supplements, physical activity/ health, neuroscience, digital humanities, pedagogy.

I am William, age 15

I have to catch a bus to school each day dragging all my stuff – three bags – school bag, guitar, art stuff, PE stuff, training gear. I bring two lunches and money, JUST in case. I am always hungry. LOL. Mom tells me I could live in the fridge. It's very loud in our house in the mornings – actually ALL THE TIME. I have younger twin brothers, Rory and Michael aged ten, and a little sister called Ellie. Rory and Michael do my head in . . . they wreck my stuff AND they will be coming to my school next year. Great, eh? Ellie is six and follows me everywhere . . .

Every evening, I have to walk the dogs (Salt and Pepper – two crazy Labradors) . . . After tea, Tommy, Chris and Joe call with their *hurleys*[1] asking me to go to the local pitch for a "puck around". Sometimes, I feel too wrecked to do this but I always go. The lads all go to the local secondary school, but I go to the city to Treetops Boys' Secondary School because my Dad and Grandad went there. On Tuesday, Thursday and Saturday, I am *dragged* out of my BED and into the car at 5am to go the Rowing Club. It's not so bad once I get there. I HATE mornings . . . The only sleep-in is Sunday, and that is wrecked as the whole family has to go to Church . . . Mass every Sunday! I really want to get good at this sport, so I have decided to save for a rowing machine. I do lots of jobs – mowing the lawn, and even "cleaning up my room" which I HATE. I can never find anything after☺. I can't believe that I actually came second in the County Schools Rowing Competition in Schull last Saturday. No one is more surprised than me☺ OMG I can't believe it. I have trained hard, but still didn't think that this would happen. I am the only one in my village who does rowing. School is different; we have a big club with about 50 rowers. Great buzz.

In September, the PE teachers, Mr. Kennedy and Mr. Bourke, entered the school in this on-line rowing competition. It is such *craic.*[2] Every lunchtime, the rowing team members get on the rowing machines and try to get to the top of the National Leader

Board by doing the most miles. We are at number 16 on the Leader Board, BUT are aiming for the "big time".

School is deadly, and all my friends are brilliant. I like Spanish and Science and Maths, all subjects except religion. PE is good craic but it "does my head in" when some people won't get involved. The teacher tries to do lots of different types of stuff but mostly games, which lots of the lads like . . .

I have spent the last couple of weeks doing an experiment for the Young Scientist competition. I wanted to see the impact of running on the lower limbs. I worked it out myself by multiplying mass by number of strides in a kilometre. Another thing, I could do ALL day is music – Jazz is my favourite – I can't pass the piano without playing it. I play lots of instruments: ukulele, classical guitar, and I REALLY want a saxophone.

A weird thing happened at GAA[3] training the other night. One of the older lads was talking about "bulking up"? Joey takes whey protein shakes and this thing called creatine. He got it on-line. It's the first time that I have looked at myself properly. I am six foot four and skinny and I would definitely like to be more buff. I know three rugby guys at school who buy supplements on-line, using their parents' credit cards . . . How do they get away with THAT?

I don't really like training. It's BORING. We all have to do the SAME thing. Once, I did manage to break my glasses – now that was a crazy session. I have been going to the Shanmore Club since I was six. My annoying brothers play too. . . . Even Ellie is on the under-eights *Camogie*[4] team. My Dad and my Granddad played for the Club too. Granddad won an All-Ireland Hurling medal for Cork in 1955 against Wexford. The score was Cork 1–9 to Wexford 1–6.[5] He is FAMOUS around here – actually all over Cork. I actually find training quite easy at the moment. Sometimes my Coach can't answer my questions – now, THAT is so annoying. I often go on-line to find things out . . .

Most nights, I get to bed and I wonder HOW did I get through the day? Up at 5am training on the River Lee for two hours, then on to school, GAA training, homework, meeting the lads, and Facebook time. There's a girl in Ravendale Girls' School who "like-likes" me on Facebook. I see her on the bus everyday. She does NOTHING apart from shopping and hanging out with friends but she is very, very funny, LOL. Now I am hungry again. I wonder whether I can sneak downstairs and get some food? LOL. Oh, Oh, I forgot to feed my turtle . . . now I have an excuse to go downstairs. Ha Ha.

A physical activity perspective on William's case

From the perspective of the physical activity (PA) and public health practitioner, William is a model subject. He meets, and indeed exceeds, the physical activity guidelines for his age. The current guidelines state: one hour of moderate to vigorous physical activity daily, engaging also in regular muscle-strengthening, flexibility and bone-strengthening exercises (Department of Health and Children 2010). William is at the opposite end of the spectrum to the challenge which is usually faced by PA practitioners, which is the increasing prevalence of inactivity among children and adolescents. The latest report from World Health Organization (WHO) Health Behaviour in School-aged Children (HBSC) study, on 11-, 13- and 15-year-old pupils in 35 countries of the European Region as well as North America, found that more than two thirds of young people do not meet the current recommendation for physical activity of 60 minutes per day, 5 or more days a week (Currie *et al.* 2012).

A useful blueprint has recently been published by the WHO to help practitioners ensure that physical activity is youth-friendly, appealing and enjoyable (Kelly, Matthews and Foster 2012). The document was developed on the basis of the perspectives and views of young delegates from the Children's Environment and Health Action Plan for Europe Network. Three categories, encompassing eighteen different points, were devised from the consultation process and case studies are used to illustrate the points identified by the youth delegates. Using this blueprint as a guide, William's experience of sport and physical activity can be judged as overwhelmingly positive. The blueprint highlights some areas that might enhance William's experience; for example, the use of mentors to guide his emerging talent in rowing, health awareness regarding his curiosity around performance-enhancing nutritional products, the inclusion of relaxation as a vital element and a means of avoiding injury and overtraining, and continuing to ensure that fun is central to all he experiences.

It is not unusual for a talented athlete such as William to engage in several sports and lead exceptionally busy lives. This is not, in itself, a particular cause for concern from a physiological or mental health perspective, particularly given his interests in non-sporting pursuits like music, his academic studies and girls! William's comments about hating early mornings, doing chores, and his annoying younger siblings are all testament to the balance and normality of his life, and this should be commended and preserved. Indeed, the number of hours William invests in sport is probably a necessity for him to succeed. The notion that it takes at least 10 years, or 10,000 hours of deliberate practice to excel in sport is a core element of the Long Term Athlete Development (LTAD) model. The model was devised by Istvan Balyi in the early 1990s, and has been applied widely across sports worldwide (Balyi and Hamilton 2004). The sport of rowing, which William favours, is classified by Balyi as a *late specialization sport* requiring a generalized approach to early training. Specialization prior to age ten is not recommended since research suggests it contributes to early burn out and drop out. In this case, therefore, William's interest in hurling is helpful rather than a distraction.

William's coaches and mentors will be vital to his future development at this vital phase of training to win. Ideally, his hurling and rowing coaches should understand the LTAD model and come to an agreement about how they will shelter William from the dangers of over-training and injury. There are some excellent web resources on the application of the LTAD model to rowing (e.g. the Association of Rowing Coaches, South Africa http://arcrsa.blogspot. ie/2011/10/12-fundamental-principles-for-building.html). The commitment of the GAA to the long-term welfare of developing players is also evident, and coaches can undertake a Certificate in Athlete Player Development for Youth Coaches (HETAC Level 6).[6] Nonetheless, with the best will in the world, the likelihood is that each discipline will probably compete for William's talents and the involvement of an independent third party may be advisable. This independent third party should be capable of taking a holistic view of William's development, including nutritional concerns and life-sport balance.

A neuroscience perspective

Exercise and cognition

As a 16-year-old boy, William's main day-to-day routine revolves around school and learning. Experimental evidence tells us that physical exercise has profound benefits on brain health, particularly on cognition. Exercise promotes a process called neurogenesis in the hippocampus of the brain, which is the region of the brain responsible for learning and memory (van Praag 2008). Neurogenesis is the birth of new neurons in the brain, a process by which neurons are generated from stem cells and functionally integrated into the hippocampal circuitry. It is now believed that this process underlies much of our ability to learn new tasks and to remember new information as an adult (Deng, Aimone and Gage 2010). As well as stimulating the proliferation and survival of these endogenous stem cells, it has been proposed that exercise increases the rate of oxygen consumption which is associated with increases in cognitive function (Kramer *et al.* 1999). Exercise also increases the concentration of brain neurotransmitters which facilitate information processing (McMorris *et al.* 2008), and the concentration of neurotrophins such as brain derived neurotrophic factor (BDNF) that supports the survival and function of neurons (Schinder and Poo 2000).

The relationship between exercise and academic performance in children and young adults is rapidly becoming an area of intense research interest. For example, a study on school-aged children (4–18 years of age) has reported a beneficial relationship between physical activity and cognitive performance including IQ, verbal tests and maths tests (Sibley and Etnier 2003). In preadolescent children, better academic performance following acute treadmill walking has also been reported (Hillman *et al.* 2009). Similar results were obtained in young adults after 12 weeks of training, which also correlated with an increase in neurogenesis in the hippocampus (Pereira *et al.* 2007). Interestingly, it has been found that a positive correlation exists between physical activity in young adults and improved cognition in later life (Dik *et al.* 2003), and it has been suggested that aerobic exercise in childhood might be vitally important for cognitive health throughout adulthood (Hillman *et al.* 2008). Indeed, in aging humans, it is well documented that physical activity is associated with improved cognitive function and increased neurogenesis, and may even contribute to decreasing the risk of developing age-related dementias such as Alzheimer's disease (Voss *et al.* 2011).

William complains that it "does my head in" when classmates don't get involved in physical exercise in school. With the increased demands on children to achieve high levels of academic performance, some opt out of what they may perceive as "time-wasting" subjects such as PE. Evidence from the literature tells us this is not a wise choice. Several studies have suggested that an increase in time spent on physical education and other forms of PA is not accompanied by a decrease in academic performance but rather that physical exercise has a positive effect on academic performance (Hillman *et al.* 2008, Rasberry *et al.* 2011).

Exercise and mood

William is excited about his participation in rowing competitions and he gets a "great buzz" from it. Research has demonstrated that exercise promotes an increase in production of the opioid β-endorphin in the brain which is released into the bloodstream. Opioids are mood-elevating hormones, and increased release of endogenous opioids in frontolimbic regions of the brain that are involved in mood regulation are reported to be responsible for increased levels of euphoria after running (the so called "runner's high") (Boecker *et al.* 2008). Interestingly, animal experiments using mice exposed to voluntary wheel running showed that mice that produced β-endorphin showed an increase in neurogenesis in the hippocampus (Koehl *et al.* 2008).

At moderate intensity, exercise is also known to reduce the harmful effects of stress. In William's situation, therefore, this may help him cope with the potential stressors in his life such as a busy household, early morning training, homework, and household chores. It is known that stress can inhibit neurogenesis and contribute to a depressed mood (Warner-Schmidt and Duman 2006). Belief in the possible involvement of hippocampal neurogenesis in mediating the beneficial effects of physical exercise on counteracting stress and depression is gaining credence (Yau, Lau and So 2011). Exercise also increases levels of BDNF in the hippocampus, while stress decreases it, and in this respect it has the same mechanism of action as an antidepressant (Russo-Neustadt, Beard and Cotman 1999). Increases in BDNF are also associated with learning, memory and hippocampal neurogenesis (Duman 2005), suggesting a central role for BDNF in the positive effects of exercise on both mood and cognition. William mentions, "Another thing I could do ALL day is music". Interestingly, it has recently been reported that music can increase BDNF in the hippocampus of mice (Li *et al.* 2010), thus one could speculate that music may even have similar beneficial effects on neuronal function as exercise.

Exercise, diet and brain health

William is "always hungry" and so his diet is very important for brain health both from a cognitive and mental health perspective. Much like physical activity, a healthy diet can benefit neuronal function (Gomez-Pinilla 2008). As yet, however, there is a lack of rigorous research on the mechanisms of an array of nutrients on the brain. Omega-3-fatty acids which are found in nuts, eggs and oily fish such as salmon, herring, mackerel and sardines have been shown to increase learning ability (Frensham, Bryan and Parletta 2012), and also to enhance the effects of exercise on cognition (Wu, Ying and Gomez-Pinilla 2008). Like exercise, Omega 3 also promotes neurogenesis (Kawakita, Hashimoto and Shido 2006) and increases hippocampal levels of BDNF. William's thoughts about supplementing with creatine "to be more buff" should, however, be treated with some caution. Creatine is a constituent of protein-based foods such as milk and meat, and at carefully controlled levels has been shown to improve cognition in the elderly (Rawson and Venezia 2011) when brain creatine is shown to be reduced (Laakso *et al.* 2003). In two human trials, however, negative changes in mood, anxiety or aggressiveness following supplementation with creatine have also been documented (Roitman *et al.* 2007, Volek *et al.* 2000).

In conclusion, evidence suggests that physical exercise is a non-invasive, non-pharmacological approach to improving cognition and mood across the lifespan. Accordingly, highlighting the importance of physical activity during the early years will serve to promote brain health and quality of life in later life.

A digital humanities perspective

> Digital life describes the media world our kids inhabit 24/7 – online, on cell phones and mobile devices, and anywhere media is displayed. By definition, digital media is participatory. The users create the content, and anything created in this digital life becomes instantly viral, scalable, replicable, and viewable by vast, invisible audiences. Kids use digital media to socialize, do their homework, express themselves, and connect to the world. New technologies give our kids unprecedented powers of creation and communication, making the world more accessible and comprehensible at earlier and earlier ages.
>
> (Common Sense Media 2009)

It is clear that sport and activity must engage with emerging social practice to leverage the combined potential of students and new media. The common goal is the development of an active and participatory knowledge society:

> *Digital technologies and new media are now prevalent in many aspects of day-to-day public and private life. For some commentators this is a cause for celebration and for optimistic predictions about life, work and learning in a networked society. . . . Critics, though, have concerns about how technology and media are impacting negatively on human relationships, individual psychologies and the entire social fabric.*
>
> (Hague and Williamson 2009: 4)

Online community engagement is a positive influence in William's case. His active engagement in a competitive (rowing) gaming community online relates to activity in his school. This represents an ideal online "community building" experience that both augments and sustains William's participation in the sporting culture of his school. The focus on external competition outside his school environment creates a positive sense of both achievement and camaraderie amongst the real-time local participants. The activity has real-time results, contributes to a team endeavour as part of the school "clocking the kilometres online", and enables an engaged socialisation that could be missing ordinarily in a solitary sport. This aspect of online engagement is under-acknowledged as a potential positive outcome of online activity.

The online rowing competition has been initiated by teachers throughout Ireland who are engaged with this methodology, and who know that the activity is safe. This type of virtual or digital community building is acknowledged as a positive experience for the young person, and very much a part of their contemporary social development:

> *. . . Peer groups are important for the development of adolescents' identity and values. The study (by Lehdonvirta) addresses the question of whether online groups are standing in for traditional peer groups that are thought to be weakening in some developed countries. The results confirm that online groups can act as strong psychological anchoring points for their members. The authors conclude that social networking sites and other online hangouts should be seen as crucial contexts for youths' identification and socialization experiences.*
>
> (Nauert 2011: 1)

Clearly this online competition generates the high levels of involvement William expects and enjoys from sport, and one that is often lacking in his actual PE classes. As William puts it: "*BUT it 'does my head in' when some people won't get involved*".

There is little evidence in this case of the concerns expressed by Lehdonvirta (cited in Nauert 2011) about a causal relationship between activity in online spaces and a breakdown in traditional communities. William participates locally in the GAA and has a profound sense of local, national and family tradition within the sport of hurling. This stated awareness, together with his friends calling in the evening "to puck a ball", suggests that online activity – including Facebook – is simply another part of this active teenager's life.

Two crucial aspects of online engagement become critical for William: the search for information prompted by the activity of peers, and by the unwillingness or inability of coaches to answer his questions. Ingesting substances bought over the Internet can have profound, and perhaps fatal repercussions for a young person. Creatine use amongst William's peers is a potential catalyst for risky online behaviours. Both this and William's need for answers to training questions are important reasons for digital literacy to be a keystone in all aspects of education for contemporary youth. There is a huge and disorganized online community around sport that goes well beyond the carefully structured online rowing environment that has been developed by educators at a national level. The potential for young people to (easily) find information that is both incorrect and dangerous is well documented. Part of the education process must facilitate digital literacy for all – including educators themselves – to empower young people to take an active participation in sport within the knowledge society. It is also interesting to note that the accessibility of a parent's credit card was integral to William's peers and their risky online activity. As with all such initiatives, parents play a vital role and their participation and awareness of digital literacy is as necessary online as it is in real-world situations. Digital literacy will help young people (and their parents) to negotiate the myriad of online sources and discern those that are to be trusted, and those that are not.

A pedagogical understanding of William's case

William as learner

It is clear that William is a keen sports person at this point in his life. In order to sustain his interest and optimise physical activity levels across his lifespan, it is critical that the most appropriate pedagogies are employed by both his PE teachers and coaches.

Pollard (2010) explains the notion of pedagogy as follows:

> *"Pedagogy" is the practice of teaching framed and informed by a shared and structured body of knowledge. This knowledge comprises experience, evidence, and understanding moral purpose and shared transparent values.*

> (p. 5)

Pollard contends that pedagogy, curriculum and assessment are intertwined, and that teachers (and, of course, youth sport coaches) must be expert in both curriculum and assessment as part of their pedagogic repertoire. He describes pedagogy in three ways: (a) the science of teaching (research informed decision-making), (b) the craft of teaching (mastery of a full repertoire of skills and practices); and (c) the art of teaching (responsive, creative and intuitive practices). McShane (2007: 1) describes the professional commitment needed for the development of an effective pedagogy, and also the teaching/coaching skills required: "*Pedagogy is about service, an educative journey, interrelationships and to a certain extent rhetoric and persuasion*". When teaching William, coaches and teachers need to be mindful of the purposes and nature of pedagogy.

The "pedagogical encounter" in sport is defined as:

> *That precise moment where a teacher, coach or instructor seeks to support a learner in sport, physical activity or exercise settings. The learning needs of the target learner are paramount in the pedagogical encounter.*

> (Armour 2011: 3)

Each pedagogical encounter with William involves the interaction of *"knowledge in context, learners and learning and teachers and teaching/coaches and coaching"* (ibid). Berliner (1991) outlines the nature of pedagogical knowledge in context, and his comments can be applied to William's case. Hence, William's teachers and coaches need to consider knowledge about William as a learner and the creation of appropriate learning environments, classroom management, assessment, methods for encouraging student motivation, and social-interactional skills.

The separation of pedagogical skills and teacher/coach personal qualities is not helpful in considering effective pedagogies. William's teacher/coach is, inevitably, a "person–pedagogue" (Armour and Fernandez-Balboa 2001) who brings his/her biography to each pedagogical encounter. In so doing, the person–pedagogue can embrace a view of pedagogy which, according to Van Manen (1994), incorporates a relational knowledge of children. This knowledge entails understanding children and youth, how they experience things, what they think about, how they look at the world, and how each child is a unique person. This view supports Shulman's (1986: 8) suggestion that all educators should have a clear "knowledge of learners". Jewett, Bain and Ennis (1995) urge us to bear in mind the all-inclusive and rounded learner:

> *Persons are holistic beings, continuously in the process of becoming, who can intend what they will do . . . and for what purpose. The primary concern of physical education is the personal search for meaning by the individual moving in interaction with the environment.*
>
> (p. 271)

Gard, Hickey-Moodey and Enright (2013) encourage physical educators to enrich:

> Our palette of pedagogical possibilities . . . by a knowledge of how young people "do culture" in order to ensure that physical education remains relevant to Youth Culture . . . we might take more seriously the things young people want from culture and, most important, learn from the techniques they use to navigate it.
>
> (p. 111)

Importantly, these authors remind us that *"there is a difference between trying to be responsive to youth culture (curriculum) and being relevant to youth (pedagogy)"* (ibid). Indeed, Gard *et al.* (2013) argue for a radically different consultative approach to the design of culturally relevant PE experiences for students, for example, co-creating meaningful pedagogies with young people, such as William and his peers.

Ennis (2013: 115) argues that *"Our children throughout the world need to find personally meaningful, engaging, and reflective approaches to be 'in' movement"* so that they continue to be physically active throughout their lives. In order to meet the needs of William, but also his less active peers, PE programmes need to include pedagogical encounters that have specific characteristics; for example that are:

> *. . . boundless, integrated, and cross disciplinary with pedagogy and assessment woven as one seamless educative enrichment. Assessments will be authentic and provide information to students about their progress and improvement.*
>
> (Ennis 2013: 115)

In William's case, it is clear that sport and physical education experiences are meaningful. Perhaps the teacher/coach has used reflexive strategies to help William to develop "learning autonomy" (James et al, 2006). In so doing, William is supported to internalize his experiences in sport and physical education and take charge of his learning. In employing such strategies, William is more likely to be active through the lifecourse. Hastie, Rudisill and Wadsworth (2013) draw on the work of Reeve (2006) to describe ways in which autonomy might be fostered:

> There are immutable aspects of teaching that cannot be compromised if one is to call the climate as autonomy supportive. These include (1) providing choices, (2) encouraging students' experimentation and self-initiation, (3) fostering students' willingness to take on challenges, explore new ideas and persist at difficult activities, (4) offering optimal challenges (neither too easy, nor too difficult), (5) providing feedback that is not evaluative of the person, (6) and giving a meaningful rationale for requested behaviour.
>
> (Reeve 2006, cited in Hastie *et al.* 2013: 51)

With respect to the inclusion of choice for William in sport and PE settings, Stefanou *et al.* (2004, cited in Hastie 2013: 52) suggest that instructional choices can be provided at three levels: (a) cognitive (such as allowing students to ask questions), (b) organizational (which includes letting students choose who they work with) and (c) procedural (such as allowing students to choose from a number of tasks or a level of challenge within a task). Hastie and colleagues (2013: 52) have found that offering choice at these three levels *"is a strong motivator for engagement"*. Pope and Grant (1996) concur and have found that students like to exert control over what they do in sport and PE settings, and this may also be true for William.

William and life-sport balance

Much of the literature on Life-Sport Balance pertains to elite athletes (e.g. Mayocchi and Hanrahan 2000) although there is some resonance with William's case. William reports trying to establish a workable Life-Sport Balance, and he appears able to juggle most of his commitments successfully. He does struggle, however, to build relaxation time into his schedule, and this could become a concern. When a balanced lifestyle state is reached, Brettschneider (1999) reports that athletes are able to use their limited free time very wisely. By managing his diverse interests, including music, Price, Morrison and Arnold (2010) would argue that William is more likely to be able to maintain a high level of motivation for sport training while also developing other *transferable skills* (Mayocchi and Hanrahan 2000).

It was suggested in an earlier section that it may be helpful to have one relatively independent person to oversee William's progress. A collaborative approach could also work to ensure William has a sport/academic programme that views him from a biopsychosocial standpoint. In their design of an applied sport-programming model of positive youth development, Fraser-Thomas, Côté and Deakin (2005) championed programmes that have a holistic focus on the athlete. The goal is to develop healthier, more psychosocially competent people, rather than merely technically skilled individuals. Their model identifies the critical role of coaches in implementing programs on a day-to-day basis, and of parents in supporting their children throughout involvement in sport programs.

William the Millennial

William is a Millennial. *Millennial* is an abbreviation for *millennial generation* and is a term used by demographers to describe a segment of the population born between approximately 1980 and 2000. Sometimes referred to in the media as "Generation Y," Millennials are the children of the post-World War II baby boomer generation. According to the Pew Research Centre Report (Taylor & Keeter, 2010) entitled *"Millennials: Confident. Connected. Open to Change"*, Millennials embrace multiple modes of self-expression. For example: three-quarters of this group have created a profile on a social-networking site; and one-in-five has posted a video of themselves on line. In America, it has been argued that Millennials are on track to become the most educated generation in American history, as they are pushed by the requirements of a modern knowledge-based economy (Taylor and Keeter 2010).

As a Millennial, William is also a "digital native" (Prensky 2001). He has access to knowledge at the touch of a button. The challenge for PE teachers and coaches who work with William is to help him to become a critical consumer of sport and physical activity knowledge and of "public pedagogies" (Giroux 2004) presented to him through the media. The role of the PE teacher and coach in this instance is:

> To help young people know where to find knowledge, to know what to do with it when they get it, to know "good" knowledge from "bad" knowledge, to know how to use it, to apply it, to synthesize it, to be creative with it, to add to it even, to know which bits to use and when and how to use them and to know how to remember key parts of it – in other words all the things computers can't do yet.
>
> (Gilbert 2010: 24)

Conole *et al.* (2006) point out that today's students turn to the Web as their first port of call when seeking information (p. 4). She also noted, however, that students are developing *"new forms of evaluation skills and strategies (searching, restructuring, validating) which enable them to critique and make decisions about a variety of sources and content"* (p. 5). Moreover:

> The use of these tools is changing the way they gather, use and create knowledge . . . shifting from lower to higher regions of Bloom's taxonomy . . . to make sense of their complex technologically enriched learning environment.
>
> (p. 6)

Trinder *et al.*'s (2008) report "Learning from Digital Natives: Bridging Formal and Informal Learning" warns that there is a mismatch between the culture of schools and learners' lives outside school. In school, students encounter:

> A pedagogic regime that is fundamentally premised on the transmission and testing of decontextualised knowledge and skills, and which is dominated by old-generation technologies (Web 1.0) underpinned by a radically different philosophy and a different set of affordances . . . Outside school, individuals act as active participants navigating their way independently through complex multimodal digital environments.
>
> (ibid. p. 5)

Pedagogical practices that may enhance William's ability to capitalize on his position as a digital native include:

1. Using on-line participatory learning spaces – such as the Rowing Competition – to engage imagination and the enthusiasm;
2. Using mobile phones to take photos, podcasts, video, record interviews, calculate results, create animations, and search the Internet in classes and coaching sessions;
3. Designing and using an e-Learning Wall, which is interactive and guides student learning (Luttrell & Chambers 2013).

Conclusion

The opportunity to view William's case through three lenses: Physical Activity, Neuroscience and Digital Humanities offers insights that can lead to the development of effective pedagogies for William in Sport, PA and PE. Clearly, coaches, teachers and parents need to collaborate to create programmes that work for William as an individual. Perhaps most important of all, however, is the realization that understanding William's status as a Millennial – and a digital native – are key factors in understanding and meeting William's needs as a learner in sport, PA, PE.

Notes

1. A hurley is the stick used in the Irish game of hurling, similar to a field hockey stick but with a wide, flat blade.
2. Craic: fun and entertainment, especially good conversation and company.
3. The Gaelic Athletic Association/Cumann Lúthchleas Gael is an Irish sporting and cultural organization that has a presence on all five continents. It is Ireland's largest sporting organization and is celebrated as one of the great amateur sporting associations in the world today. The GAA is a volunteer led, community based organization that promotes Gaelic games such as Hurling, Football, Handball and Rounders and works with sister organizations to promote Ladies Football and Camogie. It is part of the Irish consciousness and plays an influential role in Irish society that extends far beyond the basic aim of promoting Gaelic games (Gaelic Athletic Association, 2013).
4. This is an Irish stick-and-ball team sport played by women; it is almost identical to the game of hurling played by men.
5. 1 goal and 9 points to 1 goal and 6 points.
6. GAA Certificate for Mentors interested in improving concepts to improve Athletic Development in Children & Young People (U15 and below).

References

Armour, K.M. (2011). *Sport Pedagogy: An Introduction for teaching and Coaching.* London: Pearson.

Armour, K.M. and Fernandez Balboa, J.-M., (2001). 'Connections, pedagogy and professional learning,' *Teaching Education,* 12(1): 103–118.

Balyi, I. and Hamilton, A. (2004) 'Long-term athlete development: trainability in childhood and adolescence: Windows of opportunity, optimal trainability'. Victoria, Canada: National Coaching Institute British Columbia & Advanced Training and Performance.

Berliner, D.C. (1991). 'Educational psychology and pedagogical expertise: New findings and new opportunities for thinking about training,' *Educational Psychologist,* 26(2): 145–155.

Boecker, H., Sprenger, T., Spilker, M.E., Henriksen, G., Koppenhoefer, M., Wagner, K.J., Valet, M., Berthele, A. and Tolle, T.R. (2008) 'The runner's high: opioidergic mechanisms in the human brain', *Cerebral Cortex,* 18: 2523–2531.

Brettschneider, W. (1999) 'Risks and opportunities: adolescents in top-level sport – growing up with the pressures of school and training', *European Physical Education Review,* 5(2): 121–133.

Common Sense Media (2009) *Digital literacy and citizenship in the 21st century: Educating, empowering, and protecting America's kids – a common sense media white paper.* Online. Available HTTP: <www.itu.int/council/groups/wg-cop/second-meeting-june2010/CommonSenseDigitalLiteracy-CitizenshipWhitePaper.pdf> (accessed 1 October 2013).

Conole, G., de Laat, M., Dillon, T. and Darby, J. (2006) *LXP: Student experience of technologies: Final report. JISC, UK.* Online. Available HTTP: <www.jisc.ac.uk/whatwedo/programmes/elearning_pedagogy/elp_learneroutcomes.aspx> (accessed 1 October 2013).

Currie, C., Zanotti, C., Morgan, A., Currie, D., de Looze, M., Roberts, C., Samdal, O., Smith, O.R.F. and Barnekow, V. (2012) *Social determinants of health and well-being among young people. Health Behaviour in School-aged Children (HBSC) study: international report from the 2009/2010 survey.* Copenhagen, WHO Regional Office for Europe, 2012 (Health Policy for Children and Adolescents, No. 6).

Deng, W., Aimone, J.B. and Gage, F.H. (2010) 'New neurons and new memories: how does adult hippocampal neurogenesis affect learning and memory?' *Nature Reviews Neuroscience,* 11: 339–350.

Department of Health and Children (2010) *The National Physical Activity Guidelines for Ireland.* Dublin: DOHC. Online. Available HTTP: <www.getirelandactive.ie/get-the-guidlines/children-and-young-adults/> (accessed on 1 October 2013).

Dik, M., Deeg, D.J., Visser, M. and Jonker, C. (2003) 'Early life physical activity and cognition at old age', *Journal of Clinical & Experimental Neuropsychology,* 25: 643–653.

Duman, R.S. (2005) 'Neurotrophic factors and regulation of mood: role of exercise, diet and metabolism', *Neurobiology of Aging,* 26(Suppl. 1): 88–93.

Ennis, C.D. (2013) 'Implementing meaningful, educative curricula, and assessments in complex school environments', *Sport Education & Society,* 18(1): 115–120.

Fraser-Thomas, J., Côté, J. and Deakin, J. (2005) 'Youth sport programs: An avenue to foster positive youth development', *Physical Education & Sport Pedagogy,* 10: 19–40.

Frensham, L. J., Bryan, J. and Parletta, N. (2012) 'Influences of micronutrient and omega-3 fatty acid supplementation on cognition, learning, and behavior: methodological considerations and implications for children and adolescents in developed societies', *Nutrition Reviews,* 70: 594–610.

Gaelic Athletic Association (2013). *Our Games.* Online. Available HTTP: <www.gaa.ie/about-the-gaa/our-games/> (accessed on 21 October 2012).

Gard, M., Hickey-Moodey, A. and Enright, E. (2013) 'Youth culture, physical education and the question of relevance: after 20 years, a reply to Tinning and Fitzclarence', *Sport Education & Society,* 18(1): 97–114.

Gilbert, I. (2010). *Why do I need a teacher when I've got Google?: the essential guide to the big issues for every 21st century teacher.* London: Routledge.

Giroux, H.A. 2004. *The terror of neoliberalism.* Boulder, CO: Paradigm.

Gomez-Pinilla, F. (2008) 'Brain foods: the effects of nutrients on brain function'. *Nature Reviews Neuroscience,* 9: 568–578.

Hague, C. and Williamson, B. (2009) *Digital participation, digital literacy, and school subjects: a review of the policies, literature and evidence.* Online. Available HTTP: <www2.futurelab.org.uk/resources/documents/lit_reviews/DigitalParticipation.pdf> (accessed 1 October 2013).

Hastie, P.A., Rudisill, M.E. and Wadsworth, D.D. (2013) 'Providing students with voice and choice: lessons from intervention research on autonomy-supportive climates in physical education', *Sport Education & Society,* 18(1): 38–56.

Hillman, C.H., Erickson, K.I. and Kramer, A.F. (2008) 'Be smart, exercise your heart: exercise effects on brain and cognition', *Nature Reviews Neuroscience,* 9: 58–65.

Hillman, C.H., Pontifex, M.B., Raine, L.B., Castelli, D.M., Hall, E.E. and Kramer, A.F. (2009) 'The effect of acute treadmill walking on cognitive control and academic achievement in preadolescent children', *Neuroscience,* 159: 1044–1054.

James, M., Black, P., Carmichael, P., Conner, C., Dudley, P., Fox, A., Frost, D., Honour, L., MacBeath, J., McCormick, R., Marshall, B., Pedder, D., Procter, R., Swaffield, S. and Wiliam, D. (2006*) Learning how to learn: tools for schools.* Abingdon: Routledge.

Jewett, A.E., Bain, L.L. and Ennis, C.D. (1995) *The curriculum process in physical education.* Dubuque, IA: Brown and Benchmark.

Kawakita, E., Hashimoto, M. and Shido, O. (2006) 'Docosahexaenoic acid promotes neurogenesis in vitro and in vivo'. *Neuroscience,*139: 991–997.

Kelly P., Matthews A., Foster, C. (2012) *Young and physically active-a blueprint for making physical activity appealing to youth.* World Health Organization Regional Office for Europe, WHO, Copenhagen. Online. Available HTTP: <www.euro.who.int/en/what-we-publish/abstracts/young-and-physically-active-a-blueprint-for-making-physical-activity-appealing-to-youth> (accessed on 1 October 2013).

Koehl, M., Meerlo, P., Gonzales, D., Rontal, A., Turek, F.W. and Abrous, D.N. (2008) 'Exercise-induced promotion of hippocampal cell proliferation requires beta-endorphin', *Journal of the Federation of American Societies for Experimental Biology,* 22: 2253–2262.

Kramer, A.F., Hahn, S., Cohen, N.J., Banich, M.T., McAuley, E., Harrison, C.R., Chason, J., Vakil, E., Bardell, L., Boileau, A. and Colcombe, A. (1999) 'Ageing, fitness and neurocognitive function', *Nature,* 400: 418–419.

Laakso, M.P., Hiltunen, Y., Kononen, M., Kivipelto, M., Koivisto, A., Hallikainen, M. and Soininen, H. (2003) 'Decreased brain creatine levels in elderly apolipoprotein E epsilon 4 carriers', *Journal of Neural Transmission,*110: 267–275.

Lehdonvirta, V. and Räsänen, P. (2011) 'How do young people identify with online and offline peer groups? A comparison between UK, Spain and Japan'. In Nauert, R. 'Teens bond with online communities – Psych Central News'. *Psych Central.com.* Online. Available HTTP: <psychcentral.com/news/2010/08/24/teens-bond-with-online-communities/17205.html> (accessed 1 October 2013).

Li, W.J., Yu, H., Yang, J.M., Gao, J., Jiang, H., Feng, M., Zhao, Y.X. and Chen, Z.Y. (2010) 'Anxiolytic effect of music exposure on BDNFMet/Mettransgenic mice', *Brain Research,* 1347: 71–79.

Luttrell & Chambers 2013

Mayocchi, L. and Hanrahan, S.J. (2000)'Transferable skills for career change', in D. Lavallee and P. Wylleman (eds.), *Career transitions in sport: International perspectives* (pp. 95–110). Morgantown, WV: Fitness Information Technology.

McMorris, T., Collard, K., Corbett, J., Dicks, M. and Swain, J.P. (2008) 'A test of the catecholamines hypothesis for an acute exercise-cognition interaction', *Pharmacology Biochemistry & Behavior,* 89: 106–115.

McShane, J. (2007) *Pedagogy – what does it mean? Learning and teaching update,* Optimus Professional Publishing Limited. Online. Available HTTP: <www.teachingexpertise.com/articles/pedagogy-what-does-it-mean-2370> (accessed 1 October 2013).

Nauert, R. (2011) 'Teens bond with online communities – Psych Central News'. *Psych Central.com.* Online. Available HTTP: <http://psychcentral.com/news/2010/08/24/teens-bond-with-online-communities/17205.html> (accessed 1 October 2013).

Pereira, A.C., Huddleston, D.E., Brickman, A.M., Sosunov, A.A., Hen, R., McKhann, G.H., Sloan, R., Gage, F.H., Brown, T.R. and Small, S.A. (2007) 'An in vivocorrelate of exercise-induced neurogenesis in the adult dentate gyrus'. *Proceedings of the National Academy of Sciences in the United States of America,*104: 5638–5643.

Pollard, A. (2010) *Professionalism and pedagogy: A contemporary opportunity.* A Commentary by TLRP and GTCE. London: TLRP.

Pope, C.C., & Grant, B.C. (1996). 'Student experiences in sport education.' *Waikato Journal of Education,* 2: 103–118.

Prensky, M. (2001). 'Digital natives, digital immigrants.' *On the Horizon* (MCB University Press), 9(5): 1–6.

Price, N., Morrison, N. and Arnold, S. (2010) 'Life out of the limelight: understanding the nonsporting pursuits of elite athletes'. *International Journal of Sport and Society,* 1(3): 69–80.

Rasberry, C.N., Lee, S.M., Robin, L., Laris, B.A., Russell, L.A., Coyle, K.K. and Nihiser, A.J. (2011) 'The association between school-based physical activity, including physical education, and academic performance: a systematic review of the literature', *Preventive Medicine,* 52(Suppl. 1): S10–20.

Rawson, E.S. and Venezia, A.C. (2011) 'Use of creatine in the elderly and evidence for effects on cognitive function in young and old', *Amino Acids,* 40:1349–1362.

Reeve, J. (2006) 'Teachers as facilitators: what autonomy-supportive teachers do and why their students benefit', *Elementary School Journal,* 106: 225–236.

Roitman, S., Green, T., Osher, Y., Karni, N. and Levine, J. (2007) 'Creatine monohydrate in resistant depression: a preliminary study', *Bipolar Disord,* 9: 754–758.

Russo-Neustadt, A., Beard, R.C. and Cotman, C.W. (1999) 'Exercise, antidepressant medications, and enhanced brain derived neurotrophic factor expression', *Neuropsychopharmacology,* 21: 679–682.

Schinder, A.F. and Poo, M. (2000) 'The neurotrophin hypothesis for synaptic plasticity', *Trends in Neurosciences,* 23: 639–645.

Shulman, L. (1986). Those who understand: Knowledge growth in teaching. *Educational Researcher,* 15(2): 4–14.

Sibley, B.A. and Etnier, J.L. (2003) 'The relationship between physical activity and cognition in children: a meta-analysis', *Pediatric Exercise Science,* 15: 243–256.

Stefanou, C.R., Perencevich, K.C., DiCintio, M. and Turner, J.C. (2004) 'Supporting autonomy in the classroom: ways teachers encourage student decision making and ownership', *Educational Psychologist,* 39: 97–110.

Taylor, P. and Keeter, S. (2010) *The Millennials: Confident. Connected. Open to change.* Online. Available HTTP: <www.pewresearch.org/millennials/> (accessed 1 October 2012).

Trinder, K., Guiller, J., Margaryan, A., Littlejohn, A. and Nicol, D. (2008) *Learning from digital natives: bridging formal and informal learning: Research project report.* The Higher Education Academy. Online. Available HTTP: <www.engsc.ac.uk/assets/documents/LDN%20Final%20Report.pdf> (accessed 1 October 2013).

van Manen, M. (1994) 'Pedagogy, virtue, and narrative identity in teaching', *Curriculum Inquiry,* 4(2): 1–35.

van Praag, H. (2008) 'Neurogenesis and exercise: past and future directions', *NeuroMolecular Medicine,* 10: 128–140.

Volek, J.S., Duncan, N.D., Mazzetti, S.A., Putukian, M., Gomez, A.L. and Kraemer, W.J. (2000) 'No effect of heavy resistance training and creatine supplementation on blood lipids', *International Journal of Sport Nutrition & Exercise Metabolism,* 10: 144–156.

Voss, M.W., Nagamatsu, L.S., Liu-Ambrose, T. and Kramer, A.F. (2011) 'Exercise, brain, and cognition across the life span', *Journal of Applied Physiology,* 111: 1505–1513.

Warner-Schmidt, J.L. and Duman, R.S. (2006) 'Hippocampal neurogenesis: opposing effects of stress and antidepressant treatment', *Hippocampus,* 16: 239–249.

Wu, A., Ying, Z. and Gomez-Pinilla, F. (2008) 'Docosahexaenoic acid dietary supplementation enhances the effects of exercise on synaptic plasticity and cognition', *Neuroscience,* 155: 751–759.

Yau, S.Y., Lau, B.W. and So, K.F. (2011) 'Adult hippocampal neurogenesis: a possible way how physical exercise counteracts stress', *Cell Transplant,* 20: 99–111.

15

LAURA

Enduring – or enjoying – endurance training

Marc Cloes, Stéphanie Hody, Boris Jidovtseff, Anne-Marie Etienne and Alexandre Mouton

DEPARTMENT OF SPORT AND REHABILITATION SCIENCES, GIGA-NEUROSCIENCES, DEPARTMENT OF PSYCHOLOGIES AND CLINICS OF HUMAN SYSTEMS, UNIVERSITY OF LIEGE, BELGIUM

Key words: 15-year-old female, puberty, overweight, drop in blood pressure, physiology, fitness training, psychology, pedagogy.

Laura

Laura is a 15-year-old girl who lives in Liege, in the French-speaking region of Belgium. She is in the middle of her puberty period, and has developed a little later than most of her class-mates. Laura is of normal height with a BMI of 28 (calculated by her family physician during a recent visit). Her parents try to cook healthy meals although both Laura and her brother prefer "junk" food including chocolate, chips and soda. Laura's father makes a big fuss about eating breakfast. He says that children can't concentrate at school without a good breakfast but, like many teenagers, Laura and her brother prefer to sleep longer in the morning than make time for breakfast. Laura is aware that she is a little overweight and she would like to be slimmer, but she is not sure how to go about it although she knows that she probably ought to exercise more than she does.

Laura has never encountered any problems at school and is now in her fourth secondary school grade. She is very well integrated in her class, having good relationships with both girls and boys. Teachers regard Laura as a satisfactory student although they recognize that she is not, perhaps, reaching her full potential. Physical education (PE) is Laura's least favorite lesson because she feels that she is not talented. Laura scored between P_{25} and P_{40} in the last evaluation of the motor and fitness assessment. This is a set of fitness tests organized by the school at the end of the previous school year using the tools suggested by the Sports Administration (Ministère de la Communauté française 2003).

Laura does not have a boyfriend yet but she is interested in one boy at a youth movement group that meets each Saturday afternoon. Similar to other girls in her friendship group, she has little interest in physical activity and sports out of school. Furthermore, while the males in Laura's family play soccer in community clubs, she prefers to read books and chat on Facebook with her relatives.

Laura's school is located in the city center. It is one of the biggest and best known schools in the city with 1,200 students. This publicly funded school offers only general education (no vocational or technical education) and admits students from the whole region. Students mainly come from middle to high socio-economic backgrounds. The school policy is focused most strongly on cognitive development rather than on wider personal development, so activities such as sport and art are considered to be a low priority. The school does, however, have a number of sports facilities available including a sports hall able to accommodate three parallel basketball courts, a gymnasium, a former basement transformed into a place to play table tennis or adapted games, and a large paved playground that is near one of the main roads of the city. Nearby there is also a "green" area along the river with a former towpath.

Laura's school is large so it requires a team of 10 PE teachers. Classes are taught single sex with female teachers teaching the girls. Laura's PE class comprises 26 students aged 14 to 16 years. Among these girls, only three are involved in competitive sports and two are involved in sport as a leisure activity. The remaining pupils are virtually inactive physically, although several participated in sport clubs or dance schools when they were younger. Laura and her classmates have a good relationship with their PE teacher who is relatively young (27 years old) and is new to the school. This teacher arrived in the school at the beginning of the school year, two weeks ago. Unlike her predecessors, she appears to be concerned about the all-round PE and development of individuals rather than just being interested in sport performance. Very few of the students report that they preferred their previous teacher.

There are two lessons of PE each week at Laura's school: one period of 100 minutes on Tuesday morning (8:30 to 10:10 a.m.) and a second of 50 minutes on Friday afternoon (1:30 to 2:20 pm). The first quarter of the school year comprises 16 weeks between 1st of September and Christmas with a week's holiday scheduled in early November. Improving endurance is one of the key aims of PE, so Laura's class must follow a unit on endurance. An assessment of pupils' progress is mandatory, and the school policy recommends that PE teachers should devise plans that specifically enhance endurance. The class will take place outside on Tuesday while one of the indoor facilities will be available for the Friday lesson. Laura's PE teacher is free to select the activity to be taught during this second lesson. Facilities are available for showering after PE lessons but most girls avoid showers. They say that they do not like to use them at school and they explain that they avoid all activities that make them sweaty (e.g. endurance units or exercises at a high intensity level during PE lessons).

During the first quarter of the school year, the weather is typically autumnal. This means that whereas there are some lovely sunny days through September and into mid October, rain and cold temperatures follow. Laura and her friends do not feel particularly motivated to go outside when it is wet and cold. Often they will even provide medical certificates to avoid these lessons.

The autumn term started two weeks ago and since that time, Laura has experienced drops in blood pressure in the early morning during the first lesson. It has happened twice in classroom activities and also in last Tuesday's PE lesson. Teachers mentioned these incidents during one of the regular staff meetings and those who had taught Laura in previous years reported there had been no similar problems in the past. The local school health department could be informed as it is in charge of the medical follow up of the students including individual health analyses and vaccination policy. Unfortunately, it will not be operational until the middle of October.

Laura's PE teacher is somewhat concerned by this occurrence, and she is uncertain about how she should manage it safely. As for Laura, she is concerned that engaging in physical activity might make the problem worse especially as she feels so out of breath when she exercises at any intensity. Meanwhile, endurance is on the curriculum . . .

A perspective from physiology

Laura's PE teachers will probably be aware that Laura's BMI of 28, is considered to be overweight and is generally associated with higher levels of body fat than is optimally healthy. Many teachers will also be aware that, simplistically, weight gain occurs when the energy intake from food exceeds energy expenditure. At a more complex level, there are three mechanisms that contribute to daily energy expenditure, and these act in different proportions depending on the individual. The three mechanisms are basal metabolism rate, diet-induced thermogenesis and the energy cost of physical activity (Wilmore, Costill and Kenney 2008). Moreover, although weight is influenced by numerous biological, genetic and socio-environmental factors, Laura's free time activities might point to lack of physical activity and poor diet as issues that could be addressed.

Laura's drops in blood pressure (hypotension) in the early morning require further consideration. In healthy adolescents, hypotension is primarily caused by gravity-induced blood pooling in the lower extremities, which compromises venous return resulting in reduced arterial pressure. This phenomenon, named orthostatic hypotension, is a common phenomenon when suddenly shifting body position. Fatigue is a contributory factor, and since the incident was reported at the beginning of the school year, it is possible that Laura has encountered changes to her sleeping habits. This would not be surprising because dramatic changes in sleep occur during puberty, mainly due to biological circadian factors (Colrain and Baker 2011). Furthermore, a link between short sleep and increased BMI has been reported because of modifications in hormones involved in satiety and hunger (Taheri and Mignot 2010).

An alternative explanation to be considered is that symptoms of hypotension are often confounded with those of hypoglycemia (low blood sugar). One of the most frequent times for the blood sugar to dip too low is early in the morning when an individual has not eaten since the previous evening. Since Laura said that she had no time to have breakfast, hypoglycemia is a very likely cause of her repeated faintness. Yet, Laura's father is correct: breakfast is the most important meal of the day for a number of physiological reasons. Considering the importance of glucose as a brain substrate, long periods without food can create physical, intellectual, and behavioral problems. Adolescents who regularly skip breakfast may fail to get the daily recommended amount of vitamins because other meals eaten later in the day can't recoup the nutritional deficit (Giovannini *et al.* 2008). While a desire to be thin is a common reason for adolescents to skip breakfast, it is widely recognized that skipping meals can actually make weight control more difficult. According to research, breakfast skippers tend to eat more food than usual at the next meal (Szajewska and Ruszczynski 2010).

In non-obese individuals, weight gain is associated with an increase in size of the adipocytes to store excess energy intake. When these fat cells reach their maximal size, further weight gain is achieved by proliferation of new fat cells. Since hyperplasia of adipocytes is not reversible, weight reduction is difficult after cell proliferation because the fat cells must become smaller than their normal size. This biochemistry mechanism constitutes a strong argument to focus on the *prevention* of obesity more than its treatment. Added to this is the concern that being overweight in adolescence has an association with later life metabolic or cardiovascular diseases (van Dam *et al.* 2006). It is also well known that regular physical activity causes numerous metabolic adaptations, which can be considered advantageous in the prevention of metabolic disorders associated with obesity (Wilmore, Costill and Kenney 2008).

Weight management is not the only consideration in planning a "healthy" PE class for Laura and her friends. The Tuesday morning PE lesson is scheduled to take place outside. Since the school is located in the city center, the potential deleterious effects of outdoor air pollution on human health should be taken into account. When doing aerobic exercise, the air goes deeper into the lungs than in normal activity, and lung deposition of emission-related pollutants is higher because of increased ventilation. There is also a tendency to breathe in through the mouth during exercise, which bypasses filters present in the nose. These are important points that identify unintended negative consequences for people who are physically active outdoors. Nonetheless, research is clear that the benefits of exercising far outweigh the risks of inhaling pollutants. In other words, Laura's teachers can still encourage exercise even though the school is in a city centre but some practical preventive measures should be considered. For example, if students wish to do extra running they can benefit from better air quality early in the morning or late at night (if it is safe), and they should be encouraged to avoid running near heavy traffic. If the times for exercise cannot be changed, such as a scheduled physical education class, the teachers should try to ensure that strenuous physical activity is undertaken in designated parks or away from main roads.

Like many adolescents, Laura resists outdoor exercise in cold weather. Yet, it is possible to keep safe, warm and even enjoy outdoor winter exercise. The key to comfort and safety in exercise during cold or windy weather is balancing the body's heat production and loss to prevent both overheating and overcooling. One of the biggest mistakes while exercising in cold weather is to dress too warmly. Indeed, sweat moistens both the skin and clothing, and increases the rate of cooling resulting in shivering and miserable young people! Instead, pupils should be instructed to dress in several thin layers, which will keep them warmer than one heavy layer, and to cover the head, since an exposed head and neck represents a large contributor to total body heat loss (Carlson 2012). Finally, teachers might like to mention to adolescent girls who are keen to lose weight that running in the cold burns more calories compared to the same exercise in a normal temperature.

A fitness training perspective

Physical fitness is one of the determinants of any athletic performance, and it also contributes to general health. Among physical qualities, endurance represents the most valuable factor because it corresponds to the ability to resist fatigue. For athletes, endurance means maintaining the highest possible level of performance during the longest possible period. For the normal citizen, endurance supports the ability to sustain physical activity of low to medium intensity in daily life.

Endurance is mainly linked to aerobic resources of the body. Individual aerobic characteristics are, in part, genetically determined, but can also be greatly influenced by environmental factors such as engaging in physical exercises and training. Two physiological qualities are linked to the aerobic system: Aerobic power and capacity. Aerobic power training aims to improve the VO2max. The different training methods available (fartlek, interval, intermittent) are characterized by the repetition of exercise bouts at a high level of VO2max (>80%), alternated with short recovery time. Some examples are available on the Internet (e.g. www.brianmac. co.uk/vvo2max.htm; http://en.wikipedia.org/wiki/Fartlek; http://en.wikipedia.org/wiki/Interval_training; http://en.wikipedia.org/wiki/High-intensity_interval_training). Training of aerobic power is linked in the field by the concept of maximal aerobic velocity (MAV) because it is the running speed at which aerobic energy production is at its maximum. Aerobic capacity training aims to increase running time at steady state velocity. Long duration (>20 minutes) exercises are done at moderate intensity, and this is the typical effort of joggers.

In a sports context, VO2max becomes a determining parameter because it underlines an athlete's potential to perform. Although working at a low to moderate intensity is often recommended to get maximum oxidation of the lipids, this approach remains controversial as recent studies suggest that higher levels of VO2max have a better impact on mortality than weight reduction (Tjonna *et al.* 2009). A negative relationship has also been demonstrated between VO2max and body fat (Ekelund 2001).

Moreover, long duration exercise is not recommended for prepubescent children because of thermoregulation limitation and risks of injuries. Prepubescent youth seem better equipped to recover from performing exercises at high aerobic power (100–120% MAV) than from performing long duration/low intensity exercise (70–85% MAV). From adolescence, however, aerobic capacity training with longer running duration is better tolerated, both physiologically and psychologically. Endurance training with young people should be organized from aerobic power to capacity and not the reverse, as is often the case (Baquet, Van Praagh and Berthoin 2003; Gerbeaux and Berthoin 1999). It means that with young people, aerobic training should first focus on intermittent exercises and interval training rather than long duration endurance training that should, instead, be introduced progressively during adolescence.

Developing aerobic endurance is a health priority for children and adolescents, so schools and teachers should focus on this aspect of fitness. Several principles should be respected, however, in order to have the best chance of success (Aubert and Choffin 2007; Pradet 2006):

1. Organizing activities involving more than 2/3 of the body muscles as well as sufficient and consistent workloads in each session;
2. Selecting intensity levels that will really challenge the energy systems;
3. Focusing on endurance with an emphasis on aerobic power exercises;
4. Individualizing the physical load according to the youth maximal aerobic velocity (MAV);
5. Maintaining endurance training throughout the school year by diversifying aerobic solicitations through several sports and activities.

There is research available that offers general aerobic training recommendations for children and youth (Baquet *et al.* 2003; Strong *et al.* 2005). Three or four sessions from 30 minutes to 1 hour appears to be the best option to improve maximal oxygen consumption (VO2max), however, even two sessions per week can result in significant changes. In both children and adolescents, intensity higher than 80% of maximal heart rate (HRmax) is recommended to improve aerobic fitness.

To control exercise intensity, three different feedback approaches can be used with young people: conversation method, heart rate and maximal aerobic velocity (MAV) (Gindre 2012). Breathing facility and the ability to hold a conversation can be used to regulate endurance training. Students should be able to hold a conversation during aerobic capacity training, but not during more intense aerobic power training. Heart rate is a valid indicator of intensity for exercise undertaken beyond a minimum of two minutes (Billat 2003). Young people are characterized by large inter-individual variability in HRmax, so it is important to consider relative values of HRmax based on resting heart rate (Baquet *et al.* 2003). As most schools are not equipped with

HR monitors, HR has to be estimated by counting the beats in a set period of time (at least 15 to 20 seconds). The most effective point for measuring HR is the carotid artery in the neck and to be representative of exercise intensity, the manual HR measurement must be done directly after exercise. Students can take this measurement themselves but they must be trained.

The determination of MAV is probably the most important method for quantifying individual running intensity. In the educational context, a field–test requiring limited equipment can be used to estimate the MAV. Constant intensity (12 minutes Cooper test, 2000m test) and graded field tests (20m shuttle run tests, University of Montreal Track Test) are widely used by teachers to assess aerobic power level and to determine MAV. The use of individual MAV would allow every student to run at a velocity that is proportionate to his or her aerobic fitness level (Gerbeaux and Berthoin 1999). Different training schedules based on individual MAV and usable at school have been designed for both aerobic capacity (60–80% MAV) and power (80–120% MAV) training (Gerbeaux and Berthoin 1999, Aubert and Choffin 2007).

For adolescents, like Laura and her classmates, endurance training should consist of a mix of aerobic capacity and aerobic power (Méar 2012). An optimal approach would involve a range of different content and organization in order to break training monotony and to maintain motivation (particularly during aerobic capacity training). This means that while improving aerobic fitness remains the main target, staged activities and objectives can also be introduced to vary the training, for example: (1) controlling different running velocities (aerobic capacity velocity; anaerobic threshold velocity; MAV); (2) running at constant velocity; (3) reducing walking periods and stops; or (4) improving mental strength during exercise. These alternative objectives can also be added to the student assessment process (Aubert and Choffin 2007).

While the general principles outlined above are useful, they need to be tailored to the needs of individual pupils. Overweight students like Laura need particular attention because running activities may be problematic. In fact, due to mechanical constraints, risk of injuries such as micro trauma resulting in periostitis and tendinopathies is higher in overweight individuals (Strong *et al.* 2005). The prevalence of injuries can be minimized by three approaches: (1) the use of proper equipment and especially the choice of suitable running shoes; (2) the choice of soft ground on which to run, such as soil or grass; and (3) a gradual increase in physical load that should not exceed a 10% increase per week. Moreover, in most cases, overweight people are only able to run for short sequences, and this is followed by a very slow recovery.

Considering the specific case of Laura, teachers should emphasize the importance of nutrition and hydration and advise students that exercise is more difficult with hypoglycemia. Two recommendations are suggested in the literature (e.g. Bar-Or 2000) although more research is required: (1) even though young athletes usually have enough protein in their daily diets, special attention must be given to those who curtail their food intake to maintain or lose body weight; and (2) one should be sure that youths arrive fully hydrated for a physical activity session, and drink pauses should be planned every 15–20 min during aerobic activities, even if young people do not feel thirsty.

A psychological perspective

Adolescence is a period characterized by physical changes associated with puberty including hormonal and psychological changes and the impact of diverse life experiences. In combination, this set of changes influences personal development. As a result of their life experiences, teenagers adopt healthy behaviours such as regular physical activity and healthy eating, or engage in risky behaviours such as smoking and drinking alcohol. To make informed choices, personal skills such as managing emotions, self-esteem and social skills are essential (Wild *et al.* 2004). Yet, there is a stereotype associated with adolescence suggesting it should be a period of crisis and rebellion. In response to this stereotype, teenagers tend to contradict the views and choices preferred by adults such as parents and teachers (Gross and Hardin 2007). Regarding Laura, therefore, an analysis of two psychological themes will be helpful: the importance she attaches to physical health and her degree of ambivalence towards engagement in physical activity.

To explore the importance that Laura accords to physical health, it is likely that two attitudes will emerge: (1) physical health is simply not a priority area for her life; and (2) she amplifies physical sensations and dramatizes their importance. In the first case, the PE teacher might make use of the theories of *operant conditioning,* which suggests that the best way to understand behaviour is to look at the causes of an action and its consequences. Cungi (2005) recommends a simplified functional analysis of the situation: there are vicious circles that have elements that can be isolated (triggering situations, cognitions, emotions, behaviours and consequences). Regarding Laura's drop in blood pressure – which she may feel is a limiting factor in engaging in physical activity – a PE teacher could ask Laura to describe what happens just before the drop in blood pressure. Questions could be asked such as: What were you doing just before you felt unwell? Fifteen minutes before? What did you feel like just after?

Questions such as these will provide information about Laura's capacity to anticipate or not the arrival of the drop in blood pressure, the physical sensations during and after the event and the emotional nature of this event. The ability to anticipate behaviour gives the person a sense of control or mastery. In this context, Laura and the PE teacher can think about implementing actions to reduce the likelihood of the drop in blood pressure. The triggers for the event could be an inadequate breakfast or a set of stressors in her life in the early morning. Simple strategies discussed with the teacher could include ensuring Laura has time for a balanced breakfast that can be eaten without rushing. This simple exchange of information about the link between food, stress and blood pressure offers a relational point of view that might help an adolescent to take appropriate decisions.

Laura's answers to these questions will also provide clues about how she interprets the physical sensations connected to drops in blood pressure and also about her experience with physical symptoms and their management. In 1985, Reiss and McNally (cited by Stassart *et al.* 2013) introduced the concept of anxiety sensitivity (AS). This concept refers to the fear of anxiety-related bodily sensations due to beliefs that these sensations will lead to catastrophic outcomes such as physical illness, social embarrassment, and mental incapacitation. AS refers to individual differences in what people think would happen to them if they felt anxious. For example, heart palpitations will seem very alarming if someone believes they might have a heart attack; and some people panic as soon as they start to tremble or perspire in public because they believe these reactions will make them look ridiculous. For other people, "dyscontrol" or difficulty to concentrate can be worrying if they think it is a symptom of a serious mental disorder. Others interpret difficulty breathing or pain in the chest as a sign of physical danger. On the other hand, a person with low AS will not perceive these physical feelings as dangerous but simply as unpleasant and/or normal.

Laura has an underlying interest in being slimmer, but the physical sensations associated with physical activities (and indirect consequences such as drop in blood pressure) may develop a Pavlovian conditioning by contiguity of the two temporal stimuli. Over time, in order to escape the unpleasant physical sensations, Laura could choose to avoid any form of physical activity in the morning. Again, from a relational point of view, the PE teacher could adopt a psycho-educational approach. So, to put into context the physical sensations (the functional symptoms), the teacher can encourage Laura to compare her perceptions to those felt by other people or in other situations (climb the stairs, for example). This process can help Laura to restructure the physical feelings such that they are viewed as not dangerous, but simply unpleasant and/or normal.

If Laura does not "buy in" to any of the proposals made by the teacher to practice physical activity, a second approach can be taken to address *ambivalence* (simultaneous and contradictory attitudes or feelings toward an object, person, or action). So, Laura might be thinking: "On one hand the PE teacher, an important person for me, says that my behaviour must change and on the other hand I do not want to change my behaviour". To explore the degree of ambivalence, a PE teacher could use the technique of motivational interviewing (Rollnick and Miller 2009). This is a method that works by facilitating and engaging intrinsic motivation within a person in order to change behaviour. From a relational point of view, the PE teacher would take an empathetic approach and invite Laura to analyze her resistance and her intrinsic motivation. The PE teacher would not contradict Laura's perceptions about practice, physical activity, being healthy and being slim. Instead (pending the opening of the health department who may become involved) she allocates time before the course begins to discuss these issues with all students. The best strategy is to try to understand resistance and, rather than arguing, to counter it with information. Hopefully Laura will gradually take ownership of new information and will test other new – and more positive – health-related behaviours.

A perspective from pedagogy

In Wallonia, as in many other regions of the world, PE is not always highly valued in schools (De Knop *et al.* 2005). For example, although there is an expectation that PE is the place to learn motor skills and develop fitness, there is also a view that it is as an opportunity to relax, socialize, and discover a range of interesting physical activities. Moreover, PE teachers are unhappy with the low number of weekly PE lessons (two to three on average), low level of effective lesson time, poor student motivation for difficult tasks, and poor facilities. Yet, there are also efforts being made in many schools to place more emphasis on physical literacy and accountability during PE lessons.

As noted earlier, endurance is an important component of health and physical fitness. Running is an activity that is associated with physical fitness but secondary school students – particularly girls – are mostly not in favor of this activity. Students' absenteeism and non-participation increase dramatically when endurance training is planned in PE lessons, with numerous excuses being provided by parents or even physicians (Delfosse *et al.* 1997). Thus, PE teachers need to structure endurance classes in pedagogically sound ways in order to motivate their pupils. Chaumont and Carlier (2006) identified three ingredients that are necessary to deliver a successful running unit: students' learning (clear improvements, adaptation to the environment), students' pleasure (activities providing fun), and the teacher's focus on students' self esteem. Furthermore, the

French-speaking professional literature proposes specific resources that PE teachers could use to improve, diversify, and update their lessons, including in endurance. Examples include journals, books, and websites such as those published by the "Revue EPS" (www.revue-eps.com/).

It is also clear that Laura's PE teacher should adopt a twofold strategy in her particular case: (1) to manage the issue of drops in blood pressure by taking an individual approach: and (2) to plan a running unit that can be successful for the whole class, taking into account the inter-individual differences among the girls.

To manage Laura's individual issue with blood pressure, the PE teacher may need to engage other professionals. Initially, as suggested earlier, the teacher should have an individual discussion about Laura's thoughts and actions just before an event happens. If Laura shows that she is ready to talk about these events, the PE teacher may set aside time and space to discuss her feelings and whether her parents are aware that she has had such incidents at school. If the student has not shared information with her parents, the teacher will need to weigh the pros and cons of respecting Laura's rights and the requirement to safeguard her health. Different schools, localities and countries will have different guidelines on this for young people under the official age of consent. In Belgium, youth under the age of 18 are the responsibility of their parents and the school's authorities must refer to parents in the case of any problems. The key point to be made is that the PE teacher should try to respect Laura's views as far as possible, but must also respect the school's health guidelines in such cases.

Regarding the endurance lesson for the whole class, the big challenge is to organize a lesson that will motivate 26 students of mixed ability who are − at best − ambivalent about running. One approach would be to deliver a 12-week session entitled: "*I run to be fit*". This ready-to-use programme is well established in local communities and is based on alternate running and individualized recovery periods, ending in a 5km run (Gindre 2012). This programme could be the vehicle for an experimental course focusing on the benefits of physical activity (running in particular). Drawing on sound pedagogical principles, the lessons will: place students at the center of the learning process; offer opportunities for decision-making (autonomy); support them to work in groups (relatedness); maximize all their achievements (competence); structure enjoyable learning situations (pleasure); ensure the activities are sustainable (lifelong); and adapt the requirements to the needs of the individual (Ayers and Sariscsany 2010; Florence, Brunelle and Carlier 1998).

An example of a 12-week endurance programme for adolescent girls using the "I run to be fit" programme

Step One: Planning

The first step would consist of designing lesson plans, fixing the schedule and preparing information for the students. To make it easy and to enhance the PE programme within the school, the PE teacher has convinced the School Principal to adopt an ePortfolio approach (e.g. www.eduportfolio.org). This tool corresponds to an online collection of works that reflect an individual's efforts, progress and accomplishments. This window into students' achievement has many benefits: broader knowledge, facilitated communication, and a skills assessment resource for teachers (Jafari and Kaufman 2006). This should be a tool that can facilitate communication between the students and teacher in this and other areas of the curriculum.

The Principal will send a letter to parents explaining the objectives of the PE project and focusing on the potential benefits of the programme for the youths. The Principal will officially support the initiative. Moreover, it will be made clear that individual shower cubicles will be available after the sessions. This measure should limit the problem of non-participation (Mahler *et al.* 2005). The 12-week unit will alternate running lessons on Tuesdays with various intermittent activities to result in a substantial increase of the heart rate on Fridays.

Step two: introducing and informing

The programme will start with a Friday session during which the PE teacher will explain the general organization of the lessons and the use of the ePortfolio. Students will be informed that during the next Tuesday session, they will be engaged in a brainstorming session on the key topics of health, fitness, exercise and running.

The brainstorming lesson will involve discussions in small groups followed by shared analysis of views on the key topics. Practical activities will increase students' engagement with the topics through game-like situations (e.g. Going for Gold quiz, Arguments for and against, Give us an example) and use of additional material (e.g. popular topics about science and health from the national press including articles and DVDs). At the end of the lesson, a summary paper will be posted on the ePortfolio summarizing the benefits of running and also countering arguments that lead to the common excuses provided by those who do not want to run (Jutel 1994). In addition, the basic principles of running will be illustrated using links to informative and interesting websites and videos. Areas of advice would include: appropriate apparel for running in autumn and winter, especially footwear and a supportive sport bra; nutrition and hydration for running (especially interesting for Laura); advice on running with some specific conditions such as asthma, back pain, overweight, viruses and infections, and menstruation. Other topics will be developed during the unit in order to provide written resources and emphasize the relationships between the content of the practical lessons and the additional knowledge that students need to acquire in order to be successful (i.e. to enjoy and sustain the activity). Over time this might include information on measuring one's own pulse, evaluating physical effort using, for example, the Borg scale (Gindre 2003), effective running form and technique, and use of a heart rate monitor.

Step three: almost running . . .

The next two lessons will be used to introduce running on the field. For the first contact, students will walk to the "green" area along the river towpath where the PE teacher will demonstrate recovering and brisk walks. During these lessons, students will practice technical drills and learn from models on video (tablet computer). The teacher will also provide video feedback on their running skills. All videos will be posted on the individual sessions of the ePortfolio to offer further opportunities for analysis. These first lessons will also teach the specific organization of intermittent training. The physical load of these lessons will be low in order to avoid the pain and stiffness felt in muscles several hours to days after unaccustomed exercise (Delayed Onset Muscle Soreness – DOMS). On the next Friday, a MAV test will be organized and students' performances will be posted on their personal ePortfolios with a short description of the individual programme that will be planned for the further running unit.

Step four: being physically active 2–3 times each week

In order to improve the impact of the endurance training, the *"I run to be fit"* programme suggests that participants should be active 2 to 3 times per week. So, students will be encouraged to run at least once each week outside school. The PE teacher will suggest organized activities or specific places that students will be able to access by themselves. Before each Friday lesson, the PE teacher will check the students' ePortfolios to verify that all members of the class have completed their individual diary (online file). Moreover, to further strengthen the impact of the experience, the teacher will suggest that students record all activities that were undertaken with other people who were initially inactive (e.g. walking with a grandparent, swimming with a friend etc.).

By the third Tuesday lesson, the individualized *"I run to be fit"* programme will be underway. Each student runs according to her own level but systematic grouping during the intermittent activity is central to the organization of the session in order to maintain team working effect. Moreover, aerobic power-centered game-like situations will be included to adapt the original programme to the school context (Méar 2012). Regular self assessments will be planned and the learners will be invited, anonymously, to provide feedback on the process (Desplanques 2012). An interesting challenge is that students will be allowed to participate voluntarily in a popular race organized in the city in mid December (*"La Belle Hivernoise"* – see www.couriraliege.be/).

There will be some occasions at this time of the year when poor weather will constrain running activities. On these occasions, the PE teacher will plan to replace running by rope skipping in the covered playground. Moreover, as the teacher has managed to borrow four heart rate monitors, she will suggest that the students experiment with this tool. Students will be asked to measure their resting heart rate in the morning and to compare the values to those obtained during the PE lessons. This activity will be planned each week and an individual graph will be drawn by each student. This will help Laura to check whether her health is under control. The evolution of this variable over time will be the focus of discussion at the end of the programme during a final meeting with all participants.

The *"I run to be fit"* programme can be adapted in many ways by teachers to meet the needs of different individuals and groups. The core principles, however, should be retained as they are based on research that identifies the most pedagogically sound ways to support young people to enjoy – rather than endure (and resist) – endurance training.

References

Aubert, F. and Choffin, T. (2007) *Athlétisme: 3. Les courses*, Paris: Revue EP&S.

Ayers, S.F. and Sariscsany, M.J. (2010) *Physical Education for lifelong fitness: The Physical Best teacher's guide*, Champaign IL: Human Kinetics.

Baquet, G., Van Praagh, E. and Berthoin, S. (2003) 'Endurance training and aerobic fitness in young people', *Sports Medicine*, 33(15): 1127–1143.

Bar-Or, O. (2000) 'Nutrition for child and adolescent athletes', *Sports Science Exchange*/Gatorade Sports Science Institute, 13(2): 1–4.

Billat, V 2003, 'Physiologie et méthodologie de l'entraînement. De la théorie à la pratique', Brussels: De Boeck.

Carlson, M. (2012) 'Exercising in the cold', *ACSM's Health & Fitness Journal*, 16(1): 8–12.

Chaumont, E. and Carlier, G. (2006) 'La course de durée à l'école: ce qu'en disent des enseignants', in G. Carlier, D. Bouthie and G. Bui-Xuân (eds.) *Intervenir en éducation physique et en sport. Recherches actuelles* (pp. 187–193). Louvain-la-Neuve: Presses universitaires de Louvain.

Colrain, I.M. and Baker, F.C. (2011) 'Changes in sleep as a function of adolescent development', *Neuropsychology Review,* 21(1): 5–21.

Cungi, C. (2005) *Savoir s'affirmer,* Paris: Retz.

De Knop, P., Theeboom, M., Huts, K., De Martelaer, K. and Cloes, M. (2005) 'The state of school physical education in Belgium', in U. Pühse and Gerber, M (eds.) *International comparison of Physical Education: Concepts, Problems, Prospects* (pp. 104–131). Oxford: Meyer & Meyer Sport.

Delfosse, C., Ledent, M., Carreiro da Costa, F., Telama, R., Almond, L., Cloes, M. and Piéron, M. (1997) 'Les attitudes de jeunes Européens à l'égard de l'école et du cours d'éducation physique'. *Sport,* 159/160: 96–105. Online. Available HTTP: http: <http://hdl.handle.net/2268/30145> (accessed 1 October 2013).

Desplanques, F. (2012) 'Perception et analyse des sensations en course en durée', Revue EP&S - Le Cahier des 12 ans et plus, 353: 23–26.

Ekelund, U., Poortvliet, E., Nilsson, A., Yngve, A., Holmberg, A. and Sjöström, M. 2001, 'Physical activity in relation to aerobic fitness and body fat in 14- to 15-year-old boys and girls', *European Journal of Applied Physiology,* 85(3-4): 195–201. doi:10.1007/s004210100460

Florence, J., Brunelle J. and Carlier G. (1998) *Enseigner l'éducation physique au secondaire. Motiver, aider à apprendre, vivre une relation éducative,* Bruxelles: De Boeck Université.

Gerbeaux, M. and Berthoin, S. (1999) *Aptitude et pratique aérobies chez l'enfant et l'adolescent,* Paris: Presses Universitaire de France.

Gindre, C. (2003) 'Comprendre et contrôler l'effort', *Revue EP&S,* 301: 53–55.

Gindre, C. (2012) *Je cours pour ma forme,* Beaume-les-Dames: Volodalen.

Giovannini, M., Verduci, E., Scaglioni, S., Salvatici, E., Bonza, M., Riva, E. and Agostoni, C. (2008) 'Breakfast: a good habit, not a repetitive custom', *Journal of International Medical Research,* 36(4): 613–624.

Gross, E.F. and Hardin, C.D. (2007) 'Implicit and explicit stereotyping of adolescents', *Social Justice Research,* 20(2): 140–160.

Jafari, A. and Kaufman, C (2006) *Handbook of research on ePortfolios,* Hershey, PA: Idea Group.

Jutel, A. (1994) *La course à pied au féminin,* Paris: Vigot.

Mahler, P., Bouvier, P., Kurer, P., Cuenod, J.J. and Houlmann, M. (2005) 'Certificats médicaux de dispense de gymnastique scolaire, la situation à Genève', *Revue Médicale Suisse,* 28. Online. Available HTTP: <http://revue.medhyg.ch/article.php3?sid=30584> (accessed 27 July 2005).

Méar, B. (2012) 'La course en durée', in B. Méar and S. Durali (eds.) *Enseigner les activités physiques d'entretien: Musculation, course en durée, step et aérobic, natation en durée* (pp. 47–70). Paris: Editions EP&S.

Ministère de la Communauté française (2003) *Clés pour la forme. Traitement des Résultats,* Bruxelles: Cdrom, ADEPS.

Pradet, M. (2006) 'L'endurance en milieu scolaire', in G. Milet (ed.) *L'endurance* (pp. 85–102), Paris: Editions Revue EP&S.

Rollnick, S. and Miller, W.R. (2009) *Pratique de l'entretien motivationnel,* Paris: InterEditions.

Stassart, C., Hansez, I., Delvaux, M., Depauw, B. and Etienne, A-M. (2013) 'A French translation of the revised Childhood Anxiety Sensitivity Index (CASI-R): Its factor structure, reliability, and validity in a nonclinical sample of children aged 12 and 13 years old', *Psychologica Belgica,* 53(1): 57–74.

Strong, W.B., Malina, R.M., Blimkie, C.J., Daniels, S.R., Dishman, R.K., Gutin, B., Hergenroeder, A.C., Must, A., Nixon, P.A., Pivarnik, J.A., Rowland, T., Trost, S. Trudeau, F. (2005) 'Evidence based physical activity for school-age youth', *The Journal of Pediatrics,* 146(6): 732–737.

Szajewska, H. and Ruszczynski, M. (2010) 'Systematic review demonstrating that breakfast consumption influences body weight outcomes in children and adolescents in Europe', *Critical Reviews in Food Science and Nutrition,* 50(2): 113–119.

Taheri, S. and Mignot, E. (2010) 'Sleep well and stay slim: dream or reality?', *Annals of Internal Medicine,* 153(7): 475–476.

Tjonna, A.E., Stolen, T.O., Bye, A., Volden, M., Slordahl, S.A., Odegard, R., Skogvoll, E. and Wisloff, U. (2009) 'Aerobic interval training reduces cardiovascular risk factors more than a multitreatment approach in overweight adolescents'. *Clinical Science,* 116(4): 317–26. doi:10.1042/CS20080249

Van Dam, R.M., Willett, W.C., Manson, J.E. and Hu, F. (2006) 'The relationship between overweight in adolescence and premature death in women', *Annals of Internal Medicine*, 145(2): 91–97.

Wild, L.G., Flisher, A.J., Bhana, A. and Lombard, C. (2004) 'Associations among adolescent risk behaviours and self esteem in six domains', *Journal of Child Psychology & Psychiatry*, 45(8): 1454–1467.

Wilmore, J.H., Costill, D.L. and Kenney, W.L. (2008) *Physiology of sport and exercise*, Champaign, IL: Human Kinetics.

16

JOSHUA

Optimising assets: (dis)ability and the path to active participation

Doune Macdonald, Emma Beckman, Don Bailey, Cliff Mallett and Stewart Trost

SCHOOL OF HUMAN MOVEMENT STUDIES, THE UNIVERSITY OF QUEENSLAND, AUSTRALIA

Key words: 15-year-old male, amputee, low motivation, functional anatomy, positive youth psychology, exercise physiology/classification/disability studies, pedagogy.

Introduction to reading this case

This case is not one of a young man moving from exclusion – based upon a physical disability – to inclusion, although at first reading it may seem that way. Rather, participation in physical activity for all children and young people should be understood as complex, messy and ever-changing (Flintoff and Fitzgerald 2012). As has been suggested elsewhere:

> Exclusion and inclusion discourses of sport are not binary (p. 9) . . . (and) need to take account of the shifting positions of children and young people; that they as individual or members of a (problem) group may move fluidly across the sporting landscape and so sedimented readings of their position should be avoided.
>
> (Macdonald *et al.* 2012: 11)

That said, Joshua, with the help of a creative and interested Physical Education teacher, knowledge and practices from a range of physical activity and movement scientists, and a supportive family and health professional team, is poised to move back into physical activity participation. Underpinning our analysis is a concern to build on the strengths or assets that Joshua has, or has access to, including both personal assets (his health, interests, motivation etc.) and contextual assets (his family, teacher, school, curriculum, sporting associations, practitioners and scientists etc.).

Joshua

At the age of 9, Joshua was involved in an accident where his leg was trapped underneath a lawn mower. Joshua was airlifted from his rural hometown to the nearest metropolitan hospital in Brisbane, Australia, where emergency doctors and orthopaedic surgeons made the decision to perform a trans-tibial amputation of his right leg. Following surgery, Joshua was discharged from hospital, and he and his mother Jane stayed in temporary hospital accommodation while Joshua attended the children's amputee clinic. Here, following two weeks of stump bandaging to shape the stump, Joshua was fitted with an interim prosthesis and in the next six weeks underwent rehabilitation with a multidisciplinary team including physiotherapists, social workers and occupational therapists. The team concentrated on adjusting Joshua's balance to decrease his risk of falls and making sure that the stump was tolerating the load-bearing of the new prosthetic limb. Following the fitting of Joshua's definitive prosthesis eight weeks after his initial surgery, Joshua and his mother returned home to Dalby, a rural town about four hours drive west of the city. Joshua's father Peter had stayed home to care for Joshua's brother, Nathan, and manage his practice where he is the principal dentist.

Six years on from Joshua's accident and subsequent amputation, he attends the local high school and is now in year 10 (age 15). He and his mother drive to Brisbane annually for check-ups with the amputee clinic, where they meet with the clinic physiotherapist and his prosthetist. Joshua is fitted every year for a new prosthesis for general mobility, fully funded by the government's amputee limb service. At the same time, he is seen by a physiotherapist at the amputee clinic to make sure he is walking and moving well. The amputee clinic staff have been happy with Joshua's progress over the years, however, at the last visit the physiotherapist mentioned to Jane that over the last two years, Joshua had put on weight beyond growth expectations. It was pointed out that if this trend were to continue, it would impact negatively on the health of his residual limb, his movement and his prosthetic fit.

Joshua's performance in school is recorded as average with broadly satisfactory grades across all subjects. The only subject at school that has been difficult for Joshua has been Health and Physical Education (HPE).[1] Despite the amputee clinic's assurances that Joshua would be able to participate in physical activity to whatever level at which he felt comfortable, Joshua's teachers have been wary of causing him pain or triggering falls and, in the first few years following his amputation, he has been assigned regularly to the role of scorer or umpire.

Prior to his amputation Joshua was naturally "sporty", self-motivated and with favourable anthropometrics for most athletic endeavours: long legs, ectomorph body type and excellent hand-eye coordination. More recently, Joshua has become comfortable with the more passive roles in HPE and school sport, especially given that when he most recently participated in the school sports day he came last in all of his races. Although Joshua is popular at school, most of the boys in his year level spend their lunch time playing handball or football and have not approached Joshua to play with them, nor has Joshua requested to be involved. Joshua spends most of his lunch break reading.

Joshua's family has always been involved with sport, and Nathan plays soccer for the local under-13's team. When Peter and Nathan practice skills in the backyard on the weekends, Joshua prefers to play video games. Jane has noticed that Joshua almost always finds excuses so that he does not have to walk to school, go out, or play with friends. He has also lost his interest in watching sports on TV. Jane has approached the school for access to visiting physiotherapists in the hope that if Joshua could become more confident with his prosthesis, he might return to being physically active.

During year 10, a new HPE teacher, Karen, joined the school and immediately noticed Joshua's reluctance to being involved in physical activity. Karen is sensitive to Joshua's capacities and suggests ways to adapt rules and equipment to make Joshua's mobility issues less noticeable during classes. She shows the class YouTube videos of athletes with disabilities participating in Paralympic sport. Joshua is excited and inspired by the videos having never seen footage of amputees engaging in high level sport. He asks Karen if she can help him run like the athletes on the videos because he suddenly thinks he can see himself becoming an elite Paralympian runner. The following sub-disciplinary knowledge will help Karen to build on Joshua's assets to help him attain his goals.

Growth, development and promoting physical activity participation

Like many sedentary children, Joshua is ambivalent about the prospect of engaging in regular physical activity. Joshua understands and values the benefits of physical activity, and has recently demonstrated some interest in athletics. On the other hand, he continues to value the benefits of remaining sedentary (enjoys playing video games) and thinks about potential costs of becoming physically active (pain and embarrassment from falls). Helping Joshua to explore this ambivalence is crucial to increasing Joshua's motivation to engage in regular physical activity (Miller and Rollnick 2002). As a first step, Joshua's parents and HPE teacher could work with Joshua to complete a *decisional balance sheet*. This task would allow Joshua to identify and explore the costs and benefits of remaining sedentary and the costs and benefits of becoming active. Using some of the counselling techniques of motivational interviewing (open-ended questions, affirmations, reflective listening) may be helpful in creating a decisional balance in favour of regular physical activity and identifying the gap between Joshua's current activity status and where he sees himself in the future.

Joshua's progression towards a physically active lifestyle will also depend heavily on the provision of social support from his family. In this scenario, emotional and instrumental support will be especially important (Loprinzi and Trost 2010). Emotional support is the provision of empathy, love, trust and caring. Hence, it is important for the family to tell Joshua that they care about him and fully support his interest in becoming more active through athletics. Instrumental support is the provision of tangible aid or services that directly assist a person in need. In Joshua's situation, instrumental support could be in the form of contacting the organization Australian Athletes with a Disability (www.sports.org.au/) to learn more about opportunities to participate in athletics, and subsequently providing the resources needed to purchase specialized equipment and fund travel to athletics carnivals.

Enhancing Joshua's self-efficacy expectations or confidence in his ability to participate in athletics will be crucial. According to Bandura (1986), self-efficacy expectations are derived from four sources: past mastery experiences, observation learning, positive reinforcement, and physiological/emotional states. Consequently, to enhance Joshua's self-efficacy expectations, it would be very helpful for Joshua to observe other amputees successfully participating in athletics (observational learning), possibly travelling to Brisbane and seeing some Para-athlete trials. Watching participants of a similar age and ability level would be particularly helpful. To facilitate positive mastery experiences, it will also be important to establish meaningful short- and long-term performance goals that focus on individual improvement rather than relative performance. This is something that could occur as a class activity in HPE for all students.

Karen, when meeting with Joshua's mother, also mentions that Joshua appears to be putting on weight. This factor, combined with reduced weight-bearing on the skeleton, suggests that it is important to structure a broad-based, individualized activity program for Joshua. One of the primary roles of the skeleton is to provide locomotion and movement. At any given age, the skeleton is continually adapting to the functional requirements placed upon it by the mechanical environment. Dynamic mechanical loading has been shown to be osteogenic (improve bone mass) (Rubin and Lanyon 1984), and this is particularly true during the growth years (Judex and Zernicke 2000). Peak bone mass (the amount of bone mineral in the skeleton following maturation) is considered to be an important factor in determining fracture risk as an adult (Rizzoli *et al.* 2010). On average, one quarter of adult bone mineral accrues during a small window of time during adolescence (Bailey *et al.* 1999). This is why it has been suggested that adult skeletal fragility, leading to the risk of fractures, has its beginnings during the growing years (Bailey and McCulloch 1992). Since Joshua, at 15, fits right into this critical time frame and since his mechanical loading pattern has been altered because of his accident, the integrity of his skeleton and an active lifestyle are particularly important. Karen learns that physical activity programs specifically targeting the growing skeleton have been successfully applied in school settings (McKay *et al.* 2000), and she will investigate how such school-based programs could be introduced across the school.

Joshua's exercise program could involve walking regularly to and from school as well as appropriate weight-training using a mix of school and simple home equipment. Karen also suggests that the amount of time Joshua spends watching TV or videos, playing video games, or playing and surfing on the web, should be monitored. Excessive screen time is associated with an increased risk of obesity and a reduction in physical activity (Hills, King and Armstrong 2007). Guidelines developed by the American Academy of Pediatrics in 2001 recommend no more than 1 to 2 hours of TV screen time per day. Jane is keen for their family to support Joshua to make these positive changes.

Positive youth psychology

From a psychological perspective, it is possible that Joshua initially experienced some post-traumatic stress from the accident. In the early stages of assimilating back into school and family life post-accident, it appears that Joshua and those around him often focused on what he could not do (a deficit model approach) rather than what he could do (strengths-based approach). This attention to Joshua's physical limitations may have contributed towards some initial sense of a lack of autonomy and competence, and subsequent amotivation. It is also possible that he began to develop some learned helplessness. In contrast, a strengths-based approach is about making people stronger and more productive and contributing to their human potential and their quality of life (Seligman and Csikszentmihalyi 2000).

There was (and remains) a general concern to protect Joshua from further pain, discomfort, and potential falls. Inadvertently, this focus on protecting him has not enabled Joshua to develop coping resources and resiliency to deal with daily challenges. Moreover, it may have contributed to his disengagement from sport. Joshua had become passive and alienated partly as a function of his inability to master his social environment. More specifically, the way in which he and significant others have responded to his disability has likely contributed to some thwarting of psychological need satisfaction and subsequent lack of psychological growth and development (Deci and Ryan 1985). Unfortunately, it appears that Joshua has lost some meaning in his life since the accident and experienced significant amotivation towards sport participation. Karen has, however, rekindled his flame (self-motivation) and provided an increased sense of purpose, which has the potential to change the quality of Joshua's interactions with his social context (sport). Over time, this adaptive self-motivation might extend to other life domains – such as school – and subsequently foster Joshua's wider personal growth and development (Vallerand 1997).

In assisting Joshua to re-engage with sport and physical activity we might be mindful of how learning environments have the potential to influence psychological growth and development. Specifically, we might think of Joshua's self-motivation towards sport and physical activity. To foster his self-motivation towards sport he needs an adaptive learning environment that fuels the psychological needs of satisfaction and perceptions of autonomy, competence, and belonging (Deci and Ryan 1985; Mageau and Vallerand 2003).

Currently, Joshua aspires to become an elite athlete with a disability. To do so requires him to be self-motivated towards his sport participation in order to promote positive outcomes such as persistence and effort, and reduce fear of failure (Mageau and Vallerand 2003). First, Joshua has to want to play sport for mostly internal reasons, i.e. a sense of accomplishment through personal mastery, excitement, and enjoyment of playing sport (Ryan and Deci 2000). He needs to be self-referenced in his goals rather than ego-referenced (Duda 2001) and personally value his reasons for training and competing (Mageau and Vallerand 2003). Joshua's perception of competence is key to reducing his amotivation towards sport (Ryan and Deci 2000). Second, significant adults in Joshua's life (parents, teachers, health professionals) can play an important role in fostering an adaptive learning environment that facilitates his needs for autonomy, competence and belonging that, in turn, promotes self-motivation. In creating adaptive learning environments, teachers and coaches should consider a pedagogical approach that fosters the need for satisfaction. In other words, how might Karen (as the architect of the learning environment) foster Joshua's perceptions of autonomy, competence, and belonging that will promote self-motivation and positive engagement in sport?

The catalyst for a shift in Joshua's thinking emerged from Karen who has shown him what is possible, rather than what is not possible. Karen can play a significant role in developing Joshua's support network, which is critical for his psychological well-being. Research suggests that sport has the potential to contribute towards Joshua's improved psychological well-being, social reintegration, and improved physical functioning (Bragaru et al. 2011).

Peers are one of the strongest influences on adolescents (Hellstedt 1995) often being more influential than teachers, coaches and parents. Joshua's avoidant behaviours, however, have thwarted adaptive social relations with peers. Hence, consideration of how Joshua and his parents might develop a stronger sense of affiliation with his peers, both within and beyond the school, is central to developing a positive sense of self. Moreover, Joshua's family might be experiencing some psychological distress due to his injury. If this is the case, family therapy and individual counselling may be efficacious for dealing with possible vicarious trauma and helping them to move forward to re-engage Joshua in sport and other meaningful activities.

Exercise physiology/classification

Joshua's new motivation to be an elite runner stemmed from his observation that the Paralympic Movement provides opportunities for athletes with disabilities to participate in sport that is elite, exciting and inspiring (Tweedy and Howe 2011). Prior to this discovery of Paralympic sport, Joshua expressed his disappointment with coming last on sports day when he participated against his able-bodied peers. Competition has been shown to be a potent motivator for participation in sports (Gill 1993; Vallerand and Rosseau 2001), therefore when competition is seen as "unfair" participation is reduced. This may lead to reduced participation in sports and physical activity by children with a disability if avenues in disability sports are not identified and pursued.

Classification systems have always existed in non-disabled sports. Competitions are routinely divided by characteristics such as sex (classes for boys and girls), size (heavy and light weight classes in boxing and rowing) and age (junior, open and masters divisions) (Tweedy and Vanlandewijck 2010). Classification in Paralympic sport aims to minimise the impact impairment has on the outcome of competition (Tweedy and Vanlandewijck 2010). Classification is the method through which success in Paralympic sport is legitimised, ensuring that athletes who succeed do so because of training, motivation and talent, not because their disability is less severe than the athletes against whom they compete (Tweedy and Howe 2011).

In Paralympic athletics, limb deficiency is an eligible impairment type. Joshua would be required to go through the classification process to first determine his eligibility for competition and then to assign a class in which he can compete with others who experience similar difficulties. It will be important for Joshua and his support network to initiate the classification process, and Joshua and his parents should contact the Australian Paralympic Committee to discover how to go about this. Once Joshua has been assigned a classification, his performance can mean something to both himself and others and he can use qualification standards that are relevant to his classification.

If Joshua wants to reach his goals of becoming an elite runner, it is important that he begins to engage in appropriate levels of physical activity. In Australia in 2003, 24% of adults with disabilities participated in organized sports compared to 62.4% of non-disabled adults (Australian Bureau of Statistics 2006). The physiotherapist's observation of Joshua's increased body mass is common in lower limb amputees, with research indicating lower levels of physical fitness (Bussmann *et al.* 2008; Sawamura *et al.* 2002), increased risk of cardiovascular diseases (Naschitz and Lenger 2008) and other conditions such as osteoarthritis (Lloyd *et al.* 2010) in lower limb amputees. This is often a result of the increased difficulty of performing physical activity for lower limb amputees, with studies indicating that children with lower limb amputations have a 15% greater oxygen consumption during walking than children without amputation (Herbert *et al.* 1994). Cardiorespiratory training has been shown to lessen these discrepancies, with regular physical activity shown to increase gait velocity, decrease the energy cost of ambulation and increase ability to perform activities of daily living (Ward and Meyers 1995). Overall, the body of research indicates the importance of general fitness training for Joshua.

As Joshua begins to run, Karen might suggest to Jane and Peter that a physiotherapist or biomechanist spend some time ensuring that his gait is efficient in order to minimise the risk of injury (Klenck and Gebke 2007). Research has shown greater demands are placed on the hip muscles of lower limb amputees, indicating that initial strengthening of muscles through resistance training is important in amputee running (Czerniecki and Gitter 1992; Croisier *et al.* 2001; Nolan 2009, 2012).

Once Joshua is given a classification for Paralympic sport and advice on the types of training that will be important, and with the help of Karen, his school, family, health support team, and relevant sporting organizations, he can adopt new routines and activities that will move him towards his dream.

Pedagogical synthesis

The movement sciences can provide Karen with the knowledge, authority and confidence to partner Joshua and his family in making important changes to his everyday practices. Some of the key lessons for Karen have implications not only for what and how she teaches but also the school's extra-curricula programs and the partnerships that can and should be built beyond the school gates.

Curriculum and pedagogy

Australia's incoming new national curriculum for HPE takes a strong position on inclusion (Australian Curriculum, Assessment and Reporting Authority, ACARA, 2012) as is the case for many curricula globally. What is refreshing and a signpost for Karen is that it avoids identifying specific "groups" as "problems" that require particular assistance (Goodman and Peers 2012).

> Health and Physical Education must allow for inclusive teaching practices that account for the strengths and abilities of all students; to understand and respect difference through the selection of learning experiences, language, feedback and assessment practices. In Health and Physical Education contexts, inclusive language, valuing of difference and supportive teaching strategies are necessary for all students to remain engaged in their learning.
>
> (ACARA 2012)

The advice of movement scientists is that Joshua needs confidence and competence in a range of physical activities. Karen can, through the HPE curriculum, offer opportunities for Joshua and his peers to develop knowledge and skills across several physical activities (e.g. weight-bearing, individual challenge, fitness, team sports etc.). As noted in the case narrative, Karen included in her HPE curriculum materials related to Paralympic sport (possibly in a unit on the history of the Olympics; technology and sport; or refining athletic performances) in such a way that it was a celebration of achievement, sending an inclusive message to all students. Similarly important to all students is their ability to set and meet goals. The self-efficacy survey, suggested in an earlier section, would be relevant to Joshua and his classmates. A school trip to Brisbane to gain insights into opportunities to participate in organized sport beyond school, and the pathways and support for elite sport, could also be valuable. Visiting, for example, the Queensland Academy of Sport Para-athlete Programme or the Sporting Wheelies and Disabled Association (for observational learning) could offer motivational insights. Interestingly, Karen sees an important pattern emerging: what is good for Joshua is, in fact, good for all students.

Karen is clearly committed to a student-centred, critical pedagogy having graduated from a university programme that engendered these values (e.g. Macdonald and Brooker 1999). She was the first HPE teacher to make the time to talk with Joshua about his aspirations, having shifted the curriculum to become contemporary and inclusive. She is also inspired to revisit her pedagogy on the basis of the advice she received about the importance of promoting students' sense of autonomy and belonging. As 21st century learners, all students need to develop lifelong investigative and problem-solving skills. Karen will, therefore, include learning experiences that provide the knowledge and skills to access and understand the ever-changing knowledge bases for physical activity development, motor learning, sports psychology, and the like. This knowledge is integral to optimising the performance of Joshua and his classmates at and beyond school.

School environment and extra-curricula activities

Much of the advice provided by the movement scientists sought to ensure a supportive environment was developed for the promotion of physical activity for all students. Active transport is one avenue that Karen could discuss with students, school administrators, and the local council to ensure that it will be valued, timely and safe. She can also raise the possibility, with school leaders, of introducing short periods of daily physical activity as suggested earlier.

The after-school activity programme also provides opportunities that Joshua has been lacking for skill development, the setting and meeting of personal goals, and affiliation. Karen, with the help of teachers and the local athletics association, will establish a school Athletics Club that is inclusive of all students who are interested in developing their skills and sharing their enthusiasm with others. Finally, Karen has been convinced of the potential of having a school gymnasium to support curricula and extra-curricula activities. She intends to include a unit in year 10 HPE for students to plan what would be required in a school gym and how the school could raise the funds to equip a newly released space. As was noted earlier, there are likely to be grants available to purchase specialised equipment.

School-community partnerships

Much of Joshua's and Karen's progress will rely on partnerships – across the school, families, the local community, government agencies, sporting associations, health professionals etc. Karen has already begun the important conversation with Joshua's mother and, following her research, has a strong appreciation of how important this partnership will be if Joshua is to achieve his goals. When trust has been established, Karen can raise with Jane the possibility of talking further with the school counsellor, and that may open pathways to psychological support that Joshua or the family may consider helpful. Karen has also become better informed about the roles of other allied health professionals/services (physiotherapists, exercise physiologists, gait clinic) with whom she can liaise to enhance Joshua's progress.

From reading current state and national policies for the provision of sport, Karen has become aware of the direction to take in order to bridge school and community sport through the sharing of personnel, facilities, equipment, and programmes. This is a complex undertaking and requires time and good will on the part of the organizations involved (Abbott *et al.* 2011). Nevertheless, Karen envisages the benefits to Joshua and other students if their local community can coordinate resources for athletics as well as other sports. The time required to build this cooperation, together with nurturing other partnerships previously mentioned, should be recognised by the school Principal in Karen's workload.

Strengths-based approach

Underpinning the initiatives outlined above is a strengths-based approach to young people, their health and learning. This approach is of growing international interest largely founded on the salutogenetic model of health as well as its parallel iterations in positive psychology (e.g. Antonovsky 1987; Becker 2007; Park and Peterson 2008). *Salutogenesis* is defined as the process of movement toward the health end of a health-ease/dis-ease continuum; understanding what creates health rather than emphasising limitations to health and causes of disease (Antonovsky 1987). This model therefore prioritises "what keeps people healthy or active?" rather than taking a deficit, pathogenic-curative approach (Quennerstedt 2008; Simonelli *et al.* 2010). It supports a critical view of HPE, challenges the risk factor/deficit model, and is enacted through resource-oriented and competence-raising approaches to learning. The prevailing emphasis on risk factors in physical activity, and identifying groups as being "at risk" (e.g. people with disabilities, Indigenous Australians, ethnic minorities etc.) has been widely criticised for unnecessarily alienating and isolating young people and placing blame on their personal failures to conform to expectations of self-management and participation (Macdonald *et al.* 2009). The strength-based approach, on the other hand, is widely supported in Europe and particularly Scandinavia (Lindstrom and Eriksson 2010). It is consistent with preventive health aspirations and a future-orientation for positive schooling that is interdisciplinary and learner-centred.

Conclusion

In this case, Karen, the HPE teacher, has accessed relevant bio-physical and behavioural knowledge to assist Joshua, an amputee, to begin participation in athletics. Each of the contributing scholars (functional anatomy; physical activity and health; sports psychology, and exercise physiology) has identified relevant knowledge and practices that can assist Karen, Joshua and those around him. Other sub-disciplines could also make a valuable contribution to understanding our case. For example, a sport sociologist could contribute insights into sport and its significance to and for dominant masculinities in Australia; and how and why the Paralympics have become such an inspiration on the global sporting stage. A scholar in cultural studies could explain how and why sport is configured to play such a strong community role in regional Australia. Nutritionists could also make valuable contributions on the optimisation of Joshua's bone density, muscle mass, endurance and general health. Our point is that a wide range of biophysical, behavioural and sociocultural sub-disciplines can contribute to richness of understanding and evidence-based action. Taking a case-based approach to learning reminds us that, if boundaries are not challenged and crossed, (sub)disciplinary knowledge boundaries are artificial and transient constructions that can limit rather than enhance problem-solving.

Joshua is fortunate to have a HPE teacher and family who are willing to be learners themselves in order to adjust and support him. In particular, Karen is taking her professional responsibility as a learner seriously which is an expectation for all teachers in Australia (Australian Institute for Teaching and School Leadership 2011) as elsewhere. As a movement sciences practitioner, this requires her to have a work environment that values professional reading time, provides access to the Internet, supports attendance at a variety of seminars and conferences, and encourages postgraduate study (e.g. Armour 2006). This commitment, alongside Karen's strengths-based orientation to teaching and her creative use of resources, will provide the optimal environment not only for Joshue to thrive, but for the whole school and its community.

Note

1. Throughout Australia, Health and Physical Education tends to be taught in a learning area that integrates knowledge, skills and understanding related to movement, physical activity, health literacy, relationships etc. in a broad curriculum taught by specialist teachers in secondary schools.

References

Abbott, R., Macdonald, D., Hay, P. and McCuaig, L. (2011) '"Just add facilitators and stir": stimulating policy uptake in schools', *Education, Management, Administration and Leadership*, 39(5): 603–620.

American Academy of Pediatrics (2001) 'Children, adolescents, and television', *Pediatrics*, 107(2): 423–426.

Antonovsky, A. (1987) *Unraveling the mystery of health. How people manage stress and stay well*, San Francisco: Jossey Bass.

Armour, K. (2006) 'Physical education teachers as career-long learners: A compelling research agenda', *Physical Education and Sport Pedagogy*, 11(3): 203–207.

Australian Bureau of Statistics (2006) *Sport and recreation: A statistical overview*, Canberra, Australia: ABS.

Australian Curriculum, Assessment and Reporting Authority (2012) *Shape paper for the Australian curriculum: Health and physical education,* Sydney: ACARA.

Australian Institute for Teaching and School Leadership (2011) *National Professional Standards for Teachers,* Melbourne: AITSL.

Bailey, D.A. and McCulloch, R. (1992) 'Osteoporosis: Are there childhood antecedents for an adult health problem', *Canadian Journal of Pediatrics,* 4: 130–134.

Bailey, D.A., McKay, H.A., Mirwald, R.L., Crocker, P.R. and Faulkner, R.A. (1999) 'A six-year longitudinal study of the relationship of physical activity to bone mineral accrual in growing children', *Journal of Bone and Mineral Research,* 14: 1672–1679.

Bandura, A. (1986) *Social foundations of thought and action: A social cognitive theory,* Englewood Cliffs, NJ: Prentice Hall.

Becker, C. (2007) 'Salutogenesis: A guide for wellness programs in the 21st Century'. *Wellness Management – National Wellness Institute Member e-newsletter,* 21(3): 1, 3.

Bragaru, M., Dekker, R., Geertzen, J.H.B. and Dijkstra, P.U. (2011) 'Amputees and sports: A systematic review', *Sports Medicine,* 41(9): 721–740.

Bussmann, J., Schraulven, H.J. and Stam, H.J. (2008) 'Daily physical activity and heart rate response in people with a unilateral traumatic transtibial amputation', *Archives of Physical Medicine & Rehabilitation,* 89(3): 430–434.

Croisier, J., Maertens de Noordhout, B., Marqyet, D., Camus, G., Hac, S., Feron, F., De Lamotte, O. and Crielaard, J.M. (2001) 'Isokinetic evaluation of hip strength muscle groups in unilateral lower limb amputees', *Isokinetics & Exercise Science,* 9(4): 163–169.

Czerniecki, J. and Gitter, A. (1992) 'Insights into amputee running: A muscle work analysis', *American Journal of Physical Medicine & Rehabilitation,* 71(4): 209–218.

Deci, E.L. and Ryan, R.M. (1985) *Intrinsic motivation and self-determination in human behaviour,* New York: Plenum.

Duda, J.L. (2001) 'Achievement goal research in sport: Pushing the boundaries and clarifying some misunderstandings', in G.C. Roberts (ed.) *Advances in motivation in sport and exercise* (pp. 129–182). Champaign, IL: Human Kinetics.

Flintoff, A. and Fitzgerald, H. (2012) 'Theorizing difference and (in)equality in physical education, youth sport and health', in A. Flintoff, H. Fitzgerald and F. Dowling (eds.) *Equity and difference in physical education, youth sport and health: A narrative approach* (pp. 11–36). Abingdon: Routledge.

Gill, D. (1993) 'Competitiveness and competitive orientation in sport', in R. Singer, M. Murphy and L. Tennant (eds.) *The handbook of research on sport psychology* (pp. 314–327). New York: Macmillan.

Goodman, D. and Peers, D. (2012) 'Disability, sport and inclusion', in S. Dagkas and K. Armour (eds.) *Inclusion and exclusion through youth sport* (pp. 186–202). London: Routledge.

Hellstedt, J.C. (1995) 'Invisible players: A family systems model', in S. Murphy (ed.) *Sport psychology interventions* (pp. 117–146). Champaign, IL: Human Kinetics.

Herbert, L., Engsberg, J.R., Tedford, K.G. and Grimston, S.K. (1994) 'A comparison of oxygen consumption during walking in children with and without below-knee amputations', *Physical Therapy,* 74(10): 943–950.

Hills, A.P., King, N.A. and Armstrong, T.P. (2007) 'The contribution of physical activity and sedentary behaviors to the growth and development of children and adolescents: Implications for overweight and obesity', *Sports Medicine,* 37(6): 533–545.

Judex, S. and Zernicke, R.F. (2000) 'High-impact exercise and growing bone: Relation between high strain rates and enhanced bone formation', *Journal of Applied Physiology,* 88(6): 2183–2191.

Klenck, C. and Gebke, K. (2007) 'Practical management: Common medical problems in disabled athletes', *Clinical Journal of Sports Medicine,* 17(1): 55–60.

Lindstrom, B. and Eriksson, M. (2010) 'A salutogenic approach to tackling health inequalities', in A. Morgan, M. Davies and E. Ziglio (eds.) *Health assets in a global context* (pp. 17–40). New York: Springer.

Lloyd, C., Stanhope, S.J., Davis, I.S. and Royer, T.D. (2010) 'Strength asymmetry and osteoarthritis risk factors in unilateral trans-tibial, amputee gait', *Gait & Posture,* 32(3): 296–300.

Loprinzi, P.D. and Trost, S.G. (2010) 'Parental influences on physical activity behavior in preschool children', *Preventive Medicine,* 50(3): 129–133.

Macdonald, D., Abbott, R., Knez, K. and Nelson, A. (2009) 'Taking exercise: Cultural diversity and physically active lifestyles', *Sport, Education & Society*, 14(1): 1–19.

Macdonald, D. and Brooker, R. (1999) 'Articulating a critical pedagogy in physical education teacher education', *Journal of Sport Pedagogy*, 5(1): 51–63.

Macdonald, D., Pang, B., Knez, K., Nelson, A. and McCuaig, L. (2012) 'The will for inclusion: Bothering the inclusion/exclusion discourses of sport', in S. Dagkas and K. Armour (eds.) *Inclusion and exclusion through youth sport* (pp. 9–23). London: Routledge.

Mageau, G.A., and Vallerand, R.J. (2003) 'The coach-athlete relationship: A motivational model', *Journal of Sports Sciences*, 21(11): 883–904.

McKay, H.A., Petit, M.A., Schutz, R.W., Prior, J.C., Barr, S.I. and Khan, K.M. (2000) 'Augmented trochanteric bone mineral density after modified physical education classes: A randomized school-based exercise intervention study in prepubescent and early pubescent children', *Journal of Pediatrics*, 136(2): 156–162.

Miller, W.R. and Rollnick, S. (2002) *Motivational interviewing: Preparing people for change*, 2nd edn, New York: Guilford Press.

Naschitz, J. and Lenger, R. (2008) 'Why traumatic leg amputees are at increased risk for cardiovascular diseases', *Quarterly Journal of Medicine*, 101(4): 251–259.

Nolan, L. (2009) 'Lower limb strength in sports-active transtibial amputees', *Prosthetics & Orthotics International*, 33(3): 230–243.

Nolan, L. (2012) 'A training programme to improve hip strength in persons with lower limb amputation', *Journal of Rehabilitation Medicine*, 44(3): 241–248.

Park, N. and Peterson, C. (2008) 'Positive psychology and character strengths: Application to strengths-based school counseling', *American School Counselor Association*, 12(2): 85–92.

Quennerstedt, M. (2008) 'Exploring the relation between physical activity and health – A salutogenic approach to physical education', *Sport, Education & Society*, 13: 267–283.

Rizzoli, R., Bianchi, M.L., Garabedian, M., McKay, H.A. and Moreno, L.A. (2010) 'Maximizing bone mineral mass gain during growth for the prevention of fractures in adolescents and the elderly', *Bone*, 46(2): 294–305.

Rubin, C.T. and Lanyon, L.E. (1984) 'Regulation of bone formation by applied dynamic loads', *Journal of Bone & Joint Surgery (American)*, 66(3): 397–402.

Ryan, R.M. and Deci, E.L. (2000) 'Self-determination theory and the facilitation of intrinsic motivation, social development, and well-being', *American Psychologist*, 55(1): 68–78.

Sawamura, C., Fujita, H., Nakajima, S., Oyabu, H., Nagakura, Y., Ojima, I., Otsuka, H. and Nakagawa, A. (2002) 'Physical fitness of lower limb amputees', *American Journal of Physical Medicine & Rehabilitation*, 81(5): 321–325.

Seligman, M.E.P. and Csikszentmihalyi, M. (2000) 'Positive psychology: An introduction', *American Psychologist*, 55(1): 5–14.

Simonelli, F., Fernandes Guerreiro, A., Simonelli, I. and di Pasquale, C. (2010) 'Six assertions about the salutogenic approach and health promotion', *Italian Journal of Public Health*, 7(2): 94–101.

Tweedy, S. and Howe, D.P. (2011) 'Introduction to the Paralympic Movement', in Y. Vanlandewijck and W.R. Thompson (eds.) *The Paralympic athlete* (pp. 19–30). West Sussex, UK: Wiley-Blackwell.

Tweedy, S. and Vanlandewijck, Y.C. (2010) 'International Paralympic Committee position stand – Background and scientific rationale for classification in Paralympic sport', *British Journal of Sports Medicine*, 45(4): 259–269.

Vallerand, R.J. (1997) 'Toward a hierarchical model of intrinsic and extrinsic motivation', in M.P. Zanna (ed.) *Advances in experimental social psychology* (pp. 271–360). San Diego: Academic Press.

Vallerand, R. and Rosseau, F.L. (2001) 'Intrinsic and extrinsic motivation in sport and exercise', in R. Singer, H.A. Hausenblaus and C.M. Janelle (eds.) *Handbook of sport psychology*, 2nd edn, (pp. 389–416). New York: John Wiley & Sons.

Ward, K. and Meyers, M.C. (1995) 'Exercise performance of lower-extremity amputees', *Sports Medicine*, 20(4): 207–214.

17

ILONA

'Tweeting' through cultural adjustments

Laura Purdy, Gyozo Molnar, Lisa Griffiths and Paul Castle

INSTITUTE OF SPORT AND EXERCISE SCIENCE, UNIVERSITY OF WORCESTER, ENGLAND

Key words: 15-year-old female, migration background, English language support, homesick, declining sport performance, sociology, psychology, physiology, pedagogy.

Ilona

Ilona Wiszniewski is a 15-year-old female who recently migrated from Poland with her parents with the intention of settling in the UK. In her new school, Ilona is receiving language support but she is still finding it difficult to communicate beyond basic conversation. This not only causes Ilona to feel stressed and insecure about her studies, but it is also affecting her ability to develop friendships. A generally outgoing and friendly girl, Ilona now spends most of her time on her own in her new school which has further increased her feelings of isolation and insecurity. Outside of school, the local Polish community has not been particularly welcoming, and so Ilona tends to stay in her room, communicating with her friends in Poland via the Internet. Such (virtual) social links are becoming increasingly important for Ilona as she struggles to see the positive aspects of the relocation and finds it difficult to develop new social connections with her age group peers. Concerned about Ilona's cultural isolation, her parents have contacted the local rowing club to ask if Ilona could join them despite it being mid-season. Given that Ilona enjoys sport and has considerable rowing experience acquired in Poland, her parents hope that a familiar activity such as rowing will help Ilona to feel more 'settled' in her new environment so that she can begin developing social networks.

The rowing club is one of the most popular sporting venues in the local area and one of the most competitive clubs in the region. It boasts numerous crews and regularly achieves strong performances. Ilona loves rowing, and she was at the top of the region for her age group in her home country. Before leaving Poland, Ilona had aspirations to represent her country in international competitions and she believes she can still reach that goal. Based on her recorded previous successes, the coaches at her new club expected that Ilona would be the leading rower in her category but, as yet, she is not meeting their expectations. Ilona frequently arrives late for training, often still wearing her school uniform, which requires even more time to get ready for the session. Adding to the existing communication difficulties, she is reluctant to adopt the ways of the new rowing club and prefers the methods with which she is familiar. Consequently, Ilona has been moved out of the crew boat into a single scull, which has restricted her ability to make social links and has made her feel even more isolated. She is concerned that her training results are not consistent with her previous achievements; despite increasing her training volume it appears that she has hit a performance 'slump'.

Neither her former coaches (with whom she still communicates) nor her new coaches can fully understand why Ilona's performance has deteriorated so markedly. The problem is compounded by feelings of frustration with the change in her performance, and she is now starting to worry that her chances of representing Poland at an international level are declining daily. Ilona regularly uses social media, particularly Twitter, to communicate her ongoing fears and frustrations to friends in her home country.

Sociological perspective

It appears that the effect of migration on Ilona has been multi-layered and complex. When her family embarked on a life-altering journey across nations with the intention to make a long term commitment to the destination country, they inevitably exposed themselves to a wide range of challenges. These challenges may include, for example, lack of legal rights, cultural differentials, personal insecurities and identity crises. To face and cope with the personal adjustments in the host environment, migrants continuously build and re-build their perceptions of their new home and, through that process, build and re-build their own self. Consequently, when seeking to understand Ilona's experiences, it is important to consider spatial, cultural and emotional facets of relocation, the needs of her individual self and the consequent changes *within* the self. Ahmed *et al.* (2003: 5) put it succinctly: 'although migrants often move across vast geographic distances, the greatest movement often occurs within the self'. This movement within the individual is predominantly triggered by the migration–driven loss of *ontological security* of the self.

IlonaWiszniewski@Ilonawioślarskich

survived 1 month in UK and am getting back onto the H20 ☺signing up @BigLakeRowingClub
thanx matka and tata xx

Ontological security is a state of mind that is derived from daily routine and understanding of and familiarity with the socio-cultural environment in which daily routines are enacted. As we learn and become familiar with our social milieu, we are able to perform a wide range of social activities and interactions successfully at a non-conscious level. Giddens (1990: 36) described this process as 'practical consciousness'. As a result of her geographical and cultural relocation, Ilona has interrupted the majority of social mechanisms in which she participated regularly and with which she was familiar. Losing the comfort of the well-known and her day-to-day routine has led to chaos in her ordered personal milieu. In addition to losing the familiar, when settling in the host environment, Ilona has also become exposed to the unfamiliar. Consequently, she has to learn new cultural formations and social practices and expectations. In other words, the process of migration has 'challenged' Ilona's personal and cultural integrity on two levels: the absence of the familiar and the presence of the foreign.

IlonaWiszniewski@Ilonawioślarskich

On the water again ☺ @BigLakeRowingClub is very different to club in Poland

---

To illustrate the extent of migration-generated socio-cultural transitions, it is helpful to refer to Goffman's (1959) work on the presentation of the self. According to Goffman, society is a stage where people perform a range of roles and engage in multiple social situations. Roles performed and situations encountered in any given society are imbued with expectations, such as how one should behave, dress and present oneself. These expectations are widely known and recognised by the majority of the given society. This means that individuals entering social scenarios and interactions know, to a large extent, what to expect from them. Simply put, there is a collective expectation of what should happen in a social situation (front) and our under-standing of that expectation (and others' expectations) is what Goffman called the *vocabulary of fronts*. Goffman (1959: 36) explains the vocabulary of fronts as follows:

> Instead of having to maintain a different pattern of expectation and responsive treatment for each slightly different performer and performance, he (observer) can place the situation in a broad category around which it is easy for him to mobilise his past experience and stereotypical thinking. Observers then need only be familiar with a small and hence manageable vocabulary of fronts, and know how to respond to them, in order to orient themselves in a wide variety of situations.

Goffman observed that to successfully carry out social roles and engage in social situations we need to have three interconnected elements present and functioning: the physical environment (the setting); the appropriate appearance and manner of the actor (personal front); and the institutionalised collective expectation (front). What this means for Ilona is that in order to participate successfully in any given social situation, she must understand the expectations in that setting so that she can adjust her personal front in appropriate ways. For instance, Ilona's new coaches would expect her to show up at the training session on time, wear the appropriate kit and be both mentally and physically focused on the task ahead. Ilona, however, tends to turn up 10–15 minutes later than the agreed time, still wearing her school uniform. This action may be perceived as a clash between the setting, expectations and the personal front.

IlonaWiszniewski@Ilonawioślarskich

went to training today and my training group had left without me ☹

Individuals are expected to know the roles that they and others should play in joint interactions. If social actors were not familiar with cultural expectations, social life would be nearly unworkable because each individual would be required to work out each situation anew every time it occurred. As Ilona lacks familiarity with her new cultural setting and the collective expectations placed upon her, she struggles to adjust her personal front appropriately.

The mastery of social situations in Ilona's native land may not be easily transferable to the host country. It is unsurprising, therefore, to find that Ilona clashes frequently with social expectations, and it is necessary to re-learn what is required of her in a new cultural setting. During this process of learning cultural expectations that are established in the host environment,

Ilona has been continuously exposed to settings in which she is unacquainted with the social expectations. The constant 'not knowing' what to anticipate and how to behave has triggered anxieties and, in turn, insecurities. In short, Ilona illustrates the point that understanding and accepting the reality of the (novel) socio-cultural setting is essential for the maintenance of her ontological security (Giddens 1990).

IlonaWiszniewski@Ilonawioślarskich

Training + study in english = TIRED

Prior to the migration event, Ilona had little understanding of the realities of moving to a new cultural environment. In the host country, she has experienced a transition period in which her level of social anxiety has become higher and her ontological security lower than in Poland. High levels of anxiety and insecurity brought on by lack of cultural awareness and migration-driven personal adjustments can be the causes of multiple issues such as homesickness, trouble with fitting in, difficulty of self-expression and stress. Ilona has endured all of these, along with other personal adjustments and, thus, care should be taken when interpreting her actions or making judgements about her social, psychological and physiological attributes. Coaches should bear in mind that a migrant athlete may appear to behave 'oddly' and is likely to operate outside of culturally acceptable boundaries. This apparent culturally contrasting behaviour may not indicate lack of respect for the coach and/or the sport, but is more likely to be the result of a lack of cultural experience and migration-driven personal insecurities. Cultural challenges can also trigger psychological insecurities, some of which will be discussed in the next section.

IlonaWiszniewski@Ilonawioślarskich

Training = ok but it is still hard to fit in ☹

Psychological perspective

IlonaWiszniewski@Ilonawioślarskich

Today training = a run. No one ran with me ☹

In her former rowing club in Poland, Ilona had enjoyed productive working relationships with her team-mates and coaches. As a newcomer to her current sport setting, Ilona has not yet developed similar relationships. An important support mechanism that is usually present amongst and between athletes and coaches does not, therefore, exist. As a result, it might be problematic for Ilona's new coaches to identify key factors contributing to performance issues. They can only observe surface information such as an increase in times over distance or a drop in stroke rate. Similarly, lack of punctuality or attendance at training may provide (only surface) evidence that can be monitored and interpreted.

A coach should explore a wide range of support options that could be helpful in developing an accurate understanding of athletes. One of these support mechanisms could include a sport psychologist. By building an in-depth picture through conversation with Ilona and those people close to her, it may be possible to identify her psychological needs. Moreover, a sport psychologist can be instrumental in educating coaches and parents such that they can support the delivery of Ilona's psychological skills training. This is imperative for young athletes (Barker, McCarthy and Harwood 2011) who rely on parents and families. Establishing a rapport with those around Ilona before and during the early stages of consultation is essential. For example, a sport psychologist in this case could helpfully spend time observing training sessions and chatting with team members as an invited guest. This process can help Ilona to share relevant information in sessions once she becomes comfortable with the athlete–psychologist relationship.

If successful, the outcome of a fact-gathering exercise such as the one outlined above culminates in the triangulation of data. This enables the array of information to be examined for similarity, consistency or discrepancy and this, in turn, enables the sport psychologist to establish an appropriate intervention. It would be a concern in Ilona's case, however, if a sport psychologist gave exclusive focus to the physical performance deficit. In an attempt to minimise this corporeal focus, it is prudent for practitioners, coaches and support staff to be aware of the remit of sport psychologists such that practice can be better informed. A chartered or accredited sport psychologist will draw upon a selection of frameworks and models to establish the psychosocial needs of the athlete. Some key models are as follows;

Gardner and Moore's Multilevel Classification System for Sport Psychology (MCS-SP) places emphasis on the wider psychosocial elements of the athlete: environmental, intrapersonal, interpersonal, behavioural and performance history, rather than on performance-related goals in isolation (Gardner and Moore 2004). In adopting the MCS-SP, it becomes possible for the sport psychologist to classify the athlete on the basis of available evidence into one of four broad categories:

- Performance Development (PD) which focuses primarily on performance enhancement;
- Performance Dysfunction (Pdy) which focuses primarily on performance 'slumps' caused, for example, by transition and adjustment to significant life events or to endogenous factors, such as a fear of failure;
- Performance Impairment (PI) which focuses primarily on psychological and behavioural dysfunction exogenous to sport-performance; and
- Performance Termination (PT) which focuses primarily on an athlete's reaction to the end of his or her career.

Each of these categories has two sub-levels (I and II). For the purposes of clarity and for quick reference by support staff, these are summarised in Table 17.1. The categories are illustrated by an example question that might be asked when interpreting Ilona's performance after the triangulation of available evidence. One must be aware that the examples below are not exhaustive, but instead are 'signposts' to associate with observable or behavioural symptoms. In order to fully comprehend specific behavioural symptoms, it would be important to consult fully with a sport psychologist who would also have the skills and knowledge to refer the athlete to a clinical psychologist or psychiatrist if appropriate.

Based on MCS-SP alone, it might be tempting to classify Ilona into PD-I, due to her age. A sport psychologist, however, should recognise Ilona's reaction to her recent transition into the

TABLE 17.1 Sub-levels within MCS-SP and guidance questions for classifying Ilona (adapted from Gardner and Moore 2004)

	Sub-level I	Sub-level II
Performance Development (PD)	Physical skills continue to develop. Psychological skills training (PST) may enhance development or performance.	A high level of physical skills exist. Psychological skills may produce consistent, optimal performance
	Does Ilona require PST to complement the development of her physical skills e.g., self-confidence, motivation, concentration, emotional control, coping with stress or anxiety?	*Does Ilona require PST to enhance existing high-level physical skills (one would need evidence that she has reached this level)?*
Performance Dysfunction (PDy)	Athlete reacts to exogenous (external) life events, resulting in performance deficits.	Athlete reacts to endogenous (internal) cognitions, elicited in response to performance deficits.
	Is Ilona finding it difficult to adapt to a significant life transition (outside of her sport)?	*Is Ilona unnecessarily seeking approval from others, overly afraid of failure or striving to seek perfectionism in her sport?*
Performance Impairment (PI)	Athlete experiences clinical issues, e.g., anxiety, eating, affective disorders outside of sport, impairing functioning in daily life.	Athlete experiences clinical issues, e.g., addictive disorder, substance abuse, anger management.
	Is Ilona displaying signs of being overly anxious, emotional, or concealing eating habits that one might be concerned about?	*Is Ilona displaying signs of taking any substances, or being unnecessarily aggressive that one might be concerned about?*
Performance Termination (PT)	Athlete experiences an expected termination of career, e.g., retirement.	Athlete experiences an unexpected termination of career, e.g., career-ending injury.
	Is Ilona approaching the end of her competitive career?	*Has Ilona suddenly lost the opportunity to continue in her competitive career?*

unfamiliar culture and social milieu of the UK and, indeed, even the region in which she lives. Given the wider psychosocial scene, therefore, it would appear that Ilona falls into the category Pdy I, as a result of her migration to the UK. This may be viewed as a significant life event for her and the sport psychologist would wish to explore Ilona's adjustment, or lack thereof, to her new environment. In doing so, the sport psychologist may recommend the use of psychological skills training (PST) in order to develop Ilona's self-confidence, motivation, emotional control, coping with stress or anxiety and to aid successful transition.

It is important to acknowledge that younger athletes have psychosocial needs which are distinct from adults, so PST programmes that work with adult populations may need to be adapted for younger performers. In the formative years, aspects of physical, emotional, cognitive and social development must all be taken into account, and practitioners must be mindful of establishing and delivering their services based on the age-specific needs of young athletes. With these points in mind, a psycho-educational framework – the Youth Sport Consulting Model (YSCM) – is suitable for young athletes between 6 and 17 years of age (Visek, Harris and Blom 2009). The YSCM can be used to help sport psychologists to structure their service delivery from inception to completion. Table 17.2 below contextualises the YSCM for Ilona's case.

TABLE 17.2 Adapted from Visek *et al.* (2009)

Phase 1: Practitioner considerations	Sport psychologist to assemble appropriate resources in advance of service delivery with Ilona.
Phase 2: Initiating contact	Sport psychologist to initiate contact with Ilona through the coach after spending some time around the rowing club as a guest/visitor. Friendly, informal conversations with Ilona and her parents could be beneficial in establishing the beginnings of a rapport.
Phase 3: Doing sport psychology	Sport psychologist to further establish rapport with Ilona, conduct a Needs Analysis/obtain baseline measures before providing psychological skills training, in accordance with YSCM framework. For Ilona this may involve: completing a performance profile (Butler & Hardy 1992) an athlete-centred measure of the qualities involved in successful performance; a Test of Performance Strategies questionnaire (Thomas *et al.* 1999) [which would require a Polish translator], alongside the sport psychologist's initial discussions and observations.
Phase 4: Ending the season	Not applicable at this stage in service delivery.
Phase 5: Assessing the consulting relationship	Although this should take place at the end of service delivery, sport psychologists should endeavour to reflect on/assess progress on an ongoing basis.
Phase 6: Termination and continuation	Not applicable at this stage in service delivery.

When considered in conjunction with the MCS-SP (Gardner and Moore 2004) the YSCM offers the sport psychologist an appropriate foundation for service delivery. It is during the 'Doing Sport Psychology' phase of the YSCM that the fundamentals of the 5Cs Coaching Efficacy Program (Harwood 2008) can be used to focus service delivery. Harwood's programme aims to shape positive psychological and interpersonal skills for young athletes by equipping them with psychosocial competencies to complement their development, and it could readily be applied to rowing. The 5Cs are: commitment, communication, concentration, control and confidence, each of which is beneficial to successful psychological development. Coaching staff need to acknowledge that equal importance should be given to psychological training and physical or technical training (Harwood 2008). With this in mind, the coach and sport psychologist should use these competencies as a frame of reference upon which to develop psychological skills training in youth athletes (Harwood 2008; Barker *et al.* 2011; Kleinert *et al.* 2012).

It is clear in the case of Ilona that she will most likely struggle with communication-related issues as a result of the language barrier. This may impinge upon at least two more of Harwood's components (i.e., concentration and control) culminating, perhaps, in a lack of or drop in confidence. From a practitioner perspective, the language barrier also renders the use of psychological interventions – such as understanding the relevance of self-talk – extremely challenging. Similarly, Ilona is seeking to become part of a cohesive team, which could be an integral element for her (and the team's) development. In addition, at her age, lack of engagement with the team may be contributing to the performance deficit. A short-term goal, during phase 3 of the YSCM, might well be to establish an effective rowing-specific technical vocabulary. It may be prudent for the sport psychologist to work with Ilona's class teacher or language tutor to discuss her rowing-specific and general language needs. This may, in turn, enable Ilona to better communicate her cognitive and emotional needs while her language skills are developing further.

IlonaWiszniewski@Ilonawioślarskich

went for a run by myself AGAIN. I REALLY REALLY miss my friends ☹

Ilona's 'running' tweets provide implicit information about her emotional state indicating (among other things) sadness. In adopting a problem-focused, along with an emotion-focused, strategy (Lazarus and Folkman 1984) a solution emerges. The problem – running alone – may be solved by facilitating running activities involving a 'buddy system' or small-group work. In either of these strategies, however, poor communication could remain an issue. A potential solution is to devise activities or tasks requiring limited verbal communication whereby the language barrier will become less significant for Ilona. In addition, this strategy might develop a degree of empathy within the English-speaking members of the team as they experience first-hand the frustration associated with limited verbal communication and having to find alternative methods of interaction. From this starting point, a series of communication-enhancing training sessions can be discussed with Ilona's coach.

It is not only psychological issues that should be addressed when examining Ilona's performance slump. Ilona's coaches should also consider the physiological issues that may emerge from the circumstances in which Ilona finds herself following migration.

IlonaWiszniewski@Ilonawioślarskich

BIG erg test tomorrow which will decide racing combinations. My times have been slow and I don't know why. Wish me luck.

Physiological perspective

Ilona is faced with a number of physiological challenges as she acclimatises to her new environment. Initially her body has to adapt to physical adjustments occurring during and post-migration. For example, she has to become accustomed to her temporary or new living arrangements, a new educational and social structure as well as potential dietary changes (Gushulak and MacPherson 2006; Wu and Schimmele 2005), all of which may have an impact on her physical well-being (Cabieses-Valdez 2011). During this time of cultural assimilation, she may have difficulty coping without her 'normal' social support structures and may demonstrate physical signs of stress, such as physical fatigue, lack of energy, feeling unwell and/or change in appetite. As previously highlighted, social barriers, including language and lack of familiarity with social structures, may prevent Ilona from discussing physical concerns with her coaches or other relevant individuals (Kristiansen *et al.* 2007) or from accessing appropriate health care (San Martin and Ross 2006; Gushulak *et al.* 2011). Collectively, these physiological stresses may have a direct impact on Ilona's athletic performance.

In addition to the physical demands associated with migration, it is important to recognise the competing physical processes of growth and maturation relating to Ilona's athletic performance. At her particular stage of biological development, Ilona may have specific physical challenges which can affect her ability to meet the high training demands associated with competitive sport. During adolescence the body undergoes a complex series of sequential alterations in neuroendocrine function. These mechanisms are responsible for regulating growth and biological maturation, including cardiovascular, musculoskeletal, reproductive and morphological developments (Naughton *et al.* 2000).

The time and rate of growth during maturation is highly individualised as there is a natural acceleration and deceleration of these systems (Ford *et al.* 2011). A recent systematic review (Quatman-Yates *et al.* 2012) highlighted that movement skills may be hindered during adolescence due to maturation, or in some instances regression, in sensori–motor function (e.g., postural stability, neuromuscular control and intersegmental/interlimb coordination). Indeed, a rapid and substantive rise in stature and/or musculature may have an immediate negative impact on Ilona's performance because a shift in the centre of balance, or change in limb length or core strength, may affect her rowing technique. These physical changes can also lead to an imbalance between strength and flexibility providing a potential explanation for an increase in 'motor awkwardness' and risk of injury often observed at this stage. Hence, as biological maturation is not necessarily a linear pathway, training programme design should be based on Ilona's biological age (i.e., age of her physiology not chronology) and her physical ability to meet the performance outcomes, acknowledging that performance capabilities will be altered accordingly.

IlonaWiszniewski@Ilonawioślarskich

Ergtest [timed 2000m on the rowing ergometer] got me in the last boat. What is going on?? I am better than this ☹ I want to go home!

Although Ilona competes regularly, the primary training focus for young adolescents (e.g., 10–15 years) particularly in late-specialising sports such as rowing should centre on the development of fundamental movement skills, aerobic conditioning, understanding training routines/techniques and overall physical capabilities (Stafford 2005). Ilona is in a sensitive period, however, as she nears the age for transition to the next developmental training phase. In order for Ilona to progress effectively to a competition-specific training programme while optimising fitness and enhancing the technical and tactical sport-specific skills, she will need to negotiate these competing physical demands.

It is worth noting that as the nature of competitive sport has become more structured, there have been increases in intensive and repetitive training demands placed upon young athletes (Micheli 1996). This has led to growing criticism of the selection of training programmes for adolescents. Specific concerns about such training include those programmes where females are required to use male training programmes, schedules based on the individual's chronological age without consideration of biological development, and programmes that are not specific to the *individual's* strengths and weaknesses (Bailey *et al.* 2010). With an increased focus on performance outcomes, frequent programme monitoring and adjustments in training volume should be made to avoid insufficient recovery of both psychological and physiological resources. It is, therefore, essential that for young athletes like Ilona who transfer onto a new training programme, individualised programmes should be prescribed. Such programmes should use appropriate training volumes with active rest and sufficient recovery to achieve developmentally appropriate outcomes.

There are several possible explanations for Ilona's decline in performance. It may be due to the lack of an age-appropriate individualised training programme, a lack of periodisation in the training/competition schedule, insufficient recovery or other psychosocial stressors unrelated to training (Brenner 2007). Other potential triggers for the performance decline might be rooted in wider health and training issues. An initial investigation to rule out infection, pre-existing conditions or other diseases is important to establish whether changes in performance are due to an underlying clinical condition. For example, young female athletes are susceptible to iron-deficiency anaemia which has been shown to negatively affect aerobic capacity, energy levels for muscular contraction and mental function (Rowland 2012). However, if an athlete experiences a persistent decrease in his or her performance, even with two weeks of relative rest, then overtraining should be considered. Overtraining is a "series of psychological, physiologic, and hormonal changes that result in decreased sports performance" (Small 2002: 659). Potential psychological and physiological symptoms of overtraining include: an increased perception of effort during exercise, frequent upper respiratory tract infections, muscle soreness/joint pain, sleep disturbances, decreased appetite, mood disturbances and/or decreased interest in training and competition (Small 2002; Budgett 1998).

Taking into account all of these considerations, it is essential that Ilona is provided with a clear development route within the squad as well as an individualised and developmentally appropriate training programme to ensure successful athlete progression. Training demands should be periodised to cycle the training load allowing for sufficient rest and recovery which are appropriate for her age and maturational development. Educating Ilona and her coaches about the evidence-based training process may enable them to better balance the bio-psychosocial demands required of training and competition.

IlonaWiszniewski@Ilonawioślarskich

Coach came to my house today to talk to me and my parents. We made a plan for ME! Watch out I'll be number 1 in UK soon ☺

Pedagogical perspective

Throughout this chapter we have provided pedagogical 'tips' aimed at coaches working with athletes similar to Ilona. These tips are underpinned by the belief that learning is a multifaceted social process. Accepting this, we draw upon Vygotsky's (1978) cultural-historical theory as one potential lens to make sense of Ilona's adjustments to a new cultural context. Vygotsky viewed social development as co-construction; a dynamic process involving interactions with others. He argued that learning occurs in the zone of proximal development, which is "the distance between the actual development level as determined by independent problem solving and the level of potential development as determined through problem solving under adult guidance or in collaboration with more capable peers" (Vygotsky 1978: 86). Simply put, the zone of proximal development is the difference between what an individual can achieve with the help of others versus what he or she can achieve on his or her own.

Linking Vygotsky's work to the case, Ilona is new to the cultural context and, limited by language, she is struggling to write herself into her new cultural landscape. This has resulted in feelings of loneliness and sadness and, in sport, a decrease in performance. However, using

Vygotsky's (1978) theory, we can view Ilona's new coaches and crewmates (and sport psychologist) as 'more knowledgeable' others. These are individuals who have better understanding of a concept than the learner, and who could/should play a role in Ilona's social as well as sporting development. As such, actively integrating Ilona into the sporting environment would enable her to learn and understand more about her new context, for example ensuring she is running with others, and including her in crew training rather than isolating her in a single scull. It could also be argued that while her new coaches and crewmates could be viewed as more knowledgeable in relation to the social landscape of her new country, Ilona could be viewed as a 'more knowledgeable other' in relation to life and sport in Poland. This knowledge could assist Ilona's coaches and crewmates in better understanding or becoming more empathetic to issues relating to migration and to the socio-cultural challenges a migrant may face in the host environment.

In this chapter we have drawn upon the disciplines of sociology, psychology, physiology and pedagogy as 'lenses' through which to view the impact of migration on a young athlete's life. The value of using these disciplines collectively, and drawing them out of disciplinary silos, lies in the potential to create an holistic picture of Ilona's transition to a new socio-cultural context. Such an approach challenges coaches not to consider Ilona's performance slump as a "problem to be solved", rather, it asks them to view Ilona via a wider lens, recognising her as a unique and complex individual, with her own voice and persona. In so doing, we have been able to consider the impact on Ilona's sense of self as she learns and adapts to new social rules and becomes more secure in her new environment.

Building on this approach, the psychological impact of a transition has been discussed through the use of three models: Gardner and Moore's Multilevel Classification System for Sport Psychology (MCS-SP), the Youth Sport Consulting Model (YSCM), and the 5Cs Coaching Efficacy Model, which may help practitioners (e.g., coaches, teachers, sport psychologists, physiologists) to recognise areas where Ilona needs specific support. Here it was identified that the performance deficit was probably due to a change in social context, and Ilona's inability to communicate was highlighted as a critical factor. As such, strategies were proposed which may better facilitate her integration into the rowing club and society in general.

Finally, we looked specifically at Ilona's sporting performance, suggesting that the slump could also be the result of stress or a possible underlying clinical condition. Further questions were raised regarding the appropriateness of Ilona's training programme and whether consideration of her biological development was at the forefront of its design.

Although throughout the chapter we have provided guidance for practitioners, there are also implications for the coaching process. By adopting a multi-disciplinary approach to Ilona's case, it has become apparent that the role of the coach extends beyond that of a subject-matter specialist and a systematic method applier (Jones *et al.* 2004) which, traditionally, is the way in which sports coaching has been characterised. From this viewpoint, coaching is understood rather simplistically as a linear, sequential process. This, of course, underplays the reality of a coach's work that occurs in a social and cultural context and is connected to a wide range of significant others. As such, it is important that the coach (and other educators) can see and understand the individual within the process as well as interpret the contextual landscape. Such a task not only requires coaches to draw upon diverse, multi-disciplinary sources of knowledge(s), but also to possess and actively engage the 'social competencies' required to read, understand and respond to the complexity of each situation. For example, as reported in her last 'tweet', Ilona's coaches met the whole family to discuss a plan that prioritised Ilona's needs. The coaches' attempts to understand Ilona's situation more comprehensively not only demonstrates empathy for the athlete but also an ethic of care. This suggests they have understood that in order to work with Ilona effectively, knowing her as an individual is imperative in helping her progress towards her sporting potential. This holistic approach may also have an impact on Ilona's wider social milieu by helping her to feel more secure and confident in her new environment. Failure to acknowledge the wider bio-psychosocial context, however, could result in a sustained decrease in performance that will affect her sense of self. At worst, this chain of events is likely to culminate in burnout-triggered disengagement and/or Ilona dropping out of her favourite sport.

References

Ahmed, S., Castaneda, C., Fortier, A-M. and Sheller, M. (2003) *Uprootings/regroundings: questions of home and migration,* Oxford: Berg.

Bailey, R., Collins, D., Ford, P., MacNamara, A., Toms, M. and Pearce, G. (2010) *Participant development in sport: an academic review,* Leeds: Sports Coach UK.

Barker, J.B., McCarthy, P.J. and Harwood, C.G. (2011) 'Reflections on consulting in elite youth male English cricket and soccer academies', *Sport & Exercise Psychology Review,* 7(2): 58–72.

Brenner, J.S. (2007) 'Overuse injuries, overtraining, and burnout in child and adolescent athletes', *Pediatrics,* 119: 1242–1245.

Budgett, R. (1998) 'Fatigue and underperformance in athletes: the overtraining syndrome', *British Journal Sports Medicine,* 32: 107–110.

Cabieses-Valdez, B. (2011) *The living conditions and health status of international immigrants in Chile: comparisons among international immigrants, and between them and the Chilean-born.* Doctoral thesis, University of York, UK.

Ford, P., De Ste Croix, M., Lloyd, R., Meyers, R., Moosavi, M., Oliver, J., Till, K. and Williams, C. (2011) 'The long-term athlete development model: physiological evidence and application', *Journal of Sports Sciences,* 29(4): 389–402.

Gardner, F.L. and Moore, Z.E. (2004) 'The multilevel classification system for sport psychology (MCS-SP)', *The Sport Psychologist,* 18(1): 89–109.

Giddens, A. (1990) *Modernity and self-identity: self and society in the late modern age,* Cambridge: Polity Press.

Goffman, E. (1959) *The presentation of self in everyday life,* London: Penguin.

Gushulak, B.D. and MacPherson, D.W. (2006) *Migration medicine and health: principles and practice,* Hamilton: BC Decker.

Gushulak, B.D., Pottie K.P., Hatcher-Roberts, J., Torres, S. and DesMeules, M. (2011) 'Migration and health in Canada: health in the global village', *Canadian Medical Association Journal,* 183(12): E952–E958.

Harwood, C. (2008) 'Developmental consulting in a professional football academy: the 5Cs coaching efficacy program', *Sport Psychologist,* 22(1): 109–133.

Jones, R., Armour, K. and Potrac, P. (2004) *Sports coaching cultures: from practice to theory,* London: Routledge.

Kleinert, J., Ohlert, J., Carron, B., Eys, M., Feltz, D., Harwood, C. and Sulprizio, M. (2012) 'Group dynamics in sports: an overview and recommendations in diagnostic and intervention', *Sport Psychologist,* 26(3): 412–434.

Kristiansen, M., Mygind, A. and Krasnik, A. (2007) 'Health effects of migration', *Danish Medical Bulletin,* 54: 46–47.

Lazarus, R.S. and Folkman, S. (1984) *Stress, appraisal, and coping,* New York: Springer.

Micheli, L.J. (1996) 'Overuse injuries in the young athlete: stress fractures', in O. Bar Or (ed.) *The child and adolescent athlete* (pp. 189–220). Oxford, Blackwell Science.

Naughton, G., Farpour-Lambert, N.J., Carlson, J., Bradney, M. and van Praagh, E. (2000) 'Physiological issues surrounding the performance of adolescent athletes', *Sports Medicine,* 30(5): 309–325.

Quatman-Yates, C.C., Quatman, C.E., Meszaros, M., Paterno, M. and Hewett, T.E. (2012) 'A systematic review of sensorimotor function during adolescence: a developmental stage of increased motor awkwardness?', *British Journal of Sports Medicine,* 46: 649–655.

Rowland, T. (2012) 'Iron deficiency in athletes', *American Journal of Lifestyle Medicine,* 6(4): 319–327.

San Martin, C. and Ross, N. (2006) 'Experiencing difficulties accessing first-contact health services in Canada', *Health Policy,* 1: 103–119.

Small, E. (2002) 'Chronic musculoskeletal pain in young athletes', *Pediatric Clinics of North America,* 49(3): 655–662.

Stafford, I. (2005) *Coaching for long-term athlete development,* Leeds: Coachwise Business Solutions/The National Coaching Foundation.

Visek, A.J., Harris, B.S. and Blom, L.C. (2009) 'Doing sport psychology: a youth sport consulting model for practitioners', *Sport Psychologist,* 23(2): 271–291.

Vygotsky, L.S. (1978) 'Interaction between learning and development' [M. Lopez Morillas, trans.], in M. Cole, V. John-Steiner, S. Scribner and E. Soberman (eds.) *Mind in society: The development of higher psychological processes* (pp. 79–91). Cambridge, MA: Harvard University Press.

Wu, Z. and Schimmele, C.M. (2005) 'Racial/ethnic variation in functional and self reported health', *American Journal Public Health,* 95: 710–716.

18

JOHN

A coordinated approach to developing an active lifestyle

Manolis Adamakis, Nektarios Stavrou, Emmanouil Georgiadis and Mary Yannakoulia

DEPARTMENT OF PHYSICAL EDUCATION AND SPORT SCIENCE, NATIONAL AND KAPODISTRIAN UNIVERSITY OF ATHENS, GREECE, DEPARTMENT OF NUTRITION AND DIETETICS, HAROKOPIO UNIVERSITY, GREECE; SCHOOL OF SCIENCE, TECHNOLOGY AND HEALTH, UNIVERSITY CAMPUS SUFFOLK, UK

Key words: 15-year-old male, academic achievement, lack of persistence, high blood cholesterol, psychology, physical activity/health, nutrition, pedagogy.

John

John is a 15-year-old high school student who lives in Greece. He lives with his parents and brother in a municipality of the western Attica region, which is characterized as a low-income district. Based on indicators of affluence/deprivation, John's family is located at the upper level of the Family Affluence Scale. Although John has to share a bedroom with his brother, the family is quite comfortable and they have most of what they need, including two personal computers (PCs).

Both of John's parents work and, during their leisure time, the family watches TV and rests. John's mother does all the housework and cooking, but she does not have much time to spend on preparing meals. Often, she feels tired when she returns home from work, and she finds it difficult to plan ahead at the weekend for meals for the entire week. As a result, the family eats quite a lot of convenience food. Both of John's parents believe that physical activity (PA) is vital for personal fitness and health, but they have very limited leisure time so they are rarely physically active.

Apart from attending school, John's daily schedule includes at least two to three hours of private home lessons and the same amount of time spent on school homework. John does not believe that private home lessons are necessary; he finds them boring and resents the fact that he is forced to do so much extra work. The whole process of extra lessons, and the distance he has to travel (usually on foot) to attend them is very tiring for John and he experiences frequent headaches. His parents, however, believe that education is a necessity because it is the "passport" for a better future life, and they feel that private home lessons are essential to supplement school provision.

In his spare time, John watches TV, plays PC games or surfs on the Internet as relaxation from all the studying. Although he would prefer to go for long walks, play football or basketball, or hang out with his friends, John rarely does these things. There are few places near to his home where physical activity is possible, and this limits his options. For example, he would love to practice tennis, but there is no tennis court nearby. The only accessible space is the school yard and he does go there sometimes on the weekends to play basketball with his friends. John really enjoys basketball and he would like to play it more regularly, and even participate in a basketball team if he had the chance. John does, however, attend a private drama school. This was his father's idea and John very much enjoys the sessions, even though the drama school is a long way from home. John derives great personal satisfaction from this activity, even though it is only at an amateur level.

In the past, John participated in a wide variety of sports, and he enjoyed most of them. At one time, he was a member of his local football team, a swimming team and a karate team. Little by little, and for different reasons, he dropped out of all these activities. He quit football, even though he enjoyed it, because his parents would not allow him to attend the evening training sessions. They used to complain all the time because they believed he was "losing" too much time that would be better spent on studying. Furthermore, the stadium was a long way from home, John's parents could not drive him there, and he was not allowed to walk alone because the area is regarded as unsafe in the evenings.

John undertook swimming training when he was younger. At first he enjoyed it but after a while he also quit this activity because he found the training to be quite boring. He commented that "in other sports you may be bored sometimes, because you have to run all the time, but the other sports have ball contact and you can play more". As swimming lacks this variety, John thought it would be a good idea to try to play water polo, but there was no team nearby. Comparing football and swimming, John reflects that he was most happy when he was playing football. He remembers that during his swimming years, he was very afraid when the coach forced him to jump off the diving board. These kinds of experiences made swimming an even more negative experience for John.

Six years ago, John joined a karate team, but just as with the earlier activities, he soon stopped. The main reason was that, once again, the training schedule did not fit his studying schedule. John also noticed that the difficulty of the tasks was increasing over time, and he believed that he was unable to meet the new, more challenging motor skill requirements. So, although karate was an enjoyable activity at the beginning, his enjoyment soon diminished. On top of all that, there was also a financial problem that he had not anticipated. Every year, John was required to buy a new karate uniform, and this was a very expensive item for his parents to afford.

Nowadays, John's involvement in sporting activities is limited to the basketball and football he plays informally with his friends in the schoolyard. He tries to play on Saturdays, but even then his free time is limited because his weekend schedule of additional studying is similar to that on weekdays. The time allocated to Physical Education (PE) at school is very limited, so this does not offer him a significant amount of physical activity. The only sports activity to which he is fully committed is as a spectator at his local team's football matches almost every Sunday.

John has constant battles with his parents over food because they do not approve of his dietary habits. Over time, the range of food he consumes has been significantly reduced to mainly pasta, pizza and milkshakes. Sometimes he eats other things, but on the whole he prefers snacks. He will often eat a large amount of one specific meal that he enjoys (i.e. pasta

Bolognese) but then very little until he is offered something that he regards as delicious. In the mornings, he rarely eats breakfast at home, preferring instead to buy croissants or donuts with his pocket money at school. During the day, he will eat anything as long as he finds it tasty and delicious. He often experiences intense feelings of hunger and fatigue, and when that happens he buys one or more boxes of cookies and eats them all. There is evidence that John, due to reduced mobility and inefficient dietary habits, is beginning to put on weight. In addition, at his last health check, John's blood cholesterol levels were above the normal range, and this worried his parents even more. For this reason, they decided to consult a team of specialists on health, PA and nutrition.

A perspective from sport and exercise psychology

It is widely recognized that engaging in regular exercise has numerous positive health outcomes. Even though parents are often aware of the importance of exercise for children's physical and emotional health and well-being, most children fail to participate in adequate levels of sport and exercise. Based on recent data, it has been suggested that 65% of European citizens are not sufficiently physically active (European Commission 2010), and furthermore, 50% of those who do start to participate in a regular exercise program terminate their participation in less than six months (Buckworth and Dishman 2002). Based on the above, understanding the motivation that sustains regular exercise participation is important for all citizens, but even more so for young people for obvious developmental reasons.

Recent theoretical approaches to exercise participation have moved from a mechanistic behavioral explanation to a social-cognitive approach. Numerous motivational theories have been proposed such as self-determination theory, social-learning theory, self-efficacy theory and achievement goal theory.

As is indicated in John's case, he displays low intrinsic motivation and low levels of interest in participation in any exercise program. He declares a lack of interest in a range of sporting activities and appears to have a low level of self-esteem. Additionally, John shows a preference for participation in team sports, such as football and basketball, and this denotes his interest in socializing with friends. Although John is an adolescent who has participated in various sporting activities in the past, he has not sustained regular participation in any of them. The reasons behind activity termination can be addressed from a variety of approaches.

Self-determination theory could offer a helpful perspective on John's case. According to the theory, individuals constantly try to master their internal and external environments (Deci and Ryan 2012). The needs for autonomy, competence and relatedness have been shown to enhance self-motivated behavior in exercise settings. Based on Deci and Ryan (1985), motivation and persistence in the exercise setting vary according to the degree of self-determination. If, during John's participation in an exercise setting, those three psychological needs are satisfied, an enhanced level of intrinsic motivation will likely result. If, on the other hand, environmental conditions leave these three psychological needs unsatisfied, a lower level of intrinsic motivation is likely to occur (Ryan and Deci 2007). John also needs to feel competent enough to sustain his participation in a sport or exercise activity of his choice through successfully managing its demands. A coach could guide John to set personal, specific and measurable goals, thereby creating a meaningful and interesting environment of self-improvement. Personally determined, realistic and interesting goals are likely to enhance competence which is positively related to positive emotions, high self-esteem and intrinsic motivation toward increased exercise participation (Ekeland, Heian and Hagen 2005).

Evidence suggests that coaches should allow athletes to express their opinions on the decision-making and goal-setting process, thus shaping practice based on athlete preferences. Fostering a sense of relatedness with his teammates will enhance John's participation in the sport setting. He will also encounter additional opportunities to play and interact with his peers, which is clearly of importance to him.

A coach or Physical Education teacher would find it useful to educate John and also his family and friends about the benefits of an active lifestyle. In this way, the creation of a positive social context of significant others can help to facilitate increased engagement in sport and exercise (Pate *et al.* 2006). A coach can increase participation and sustain motivation by explaining the importance of trial and error for the learning process and the mastery of important sports skills. Through accurate, positive and task-related feedback, a coach can create an adaptive psychological environment for learning and positive interaction. Parents can help too, by creating opportunities for exercise activities and including choices so that John can pick the activities he prefers.

In this case, John's parents appear unable to act as positive role models for exercise participation. According to social learning theory (Sallis and Nader 1988), individuals learn attitudes towards a physically active lifestyle early in their development, through observing and imitating their parents. John's parents can help to promote an active lifestyle by encouraging him to engage in physical activity as part of everyday life. If it is feasible for them to do so, parents can facilitate participation in various exercise activities by providing transportation, access, and equipment. Parents are also in a position where they can reduce periods spent on sedentary behaviors (i.e. playing computer video games, watching television). Taking some or all of these actions could significantly improve John's interest in being physically active, and research suggests this could also influence exercise patterns later in life (Welk, Wood and Morss 2003).

John's parents are keen supporters of his academic achievement but they pay little attention to health behaviors. They may need to help John to design an efficient time plan that accommodates his rather overloaded daily schedule. Lack of time is a well-known barrier to exercise and sport participation for children and adolescents. A well-organized weekly schedule that eliminates time conflicts can create the conditions for John to feel competent in both the academic and sporting environments.

A physical activity perspective

Excess body weight makes participation in sport and exercise programs increasingly difficult. The weight creates growing levels of discomfort that constitute an additional obstacle to participation in such activities. Similarly, gradual evasion of PA could lead to other cardiovascular risk conditions. The fact that John is in the middle of his adolescent growth spurt indicates an even bigger concern. Any anomalies in health should be normalized before John reaches adulthood where reduced leisure time, increased career concerns, and other endeavors may result in further barriers to developing a healthy lifestyle.

Looking back at his previous sporting experiences, it could be argued that John has difficulty self-identifying as an exercise-schematic person, i.e. one who rates exercise behavior as critical for his self-image. Furthermore, the fact that John is an adolescent creates interesting issues. On the one hand, his lifestyle has not become fixed in sedentariness, i.e. it is not yet characterized by scarce movement opportunities caused by a largely fixed adult life pattern. This does offer opportunities to alter his current movement patterns and those for the future. On the other hand, John's ability to take more care with his life and health habits is seriously jeopardized by his immaturity and his inability to control large areas of his life, including those changes that are due to puberty. John has sedentary role models as both his parents are currently inactive. It is clear that while this family is aware of what is needed, a healthy diet and regular exercise are not the top priorities on their agenda.

Both John's parents have high aspirations for his academic achievements. In prioritizing that aspect of his development, John's parents appear less concerned about his physical and psychological health, at least until they became aware of his blood lipid problems. They seem unaware of the scientific evidence linking high levels of school achievement to frequent aerobic exercise (Ratey 2008), and also of the evidence associating frequent sitting behaviors to significant health threatening conditions (Healy *et al.* 2008; Owen *et al.* 2010). John's case is a good example of the need for parents to be fully informed about the scientific evidence linking modern lifestyles to certain health hazards, such as obesity.

The case of John, an adolescent who has already shown signs of increasing body weight and hypercholesterolemia, needs a multidimensional intervention to be tackled efficiently. This intervention should comprise: (a) an educational element aiming to change the attitudes of John and his parents; (b) a systematic attempt to reconnect John with a sport environment and his active peers to facilitate more regular participation in formal sports activities during leisure time; and (c) more PA integrated into everyday life.

A. Educational program for John and his parents

It is not always easy to link the evidence on improved human health to increased engagement in PA and exercise programs. An introduction to the mechanisms of physiology and also psychological influence is required – at the very least – so the first step is an educational programme. Such a programme could explain the ways in which the human system adapts to exercise, how cardiovascular risk factors could be reversed, and evidence that increased PA can ameliorate a wide range of chronic health problems. The delivery of such a program could be done under the guidance of the family's doctor or another health professional to ensure it engenders feelings of ability and control over health. It also needs to be accompanied by information on specific methods to support self-motivation (i.e. goal setting and stimulus control) to create an environment that is most likely to deliver success. Meeting with other families who have taken a similar step to include opportunities of increased PA and exercise in their everyday lives could also help John's parents to get started and to overcome any reluctance due to previous negative exercise experiences. Even the chance simply to talk through obstacles they may encounter as members of a family system (i.e. scheduling difficulties) can help. Similarly, the opportunity to express any lack of self-efficacy over uncontrolled conditions could also help the implementation of relevant changes toward changing PA habits.

B. Reconnecting John to the sporting environment

John needs to learn how to take responsibility for his own behavior. For this reason, the maintenance and reinforcement of his autonomy needs are essential in order to increase his intrinsic motivation to engage in a more active lifestyle. Practical ways to achieve this essential psychological goal include: offering choice or sharing decisions, acknowledging the difficulty he may encounter trying to change his behavior, providing a clear rationale for the need to change his behavior, and understanding that every behavior choice has its consequences. In this way, a facilitative setting is in place for all the necessary changes to occur while minimizing any negative reaction or reluctance (Deci and Flaste 1995; Deci and Ryan 1985). If John perceives the required behavioral changes as an obligatory chore or a bore, the chances of a successful adaption to a healthy lifestyle are going to be significantly diminished.

Trying to reconnect John with the sporting environment and regular participation in exercise and sport activities is unlikely to be successful without involving peers. As an adolescent, John's self-concept and his autonomy relate to the bonds created with peers. Thus, the more opportunities John has to be associated with peers who are actively involved in the sporting domain, the more chances there are to connect him to this domain. The school PE teacher has an important role to play in this attempted behavior shift. A PE expert can act as a role model for healthy lifestyle habits and can be an inspirational coach if he or she has the interest and motivation.

John needs to improve different aspects of his fitness level in order to be able to participate in sport and/or compete at a recreational level without risking potential injury. As John's aim will be to improve in stamina, strength and speed, he needs the expertise of his PE teacher to help him realize that his system may need additional time to adapt. With the right information (i.e. practical guidance) John can gradually start building his abilities, setting new goals and feeling increasingly competent to participate actively in the sporting domain. Through this whole process John will benefit from any support he can find in his social environment. Positive impact on the sustainability of his efforts to be active can be offered by significant others and specialists in the form of emotional, informational, and instrumental guidance (Lox, Martin-Ginnis and Petruzzello 2010).

C. Increased PA in everyday life

There is already some evidence that John engages in walking in order to get to school and other activities. Active travel to and from various destinations will create an additional energy cost for John, helping him to normalize his cholesterol levels. If John is aware of this, he might enjoy the walking rather than viewing it as a chore. To build on this start, John needs to be supported by an environment that creates numerous opportunities for PA. These opportunities could include parks, biking paths, sidewalks, proximal distances and a secure environment included in a social system that promotes active living (Spence and Lee 2003). The development of such an environment is, of course, the responsibility of policy makers and public bodies that need to support policies for active transportation and increased "walkability".

A nutritional perspective

Genetic predisposition and environmental influences interact to result in energy balance. A positive energy balance leads to excess body weight, and this is beginning to be evident in the case of John. Weight management for the treatment of obesity aims to modify the key factors of energy disequilibrium, i.e. dietary intake and PA. The Expert Committee, that was convened in 2005 by the American Medical Association, in collaboration with the Health Resources and Service Administration and the Centers for Disease Control and Prevention, published specific lifestyle recommendations for primary care physicians or any other allied health care providers involved in paediatric weight management programs (Spear *et al.* 2007). The behaviors that should be targeted, following these recommendations, are: consumption of ≥ 5 servings of fruits and vegetables per day; minimization or elimination of sugar-sweetened beverages; limits of ≤ 2 hours of screen time per day and no television in the room where the child sleeps; ≥ 1 hour of PA per day; eating breakfast daily; limiting meals taken out of home (including fast food venues and other restaurants); eating family meals at least 5 or 6 times per week; and allowing the child to self-regulate his or her meals while avoiding overly restrictive behaviors.

Schools provide a unique environment for tailoring children's food choices. Within schools, teachers, trainers, coaches and other instructors may influence students' eating behaviors by adopting a number of strategies. These adults, for example, have important knowledge about health behaviors. They act as authority figures and serve as role models through their own food practices. There is no doubt that young people are more likely to make healthy eating choices when they receive constant messages in an encouraging school environment (Perez-Rodrigo and Aranceta 2003). All professionals working with young people, therefore, should focus on the promotion of healthy lifestyle behaviors in the school context, but without stigmatizing over-weight children or supporting restrictive regimes and "unhealthy" dieting practices. The concept of "eating differently, not necessarily less" is the cornerstone of actions and interventions in this field. The evidence to date suggests that in the management of moderately overweight children and adolescents, normalization of eating habits, rather than calorie restriction *per se* (Braet 1999) is the most effective approach. In other words, the focus should be less upon restraint in dietary manipulations because there is evidence that flexible – rather than rigid – dietary restraint is associated with more successful long-term weight control (Westenhoefer 2002).

A series of general actions could be taken at the school level to support healthy eating:

- Teachers and other instructors could act as role models for fruit consumption. This approach may be more effective than traditional educational interventions.
- School feeding programs and meal times provide an important nutritional resource for all students. Specifically for John, this could provide an opportunity for increasing his expo-sure to "new" tastes and foods, as well as to healthy eating.
- Advertising healthy snacks, such as fruits and whole grain cereals, is an easy step to take; i.e. by focusing on their inclusion in as many school activities as possible (prizes, games, plays, classes) and ensuring all staff are on board. In addition to the school level actions, specific actions are needed to address John's eating habits and, thus, his body weight and blood lipid profile.

John's tutor or any "significant" instructor should work with him to enhance motivation either in relation to diet or to body weight. Possible motives suggested for adopting more bal-anced eating habits might include potential changes in appearance, but should also emphasize changes in physical endurance and cognitive parameters (such as memory, concentration etc.). Misconceptions around healthy eating should also be addressed; for example, it is important to emphasize that healthy meals can also be very tasteful; that small changes – rather than dramatic ones – are needed; and that quality is better than quantity.

There is no doubt that John's family will need to be involved in the proposed changes. Parents sometimes find it difficult to acknowledge the level of their contribution to nutrition and PA issues. Indeed, parents tend to underestimate their children's degree of overweight – or even its existence – and they report low levels of readiness for and confidence in implementing changes (Rhee *et al.* 2005). Factors associated with overall parental readiness to initiate change include beliefs that their child's weight is a health problem (and not just an appearance-related issue) as well as whether they perceive themselves to be overweight. Information on both issues may be important in ensuring that parents are actively involved in any action or intervention.

The literature is not conclusive on the most effective parental role or the precise degree of parental involvement that will lead to positive outcomes. Nonetheless, a supportive role for parents is recommended, with reducing involvement as the child gets older (Barlow 2007). In practical terms, this means that John's family is strongly encouraged to adopt, as far as is possible, strategies including: eating meals together as a family, ensuring vegetables are served as part of most meals, limiting consumption of ready-to-eat or convenience foods, and promoting the preparation and cooking of healthy meals. It is also possible, of course, that if required, John could be referred to a more structured weight management protocol, delivered by a health care provider who is highly trained in weight management in adolescents.

A pedagogical perspective

John's case is typical of many young people in contemporary Greece. Like large numbers of Greek adolescents, his daily schedule and free time are mainly occupied by school and academic activities. As a result of this, there is evidence of a drift away from physical activities as part of everyday lifestyles, and this can also be observed across Western developed countries (Bauman *et al.* 2009; Dumith *et al.* 2011). This trend has resulted in a loss of awareness about the importance of movement development in early childhood, and in the case of John, neither his parents nor his teachers appear to be taking responsibility for this aspect of his development. There is evidence in the case narrative that John still seems to be intrinsically motivated to take part in some physical activities and sports. He likes to play informal football and basketball with his friends and particularly enjoys physical activities that include interacting with a ball. John is, however, at a very important age, and he needs all the social support he can find in his environment in order to ensure he does not develop entrenched inactive behaviors.

"Physical Literacy" refers to an individual who has the "motivation, confidence, physical competence, knowledge and understanding to maintain PA throughout the lifecourse" (Whitehead 2010: 5). This concept consists of six main dimensions: (a) motivation, (b) competence, (c) environment, (d) sense of the self, (e) expression and interaction with others, and (f) knowledge and understanding. So Physical Literacy is important because basic skills for an active lifestyle need to be developed at an early age. At this point in his life, John could be regarded as a moderately physically literate individual. Whitehead (2010) has argued that motivation arises from confidence and self-esteem acquired through positive experience, that is, experience that has been perceived as successful and has been recognized as such. John did have positive experiences with football and basketball, but he also had some negative ones, particularly in swimming and karate. He still seems to have the desire to be active in order to improve his physical competence, but he struggles to persist with an activity, even if he enjoys it. There is evidence of damaged motivation in some activities (Whitehead 2010). At the age of 15,

John's movement vocabulary, movement capacities and movement patterns are at a level below where they might be, thereby decreasing his competence and perceived confidence. Finally, even though he can "read" simple and structured PA settings, John does not have the ability to respond to these "readings", as he does not participate in any kind of extracurricular exercise.

Perhaps the key problem for John and his family is the parental belief that John needs to spend virtually all of his time on activities that improve his cognitive development. John's parents are role models for physically inactive and sedentary lifestyles, and they also have increased body weight. At the same time, they have busy and demanding jobs, and this case illustrates the reported relationship between the overweight status of children and their parents, especially in low income areas (Manios *et al.* 2007). The simplest advice for parents such as these would be to start doing any kind of exercise, because it is widely accepted that it is easier to prevent obesity than to cure it (Malindretos *et al.* 2009). Clearly, John's parents could also encourage active travel from one activity to another and, if possible, they should try to walk with him at least some of the time.

PE teachers and coaches can also act as active role models. With their attitude and guidance, John could be persuaded to become part of the sporting environment once more. In order to achieve this, the focus should not be primarily upon motor skills and sport perfectionism because, while "it may energize large quantities of motivation, in many cases it may also serve to undermine the potential for participation in sport to be a fulfilling experience for junior athletes" (Mallinson and Hill 2011: 682). More specifically, concerns over mistakes and perceived pressure from coaches are common reasons for individuals experiencing exercise as need-thwarting.

It was noted in an earlier section that John's PE teachers have an important role to play in supporting John to develop an active lifestyle. It may be more successful for them in this case to focus on a teaching orientation, rather than a coaching one. According to Figone (1994), teaching and coaching are two different occupational roles in terms of their instructional objectives, motivation, student skill levels, time available and facilities. Both PE teachers and coaches are pedagogues, although it has been argued that coaches devote rather less attention to the pedagogical aspects of their work (Tinning 2010). John is not an athlete with an elite level competitive background, so he should not be treated as an athlete. Instead, he is more likely to respond to being treated as an individual who wants to socialize through sports, enjoy himself and, as part of this, improve his health. Teachers (and coaches) who take an "empowering" approach tend to provide more space for students to engage in democratic decision-making (Kwon, Pyun and Kim 2010). Individuals aspiring to be elite athletes, on the other hand, may perceive the coach to be poor at teaching by not providing useful instruction, not individualizing it to fit the unique athlete's needs and not knowing the qualities and skills needed to teach effectively (Gearity 2012). Moreover, sport practitioners with a teaching orientation tend to emphasize non-competitive sport activities, and the social aspect is a key ingredient of all non-competitive sports. This would suit John very well indeed.

The rules in non-competitive sport can be changed to suit the participants and environment to ensure that everyone can participate and no one is excluded. One method that might help John to participate in a sport activity is to use the curriculum model: Teaching Games for Understanding (TGfU). This model can offer John opportunities for autonomy, choice, intrinsic motivation, support and positive interpersonal relations. TGfU emphasizes tactical understanding and effective strategic movement more than the development of motor skills and skills-based teaching. Furthermore, TGfU has the potential to help students increase the amount of active participation, and promote enjoyment, mental and physical engagement while they develop their motor skills (Griffin and Butler 2005). Students' intrinsic motivation toward sports can be enhanced through TGfU as a result of increased interest, fun and enjoyment engendered through its games-oriented approach (Jones, Marshall and Peters 2010).

So John, who likes playing sports, is more likely to have a positive experience in TGfU since he will participate in a game that he enjoys and, perhaps most important of all, he will handle a ball. Following that, he will become aware of the tactical aspects of the game, make appropriate decisions and, finally, improve his performance through advanced skill execution. From a constraints-led approach and non-linear pedagogy, physical educators' manipulation of key task constraints can guide John toward a range of highly suitable action paths, narrowing down the time needed for exploratory behavior (Chow *et al.* 2007). It is important to remember, however, that school PE cannot be the only activity responsible for promoting children's activity and health. In order for this objective to be achieved, wider social and environmental changes are needed.

Even though John lives in the country that identified originally the importance of the mind-body connection, many contemporary "experts" still support the body-mind dualistic approach, and this influences parents and the choices they make for their children. From this view point, the superiority of a human's intellect is in contrast to the inferiority of the body. This belief is apparent in John's case as his parents discourage him from participating in extracurricular physical activities, while at the same time forcing him to take additional private lessons each day. Furthermore, the time devoted to PE in the school setting is insufficient and is constantly decreasing. According to the national curriculum guidelines, John is likely to be offered just two 45-minute PE lessons per week. This means that school PE classes cannot be responsible for improving children's physical fitness and health (Ericsson 2011). Furthermore, it has been reported as common practice in Greek schools for PE lessons to be abandoned when time is required for reading and mathematics or for revision purposes and tests on academic work (Yiallourides 1998).

PA leading to fitness may be a valuable part of PE and sport in school, but it cannot be an end in itself. There is a need to understand the importance of children's self-actualization through enhanced PA. Enhancing health and wellbeing are reasonable goals for PE but professional educators must go beyond the reductionist logic of "energy intake, energy consumption". To be effective, teachers, coaches and other significant adults need to take into account the complexity of discourses around PA, fitness, wellbeing and health. Professional practitioners in physical education and youth sport have an important role to play in educating children and parents about these key discourses.

References

Barlow, S.E. (2007) 'Expert committee recommendations regarding the prevention, assessment, and treatment of child and adolescent overweight and obesity: summary report', *Pediatrics*, 120: S164–192.

Bauman, A., Bull, F., Chey, T., Craig, C.L., Ainsworth, B.E., Sallis, J.F., Bowles, H.R., Hagstromer, M., Sjostrom, M., Pratt, M. and The IPS Group (2009) 'The International Prevalence Study on Physical Activity: results from 20 countries', *International Journal of Behavioral Nutrition and Physical Activity*, 6: 21–31.

Braet, C. (1999) 'Treatment of obese children: a new rationale', *Clinical Child Psychology and Psychiatry*, 4: 579–591.

Buckworth, J. and Dishman, R.K. (2002) *Exercise psychology*, Champaign, IL: Human Kinetics.

Chow, J.Y., Davids, K., Button, C., Shuttleworth, R., Renshaw, I. and Araújo, D. (2007) 'The role of non-linear pedagogy in physical education', *Review of Educational Research*, 77: 251–278.

Deci, E.L. and Flaste, R. (1995) *Why we do what we do: The dynamics of personal autonomy*, New York: Grosset/Putman.

Deci, E.L. and Ryan, R.M. (1985) *Intrinsic motivation and self-determination in human behavior*, New York: Plenum Press.

Deci, E.L. and Ryan, R.M. (2012) 'Self-determination theory', in P.A.M. Van Lange, A.W. Kruglanski and E.T. Higgins (eds) *Handbook of theories of social psychology: Vol. 1* (pp. 416–437). Thousand Oaks, CA: Sage.

Dumith, S.C., Hallal, P.C., Reis, R.S. and Kolh, H.W., III (2011) 'Worldwide prevalence of physical inactivity and its association with human development index in 76 countries', *Preventive Medicine*, 53: 24–28.

Ekeland, E., Heian, F. and Hagen, K.B. (2005) 'Can exercise improve self-esteem in children and young people? A systematic review of randomized controlled trials', *British Journal of Sports Medicine*, 39: 792–798.

Ericsson, I. (2011) 'Effects of increased physical activity on motor skills and marks in physical education: an intervention study in school 1 through 9 in Sweden', *Physical Education & Sport Pedagogy*, 16(3): 313–329.

European Commission (2010) 'Sport and physical activity (Special Eurobarometer 334)', Brussels, European Commission. Online. Available HTTP: <http://ec.europa.eu/sport/library/documents/d/ebs_334_en.pdf>

Figone, A.J. (1994) 'Teacher-coach role conflict: its impact on students and student athletes', *Physical Educator*, 51: 29–34.

Gearity, B.T. (2012) 'Poor teaching by the coach: a phenomenological description from athletes' experience of poor coaching', *Physical Education & Sport Pedagogy*, 17(1): 79–96.

Griffin, L.L. and Butler, J.I. (2005) *Teaching games for understanding: Theory, research, and practice*, Champaign, IL: Human Kinetics.

Healy, G.N., Winjndaele, K., Dunstan, D.W., Shaw, J.E., Salmon, J., Zimmet, P.Z. and Owen, N. (2008) 'Objectively measured sedentary time, physical activity, and metabolic risk', *Diabetes Care*, 31(2): 369–371.

Jones, R.J.A., Marshall, S. and Peters, D.M. (2010) 'Can we play a game now? The intrinsic benefits of TGfU', *European Journal of Physical & Health Education*, 4(2): 57–63.

Kwon, H.H., Pyun, D.y. and Kim, M. (2010) 'Perceived leadership behavior of physical education teachers-coaches: when they teach vs. when they coach', *Journal of Teaching in Physical Education*, 29: 131–145.

Lox, C., Martin-Ginnis, K.A. and Petruzzello, S.J. (2010) *The psychology of exercise: Integrating theory and practice*, 3rd edn, Scottsdale: Holcomb Hathaway.

Malindretos, P., Doumpali, E., Mouselimi, M., Papamichail, N., Doumpali, C., Sianaba, O., Orfanaki, G. and Sioulis, A. (2009) 'Childhood and parental obesity in the poorest district of Greece', *Hippokratia*, 13(1): 46–48.

Mallinson, S.H. and Hill, A.P. (2011) 'The relationship between multidimensional perfectionism and psychological need thwarting in junior sports participants', *Psychology of Sport and Exercise*, 12: 676–684.

Manios, Y., Costarelli, V., Kolotourou, M., Kondakis, K., Tzavara, C. and Moschonis, G. (2007) 'Prevalence of obesity in preschool Greek children, in relation to parental characteristics and region of residence', *BMC Public Health*, 7: 178–185.

Owen, N., Healy, G.N., Matthews, C.E. and Dunstan, D.W. (2010) 'Too much sitting: the population health science of sedentary behavior', *Exercise and Sport Sciences Reviews*, 38(3): 105–113.

Pate, R.R., Davis, M.G., Robinson, T.N., Stone, E.J., McKenzie, T.L. and Young, J.C. (2006) 'Promoting physical activity and youth: a leadership role for schools', *Circulation*, 114: 1214–1224.

Perez-Rodrigo, C. and Aranceta, C. (2003) 'Nutrition education in schools: experiences and challenges', *European Journal of Clinical Nutrition*, 57(Suppl. 1): S82–S85.

Ratey, J.J. (2008) *SPARK: The revolutionary new science of exercise and the brain*, New York: Little Brown.

Rhee, K.E., De Lago, C.W., Arscott-Mills, T., Mehta, S.D. and Davis, R.K. (2005) 'Factors associated with parental readiness to make changes for overweight children', *Pediatrics*, 116: e94–101.

Ryan, R.M. and Deci, E.L. (2007) 'Active human nature: self-determination theory and the promotion and maintenance of sport, exercise, and health', in M.S. Hagger and N.L.D. Chatzisarantis (eds.), *Intrinsic motivation and self-determination in exercise and sport* (pp. 1–19). Champaign, IL: Human Kinetics.

Sallis, J.F. and Nader, P.R. (1988) 'Family determinants of health behaviors', in D.S. Gochman (ed.), *Health behavior: Emerging research perspectives* (pp. 107–124). New York: Plenum Press.

Spear, B.A., Barlow, S.E., Ervin, C., Ludwig, D.S., Saelens, B.E., Schetzina, K.E. and Taveras, E.M. (2007) 'Recommendations for treatment of child and adolescent overweight and obesity', *Pediatrics*, 120: S254–288.

Spence, J.C. and Lee, R.E. (2003) 'Toward a comprehensive model of physical activity', *Psychology of Sport & Exercise*, 4: 7–24.

Tinning, R. (2010) *Pedagogy and human movement: Theory, practice, research*, Oxon, UK: Routledge.

Welk, G.J., Wood, K. and Morss, G. (2003) 'Parental influences on physical activity in children: an exploration of potential mechanisms', *Pediatric Exercise Science*, 15: 19–33.

Westenhoefer, J. (2002) 'Establishing dietary habits during childhood for long-term weight control', *Annals of Nutrition & Metabolism*, 46(Suppl. 1): 18–23.

Whitehead, M. (2010) *Physical literacy: Throughout the Lifecourse*, New York: Routledge.

Yiallourides, G. (1998) *Factors influencing the attitudes of 9–14-year-old Cypriot pupils towards physical education*, PhD dissertation, University of Manchester, United Kingdom.

19

MARIANNE

Training, running efficiently, and staying motivated

Jean Lemoyne, Emilie Lachance and Caroline Poulin

DEPARTMENT OF PHYSICAL ACTIVITY SCIENCES: KINESIOLOGY AND PHYSICAL EDUCATION, DEPARTMENT OF CHIROPRACTICS, UNIVERSITY OF QUEBEC AT TROIS RIVIERES, QUEBEC, CANADA

Key words: 16-year-old female, low physical activity, poor motivation, endurance training, exercise physiology, biomechanics, psychology, pedagogy.

Marianne: background

The benefits of regular physical activity are well documented, suggesting desirable outcomes for both physical and psychological health. Yet, despite all of the documented benefits associated with engagement in regular physical activity, young people still have difficulties in maintaining a sufficient level of physical activity and this often tracks into an inactive in adulthood. Scientific evidence suggests that adolescence is the stage of life where we observe the steepest decline in active behaviours, especially among girls (Duncan *et al.* 2007). During adolescence, physical education is frequently cited as an excellent opportunity to develop requisite skills and a desire to maintain an active lifestyle. Teachers, however, face considerable challenges in finding effective pedagogical interventions that will support their students to maintain an active lifestyle beyond school.

Marianne: initiating and sustaining an interest in exercising regularly

Marianne is 16 years of age. Although she takes part in regular physical education classes, she has not participated in any other form of organized sport since she was 5 years old when she played soccer in primary school. Her tendency towards being physically inactive in recent years has contributed to a modest weight gain (five to ten pounds) and, as a consequence, she is dissatisfied with her body image. Despite knowing that being more active could contribute positively to her physical health, Marianne's interest in taking regular exercise is very low. Lack of time, energy and motivation are the main reasons she cites that prevent her from being more active. Some of Marianne's friends, however, are more active, participating in the school's cheer-leading and volley-ball teams.

Marianne is not the only girl in her class who lacks interest in physical activity. Her physical education teacher is aware of the problem of physical inactivity among adolescents, especially girls' low level of motivation to engage in multiple exercise behaviours. In recent years, the teacher has been trying out a new approach to motivate his students to participate in regular exercise. Over an eight-week period, he encourages his students to take part in an exercise programme to prepare them to participate in a 5-kilometre run. The run is known as the Project 5-K, and it is an event open to all schools in the district (over 300 adolescents). The preparation involves running/jogging during the regular physical education classes and, in addition, students have to prepare themselves for Project 5-K by being active in out-of-class activities (after school and during lunch hours).

Marianne has listened to her teacher's suggestions about Project 5-K but she does not feel confident about completing the task, especially as she knows almost nothing about jogging and running. She does feel it could be an interesting opportunity for becoming more active and getting in a better shape, but she has no idea how she will continue with her training sessions outside of the physical education classes. The task seems very hard and she is not fully convinced that the physical education teacher can motivate her to change her behaviour in a sustained way.

Marianne's perceptions about her capabilities to prepare for a 5-kilometre run are not encouraging, and several of her friends feel exactly the same way. The task for the teacher, therefore, is not uncommon. Figure 19.1 illustrates Marianne's perceptions about the proposed task, and the numerous challenges faced by the physical education teacher. First, he will have to help his students to develop the necessary skills that can be transferred outside the physical education class. Secondly, the teacher is acutely aware of the potential risks for novice runners, in particular

Physical Education context: motivating students for Project 5-K		
Adolescents' perceptions regarding the proposed task Low level of fitness Low level of participation in physical activity behaviours Little motivation (lack of time, energy)	**MULTIPLE CHALLENGES** **From the students' and teachers' perspectives** **Preparing for Project 5-K** **HOW** to run? **WHY** to run 5 km? **HOW** to train? **HOW** to keep students motivated?	**Physical Education teacher goals for the task** Motivate students towards the adoption of an active lifestyle Promote lifelong learning by transferring competencies to real-life situations Developing students' skills and competencies

FIGURE 19.1 The present case: motivating adolescents to prepare for a 5-kilometre run (known as Project 5-K)

the high occurrence of running-related injuries. Finally, he faces an important challenge, regarding the motivational aspects of exercise participation, particularly if he wants his students to get involved in out-of-class activities. The teacher has spent many years trying to motivate adolescent girls to be more physically active, and he is aware that in the research literature it is reported as a common concern. He decides, therefore to seek the help of some experts.

Guiding students towards an active lifestyle: views from an interdisciplinary perspective

Which disciplinary fields have the knowledge that the teacher needs to design an efficient intervention that will motivate Marianne? It is important to acknowledge from the outset that running, despite its simplicity as a motor task is, in many respects, very effort consuming. We suggest that the teacher needs to draw on Exercise Physiology to teach Marianne *"How to prepare"* appropriately for the 5-kilometre run; Biomechanics to teach Marianne *"How to run"* efficiently and reduce injury risk; and Motivational Psychology to help her to sustain her participation when she feels tempted to give up.

Interdisciplinary challenge #1: how to train for the 5-kilometre run?

Let's talk about some exercise physiology

Running is an aerobic exercise that can increase well-being and cardiovascular capabilities. Furthermore, running is subject to dose-response relationships because the more people run, the more benefits they get. These benefits include decreasing systemic blood pressure, improving body weight control, as well as improving some blood parameters such as glycaemia control, triglycerides, and cholesterol. At first sight, running can seem like a simple task; yet running 5 kilometres continuously requires some preparation in order to ensure our bodies have the necessary capacities to perform this task with sufficient energy. To help Marianne to prepare adequately, it is essential to understand some key exercise physiology principles and concepts, physical activity guidelines for adolescents, and training principles.

Exercise physiology concepts and guidelines for adolescents

The term *exercise* refers to a form of

> leisure-time physical activity that is usually performed on a repeated basis over an extended period of time (exercise training) with a specific external objective such as the improvement of fitness, physical performance, or health.
>
> (Bouchard and Shephard 1994:77)

Exercise can be done in many forms as long as they require muscle contractions that cause coordinated movements, such as in running or jogging. Using exercise physiology terminology, a single bout of exercise is known as *acute* exercise and the addition of several bouts of exercise during several weeks is known as *chronic* exercise. The latter, if sustained in time, will produce a number of physiological changes known as adaptation, which is the positive consequence of long-term exercise training.

Principles of exercise training

Before discussing the prescription approach to exercise and training principles, it is important to specify the required *amount* of physical activity required to prepare for a 5-kilometre run. To achieve such a task, a certain frequency and intensity of exercise is required. Regarding frequency, the current recommendations suggest that adolescents (12–17 years) should accumulate approximately 60 minutes of moderate to vigorous physical activity on a daily basis, in order to obtain health benefits (Tremblay *et al.* 2011). This recommendation leads us to focus on exercise intensity. Intensity of exercise refers to the magnitude of the physiological disruption or stress caused by the activity. For an aerobic exercise, such as a 5-kilometre run, intensity of exercise is best characterized by a measure of energy expenditure (VO_2 max) or a percent of the maximal heart rate. The maximal oxygen consumption (VO_2 max) is known as the maximum volume of oxygen that can be utilized in one minute by the active muscles during maximal exercise. It is measured as millilitres of oxygen used in one minute per kilogram of body weight. Endurance is a little different from VO_2 max, and its definition is more like "the aptitudes to maintain a high percent of VO_2max during a given duration" (Thibault 2009:19). For the 5-kilometre run, duration will vary approximately between 25 and 40 minutes. This means that Marianne will need to use her aerobic energy system in most of the duration of the run.

In addition to frequency and intensity, there are five major principles of training to respect in order to improve Marianne's performance: specificity, overload, recovery, adaptation, and reversibility (Wilmore and Costill 2002). To improve running speed, it is important to perform exercises that involve a running speed component. Speed exercises, however, will improve running speed but not technique; and that is the *specificity* principle. The *overload* principle means that a muscle or ability will improve only when forced to execute beyond its customary intensity, so increasing gradually the intensity of exercise is an example of overload. *Recovery* is a training principle required to ensure an organism can recover from training. *Adaptation* occurs in the recovery period, and it is defined as the increase in strength or ability of the body to react to the training loads imposed. Finally, *reversibility* means that improvements generated by the training may disappear if the training is not sustained over time. Examples representing the five major training principles are shown in Table 19.1.

To complete the exercise physiology "section" of this chapter, it is important to consider the concept of *perceived effort*. For many years, exercise physiologists believed that skeletal muscles,

TABLE 19.1 Preparing for Project 5-K: training principles

Training principles	*5 km run training examples*
Specificity	80% of training should be done at running
Overload	Increasing progressively the intensity and frequency of trainings
Recovery	Allow 1 day off between each training
Adaptation	The decrease in perception of effort for the same training
Reversibility	Keep a regular training program in order to keep specific running adaptations

heart and lungs limited endurance performance. Recently, Marcora and Staiano (2010) demonstrated that perceived effort is an important factor limiting endurance performance. This new concept led coaches and athletes to modify their training approaches and to add perceived effort to the training prescription. Perceived effort is usually measured using a 0 to 10 scale with 0 representing being totally relaxed (such as when sitting on a couch) and 10 being the most intense effort that it is possible to maintain. A "level 5 to 8" perceived effort represents moderate to vigorous activity, similar to light jogging. The latter is a very good example of the perceived effort that should be used in the 5-kilometre run training preparation for Marianne.

Training preparation for a 5-kilometre run

In order to ensure Marianne is well prepared for her 5-kilometre run, she needs to ensure there is some progression in duration, intensity, frequency and – as a result – *volume* of training. What follows is an example of suggested training progression over 10 weeks for a beginner in exercise training. To train efficiently, Marianne must learn how to calculate her maximal heart rate. Maximal heart rate is defined as the maximum beats of heart per minute that an individual can attain when performing a very high intensity exercise. For a 16-year-old girl, we calculate this as 220 minus age (e.g. 220 –16 = 204 beats per minute). The next table shows an example of preparation that could be undertaken over a ten-week period (Table 19.2). Over the ten-week

TABLE 19.2 A 5-kilometre run training program for a youth beginner: applying the overload principle

Week	Period	Frequency (days/week)	Duration (min)	% maximal heart rate (beats per minute[bpm])	Rate of perceived effort (/10)
1	*Introduction* of lower limbs muscles to running	2–4	15–20	55–69 (112–141)	3–5
2		2–4	20–25	55–69 (112–141)	3–5
3		3–5	20–25	55–69 (112–141)	3–5
4		3–5	25–30	55–69 (112–141)	3–5
5	*Progression* in volume, frequency, and intensity	3–5	25–30	70–89 (142–182)	6–8
6		3–5	25–30	70–89 (142–182)	6–8
7		3–5	30–35	70–89 (142–182)	6–8
8		3–5	35–40	>75 (>153)	7–8+
9	*Maintenance* of physical qualities	3–5	30–45	>75 (>153)	7–8+
10		Goal: 5-km run	25–40	70–89 (142–182)	7–8+

program, exercising at different percentages of maximal heart rate will increase adaptation. This element will help Marianne to follow the Canadian government's physical activity guidelines and, consequently, improve progressively her level of fitness.

Interdisciplinary challenge #2: how to run efficiently?

Learning running techniques and preventing injuries

Despite its popularity, is running a "dangerous" or "unhealthy" sport?

Running is one of the most popular activities in the world. People seeking a healthier lifestyle or weight control tend to choose this sport because it is considered easy to integrate into most lifestyles and is relatively low cost (Taunton *et al.* 2003:239). Indeed, between 1990 and 2011 the number of road race finishers increased by 192% in the United States (www.runningusa. org). Unfortunately, injuries increased at the same rate. The reported incidence of running injuries varies greatly in studies, between 18.2% and 92.4% depending on characteristics and definitions used by the authors (Lopes *et al.* 2012). Injury is a sign of overload of a particular structure, and will typically affect the weakest link of a limb. The most frequent injuries experienced by runners are tibial stress syndrome, Achilles tendinopathy, and plantar fasciitis. Anterior tibial stress syndrome is especially frequent in novice runners. This inflammation of the bone results from a problem with the shock absorbing-mechanism and, consequently, running has to be introduced slowly with beginners.

Injury prevention

Due to the substantial incidence of related injuries, running has been considered by some in the non-running and medical communities as unhealthy because it is commonly associated with early knee degeneration. More recent research, however, has demonstrated this belief was actually false, and that the prevalence of osteoarthritis (OA), or joint degeneration was no higher in runners than non-runners (Chakravarty *et al.* 2008). Injury can be related to intrinsic or extrinsic causes. Intrinsic causes are related to the structure of the body and are not discussed here. Among the extrinsic causes, training and surface are particularly important, and these factors can easily be assessed by the physical education teacher. As mentioned earlier, one of the key points to remember when introducing running activities is to introduce and increase training load in line with the adaptation capacities of the individual. In other words, the repeated impacts associated with running will lead to injury if they exceed the tolerance threshold of an individual's bones, tendons and muscles. The threshold differs between individuals, and the only way to find it is to cross this "invisible line" which is, of course, too late. Nonetheless, a frequent error made by all types of runners is simply doing too much, too fast and too soon. Thus, when thinking about injury prevention, we cannot overemphasise the importance of an individually designed running program. In a school context, this means that a teacher will have to adapt a generic program as soon as the first injury symptoms appear.

A good way to avoid injuries when starting to run is to alternate between running and walking. Short walking breaks prevent the lower limbs from absorbing too much shock or impacts that could, over time, lead to the development of an injury. Table 19.3 shows an

TABLE 19.3 Learning to run while preventing injuries (a seven-week progression)

Run/walk (minutes)		Repetitions (number of walk-run combinations)		
		Session 1	Session 2	Session 3
Week 1	(1/1)	5	8	10
Week 2	(2/1)	4	6	8
Week 3	(3/1)	4	6	8
Week 4	(5/1)	4	5	6
Week 5	(10/1)	3	3	3
Week 6	(15/1)	2	2	2
Week 7	(30/0)	1	1	1

Note: Training program based on 3 sessions per week. Number of repetitions indicated under each session. There should always be a day off between sessions. A runner who experiences pain should not progress to the next level until she or he is pain free.

example of a run/walk training program for beginners, leading to 30 minutes of continuous running after 7 weeks. The same program can be given to a runner recovering from a serious injury.

Running technique

There has been much debate in the past about whether running technique should be taught according to common biomechanical principles, or whether an individual's natural patterns should be retained. Running is an ability acquired during early childhood, so motor patterns are deeply anchored and very difficult to change. Despite the popularity of techniques based on biomechanical principles, it is widely accepted that one technique cannot fit all individuals. On the other hand, key elements of a technique can be taught for different purposes such as injury prevention and performance improvement. When evaluating a student's or novice runner's technique, the physical education teacher can undertake a visual scan from head to feet and what follows is a review of the key points to be considered. Figure 19.2 illustrates the key running technique elements to consider, especially when working with novice runners.

Head and shoulders. The key watch-word for head and shoulders is *relaxation*. Eyes should look far ahead; shoulders should be kept low and relaxed. The first signs of a runner in difficulty are raised shoulders and face tension. Runners will lose valuable energy by contracting these muscles unnecessarily.

Arms. Unless sprinting, a runner should seek to avoid losing energy through uneconomical arm action. What is required is a flexion/extension movement of the arms, coming from the shoulder, in order to counteract the rotational moment of the pelvis and to dictate the pace. Hands should be kept low, at the level of the hips, with slightly closed fists. A frequent error made by runners is making a side-to-side movement of the elbows, as in skating.

Hips. The hips are close to the centre of mass, and should be projected forward, without flexing or extending the spine. Common mistakes are adopting a sitting posture or bending

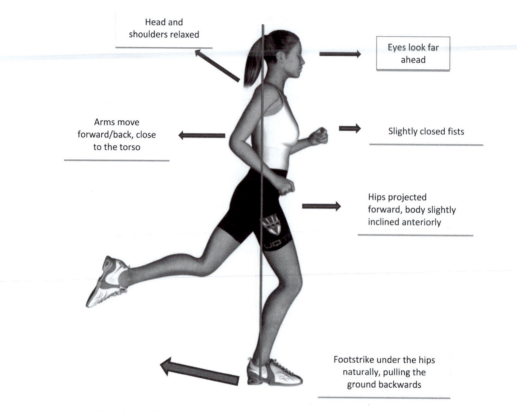

FIGURE 19.2 Running technique fundamentals (from Black & Poulin, UQTR. 2013 [unpublished])

forward from the pelvis, thereby moving the hips backwards. The body should be straight, but with a slight anterior inclination from the ankles.

Footstrike. There has been much debate in the literature about how the foot should touch the ground. Lieberman *et al.* (2010) demonstrated that a barefoot runner will tend to forefoot or mid-foot strike, compared to the majority of shod runners who are heel strikers. Sprinters also land on their toes. Consequently, many coaches instruct runners to forefoot or mid-foot strike in order to increase speed and avoid large impact loads associated with forward heel strike, even though we know that 75% of elite marathoners are heel strikers (Hasegawa, Yamauchi and Kraemer 2007). More importantly, one of the most common faults made is to over stride, or land in front of the body, often with the heel. This will lead to deceleration forces that will not only affect the efficiency of the runner, but also generate a high impact on the Achilles tendon and calf and, consequently, cause injury. After analysing the debates on this topic, we conclude that the key point is to instruct runners to land naturally under their hips, pulling the ground backwards. A good way to prevent over striding is to increase the stride frequency. Daniels (2005) found that in events ranging from 5 kilometres to marathon, elite runners had a running frequency close to 180 steps per minute. Although this number hasn't been studied extensively, it remains largely accepted as it offers a good guide when teaching runners to decrease their stride length.

Finally, it should be noted that acquiring a good running technique or adjusting an existing running form is not easy. The runner will often feel uncomfortable and inefficient during the early stages of making changes. Teachers or coaches will have most success if they try to correct some aspects of the running form, and then allow time to assimilate the new motor patterns. In case of injury, the mileage should be decreased to a comfortable level immediately. If pain is felt in daily activities or at rest, a runner should always stop running for a few days until pain has disappeared. On the other hand, a runner should do as much pain-free mileage as possible to ensure adaptations take place and capacities are increased.

Interdisciplinary challenge #3: how to stay motivated?

Thinking about behaviour change and motivation

As mentioned earlier, the literature suggests that large numbers of adolescents, particularly girls, find it difficult to feel motivated to exercise regularly. In this regard, the teacher must understand the most important motivational aspects for participation in multiple exercise behaviours. Regarding Marianne, teachers can draw upon the principles established in the exercise psychology domain and, in particular, the *Theory of Planned Behavior* (Ajzen and Fishbein 1980) is one of the most frequently cited.

The *Theory of Planned Behavior* (TPB) is a belief-based model suggesting that behaviour is directly influenced by the intentions about performing a specific behaviour. In our example, the behaviour is Marianne's participation in three (or more) weekly jogging/running sessions. But what influences Marianne's intentions to prepare for the 5-kilometre run? The TPB (see Figure 19.3) suggests that three categories of beliefs influence intentions

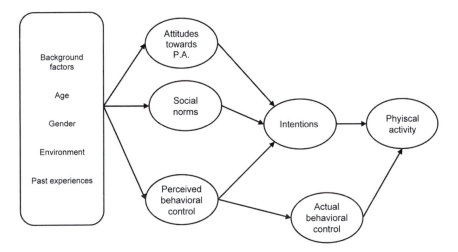

FIGURE 19.3 The Theory of Planned Behavior and the contribution of background factors (adapted from: Ajzen and Fishbein [1980] and Hagger, Chatzisarantis and Biddle [2002])

about the behaviour: 1) attitudes about the behaviour, 2) social norms, and 3) perceived behavioural control. *Attitudes* are defined as the values associated with the behaviour, and they are linked to the expected outcomes related to the behaviour. Attitudes can be conceptualized as having two components: instrumental and affective. For example, Marianne might think that jogging is good for her health (instrumental), but she does not really enjoy it (affective). *Social norms* are defined by beliefs about the necessity to act according to an individual's referents. Those influences could come from multiple social groups such as parents, peers, and teachers. For example, if Marianne respects her parents and knows that her parents want her to exercise regularly, she may be more likely to make the decision to exercise. *Perceived behavioural control* represents the beliefs individuals have about whether they are able to perform behaviour. Perceived behavioural control could be the level of control over external factors, such as the lack of time, or the fear of getting injured. It also could be associated with internal factors such as self-efficacy. Perceived behavioural control is related to actual *behavioural control*, reflecting the real capability of an individual to perform the behaviour. Developing motor skills and specific abilities is essential, and the more an individual is able to perform the behaviour (combined with favourable intentions) the more likely they are to adopt it.

Antecedent research has demonstrated that high perceived behavioural control is related with strong intentions and, consequently, adoption and maintenance of behaviour (Fishbein and Ajzen 2010: 170-176). For example, Hagger, Chatzisarantis and Biddle (2002: 293) demonstrated that autonomous intrinsic motivation were strongly related to the development of favourable attitudes and strong perceptions of control. In their study, students who were motivated intrinsically (e.g. pleasure, personal satisfaction) developed strong intentions to take part in multiple exercise behaviours. As was noted by Marsh, Papaioannou and Theodorakis (2006: 316), this underlines the potential contribution of the physical education teacher in the development of student beliefs that can lead to increases in their participation in regular exercise. Finally, *background factors* are related directly to beliefs about the behaviour and, consequently influence intentions to perform the behaviour. For example, past experiences are primordial in determining whether an individual finds jogging to be a fun activity. Gender and age are also good examples of factors that are related to different beliefs about physical activity.

Motivating students towards the adoption of regular exercise behaviours

The TPB framework offers interesting options for teachers, especially because it suggests it is possible to identify specific factors that influence intentions and, thus, influence behaviour. From this perspective, stakeholders (teachers, coaches) can design theory-based interventions that will impact positively on students' beliefs regarding the desired outcome (preparing for the 5-kilometre run). More complex, however, is an understanding of which specific approaches or strategies will contribute to behaviour change? A review by Michie *et al.* (2009), tested the effectiveness of 26 behaviour change techniques, and identified those approaches most likely to succeed in physical activity interventions. In the case of Marianne, some of these techniques (showed in Table 19.4) could be used by the teacher.

TABLE 19.4 Behaviour change techniques to motivate adolescents towards engagement in physical activity (adapted from Michie *et al.* 2009)

Influencing/reinforcing (What the teacher is trying to change in the girl's mind?)	*By doing . . .* (Teacher's strategies)	*Resulting in . . .* (Student's action)
Attitudes	Provide information about benefits (affective and instrumental) of running	Better knowledge regarding the advantages of being active and start running
Social norms/support	Prompt about others' approval regarding the task (family, peers)	Increasing social support and desire to participate with important people (friends, family)
Perceived behavioural control	Provide positive feedback on the task during lessons	Increase self-efficacy
	Prompt barrier identification (e.g. lack of time) and problem solving	Overcome barriers and other limiting factors
Intentions	Prompt intention formation (e.g. specific goal setting)	Fix goals about training and completing the 5 kilometre run
Intrinsic motivation (autonomous motives)	Provide positive experiences during classes, associated with positive feedbacks, achievement and self-enhancement	Develop autonomy and self-determination to participate in physical activity

The final section will describe how to merge these three disciplinary fields in a learning context that will influence Marianne to adopt exercise as a part of her lifestyle.

Pedagogy: structuring the learning experience – an interdisciplinary pedagogical approach

The main challenge for the physical education teacher is to try to organize a positive learning experience for each of his pupils. This is particularly challenging in the case of pupils such as Marianne who are rarely active and who doubt their capabilities. The previous disciplinary perspectives identify core knowledge to be taken into account by educators.

The teacher's challenge: what comes first?

Planning the learning experience

Table 19.5 suggests a sequence of learning activities that could guide the physical education teacher in supporting Marianne to achieve the running goal. In this case, the learning experience is structured over a period of ten weeks. At first view, this might seem like a very long period, but it is important to remember the points made earlier about progression and adaptation. Sufficient time to adapt is necessary, both from an adaptation and an injury-prevention perspective. (The programme could, however, be shortened to 6–8 weeks depending on the initial level of the students.) For Marianne, a ten-week time frame allows the teacher to organize

TABLE 19.5 Structuring the learning experience for Marianne: the path towards an active lifestyle

	Specialist Perspectives		
	Exercise Physiology	*Injury-Prevention Running technique*	*Exercise Psychology*
The initial phase Weeks 1–3	Guidelines for physical activity (frequency and intensity) The *Overload* principle Fitness testing for the 5-km goal (optional)	Running mechanics Warming up and stretching principles Running and walking	Intentions implementation Working positively on attitudes and beliefs
The development phase Weeks 4–9	The *Specificity* principle Encourage participation in running sessions The *Adaptation* principle Encourage taking part in cardiovascular activities (stair climbing, elliptical trainer) Working on the progression (increase duration)	Preventing injuries with a better running form Video: running technique analysis (on track) Running technique exercises to improve form. Focus is on running efficiency (skill development)	Stimulate social support Perceived control and autonomy Autonomous motives: sessions oriented on achievement, goal attainment and positive feedbacks during practice. Evaluating abilities and perceived competence Revising and adjusting goals
The final preparation phase Week 10	The *Reversibility* principle (emphasis on the necessity to stay active)	Determining a strategy to complete the 5-km run without getting injured Determining the amount of run-walk bouts during the challenge	Emphasis on the fun aspects of the run, less oriented on performance Completing (perceived competence) the event is the main objective

the learning in a manner that respects Marianne's individual needs. Moreover, in this plan, the three exercise specialist perspectives have integrated their knowledge with specific contents presented at specific times.

Learning to run and get motivated: a ten-week approach to develop competencies, skills and motivation to prepare for a 5-kilometre run

The initial phase (2 to 3 weeks)

The first three weeks of the intervention are primordial for the physical education teacher, because he needs to convince students to get involved in Project 5-K. The initial phase learning activities are presented in Table 19.6. As noted at the beginning of this chapter, Marianne is not convinced of the value of taking part in such a challenge, so the teacher has to be convincing at this stage. He should first explain what Project 5-K is, and put emphasis on the many benefits (health, social, personal satisfaction) associated with completing such a challenge. He should also make it clear that Project 5-K is not performance oriented but, instead, is

TABLE 19.6 The Initial Phase (4 to 6 sessions): introducing adolescents to running

Sessions	Learning Objectives	Specific Key Elements
1 to 3	Increase attitudes and values associated with regular exercise	What is Project 5-K?
		The benefits of regular exercise
	Fixing personal goals (intentions (e.g. complete Project 5-K, training more . . .)	Fixing realistic goals
		The different purposes of warming up and cooling down
	Learning a warm-up stretching routines	
	Learning running techniques	What should adolescents do in terms of exercise frequency? Physical activity guidelines
	The *Overload* Principle	
	Determining a run-walk pattern	
		Heart rate as an indicator of intensity
4 to 6	Discovering multiple exercise intensities	Training at the right intensity
	Learning running mechanics	Heel strike versus toe strike
	Integrating an "active student" routine	Keeping a running log

focussed on individual and regular physical activity. The initial phase is also important from the "exercise physiology" and "running technique" perspectives. The teacher should inform Marianne about the appropriate amount of physical activity for her (using the guidelines and overload principle). He also should provide Marianne with information about the demands (time, energy) of completing a 5-kilometre run, while taking care not to be discouraging. To help in this process, the teacher should work with Marianne to identify an attainable goal for her current ability. The teacher could use one of the recognised fitness tests, e.g. the Cooper Institute's 12-minute run (Cooper 1968: 201–204) or the 1-mile run (Cureton *et al.* 1995) as a tool to help in identifying a reasonable goal for Project 5-K. In the first sessions, the teacher should also ensure he initiates a sound warm up/cool down routine to help prevent some of the common running injuries. In this phase, and when working with a whole class of children, it is essential that the teacher provides alternatives for those like Marianne who have comparatively lower levels of ability. As was suggested in the previous section, determining an adequate proportion of running interspersed with short walking breaks is likely to be a good strategy because it lowers the risk of injury and offers a gradual approach to the integration of a new exercise routine.

The development phase (4 to 6 weeks)

The development phase (Table 19.7) is much longer than the initial phase. In this phase, Marianne, will be involved in multiple processes that will encourage her to take part in regular exercise. Furthermore, she will develop running/training skills that will help her towards the completion of Project 5-K. From an exercise psychology perspective, the physical education teacher should organize the learning experience in ways that will enhance perceived control over the desired outcome, i.e. running regularly (and preparing for Project 5-K). For example, the teacher could discuss with Marianne strategies to overcome barriers to exercise. The teacher should also focus on the enhancement of Marianne's capabilities (efficacy) by providing positive feedback during the running sessions. Marianne will also benefit from a supportive

TABLE 19.7 The Development Phase (8 to 12 sessions): developing skills and competencies to stay active

Sessions	Learning Objectives	Specific Key Elements
1 to 4	Increasing perceived behavioral control Identifying barriers and strategies to overcome Encouraging peer involvement for promoting exercise behaviors Correcting running form The *Specificity* and *Adaptation* principles	Positive feedback, emphasis put on personal achievement instead of performance Focus groups on barrier identification and strategies Offering out-of-class running sessions (with peers and or family members) Video analysis during running sessions Increasing progressively training volume (duration), and planning rest days between sessions.
5 to 12	Revising goals, evaluating skills and competencies related with regular exercise behaviors	Keeping up a running log Simulation of the Project 5-K (a 3-km run test) Revising personal goals for Project 5-K

environment (social norms). By providing lunch-hour running sessions, the teacher could try to create running groups with students who have similar running ability. For example, the teacher could offer "once a week" running group sessions to offer opportunities for peer influence to contribute to the adoption of a running routine.

During the development phase, specificity and adaptation are the training principles that should be underlined. Moreover, the teacher should emphasise the adaptation principle by encouraging Marianne to take enough rest days between running sessions. Running every two days (3 to 4 days a week), combined with other moderate intensity physical activities (e.g. walking to school) should be sufficient to meet the suggested levels of physical activity in the national guidelines. Marianne should also focus on the intensity of the running sessions by monitoring her heart rate (a process learned in the initial phase). During the developmental phase, the teacher should also emphasise the importance of good running technique for both efficiency and injury prevention. The teacher should observe Marianne's running technique and suggest adjustments. Filming students running during sessions (on a track to facilitate video recording) should help in the visualization of running form, which will then help to adjust Marianne's technique. In summary, the development phase is of primary importance because it is the learning sequence that contributes the most to developing the skills necessary to become more efficient.

The final phase (the final week before Project 5-K)

The final phase (Table 19.8) is the conclusion of the learning situation designed by the teacher. First, completion of Project 5-K is an opportunity for Marianne to see whether her preparations for the 5-kilometre run were adequate. The teacher should discuss with Marianne a strategy for completing the challenge, for example the amount of running (minutes) combined with short walking breaks (if necessary). Also, he should help her to identify other group of students

TABLE 19.8 The Final Phase (2 sessions): completing Project 5-K and reflecting about staying active

Session	Learning Objectives	Specific Key Elements
1	Revising goals for Project 5-K	Revise running logs
	Planning a strategy for completing Project 5-K	Plan adequate run-walk sections for the run
	Involving social support for completing the challenge	Regroup with people of similar capabilities
	Completing Project 5-K	
After Project 5-K	Analyzing goal attainment	Overview of Project 5-K (reflections)
	Planning, evaluating intentions about future involvement in physical activity	Fixing new goals, new challenges?
	The *Reversibility* principle	

who have similar objectives. Planning an effective strategy could certainly help Marianne feel more confident about achieving the task (perceived control). Another aspect to consider is the social support dimension. Running alongside people with similar abilities (social norms) should help Marianne to feel more confident that she can accomplish the 5-kilometre run. Finally, the teacher will have to spend some time with Marianne after completion of Project 5-K. During this period, the teacher will encourage Marianne to take up further challenges or simply to stay active for the fun and satisfaction (autonomous motives) that were part of the learning experience.

Concluding remarks

From an educational perspective, motivating adolescents to engage in a sufficient level of physical activity is not an easy task. Even if adolescents are aware that exercise is positive for their health, 50% of them remain insufficiently active. As presented in this chapter, many factors could contribute to enhancing the desire to become more active and educators, teachers and other stakeholders need to work on all these different aspects. The challenge for teachers (and coaches) is to have sufficient expertise to draw upon and then to integrate knowledge from different domains in the interests of individuals such as Marianne. In this chapter we integrated concepts from three sport sciences domains to design a specific learning experience for adolescents. Running was selected as the activity because it is popular as a participation event outside school and so could be transferable beyond school.

References

Ajzen, I. and Fishbein, M. (1980) *Understanding attitudes and predicting social behavior*, London: Prentice-Hall.

Bouchard C. and Shephard R. J. (1994) *Physical activity, fitness and health*. Champaign, IL: Human Kinetics.

Canadian Society for Exercise Physiology (CSEP) (2011) *Canadian Physical Activity Guidelines for youth 12–17 years old. Ottawa, Canada*. Online. Available HTTP: <www.csep.ca> (accessed on 15 November 2012).

Chakravarty, E.F., Hubert. H.B., Lingala, V.B., Zatarain, E. and Fries, J.F. (2008) 'Long distance running and knee osteoarthritis: A prospective study', *American Journal of Preventive Medicine*, 35(2): 133–138.

Cooper, K.H. (1968) 'A means of assessing maximal oxygen intake', *The Journal of the American Medical Association,* 203: 201–204.

Cureton, K.J., Sloniger, M.A., O'bannon, J.P., Black, D.M. & McCormack, W.P. (1995) 'A generalized equation for prediction of VO_2 peak from 1-mile run/walk performance', *Medicine & Science in Sports & Exercise,* 27: 445–451.

Daniels, J. (2005) *Daniels Running Formula,* 2nd edn, Champaign, IL: Human Kinetics.

Duncan, S.C., Duncan, T.E., Strycker, L.A. and Chaumeton, N.R. (2007) 'A cohort sequential latent growth model of physical activity from ages 12 to 17 years', *Annals of Behavioral Medicine,* 33: 80–89.

Fishbein, M., and Ajzen I. (2010) *Predicting and changing behavior: the reasoned action approach.* New York: Taylor & Francis Group.

Hagger, M.S., Chatzisarantis, N.L. and Biddle, S.J.H. (2002) 'The influence of autonomous and controlling motives on physical activity intentions within the Theory of Planned Behaviour', *British Journal of Health Psychology,* 7: 283–297.

Hasegawa, H., Yamauchi, T. and Kraemer, W.J. (2007) 'Foot strike patterns of runners at the 15-km point during an elite-level half marathon', *Journal of Strength & Conditioning Research,* 21(3): 888–893.

Lieberman, D.E., Venkadesan, M., Werbel, W.A., Daoud, A.I., D'Andrea, S., Davis, I.S., Mang'Eni, R.O. and Pitsiladis, Y. (2010) 'Foot strike patterns and collision forces in habitually barefoot versus shod runners', *Nature,* 463: 531–535.

Lopes, A.D., Hespanhol, L.C., Yeung, S.S. and Costa, L.O.P. (2012) 'What are the main running-related musculoskeletal injuries? A systematic review', *Sports Medicine,* 42(10): 891–905.

Marcora, S.M. and Staiano, W. (2010) 'The limit to exercise tolerance in humans: mind over muscle?', *Journal of Applied Physiology,* 110(6): 763–770.

Marsh, H., Papaioannou, A. and Theodorakis, Y. (2006) 'Causal ordering of physical self-concept and exercise behaviour: reciprocal effects model and the influence of physical education teachers', *Health Psychology,* 25: 316–328.

Michie, S., Abraham, C., Whittington, C., McAteer, J. and Gupta, S. (2009) 'Effective techniques in healthy eating and physical activity interventions: a meta-regression', *Health Psychology,* 28: 690–701.

Taunton, J.E., Ryan, M.B., Clement, D.B., McKenzie, D.C., Lloyd-Smith, D.R. and Zumbo, B.D. (2003) 'A prospective study of running injuries: the Vancouver Sun Run "In Training" clinics', *British Journal of Sports Medicine,* 37: 239–244.

Thibault, G. (2009) *Entraînement cardio sports d'endurance et performance* (19–20). Montréal: Vélo Québec éditions.

Tremblay, M.S., Colley, R., Duggan, M., Hicks, A., Janssen, I., Kho, M., *et al.* (2011) Canadian Sedentary Behaviour Guidelines for Children and Youth., *Applied Physiology, Nutrition, and Metabolism,* 36: 59–64.

Wilmore, J.H. and Costill, D.L. 2002. *Physiologie du sport et de l'exercice: adaptations physiologiques à l'exercice physique* (17–19). Paris: De Boeck Université.

20

KAREN

Striving to reach Olympic performance levels

Gemma van Vuuren-Cassar, Jon Swain, Claire J.L. Rossato and Diakai Chatziefstathiou

DEPARTMENT OF CHILDHOOD STUDIES, DEPARTMENT OF SPORT SCIENCE, TOURISM AND LEISURE, CANTERBURY CHRIST CHURCH UNIVERSITY, ENGLAND, UNITED KINGDOM

Key words: 16-year-old female, physically active, elite sport, Olympic dream, skill acquisition, coach–athlete relationships, socialization, pedagogy.

Karen

Karen is a sociable, physically active 16-year-old girl who has just commenced the last 2 years of secondary schooling at East Tenkerdent Sixth Form College (ET6C; a pseudonym). The college is located in the South East of England and is state-funded, mixed gender and comprehensive for pupils age 16 to 19. Karen is in her first year at college and she, like all her fellow students, is new to this educational environment having transferred at the age of 16 from a secondary school.[1] Karen is determined to work as hard as she can on her academic subjects but she is also a keen and successful volleyball player who has been training and playing for the local volleyball club since she was 9 years old. Indeed, Karen specifically chose ET6C at the age of 16 because it had recently become the home base for Tenkerdent volleyball club (also a pseudonym). In addition, one of the teachers at the Physical Education (PE) and Sports Department at ET6C, Mr. Campbell, is also a highly respected ex-player and current coach at Tenkerdent Volleyball Club. Mr. Campbell is known fondly as the "tour operator" of the club because the number of visiting clubs from Europe increased significantly since the club moved to its college base.

Over the years, Karen has worked hard to be a successful volleyball player. Now that her college is also the home ground for Tenkerdent Volleyball Club, Karen is more determined than ever to continue to improve her volleyball skills and competencies. Karen's dream is to reach Olympic performance levels. Steps towards her Olympic dream include playing for the college team, the Tenkerdent Volleyball Club and the regional Under-18 Women's Volleyball Championship League. In addition, Karen is seriously considering developing a career in physical education and school sports, while attempting to be a semi-professional national athlete in volleyball.

Karen is an only child and although she lacks siblings, she has lots of friends at the volleyball club. Karen's mother is a teacher in a primary school and her father is a policeman, and both parents work hard to offer Karen the financial support she needs to succeed in education and sport. Karen's parents also enjoy a full social life connected mainly to the volleyball club. Karen's involvement in physical activities started early when, at age 3, her mother enrolled her in a local dance school. There, Karen practiced different forms of dance such as ballet, tap and contemporary and, each year, this culminated in an annual performance by the dance school at the local theatre. Karen always looked forward to this event, especially as family and friends were invited to watch her perform. When she was 6 years old, Karen began to accompany her father on Saturday afternoons to training sessions at the local adult volleyball club. While the adults attended their training sessions, Karen played informally with the children of the other players. On match days, the families of the players joined in to support the senior teams, and Karen enjoyed these sociable sporting events.

In addition to the adult teams, the volleyball club offered training sessions for children from the age of 9. Unsurprisingly perhaps, given their familiarity with the club and the other children, Karen and some of her friends were keen to join Tenkerdent Volleyball Club juniors' programme as soon as they reached the age of 9. Other children from her school and local area also joined the club, and this marked the beginning of Karen's enduring bond with volleyball. Karen was a very active child and, until age 11, she also maintained her participation in dance lessons on Saturday mornings. Her father, in the meantime, was becoming increasingly involved in the volleyball club, taking an umpiring qualification and also officiating at matches.

Between the ages of 11 and 16, Karen attended a secondary school where she had the opportunity to participate in an after-school volleyball club that included frequent competitions against other school teams. Fortunately for Karen, a new Physical Education teacher (Miss Smith) was also a very keen volleyball player and she, too, joined Tenkerdent Volleyball club. This link made it easy for Miss Smith to refer pupils with an interest and competence in volleyball to the club. In many respects, therefore, Karen was immersed in volleyball. Karen and her father had been members of the club for many years, and Karen loved the fact that so many of her school friends were also junior members.

At school, Miss Smith extended Karen's involvement in volleyball by taking the older pupils to trials for the Under-16 regional team. Karen was selected to go to the trials at the age of 14 and, to her delight, she was selected for the Under-16 girls' regional squad. Karen's parents, club and schoolmates were very proud, and her parents were convinced that Karen's early start in volleyball as a child at her father's club had really paid off. Karen was happy and excited at the opportunity she had been given.

Selection for a regional squad meant that Karen now had to travel long distances to play against teams from other parts of the country. Most of the opposing teams comprised experienced and older players, and Karen noticed that her level of skill and decision-making abilities improved at an accelerated rate when competing against such capable volleyball players. In addition, Karen was involved in school and club volleyball tours to The Netherlands, Belgium and France, and she found the training sessions and competitive games with different squads to be inspirational and valuable. For example, she encountered British National volleyball players who trained and competed in the national leagues of these countries, and having the opportunity to play at this challenging level – even when beaten – was worthwhile. Karen discovered, however, that in order to train, play and gain valuable volleyball experience to reach national level, she needed to miss out on being with her family and friends for birthdays, funerals and other festive celebrations.

It was not long before Karen was selected for the National Under-16 squad. What an achievement! This also meant that she now qualified to receive support funding[2] and had access to new training sessions with fitness and volleyball coaches. The amount of national and international travel also increased, and this made it difficult for Karen to keep up with her schoolwork. Nonetheless, Karen had continued support from her school, club, parents and boyfriend. Karen's hunger for success and improvement in volleyball intensified further when her team won the National Championships of the Under-16 School League. Then came an historic moment: The London 2012 Olympics. The women's volleyball team of Great Britain (GB) beat Algeria (ranked over 50 places above GB in the world) 3–2; Karen was a spectator at that game, and the thought of playing at an Olympic level of performance has dominated her thoughts ever since.

Now age 16, Karen dreams of being part of the national volleyball team and playing at the Olympics. She knows, however, that she needs to improve markedly to gain a place on the Under-18 Women's regional and national teams. She was invited to attend her first trial for the Under-18 squad but had no success in securing a place, so she intends to work even harder. The feedback that Karen received from the national coach was that her decision-making was slow and that she needs to improve. Karen has been putting in extra hours of training at the school gym before school starts, devising her own personal improvement programme. Karen's parents had considered registering her at the National Volleyball Academy in another College.[3] Unlike their local sixth form (ET6C), which is state-funded, they would have to pay considerable sums of money for her education and elite training at the new College and Academy. They were reluctant to commit their limited savings in this way, and they were keen to be able to offer Karen some financial support through her years at university. They were upset when they realized that although Karen met the entry criteria for the National Academy (because she was in the Under-16 national squad) this was an expense that they simply could not afford.

Studying at the National Volleyball Academy would have given Karen a unique opportunity to combine academic study with a rigorous training schedule for her last two years of secondary schooling. However, given that this is not an option, Karen's parents are encouraging her to work hard at ET6C to get the best grades possible so she is accepted at a university of her choice. They believe that while at university, Karen will find all the support she needs to succeed in volleyball while also gaining qualifications for a career. Karen thinks so too. At the same time, Karen's teammates are suggesting that she should consider a move to a European country such as Italy, Belgium, Germany or even the United States to combine university with playing volleyball for a strong team. Karen discussed these issues with her parents, boyfriend and the coach at Tenkerdent Volleyball Club. Although she made the case that such a move might improve her level of performance and increase her chances of getting selected for team GB volleyball, the discussions did not go well. The coach said that he would hate to see her go because the team would lose a good player.

A skill-acquisition perspective

If Karen's goal of reaching the Olympics is to be fulfilled, it can be argued that she will need to engage in roughly 10,000 hours of extended training. This training must be both effective and efficient in providing relevant practice activities (Williams and Ford 2009; Ericsson, Krampe and Tesch-Romer 1993). Empirical research suggests that it is the amount of time spent practising diligently that accounts for differences between elite and sub-elite performers (Ward *et al.*

2004). Therefore the 10,000-hour metric is thought to incorporate key factors that could make the difference between gaining a podium place at the Rio 2016 Olympics and spending a summer in front of the television dreaming of success.

Whilst Karen may be prepared to commit a large amount of time to practising volleyball, it is the *nature* of that practice that will determine her development. Feedback from the national squad coaches is that Karen appears to be less decisive in her initial decisions compared to the other trialists in her playing position. As one coach described it: *"hesitant and erratic choices on court are holding her back"*. It has also been suggested that Karen has adequate technical skills but lacks *"game intelligence"*. The selection coach questions whether this *"gift"* can be taught or will ultimately become a barrier to her progression into the national squad system. A viewpoint shared by many coaches is that these skills are either innate or that they can be developed simply by accruing years of playing experience (Ward *et al.* 2004). Yet, the coaching philosophy and frameworks that underpin these beliefs can be questioned; indeed, it has been argued that they are based on tradition and intuition, rather than empirical evidence (Ward *et al.* 2008). Furthermore, whilst tradition can result in stable "tried and tested" coaching practices (e.g. *if it is not broke, why fix it?*), it can also act as a barrier to developing new knowledge. How, for example, can coaches with entrenched attitudes learn about up-to-date scientific evidence-based principles of skill acquisition? In particular, questions could be raised about whether such coaches will be able to support the skill acquisition needs of those athletes who do not fit the "perfect" development model of progression desired by coaches and sporting bodies alike (Williams and Ford 2009).

There is growing empirical evidence available on the implementation of perceptual training programmes to enhance an athlete's game awareness or intelligence (Williams *et al.* 2010). This evidence could clearly benefit Karen. High-level volleyball tactics rely on defenders' abilities to anticipate the interaction between attackers and the setter in order to block a developing attack (Bergeles, Barzouka and Nikolaidou 2009; Afonso *et al.* 2012a). At the Olympic level, quick attacks are prevalent in order to disrupt the organization of this defensive block (Afonso *et al.* 2010). It is widely accepted that good anticipation and probability-based decision-making skills are essential tools for the elite player (Williams and Ford 2009; see Mann *et al.* 2007 for a review). Developing these anticipation skills will enable Karen to prepare and execute her own responses in order to counter her opponents' tactics as well as work coherently and successfully with her teammates. Karen's ability to make good decisions whilst under the extreme time-constraints of a volleyball point will depend on a range of perceptual skills. These include her ability to use the visual system to extract relevant information from the environment (e.g. the court space and ball flight), as well as her opponents' and teammates' behaviours (postural cues) before a key event such as an opposing team's serve or set. Also, Karen will need to recognize patterns of play and probable situations from both sides of the net so that she can respond in the shortest time possible (Williams and Ward 2007).

Previous research has shown that elite volleyball players demonstrate a specific type of perceptual behaviour compared to that of sub-elite players. During a standard "setting" scenario, sub-elite players spend more time gazing at the initial ball path and then onto the setter's shoulders and hands, and as a result, disregarding the ball trajectory (Hernandez *et al.* 2004; Piras, Lobietti and Squatrito 2010). In contrast, elite volleyball players appear to use different, more active, search behaviours; they spend more time looking at the receiver and the space between the opposing attackers and blockers compared to sub-elite performers (Afonso *et al.* 2012b).

This research suggests that Karen may need to adapt her visual search behaviour to process more information related to the functional spaces on the court (i.e. gaps between players) in order to promote the necessary decision-making processes required at an elite level. Technological advances allow skill-acquisition specialists to track Karen's visual search behaviour with a good degree of accuracy without sacrificing task or environmental validity. These systems would allow the coaching team to view Karen's current behaviour and potentially modify it with the aid of a perceptual simulation training programme.

Most of the reported perceptual-based learning programmes have used film displays with a combination of field-based interventions to train players to focus on the meaningful and useful information available to them during critical events. Successful training programmes have focused on key perceptual events (e.g. postural cues of opposing players, spaces between players) and have reported a number of performance improvements in both laboratory and, more importantly, field/performance settings. Examples of improvements include reduced reaction time (Farrow *et al.* 1998); reduced response times (Williams, Ward and Chapman 2003); increased response accuracy (Williams *et al.* 2002); better awareness of teammates' positioning, and improved passing (Williams *et al.* 2005). Another approach is to provide detailed feedback comparing the player's current visual behaviour with that of a successful elite player. An example of this expert performance approach is the work of Adolphe, Vickers and LaPlante (1997). These researchers used a combination of video-based visual search feedback and field-based training over six weeks to improve the accuracy of a volleyball return. It is important to note that the improvements gained as a result of perceptual training in volleyball have been reported to last for over a year (Wilkinson 1992), which suggests it is practice time well spent.

One advantage of perceptual training approaches is that learning can be self-paced and can take place in an environment away from the volleyball court or *in situ,* with equipment that is readily available (e.g. a laptop computer, digital camera). Furthermore, the video images used can be manipulated easily to highlight or occlude various sources of information (e.g. setter's posture; Williams *et al.* 2002).

Questions remain about the scheduling of such training methods. Training programmes with high variability and contextual interference demonstrate stronger perceptual learning effects compared to incremental or blocked training schedules (Memmert *et al.* 2009). The optimal frequency and duration of perceptual training sessions is still open to debate and furthermore, the style in which perceptual information is conveyed to Karen may have an impact on her learning. Anticipatory skills can be improved using a variety of methods (e.g. explicit/implicit/guided discovery approaches) and whilst implicit approaches appear to promote sustained learning, traditional instruction-based programmes can still be effective (Abernethy *et al.* 2012). Consequently, the coach must determine how best to design, schedule and evaluate the training programme so that Karen can derive maximum benefit; in other words, the coach must adapt to Karen's specific learning needs.

It is important that any training programme is derived from the superior performance exhibited by experts and is grounded in the sporting situations in which elite players display this superiority. This can sometimes be difficult to set up, but it is an important consideration because experts react differently when faced with an unrealistic test environment (Dicks, Button and Davids 2010). It is also important for the simulation training to include both right- and left-handed elite players. Research suggests that volleyball players fail to anticipate to optimal levels when faced with a left-handed opponent over the net. It is suggested that this effect becomes more pronounced amongst skilled players because they encounter left-handed opponents so infrequently (Lofting *et al.* 2012). Finally, whilst perceptual simulation training in volleyball is still relatively infrequent, the evidence suggests that sustained and deliberate engagement with such training sessions could prove to be a welcome and worthwhile reprieve for Karen from some of those 10,000 hard-earned hours of practice on court.

A coach-athlete relationship perspective

Karen's dream of reaching the GB Olympic volleyball team seems somewhat distant, but it is clear she has the drive and passion to achieve this success. Although her teammates were supportive of the idea of moving abroad to pursue her dreams, the suggestion resulted in a negative reaction from her parents, boyfriend and coach. Karen feels somewhat conflicted about the situation because she knows the move could offer her opportunities that would otherwise not be available within Tenkerdent Volleyball Club or her school. Wylleman's (2000) relationship in sport model illustrates the ways in which athletic careers can be influenced by an athlete's relationship with a coach, peers and parents. A negative relationship with her coach could lead to discontinuation in the sport, especially if Karen feels she is no longer getting what she perceives she needs from the relationship.

Karen feels torn between the social element of her life, which includes staying close to her family, and pursuing her dreams in sport. Karen discusses her ambitions with her coach who expresses concerns about her moving abroad because the team would lose a good player. Jowett and Poczwardowski (2007: 4) defined the coach-athlete relationship as "a situation in which a coach's and athlete's cognitions, feelings and behaviours are mutually and casually interrelated". It is important, therefore, that there is a good relationship with the coach and athlete if such issues are to be discussed constructively. The coach-athlete relationship is also likely to change over time and, as Karen has experienced, she is finding that her cognitions are different to those of her coach. Once Karen has lost this complementarity with her coach, she will undoubtedly feel growing pressure when attending training sessions. Yet, it is vital for any coach to understand that the individual needs of the athlete must be the priority.

Jowett's (2005) 3+1 Cs Model of the Coach-Athlete Relationship explains that closeness (the affective meanings that the coach/athlete assign to their relationship), commitment (to maintain the relationship now and in the future) and complementarity (being co-operative) alongside co-orientation (accurately assessing what the coach/athlete is feeling) are fundamental to a positive coach-athlete relationship. The co-orientation of coach-athlete relationship takes into account assumed similarity, actual similarity and empathetic understanding (Jowett and Cockerill 2002). Assumed similarity, in this case, is what Karen actually feels about the situation and what Karen thinks her coach feels about the situation. Actual similarity is the comparison between what Karen feels and what the coach feels about the situation. Empathetic understanding refers to what Karen *thinks* her coach feels about the situation and what the coach actually feels about the situation.

It is important that the coach and athlete fully understand each other before considering important decisions about an athlete's career. For example, in their study on Olympic swimmers, Philippe and Seiler (2006) found that closeness (social relationships), communication and setting objectives/goals (co-orientation) as well as respect and acceptance of roles (complementarity) played an important part in the quality of the coach-athlete relationship. So, in the case of Karen, whereas the coach may think he is advising Karen to stay in the local area for the right reasons, Karen may not agree and the coach may not even be aware of this.

Using the 3+1 Cs model, Rhind and Jowett (2010) offer a theoretical framework to explore how coaches and athletes might maintain the quality of their relationships using the COMPASS model. This model includes conflict management, openness, motivation, positivity, advice, support and social network. In this instance, Karen and her coach need to find ways to deal with their differing ideas about a potential move to another club or abroad.

Referring back to Wylleman's (2000) relationships in sport model, it would appear that Karen is in the development stage of her career. In order to progress any further and to realize her ambition, she probably does need to move to a higher level club or an elite sports academy. Yet, Karen is facing social-contextual barriers and if these are not overcome, it seems unlikely that she will progress to realize her Olympic dream.

A family and schooling sport socialization perspective

In Karen's story there are clear illustrations of the ways in which the primary (e.g. parents) and secondary (e.g. school) socialization groups have played their roles. In terms of the family, Karen and her father had been members of the Tenkerdent Volleyball Club for many years. Since the family is a primary group for Karen's self-identification, it can be assumed that her behaviour and conduct were shaped from a young age through social interaction with her parents. In particular, Karen developed a love for volleyball through modelling her father's sporting practices, and it is clear he acted as an influential social agent and a role model in Karen's life. Birchwood, Roberts and Pollock (2008) have argued that family culture determines an individual's tendency to be involved with sport. Bourdieu described this as the development of an individual's "habitus" which he defined as a set of deeply rooted predispositions shaped by the social environment (Bourdieu 1990; Bourdieu and Wacquant 1992).

Social learning theory also considers the family as a key determinant in influencing behaviours (Bandura 1977; Ormrod 1999; Miller 2011). It is widely recognized that children are influenced by close contact with parents (or siblings) who are involved with sport or pro-sport related activities (Greendorfer 1991). On a similar note, the studies of Kirk and MacPhail (2003) and MacPhail, Gorely and Kirk (2003) emphasize the extent to which the social roles undertaken by family members (particularly parents) impact upon their children's engagement with sport. These research findings are certainly illustrated in the case of Karen. There is limited research into sport socialization, gender and parental influence, although there is some evidence in the literature that same-sex parental sport influence can be particularly strong, especially for girls (Synder and Spreitzer 1973; Greendorfer and Ewing 1981). However, findings are contradictory because in other studies, fathers have been identified as a significant role model for both boys and girls in terms of sport socialization (Lamb 1976; Greendorfer and Lewko 1978). In the case of Karen, the latter findings appear most accurate as it was her father, first as a player and later as an official in volleyball, who played a major role in shaping her sporting identity. Another notable issue is that Karen has received considerable support from her family and, as has been illustrated elsewhere, children who can broadly be defined as "middle class" tend to receive more family support to develop their talents than children from low-income families (Kay 2003; Vincent and Ball 2007). Moreover, there is evidence that sustained sports participation is more common amongst children in two-parent families than in single-parent families (Clark 2008; Quarmby and Dagkas, 2010).

Regarding Karen's socialization in school, it is evident that her environment has not only reinforced the love for volleyball that she learnt from her family but has also offered additional opportunities to play at a competitive level. As noted earlier in the chapter, a new and enthusiastic PE teacher at Karen's secondary school (Miss Smith) encouraged Karen to experience regional, national and international competitions. Currently, her new sixth form college (ET6C) for 16 to 18 year olds is also the home base of the Tenkerdent Volleyball Club and one of the ET6C PE teachers is a lead coach at the club. In both cases, Karen's teachers/coaches have helped Karen to meet older, more skilled athletes who can inspire her to improve her own skills and performance.

Within a UK-educational context, research has illustrated the significance of schools for sustained participation in competitive sport (Bailey and Dismore 2004). Participation is, however, affected by a range of school-related factors such as the type of school attended (socioeconomic status), the geographical location (access to facilities and size of community) and educational attainment levels (Côté *et al.* 2006). Another important factor in the sports socialization process is the link between schools and sports clubs. A series of UK government documents (e.g. *Sport Raising the Game; see DoNH 1995*) and strategies (e.g. *PE, School Sport and Club Links* – PESSCL; see Ofsted 2005) has emphasized the importance of establishing links between school sport and club sport. In Karen's life, such links have existed since her primary school years, perhaps also contributing to her talent development and sport participation (Bailey and Morley 2006).

Pedagogical comment

At the age of 17, Karen's opportunities to be part of the national volleyball squad seem to be within her grasp. Nevertheless, she is facing a series of potential barriers to reaching Olympic performance levels. Karen also aims to succeed academically which, in turn, will contribute to her opportunities for a "dual career" in sport performance and sport-related professions.

It is clear from our expert in motor skill acquisition that Karen will benefit from perceptual stimulation training programmes that will develop her game intelligence and awareness. Williams and Ford (2009) argued that there is a need to move towards a culture where evidence-based practice permeates all aspects in the development and preparation of Olympic athletes. They suggest that skill-acquisition theory and practice can help inform and guide movement practitioners and coaches who have a responsibility for elite performance. Although the refinement of skills is essential to performance in most Olympic sports, paradoxically, the area of skill acquisition has not impacted in a concerted and meaningful way on Karen's skill improvement goals. As Williams and Ford argue:

> Skill-acquisition specialists need to be more proactive in forging links with elite sport, whereas practitioners, coaches, and administrators need to appreciate the important role that sports scientists with a background in this area can play in helping to develop future generations of podium athletes.
>
> (2009: 1381)

Taking into consideration the suggestions offered by our expert in motor skill acquisition, it will be useful for Karen and her coaches to focus on perceptual motor approaches to visual training in order to reduce her reaction and response times, increase response accuracy, gain better awareness of team mates' positioning and improve passing. The reality is that these improvements are unlikely to materialize in the training practices used at Karen's club.

The existing coach–athlete relationship has worked well for Karen up to sub-elite level. The proposition offered by our sport psychology and sport sociology experts is that Tenkerdent Volleyball club has created a climate that MacPhail *et al.* (2003: 251) have described as "educative" with a lesser emphasis on "elite development goals". In the context of PE, Bailey *et al.* (2010) have described the flow between different, but interrelated motives for involvement. Is it possible that Karen's coach/PE teacher lacks knowledge and understanding of an effective programme for an elite volleyball athlete? Research published in the United Kingdom (North 2009) has revealed that only 3 per cent of the total coaching workforce is in full-time employment in coaching, and almost half of volunteer coaches have no formal qualification. In the absence of a coaching system with a strong emphasis on the scientific principles of athlete development and a prevalence of degree level education for coaches (Lyle 2002), a multidisciplinary team of coaches and sports scientists may be required to meet Karen's needs.

Croston (2013: 60) argued that sport education policy in England since 2000, such as "Physical Education, School Sports and Club Links" (PESSCL), has aimed to merge educational and sporting ambitions, resulting in a shift in focus "away from educational objectives towards supporting elite development". Yet, despite this:

> . . . there remains limited understanding of talent identification (ID) and as such, a danger for talent in PE and sport to be considered synonymous, resulting in a lack of clarity over the methods, purpose and focus of talent ID, and consequently notions of ability in PE.
> (Croston 2013: 60)

A key issue that is central to Karen's case is whether school-based and other sports clubs are able to support athletes who have the potential to achieve Olympic levels of performance. Bailey, Morley and Dismore (2009: 70) argued that some heads of PE have called for a "clear exit route to clubs" or "more clearly defined pathways to excellence". Yet, the talent identification system still tends to rely on "current levels of performance in school sport and club sport achievement" rather than the *potential* to achieve. Bailey *et al.* (2009) argued that this could not be described as best practice. Karen's case certainly illustrates the problems that can occur for talented young athletes caught in the loosely defined school-club links that currently exist.

Karen needs to ensure that in addition to being selected for the national volleyball squad, she also works hard to gain university entrance qualifications by achieving successful academic results through her two-year sixth form education. Her parents have ensured that Karen is aware of the fact that in addition to being a successful top-performance volleyball athlete, she also needs to think of developing her professional career since she is unlikely to earn her living through volleyball alone. The European Commission for Sport (2009) has supported this concept of a "dual career" for young sports people, advising that they are offered an education and/or professional training in addition to their sports training.

Conclusion

In conclusion, it seems clear that in Karen's case, the following steps could be taken to offer better support for her high aspirations:

1. Ensure Karen's coaches are able to work with motor skill acquisition specialists to gain an understanding of perceptual motor training. This could be achieved through the establishment of a professional multidisciplinary network that is local, county or regional based to support elite volleyball practice squads.
2. Clarify the roles of the performance and elite sports coaches while supporting realistic and sustainable school-clubs links. One practical step might be to organize for an elite coach to visit grassroots clubs to foster a better understanding of the needs of talented athletes.
3. Encourage athletes to follow dual careers, in this case, as an athlete and a sports professional. The adoption of a sport education model (Siedentop *et al.* 2011) in PE is one way to ensure that participants have opportunities to develop a broad range of skills and competencies in sport.

These suggestions may be ambitious, and clearly there are local, regional, national and international contextual factors that will influence the steps that can be taken. Nonetheless, Karen's case illustrates the challenges young talented athletes face when the "systems" are not coordinated to meet their needs.

Notes

1. A sixth form college in England is an educational institution where 80 per cent of the students are aged 16 to 19. They study for advanced school-level qualifications leading to entry into undergraduate degree courses or work. Although some secondary schools for 11–16 year olds have sixth form colleges, in England, sixth-form colleges are not part of the schools sector but independent, autonomous institutions that provide education, training, or work-based training for the 16–19 sector (DfE, 2013).
2. Funding opportunities such as the Talented Athlete Scholarship Scheme (TASS n/d) including TASS bursaries worth up to £3,500, are focused on 16 to 18 years olds studying a further education course or starting out in employment. TASS awards scholarships to talented athletes committed to combining their sport and education. It aims to reduce the drop out of talented athletes from sport and supports and develops the talent of today for sporting success in the future. Athletes must be competing at National or International level in their sport and be nominated for a TASS award by their National Governing Body. The funds for bursaries are typically raised through sponsorships, donations to charities (sports organizations) and government funding.
3. Colleges in England provide a rich mix of academic and vocational education. It may be from basic training to Higher National Diploma or Foundation Degree. Colleges in the UK that are regarded as part of the Further Education sector include General FE and Tertiary Colleges; Sixth-Form Colleges; and Specialist Colleges (e.g. Sports). Specialist colleges educate, support and train elite athletes through provision of Academies and by supporting athletes in national and international squads (Association of Colleges 2013).

References

Abernethy, B., Schorer, J., Jackson, R.C. and Hagemann, N. (2012) 'Perceptual training methods compared: The relative efficacy of different approaches to enhancing sport-specific anticipation', *Journal of Experimental Psychology: Applied,* 18(2): 143–153.

Adolphe, R.M., Vickers, J.N. and Laplante, G. (1997) 'The effects of training visual attention on gaze behaviour and accuracy: A pilot study. *International Journal of Sports Vision,* 4(1): 28–33.

Afonso, J., Esteves, F., Araujo, R., Thomas, L. and Mesquita, I. (2012a) 'Tactical determinants of setting zone in elite men's volleyball', *Journal of Sports Science & Medicine,* 11: 64–70.

Afonso, J., Garganta, J., McRobert, A., Williams, A.M. and Mesquita, I. (2012b) 'The perceptual cognitive processes underpinning skilled performance in volleyball: Evidence from eye-movement and verbal reports of thinking involving an in situ representative task', *Journal of Sports Science & Medicine,* 11: 339–345.

Afonso, J., Mesquita, I., Marcelino, R. and Antonio da Silva, J. (2010) 'Analysis of the setter's tactical action in high-performance women's volleyball', *Kinesiology,* 42(1): 82–89.

Association of Colleges (2013) *About Colleges.* Online. Available HTTP: <www.aoc.co.uk/en/about_colleges/> (accessed 25 September 2013).

Bailey, R., Collins, D., Ford, P., MacNamara, A., Toms, M. and Pearce, G. (2010) *Participant development in sport: An academic review.* Sports Coach UK and Sport Northern Ireland. Online. Available HTTP: <http://sportscoach.dnsupdate.co.uk/index.php?PageID=5&sc=23&uid=1813> (accessed 25 September 2013).

Bailey, R. and Morley, D. (2006) 'Towards a model of talent development in physical education', *Sport, Education & Society,* 11(3): 211–230.

Bailey, R., Morley, D. and Dismore, H. (2009) 'Talent development in physical education: A national survey of policy and practice in England', *Physical Education & Sport Pedagogy* 14(10): 59–72.

Bailey, R.P. and Dismore, H. (2004) *Sport in Education (SpinEd) – The role of physical education and sport in education,* Project Report to the 4th International Conference of Ministers and Senior Officials Responsible for Physical Education and Sport, Athens, Greece: MINEPS IV.

Bandura, A. (1977) *Social learning theory.* New York: General Learning Press.

Bergeles, N., Barzouka, K. and Nikolaidou, M. (2009) 'Performance of male and female setters and attackers on Olympic-level volleyball teams', *International Journal of Performance Analysis in Sport,* 9(1): 141–148.

Birchwood, D., Roberts, K. and Pollock, G. (2008) 'Explaining differences in sport participation rates among young adults: Evidence from the South Caucasus', *European Physical Education Review,* 14(3): 283–298.

Bourdieu, P. (1990) 'Structures, habitus, practices', in P. Bourdieu (ed.), *The logic of practice* (pp. 52–79). Stanford, CA: Stanford University Press.

Bourdieu, P. and Wacquant, L.J.D. (1992) *An invitation to reflexive sociology.* Chicago and London: University of Chicago Press.

Clark, W. (2008) *Kids' sport.* Statistics Canada, Canadian Social Trends, Catalogue No.11. Online. Available HTTP: <www.sportmatters.ca/Groups/SMG%20Resources/Reports%20and%20Surveys/2008-Stats%20Can%20Candian%20Social%20Trends%20-%20Kids%20Sports%20(3).pdf> (accessed 25 September 2013).

Côté, J., MacDonald, D., Baker, J. and Abernethy, B. (2006) 'When "where" is more important than "when": Birthplace and birthdate effects on the achievement of sporting expertise', *Journal of Sports Sciences,* 24(10): 1065–1073.

Croston, A. (2013) '"A clear and obvious ability to perform physical activity": Revisiting physical education teachers' perceptions of talent in PE and sport', *Physical Education & Sport Pedagogy,* 18(1): 60–74.

Department for Education (2013) *Sixth-form colleges.* Online. Available HTTP: <www.education.gov.uk/schools/leadership/typesofschools/sixth> (accessed 20 March 2013).

Department of National Heritage (DoNH) (1995) *Sport: Raising the game, London, UK.* Online. Available HTTP: <www.sportdevelopment.info/index.php/subjects/48-policy/844-sport-raising-the-game> (accessed 25 September 2013).

Dicks, M., Button, C. and Davids, K. (2010) 'Examination of gaze behaviour under in situ and video simulation task constraints reveals differences in information pickup for perception and action', *Attention, Perception, & Psychophysics,* 72: 706–720.

Ericsson, K.A., Krampe, R.T. and Tesch-Romer, C. (1993) 'The role of deliberate practice in the acquisition of expert performance', *Psychological Review,* 100: 363–406.

European Commission for Sport (2009) *Education and training in sport.* Online. Available HTTP: <http://ec.europa.eu/sport/what-we-do/doc31_en.htm> (accessed 25 September 2013).

Farrow, D., Chivers, P., Hardingham, C. and Sacuse, S. (1998) 'The effect of video based perceptual training on the tennis return serve'. *International Journal of Sport Psychology,* 29: 231–242.

Greendorfer, S.L. (1991) 'Gender role stereotypes and early childhood socialization', in G.L. Cohen (eds.) *Women in sport: Issues and controversies* (pp. 3–14). Newbury Park, CA: Sage.

Greendorfer, S.L. and Ewing, M.E. (1981) 'Race and gender differences in children's socialization into sport', *Research Quarterly for Exercise & Sport,* 52(3): 301–310.

Greendorfer, S.L. and Lewko, J.H. (1978) 'Role of family members in sport socialization of children', *Research Quarterly Exercise and Sport,* 49(2): 146–152.

Hernandez, E., Urena, A., Miranda, M.T. and Ona, A. (2004) 'Kinematic analysis of volleyball setting cues that affect anticipation in blocking', *Journal of Human Movement Studies,* 47(4): 285–301.

Jowett, S. (2005) 'On repairing and enhancing the coach-athlete relationship', in S. Jowett and M. Jones (eds.) *The psychology of coaching* (pp. 14–26). Leicester, UK: The British Psychological Society, Sport and Exercise Psychology Division.

Jowett, S. and Cockerill, I.M. (2002) 'Incompatibility in the coach–athlete relationship', in I.M. Cockerill (eds.) *Solutions in sport psychology* (pp. 16–31). London: Thomson Learning.

Jowett, S. and Poczwardowski, A. (2007) 'Understanding the coach-athlete relationship', in S. Jowett and D. Lavallee (eds.) *Social psychology in sport* (pp. 3–14). Champaign, IL: Human Kinetics.

Kay, T. (2003) 'The family factor in sport: A review of family factors affecting sports participation', *Report commissioned by Sport England,* Loughborough: Institute for Youth Sport.

Kirk, D. and MacPhail, A. (2003) 'Social positioning and the construction of a youth sports club', *International Review for the Sociology of Sport,* 38(1): 23–34.

Lamb, M. (1976) *The role of the father in child development.* New York: Wiley.

Lofting, F., Schorer, J., Hagemann, N. and Baker, J. (2012) 'On the advantage of being left-handed in volleyball: Further evidence of the specificity of skilled visual perception', *Attention Perception & Psychophysics,* 74(2): 446–453.

Lyle, J. (2002) *Sport coaching concepts: A framework for coaches' behaviour.* London: Routledge.

MacPhail, A., Gorely, T. and Kirk, D. (2003) 'Young people's socialization into sport: A case study of an athletics club', *Sport, Education & Society,* 8(2): 251–267.

Mann, D.T.Y., Williams, A.M., Ward, P. and Janelle, C.M. (2007) 'Perceptual cognitive expertise in sport: A meta-analysis', *Journal of Sport & Exercise Psychology,* 29: 457–478.

Memmert, D., Hagemann, N., Althoetmar, R., Geppert, S. and Seiler, D. (2009) 'Conditions of practice in perceptual skill learning', *Research Quarterly for Exercise & Sport,* 80(1): 32–43.

Miller, P.H. (2011) *Theories of developmental psychology.* New York: Worth Publishers.

North, J. (2009) *The UK coaching workforce.* Leeds: Sports Coach UK.

Ofsted (2005) *The physical education, school sport and club links strategy,* UK. Online. Available HTTP: <www.ofsted.gov.uk/resources/physical-education-school-sport-and-club-links-strategy> (accessed 25 September 2013).

Ormrod, J.E. (1999) *Human learning,* 3rd edn. Upper Saddle River, NJ: Prentice Hall.

Philippe, R.A. and Seiler, R. (2006) 'Closeness, co-orientation and complementarity in coach-athlete relationships: What male swimmers say about their male coaches', *Psychology of Sport & Exercise,* 7: 159–171.

Piras, A., Lobietti, R. and Squatrito, S. (2010) 'A study of saccadic eye movement dynamics in volleyball: Comparison between athletes and non-athletes', *Journal of Sports Medicine & Physical Fitness,* 50(1): 99–108.

Quarmby, T. and Dagkas, S. (2010) 'Children's engagement in leisure time physical activity: Exploring family structure as a determinant', *Leisure Studies,* 29(1): 53–66.

Rhind, D.J.A. and Jowett, S. (2010) 'Relationship maintenance strategies in the coach-athlete relationship: The development of the COMPASS model', *Journal of Applied Sport Psychology,* 22: 106–121.

Siedentop, D., Hastie, P.A. and Van Der Mars, H. (2011) *Complete guide to sport education,* 2nd edn. Champaign IL: Human Kinetics.

Synder, E. and Spreitzer, E. (1973) 'Family influence and involvement in sports', *Research Quarterly,* 44(3): 249–255.

TASS (n.d.) *Helping talent shine in education and sport*. Online. Available HTTP: <www.tass.gov.uk/> (accessed 25 September 2013).

Vincent, C. and Ball, S.J. (2007) 'Making up the middle-class child: Families, activities and class dispositions', *Sociology,* 41(6): 1061–1077.

Ward, P., Farrow, D., Harris, K.R., Williams, A.M., Eccles, D.W. and Ericsson, K.A. (2008) 'Training perceptual-cognitive skills: Can sport psychology research inform military decision training?' *Military Psychology,* 20(1): S71–S102.

Ward, P., Hodges, N.J., Williams, A.M. and Starkes, J.L. (2004) 'Deliberate practice and expert performance: Defining the path to excellence', in A.M. Williams and N.J. Hodges (eds.) *Skill acquisition in sport: Research, theory, and practice* (pp. 231–258). London: Routledge.

Wilkinson, S. (1992) 'Effects of training in visual discrimination after one year: Visual analysis of volleyball skills', *Perceptual & Motor Skills,* 75(1): 19–24.

Williams, A.M. and Ford, P.R. (2009) 'Promoting a skills-based agenda in Olympic sports: The role of skill-acquisition specialists', *Journal of Sports Sciences,* 27(13): 1381–1392.

Williams, A.M., Ford, P.R., Eccles, D.W. and Ward, P. (2010) 'Perceptual-cognitive expertise in sport and its acquisition: Implications for applied cognitive psychology', *Applied Cognitive Psychology,* 25: 432–442.

Williams, A.M., Heron, K., Ward, P. and Smeeton, N.J. (2005) 'Using situational probabilities to train perceptual and cognitive skill in novice soccer players', in T. Reilly, J. Cabri and D. Arajuo (eds.) *Science and football V.* (pp. 337–340). London: Taylor & Francis.

Williams, A.M. and Ward, P. (2007) 'Perceptual-cognitive expertise in sport: Exploring new horizons', in G. Tenenbaum & R. Eklund (eds.) *Handbook of sport psychology,* 3rd edn (p. 203–223). New York: Wiley.

Williams, A.M., Ward, P. and Chapman, C. (2003) 'Training perceptual skill in field hockey: Is there transfer from the laboratory to the field?' *Research Quarterly for Exercise & Sport,* 74(1): 98–103.

Williams, A.M., Ward, P., Knowles, J. and Smeeton, N.J. (2002) 'Anticipation skill in a real-world task: Measurement, training, and transfer in tennis', *Journal of Experimental Psychology: Applied,* 8(4): 259–270.

Wylleman, P. (2000) 'Interpersonal relationships in sport: Uncharted territory in sport psychology research', *International Journal of Sport Psychology,* 31: 555–572.

INDEX

Please note: page numbers in *italics* followed by *f* indicate figures and by *t* indicate tables.